The Kaiser's Holocaust

Dedicated to the memory of
Jørn Wulff
Karen Wulff
&
Olorunjube Franklin Ojomo

THE KAISER'S HOLOCAUST

Germany's Forgotten Genocide and the Colonial Roots of Nazism

DAVID OLUSOGA

and

CASPER W. ERICHSEN

First published in 2010 by Faber and Faber Ltd
Bloomsbury House
74–77 Great Russell Street
London WC1B 3DA

Typeset by RefineCatch Limited, Bungay, Suffolk
Printed and bound in the UK by CPI Mackays, Chatham

A CIP record for this book
is available from the British Library

ISBN 978-0-571-23141-6

2 4 6 8 10 9 7 5 3 1

Contents

INTRODUCTION

Cell 5

At 10.30 p.m. on 14 October 1946, Private Harold F. Johnson of 'C' Company, 26th US Infantry, walked along the corridor leading to Cell 5. Taking up the position he was to occupy for the next few hours, he leaned forward and peered through the viewing hole into the cell. 'At that time', Johnson later informed a Board of Inquiry, the prisoner was 'lying flat on his back with his hands stretched out along his sides above the blankets. He stayed in that position for about five minutes without so much as moving.' At about 10.40, Johnson informs us, the captive man 'brought his hands across his chest with his fingers laced and turned his head to the wall . . . He lay there for about two or three minutes . . . Later he seemed to stiffen and made a blowing, choking sound through his lips'. Private Johnson raised the alarm. He shouted for the Corporal of the Relief, Lieutenant Cromer, who ran noisily down the spiral staircase from the corridor above, quickly followed by the Prison Chaplain, Captain Henry F. Gerecke. Only when all three were assembled did Johnson unlock and swing open the cell door. Cromer rushed past and was the first inside, followed by the Chaplain; Johnson came in behind 'holding the light'. Chaplain Gerecke leaned down and grasped hold of the prisoner's right arm, which hung limply over the edge of his metal bunk. He searched frantically for a pulse. 'Good Lord,' he said, 'this man is dead.'[1]

The prisoner who lay in Cell 5 of the Nuremberg Prison, with shards of glass from an ampoule of cyanide still in his mouth, had once been Prime Minister of Prussia and President of the Reichstag. He was the former Commander-in-Chief of the most feared air force in Europe and a ruthless administrator who had overseen the deadly exploitation of Eastern Europe. He considered himself – as he had boasted to his jailers only weeks earlier – a 'historical figure', and was convinced that 'in fifty or sixty years' statues in his image would be erected all across Germany. He was Hermann Göring, and in the last twist of his strange life he had cheated the hangman, committing suicide just two hours before his execution.

Seven months earlier, in one of the opening addresses of the Trial of German Major War Criminals, one of the American prosecutors, Robert Kemper, had described the Nuremberg Trials as 'the greatest history seminar ever'. The case for the prosecution was in itself a monumental piece of historical research. Outside the chamber, a team of historians, translators, archivists and documentary filmmakers had assembled to catalogue and file, estimate and quantify the litany of aggression and murderous criminality committed during the twelve years of Hitler's 'Thousand-Year Reich'. From millions of individual tragedies, they had formed a prosecution case. The documents linking these crimes to the twenty-three accused men had been duplicated, indexed and translated into French, Russian and English. The indictment alone ran to twenty-four thousand words. The preparation of the case for the prosecution could perhaps have lasted longer than Nazi rule itself. As it was, the first three days of the trial were entirely taken up just reading the indictment into the official record.

Over the course of the trial, the defendants were condemned by the records from their pasts. Their own signatures, on their own documents, were submitted against them. The minutes of incriminating meetings they had attended were recited to them; their speeches and edicts read, sometimes shouted, back at them. Those who had escaped their prisons and concentration camps recounted their appalling stories. Perhaps at no other time and in no other place has the work of historians and archivists been put to such dramatic effect. In our time, only the Truth and Reconciliation Committees of post-Apartheid South Africa have come close to replicating the drama of Nuremberg.

What happened at Nuremberg between November 1945 and October 1946 was more than a trial: it was the elaborate centrepiece of an enormous act of national exorcism. The Allied powers believed that the prosecution of the surviving members of the Nazi elite would be a key step in the 'de-Nazification' of the German people. The post-war settlement was, in part, predicated upon the willingness of Germany's battered and exhausted population to reject Nazism. With every major city in ruins, five million Germans dead and four armies of occupation on German soil, all but the most fanatically pro-Nazi were willing to acknowledge that the Third Reich had been an unparalleled national calamity. When confronted at Nuremberg with the stark truth of what Germany had done under the Nazis, some came to other conclusions. The Nazi leaders in the dock, and the thousands of henchmen who had enacted their decrees, came to be seen as 'other'. Their actions had showed them to be inhumane; perhaps, therefore, they were unhuman. Led by such men, the Third Reich had been capable of crimes that were both terrible and unique in history. Nazism, so the argument went, had been an aberration in European history, a discontinuity.

This is the great post-war myth: the comforting fantasy that the Nazis were a new order of monsters and that their crimes were without precursor or precedent. They were not. Much of Nazi ideology and many of the crimes committed in its name were part of a longer trend within European history. Nazism was both a culmination and a distortion of decades of German and European history and philosophy. It was, in part, the final homecoming of theories and practices that Europeans had developed and perfected in far-flung corners of the world during the last phase of imperial conquest. There is nothing within that historical subsoil that made the ultimate flowering of Nazism inevitable, but there is much that makes it understandable. At Nuremberg, however, all such historical precedent was plunged into darkness. 'The greatest history seminar ever' did not look back far enough into history.

The Nuremberg Trials took as their start date the year in which a new age of barbarism had seemed to overwhelm Europe – 1914. This was year zero for the prosecuting nations, all of whom agreed that World War I had been the calamity that set Europe on course for the greater tragedies of World War II. The generation who had mutilated their own continent had, in the process, been disfigured politically and ideologically. The national enmities and the trauma of mass, mechanised killing had sown the seeds for the savagery that lay at the heart of Nazism. At Nuremberg, everything before the Somme, Verdun and Ypres was regarded as mere detail, as it was presumed that Nazism as an ideology had emerged fully formed from the chaos and resentment following Germany's defeat in 1918.

In its narrow historical focus, if in no other way, the trial of Hermann Göring was typical. When questioning began, on the morning of 13 March, Göring was asked for a 'short account of his life up to the outbreak of the First World War'. The president of the court repeatedly stressed the need for brevity. It was only when Göring's account reached 1914 that he was encouraged to elaborate and detailed questioning began.[2] Over the course of the 218-day trial, Hermann Göring, the lead defendant, delivered only four sentences about his life before World War I and the role of his family in Germany's longer history.

Had the Nuremberg prosecutors looked further into Göring's past, and his nation's, they would have discovered another story of death camps and racial genocide. They would have seen that the ideas of many of the philosophers, scientists and soldiers whose theories inspired Hitler had underpinned an earlier, forgotten holocaust. Perhaps they might have recognised a continuity in German history and understood that Nazism was anything but unique. They might also have grasped the importance of the few sentences Göring uttered at the start of his cross-examination, in which he described his family background and the world before 1914 that had formed him and his generation.

Göring, for his own reasons, was determined to use his last stand in the dock at Nuremberg as an opportunity to place the Third Reich within the mainstream of world history. One strand of his defence strategy was to claim that Nazism and the principles on which it had been founded were not unique but merely Germanic incarnations of the same forces with which the prosecuting powers had built up their own empires and expanded their own power.

On the second day of direct examination by his defence counsel Dr Otto Stahmer, Göring was asked for his definition of the term *Lebensraum* – the theory of living space on which the Nazis' invasion of the USSR and their plans for its later colonisation had been founded. He replied: 'That concept is a very controversial one. I can fully understand that the Powers – I refer only to the four signatory Powers – who call more than three-quarters of the world their own explain this concept differently'.[3]

Speaking a few days later in Cell 5 to G. M. Gilbert, the psychiatrist given access to the Nuremberg defendants, Göring directly compared the crimes he was defending in court with those perpetrated in the empires of the victor nations. The British Empire, he claimed, had 'not been built up with due regard for principles of humanity', while America had 'hacked its way to a rich Lebensraum by revolution, massacre and war'.[4]

Göring's attempts to compare the crimes of the Third Reich to the genocides and massacres of the age of empire could easily be dismissed as a desperate defence tactic. But behind the bluster, arrogance and amorality of a man who was patently unable to confront his own crimes, there is an uncomfortable truth.

When Göring was asked to speak briefly about his life before 1914, he outlined what he called 'a few points which are significant with relation to my later development'. He told the court of his father, who had been the 'first Governor of South-West

Africa', pointing out that in that capacity the elder Göring had had 'connections at that time with two British statesmen, Cecil Rhodes and the elder Chamberlain'.[5]

Hermann Göring's father, Dr Heinrich Göring, had indeed been a key factor in his son's 'later development'. In 1885 he had been appointed by Chancellor Bismarck to help establish the German colony of South-West Africa, today the southern African nation of Namibia. Dr Göring's role was one of slow negotiations with the indigenous African peoples, with no garrison and little funding. Fifty years later, an official Nazi biography of Hermann Göring shamelessly attempted to glamorise the elder Göring's record as an empire-builder. It describes how 'Young [Hermann] Göring listened, his eyes sparkling with excitement, to his father's stories about his adventures in bygone days. The inquisitive and imaginative lad was . . . thrilled by his accounts of his pioneer work as a Reichs Commissar for South-West Africa, of his journeys through the Kalahari Desert and his fights with Maharero, the black king of Okahandja.'[6]

In truth, Heinrich Göring had no fights with any of the 'black kings' of South-West Africa. For three years he travelled across the southern deserts with a wagon full of so-called 'protection treaties', desperately attempting to dupe or cajole the leaders of the local African peoples into signing away rights to their land. When his promises of protection were exposed as empty, he was recognised as a fraud and summarily expelled.

What inspired the elder Göring to volunteer for service in Africa was that, like many Germans in the late nineteenth century, he could foresee a time in which the land of that continent might become living space into which the German race could expand. It was imagined that Germany's colonial subjects – the black Africans of her new-found empire – would become the cheap labour of the German farmers. Those tribes unable or unwilling to accept their diminished status would face the industrial weapons that Göring knew would one day appear in the South-West. Those Africans who stood in the way of the German race simply had no future. Like his son fifty years later,

Dr Heinrich Göring understood that the weaker peoples of the earth were destined to fall prey to the stronger, and rightly so.

These beliefs were hardly controversial in certain political circles in the late nineteenth-century Europe. But in Germany, some writers and politicians began to draw the distinction between Europeans and what Hitler was later to call 'colonial peoples' much closer to home. In the last decades of the nineteenth century, they began to argue that Germany's destiny was to become the masters of an empire built on the continent of Europe itself. Germany was too late to take her share of Africa or Asia, but just over her eastern borders, in the lands of the Slavic peoples of Poland and Russia, was all the space she would ever need.

The Göring family perfectly encapsulates that shift in German colonial ambitions. Both father and son were committed imperialists. The father spent his brief colonial career struggling with pitiful resources to construct the most meagre foundations of a colony in the deserts of South-West Africa. More than half a century later, his son commanded the industrial energies of an expanded and mobilised Reich, and forged a short-lived but genocidal empire in the European East. While the father, whose prospective victims were black Africans, fits our view of a colonialist, the son does not. Yet the Nazis' war in the East was one of imperial expansion, settler colonialism and racial genocide.

Today that war is commonly portrayed as an epic military disaster. The battles of Kursk, Leningrad and Stalingrad are now well known, but behind the lines, in civilian areas under German control, another war was fought. Land was cleared, crops confiscated and millions enslaved. Whole villages were simply wiped off the map in punitive raids, just as thousands of villages in Africa, Asia and the Americas had been during the centuries of colonial expansion. In the fertile Ukraine, ethnic German farmers settled on the land of Ukrainian families. In many cases they were simply transplanted into the homes of Ukrainian Slavs, given their houses along with their contents, while the previous owners were driven into the camps. In Berlin, rooms full of bureaucrats spent their days planning the resettlement of millions more Germans at the expense of millions more Slavs and Jews.

Throughout the grim process of colonisation, Hitler, in his underground bunker in an East Prussian forest, sat late into the night describing to his captive audience of generals and party apparatchiks the wonders of the empire that was just beginning to emerge. He spoke endlessly of the great radial autobahns that would link the new Eastern settlements to Berlin and of the new breed of farmer soldiers who would become the masters of the East – the overlords of the Slavic hordes. Millions of those sub-humans would need to be liquidated and the rest reduced to a primitive existence – denied medicine, education and even the most basic rights. If, like the natives of previous empires, they dared to resist the will of their masters, their villages would simply be bombed from the air.

The Nazi war to build an empire in the East was classically colonial in that it was characterised by genocidal violence, much of which – particularly that ranged against Slavic civilians and Soviet POWs – has been largely forgotten. Colonial genocide has always been a drawn-out process of massacres, famines, enslavement and hidden liquidations. A form of warfare without glory or glamour, it has never been the stuff of memoirs. The wars that built the British and French empires, that kept the rubber flowing in the Belgian Congo, that cleared the Pampas of Argentina and the Great Plains of the US, have similarly been overshadowed by an alternative and more glamorous history of colonialism, focusing on great battles and notable heroic figures.

The empires of Germany's Second and Third Reichs died soon after birth. The former took with it hundreds of thousands of lives; the latter, millions. Both were inspired by a nationalist and racial fantasy that began in the late nineteenth century. What was forgotten at Nuremberg and has been forgotten ever since is that the imperial ambitions and many of the crimes committed by the Third Reich have a precedent in German history. The nightmare that was visited upon the people of Eastern Europe in the 1940s was unique in its scale and in the industrialisation of killing. The fusion of racism and Fordism was a Nazi innovation. Yet in many other respects, Germany had been here before.

Five thousand miles from Nuremberg lies the tiny Namibian town of Lüderitz. Trapped between the freezing waters of the South Atlantic and the endless dune fields of the Namib Desert, it is without doubt one of the strangest places on earth. The sea of sand dunes stops literally on the edge of town; they seem encamped, as if waiting for permission to enter. In the mornings, when the desert is screened behind a thick curtain of sea mist, Lüderitz looks completely un-tropical. It resembles an overgrown Arctic research station or a defunct whaling settlement, perhaps in the Falkland Islands or Greenland. Even on a good day the town looks half dead.

Most of the buildings are brightly painted in reds, oranges and yellows, and are randomly scattered over the half-dozen or so hills that surround the wide and blustery bay. The vivid colours of the buildings contrast with the sea-weathered rocks of the hills, which resemble wrinkled and dusty elephant hide. Recently the main avenues have been tarmacked, but the back alleys remain rough and pitted dirt tracks. Everywhere piles of dust and sand linger on street corners. A visitor arriving by ship would see nothing to indicate they were in Africa. On landing, their confusion would be compounded by a white population speaking German and hundreds of black Africans speaking the Afrikaans of the Boers.

Today most visitors to Lüderitz arrive by road. The B4 highway, an arrow-straight ribbon of black tarmac, shoots across the Namib Desert following the line of the old narrow-gauge railway that once connected the southern settlements of what was then German South-West Africa to Lüderitz Bay and from there to the great shipping lanes of Imperial Germany. Each night, out beyond the town limits, the sand dunes inch their way onto the tarmac of the B4, in their nightly attempt to suffocate the town. Each morning a huge yellow excavation machine thunders out of town to clear the highway. The desert itself seems determined to seal Lüderitz off from the outside world. Like the forests of the Congo as witnessed by Joseph Conrad, the dunes of the Namib seem to be waiting with 'ominous patience . . . for the passing away of a fantastic invasion'.[7]

In 1905 this tiny settlement was chosen as the site of a new experiment in warfare. Until perhaps only thirty years ago, Lüderitz's oldest residents had their own memories of what happened here in the first years of the twentieth century; they said nothing. Today it remains a secret. The tourist information office on Bismarck Strasse has nothing to say on the subject, none of the guidebooks to Namibia mention it and most of the history books they recommend as further reading are similarly mute. Yet what happened in Lüderitz between 1905 and 1907 makes it one of the pivotal sites in the history of the twentieth century.

The experiment took place on Shark Island, a squat, mean-looking ridge of rock that lies just across the bay, in full view of the whole town. It was in its way a resounding success, bringing to life a new device: a military innovation that went on to become an emblem of the century and take more lives than the atom bomb. For here, on the southern edge of Africa, the death camp was invented.

Today Shark Island is the municipal camping site for the town of Lüderitz. A new restaurant overlooking the island offers excellent South African wines and South Atlantic seafood. Diners are encouraged to sit out on the balcony and enjoy views of an island upon which, a century ago, three and a half thousand Africans were systematically liquidated. Just a couple of hundred yards away, beneath the waters of Lüderitz Bay, divers have reported Shark Island to be surrounded by a ring of human bones and rusted steel manacles. The human beings who were made to wear those chains and whose remains lie beneath the waves have been almost erased from Namibian and world history. The names of their tribes – the Herero, Witbooi Nama, Bethanie Nama – mean nothing to most people outside of Namibia.

Shark Island is not Namibia's only secret. There is a mass grave under the sidings of the railway station in the Namibian capital, Windhoek, and another on the outskirts of the seaside holiday town of Swakopmund. The national museum itself is housed in a German fort which was built on the site of another concentration camp.

But for most, Namibia is seen as a quaint backwater, a relic of Germany's short-lived foray into colonialism, and a microcosm of late nineteenth-century Germany that has somehow survived intact into the twenty-first. In the gift shops tourists buy postcards and picture books that depict this lost idyll. Streets are named after military commanders from aristocratic families. In the shopping malls one can buy replica hats of the *Schutztruppe*, the German colonial army. They come emblazoned with the red, white and black insignia of Germany's Second Reich – the age of the Kaisers. The German imperial flag, with its severe black eagle, is also for sale, alongside local history books that skirt over the wars that were fought under that banner – wars that almost wiped out two of Namibia's indigenous peoples.

What Germany's armies and civilian administrators did in Namibia is today a lost history, but the Nazis knew it well. When the *Schutztruppe* attempted to exterminate the Herero and Nama peoples of Namibia a century ago, Hitler was a schoolboy of fifteen. In 1904, he lived in a continent that was electrified by the stories of German heroism and African barbarism emanating from what was then German South-West Africa.

Eighteen years after the Herero-Nama genocide, Hitler became closely associated with a veteran of the conflict. In 1922 he was recruited into an ultra-right-wing militia in Munich that was indirectly under the command of the charismatic General Franz von Epp, who had been a lieutenant during Germany's wars against the Herero and Nama. As both a young colonial soldier and, later, a leading member of the Nazi party, von Epp was a fervent believer in the *Lebensraum* theory, and spent his life propagating the notion that the German people needed to expand their living space at the expense of lower races, whether in Africa or Eastern Europe. It would be an exaggeration to claim that Hitler was von Epp's protégé, but in the chaos of post-World War I Munich, von Epp, perhaps more than any figure other than Hitler himself, made the Nazi party possible. It was through von Epp, in various convoluted ways, that Hitler met many of the men who were to become the elite of the party: von Epp's deputy was Ernst Röhm, the founder of the Nazi storm troopers. Via the party's connections to von Epp and other old soldiers of Germany's African colonies, Röhm and Hitler were able to procure a consignment of surplus colonial *Schutztruppe* uniforms. Designed for warfare on the golden savannah of Africa, the shirts were desert brown in colour: the Nazi street thugs who wore them became known as Brown Shirts.

Today von Epp is viewed as a minor player in the story of Nazism. When the party came to power in 1933, his role was to campaign for the return of the colonies lost at Versailles for which he had fought as a young man. But by 1939 von Epp had become a marginal figure, excluded from Hitler's inner circle and eclipsed by younger men. His critical role in the development of the party as a political force has been overlooked. Yet in his writings before the war, Hitler recognised the role von Epp had played. In countless pictures and party propaganda films, von Epp and Hitler stand side by side.

In the last pictures taken of him, von Epp sits next to Hermann Göring. Both have been stripped of their uniforms and decorations as they await trial under American custody at Mondorf-les-Bains. The old general looks gaunt, slumped back in his chair squinting at the photographer. A generation older than many of his fellow inmates, von Epp died in custody just weeks after those pictures were taken. Had he lived to stand trial alongside Göring, might von Epp's testimony have led the prosecutors to see the continuities between the genocide he had taken part in as a young infantry lieutenant and the acts of the Third Reich?

Today the memory of Germany's empire has become detached from European history. Nineteenth-century colonialism has long been viewed as a specialist subject, a historical annexe in which events were played out in near-complete isolation from Europe. Yet in colonial history, ideas, methods and individuals always moved in both directions. Hitler's 1941 statement that he would treat the Slavs 'like a colonial people' has lost its resonance, but for the Führer it was a phrase full of meaning, a shorthand readily understood by a generation of Nazis who were boys when the Kaiser sent his armies to Africa to destroy native rebels who had placed themselves in the path of Germany's racial destiny. Our understanding of what Nazism was and where its underlying ideas and philosophies came from is perhaps incomplete unless we explore what happened in Africa under Kaiser Wilhelm II.

1

The World behind the Fog

Sometime in the late summer of 1484 two ships slipped out of Lisbon harbour, caught the wind in their sails and turned south. They were the caravels of Diogo Cão, and they were heading further south than any Europeans had ever ventured. King João II of Portugal had ascended to the throne determined to advance the age of exploration begun by his illustrious father King Henry 'the Navigator'. The prize sought by João and every navigator and explorer of the fifteenth century was a sea route to India and China. In the same year that Diogo Cão left Lisbon harbour, Portugal had officially abandoned the notion of attempting to reach India by crossing the Atlantic, an idea then being suggested by little-known navigator Christopher Columbus. In 1484 the focus of Portuguese interest was Africa, the great continent to the south, around which they were convinced lay the shortest route to India.

In the fifteenth century the Portuguese, like other Europeans, knew almost nothing of Africa. African kingdoms and peoples who had been in regular contact with Europe during the empires of ancient Greece and Rome had, from the fifth century onwards, been cut off from Europe by the rise of Islamic North Africa. For almost a millennium, black and white humanity had been separated, and in parts of Europe black Africans became almost mythological figures. Africa was imagined as a land inhabited by monstrous creatures, where the sun's heat was so intense it might prove deadly to Europeans. Yet it might also offer riches and bountiful trade, and beyond its shores more wealth might flow from India and China.

Although by the middle of the fifteenth century black Africans had been brought to Portugal and the wealth of the continent was already flowing back to Lisbon, each new discovery raised more questions and uncovered new mysteries. Despite several expeditions, no explorer had been able to map even the coast of the continent, while the interior remained completely unknown. Critically, no one had any idea how far to the south Africa stretched.

On his first expedition in 1482, Diogo Cão had discovered the Congo, a river larger and more powerful than anything Europeans had previously encountered. Yet he had failed to find a route around the continent. How large *was* Africa? What perils might lie along that seemingly endless coastline? What other great rivers, strange peoples and exotic animals were waiting to be discovered? In late 1484 Diogo Cão's two caravels sailed east along the lush green shores of West Africa. The wealth of the coast was clearly visible. Enormous kingdoms had risen and fallen over centuries. Millions populated the fertile forest belt, hundreds of miles thick, and broad rivers regularly cut into the forests, offering possibilities for future explorers and traders to penetrate the unknown interior. Tracking along the lagoons at the mouth of the River Niger, they then turned south along the coast of Cameroon, passing the mouth of the Congo. Further south they sailed past the coast of what is today Angola, finding shelter in the natural harbours that were later to become the centres of Portugal's slave empire. The further they went, the more the landscape began to change. The tangled forests of fig trees and giant baobab trees that fought for space on the shoreline of the Congo Basin began to dwindle. Mile by mile the trees became smaller, fewer and further apart.

As they passed the mouth of the Kunene River, the explorers saw a green island feeding off the Kunene's waters; this was the last dense burst of vegetation they were to encounter on their journey. South of this, the shore they surveyed was utterly desolate. Vast fields of sand dunes stretched back from the shore, a sea of yellow running parallel to the cold blue of the ocean. Dark and sombre mountain ranges were occasionally visible in the far distance, half lost in the heat haze.

Each morning a heavy sea mist would roll in and blanket the coast with a thick grey fog, as if the icy waters of the South Atlantic were turned to steam on contact with the roasting sands of the southern desert. Salt and spray hung in the air and bitter winds raked the coastline, whipping up the sands, reshaping the dunes and cutting into the faces of the sailors on deck. As they pushed further and further south, they will have seen humpback whales cruising to their breeding grounds and the broad fins of the great white sharks that still patrol the coastline. Nearer the coast, they will have come across Cape fur seals and killer whales. In the icy Benguela currents that stream up the coast from their source in Antarctica, the explorers would have encountered the bizarre sunfish and various species of sea turtle. But on the coastline there was nothing but stillness, solitude. An early twentieth-century description of this little-travelled coastline gives some indication of its desolation and danger:

> Heavy squalls and gales of wind are frequent, and often come on without warning, and with a cloudless sky. Sometimes sand is blown from the desert in large quantities, filling the air with minute particles, which are a long time subsiding; these conditions are accompanied by intense heat. The ordinary state of the atmosphere along this coast causes great refractions, and fogs are also frequent . . . the rollers frequently set in along this coast from the westward with great fury, and there is almost always a tremendously heavy swell thundering upon the shores, it is advisable to give the land a good berth . . .[1]

What Diogo Cão had 'discovered' was the coastline of modern-day Namibia, the Skeleton Coast. The dunes he viewed in the distance were those of the Namib Desert, an enormous belt of bleak coastal sands, 1,000 miles long and ranging between 30 and 100 miles in width, that sealed off the interior of south-western Africa from the rest of the world.

In January 1486 the explorers came across a small bay populated by hundreds of thousands of Cape fur seals. Here Diogo Cão and his men became the first Europeans ever to set foot in the Namib. Before landing they carefully lowered one of three stone *padrãos* they had carried from Lisbon into a launch. The *padrãos* were stone markers inscribed with the Portuguese coat of arms and a dated inscription that declared the land upon which they were planted as claimed by the King of Portugal. Cão and his men planted the *padrão* on a hill above the bay, where it stood 6 feet high, alone on the horizon in a land without trees, framed by the black hulk of the Brandberg Mountain in the far distance. The raising of the *padrão* claimed the empty desert for Portugal and King João II, but also marked the southern extent of Diogo Cão's now failed journey to find a route to India. It was not the last time the Namib would disappoint and dishearten a prospective empire-builder.

The *padrão* itself was to stand where Cão had left it for 408 years. In 1893 it was finally uprooted by sailors of the German Navy and returned to Europe, becoming a trophy of the German Naval Academy in Kiel. Today, at what is known as Cape Cross, a quarter of a million Cape fur seals, the descendants of those who greeted Diogo Cão, still sunbathe noisily at the foot of a granite replica of the missing *padrão*. Here at least, little has changed since Diogo Cão rowed ashore.

Although the Namib had been claimed for Portugal, the Portuguese never arrived to take possession or to seek out its elusive inhabitants. An order for the exploration of the coast was given in 1520, but nothing seems to have happened. This was unwanted real estate: there were no thriving coastal populations to trade with or enslave, no broad rivers slicing into the heart of the continent, no gold, spices or precious stones. This was a land which profited no one – a wasteland with a murderous coastline which only added weeks of travel and additional danger to the journey around Africa. A later Portuguese writer summarised the Namib in one line, 'All this coast is desert and without people.'[2]

For the next four centuries the Skeleton Coast and the Namib Desert beyond it became mute witnesses to the rise of the age of empire. Ships travelling to India in the sixteenth century via the Cape were so fearful of the coastline that they travelled 250 miles offshore to avoid its hidden rocks and treacherous currents.[3] The Dutch, the master navigators of their age, dared to come closer, as they headed to their empire in the East Indies. Their sailors reported that, when peering through the fog, they could on occasion spot black figures on the shores staring back at their ships. The Dutch called these unknown people *strand-loopers* – beach runners. From the fifteenth to the end of the eighteenth century this was the limit of human contact between the peoples of south-western Africa and Europe.

Although European ships occasionally sought shelter in the natural bays and harbours, those travellers never dared attempt to cross the desert or make contact with the mysterious *strand-loopers*. The only Europeans who embarked upon that hopeless journey were stranded survivors from ships wrecked in the Benguela Currents. They stumbled blindly inland until they succumbed to the heat. It was their whitened, weathered bones that gave the Skeleton Coast its name.

For a brief moment in the 1780s, it looked as though all that might change. The nation that had eventually superseded the Portuguese as the world's prime maritime power turned its attention to the Namib coast. Influenced by the spurious accounts of travellers who claimed to have ventured into the lands north of the Orange River (the modern-day border between South Africa and Namibia), a British parliamentary committee began to consider what role the Namib might play in Britain's global empire. Three centuries of inaction surely meant that Portugal's claims to ownership had lapsed, and from their comfortable offices in London the committee members speculated that the Namib might be the perfect location for a penal colony. In fact, the parliamentarians were so confident that the Namib was a suitable site for European settlement that they even debated whether it might also be offered as a new home to those loyal subjects of the crown who had fled the American colonies after the Revolutionary Wars.

A naval survey ship, the *Nautilus*, was sent out to explore the coast and find a site for the colony. Some on the committee argued that south-western Africa would offer a more hospitable climate for the convicts than the alternative location, the Gambia. One committee member, the philosopher Edmund Burke, argued that convicts sent to the Gambia would be decimated by tropical disease and attacked by the local African peoples, and hence deportation would amount to a death sentence, 'after a mock display of mercy'.[4] Had Burke known anything of the Namib he would have considered the Gambia benign by comparison.

In 1785 the *Nautilus* returned with bad news. The Namib coastline of dense fog and thunderous seas was unchanged since Diogo Cão had encountered it three hundred years earlier. Any convicts or would-be colonists sent there would face certain death. Instead, Britain's convicts were sent to Botany Bay and the colonisation of Australia began.

Behind the fog banks of the Skeleton Coast and the sand fields of the Namib Desert, there was a world that the Portuguese explorers and British colonialists could not have imagined. Hidden from the gaze of the Europeans was a land of enormous beauty. This realm of tall grasses, waterholes and hot springs was home to an array of African peoples. High on a great central plateau that lay sandwiched between the Namib and Kalahari deserts, tens of thousands of people lived in relative affluence. Some subsisted by hunting the vast herds of springbok, kudu, wildebeest and zebra that swarmed across the land in incalculable numbers. Others had forged a way of life and a culture centred on their precious long-horned African cattle. Unknown to generations of those pastoralists, these wonderful animals were not in fact their greatest asset. Rather, it was the 1,200 miles of the treacherous shoreline and impenetrable desert that had insulated them from European colonialism.

The word 'Namib' itself hints at some deeper understanding of the role the desert played in the long history of Africa's south-west. It comes from the language of the Khoi, one of the many peoples of southern Africa, and means to 'shield'. It was due to the great shield of fog, sand and heat that this region of Africa was able to progress free from outside influence. Empires were built, whole peoples had made treks, fought epic battles and displaced their enemies.

The earliest inhabitants of the region had been the San, a people otherwise known – even today – as the 'Bushmen'. For the San, south-western Africa was merely one part of a vast territory, stretching from the Cape all the way to the Great Lakes of East Africa, over which they had roamed and hunted for millennia. In the Herero language the San were known as the *Ovokuruvehi*, meaning the oldest of the earth, and, judging from their rock paintings and engravings, they had lived in the region since ancient times. Their art, that still adorns mountains and caves across modern-day Namibia, is both complex and stunning. Some paintings depict scenes of everyday life and mystical religious ceremonies; others are abstract expressions so vivid and imaginative that the white South Africans, who ruled over the mandate of South-West Africa from 1919 to 1990, convinced themselves they were the work of some lost white civilisation.[5]

Sometime around the start of the seventeenth century a wave of migrants arrived in the south-west. They were Bantu-speakers, members of a huge language group that links the deep histories of peoples from across Central Africa, from Kenya to Cameroon. The newcomers were pastoralists and they travelled south with their herds of cattle in search of new pastures. One theory is that they were refugees fleeing wars in their homelands. About half their number settled around the banks of the Kunene and Kavango, the rivers that today form the border between Namibia and Angola. This group, who became known as the Owambo, grew crops by harnessing the waters of the

Cuvelai floods that swell the Kunene and Kavango with waters from Angola each year.[6]

The rest of the Bantu invaders headed further south, into the fertile grasses of the central plateau. This second wave, the Herero, largely eschewed agriculture and remained devoted pastoralists. They found what little water there was by digging deep stone-lined wells into the network of dry seasonal rivers found across the central plateau. They settled over an area roughly the size of Holland. Over generations, they subdivided into numerous clans, but the Herero were a people who held their lands in common. The meter and rhythm of their lives was determined by the needs and movements of their herds and by the seasons of the plateau.

At the core of their identity as a people was their all-powerful deity Ndjambi.[7] So awe-inspiring was Ndjambi that no direct communication could take place between him and living men. The dead, the Herero's holy ancestors, were able to intercede on their behalf, being closer to Ndjambi than the living, and all prayers and requests were channelled through them. In every one of the hundreds of Herero settlements, holy fires were lit. These were left permanently burning to symbolise the connection between the worlds of the living and the dead. Each morning and every evening the elders sat by their fires and spoke at length to the ancestors.

Due to their ancestral religion most Herero could trace their families back several generations, but theirs was not a patriarchal society: the rights of inheritance were nuanced and complex. The Herero were a people without a king, a fact that convinced the first Europeans who encountered them that they were the scattered remnants of a once great empire, now fallen into a steep and terminal decline. They were governed by a series of local chiefs. When a chief died, a council of elders was assembled to elect a successor from among his maternal nephews and uncles. Bound by kinship and religion, Herero society, despite the great distances between their settlements, was tight-knit and conflict between the various clans was rare.

By the 1780s, as the British were contemplating building a penal colony on the Namib coast, the Herero had established themselves as the dominant force on the central plateau. One estimate, made at the end of the eighteenth century, suggests their population had reached between thirty and forty thousand. With their power seemingly assured, few among the Herero, the San or the Owambo could have dreamed that south-western Africa's age of isolation would end.

When change arrived, it did not come from the sea and it was not in the form of white colonisers. In the early years of the nineteenth century, a wave of African invaders, many of them of mixed-race, moved up slowly from the Cape in the south, bringing with them trade, new ways of life and a new method of warfare. They were the Nama, a people who became known across much of Europe by the derogatory term 'Hottentot'.[8]

The Nama sprang from the genetic and cultural whirlpool that was the Dutch Cape Colony in the eighteenth century. Most were the product of unions between Dutch colonialists and the local Khoisan peoples, the original inhabitants of the Cape. Others were escaped Khoisan slaves or the descendants of the Malay slaves brought to the Cape by the Dutch East India Company.

The Nama were a people whose culture was as mixed as their blood. Alongside Khoekhoegowab, the distinctive clicking language of the Khoisan, most also spoke the Cape Dutch of the Boers. Many were Christian, some devoutly so. In the Cape, they eked out an existence as small-scale farmers living as far from white settlement as possible. Others became outlaws, surviving by raiding cattle from the Boers and other Khoisan peoples.

The Nama were men and women who had rejected the status of slaves or landless labourers offered to them by Boer society. Yet it was the aspects of Dutch culture that they appropriated, rather than those they rejected, that made them a unique and powerful force. In the early decades of the nineteenth century, the Nama had begun to acquire the two tools that lay at the heart of Dutch power – the gun and the horse. Some, notably a subgroup known as the Oorlams, copied the Boers and formed armed, mounted bands known as commandos.

In 1833 the Abolition Act was passed by the Westminster Parliament, prohibiting slavery in Britain's dominions across the globe. It followed 'Ordinance 50', a law of 1828 that guaranteed 'free peoples of colour' rights to land and labour contracts in the Cape. Many Boers regarded these laws as unacceptable interferences by the British, and in 1836 several thousand abandoned their farms and settlements in the Cape to embark upon their famous Great Trek. While most of the 'Trek Boers' moved to the future Boer republics, some pushed north into lands occupied by the Nama. The Nama were forced to move further north and, one by one, various bands slipped over the Orange River and into the south-west.

The terrain into which the Nama moved was, at the time, uncharted and very different from the more fertile plains of the Cape. Here two great deserts – the Namib to the west and Kalahari to the east – come together, forming a thick belt of shrub desert. The southern deserts are pitted with deep canyons and pockmarked with mountains and extinct volcanoes. Human life is made possible only by the existence of underground water. As the Nama trekked north into this unknown territory, they were guided by dogs trained to sniff out hidden waterholes. Where the dogs stopped the Nama dug their wells and built their settlements.[9]

By the end of the century, twelve separate Nama bands had settled north of the Orange River. Although unified by their two languages and bound together by a common culture, each Nama band occupied its own territory. There they formed clans under the leadership of their *Kapteins* – a term borrowed from the Boers. The wonderful lyrical names of the Nama clans also come from the Dutch. The Veldskoendraers took their name from their *veldskoen*, their distinctive leather field shoes. The Rooi

Nasie, or Red Nation, were named after their copper-red skin colour, a distinctive and much-prized feature of the mixed-race Nama. The Witbooi, meaning White Boys, one of the most powerful Nama clans, were named after the white bandanas they wrapped around their wide-brimmed hats.

Another aspect of Boer life that the Nama appropriated and carried with them over the Orange River was Christianity. Once settled in an area, they built a simple church and called for a European missionary to join them. The missionaries of the south-west, incredible as it seems, secured their position in Nama society not just by offering salvation but by becoming the suppliers of a key frontier commodity: gunpowder.[10]

With scripture and black powder they bought souls and exercised huge cultural influence, pressuring the Nama to abandon what was left of their traditional festivals and ceremonies. They encouraged them to draft local constitutions and enshrine marriage. As the Namibian historian Klaus Dierks has remarked, 'The missionary campaign to Christianise Africa not only converted "heathens" into Christians but also tried to convert Africans into Europeans.'

The missionaries also opened schools, and the ruling elites of both Nama and Herero society began to send their children and their wives to the classrooms. In these early days the missionaries, despite their undoubted influence, remained guests and the Africans kept a tight hold of the commodities that really mattered: land and cattle.

These were the years before the arrival of cameras in the south-west, and yet a picture of this world is clear enough. It was mainly scrub desert, green and fertile in the short dry winter, baked golden yellow in the long wet summer. Between the canyons and mountains were small settlements of mud-brick huts, clustered around whitewashed churches from which missionaries distributed barrels of gunpowder, struggling to interest their flocks in scripture more than trade. During these decades of change, whole societies vacillated between ancient traditions, recently borrowed Boer customs and new ideas from Europe.

The local elites – both Herero and Nama – took to wearing tailored jackets and Boer-style military tunics, while the ordinary Herero still wore traditional leather skirts and covered their skin with red ochre and cow fat to block out the sun.

Between the settlements were endless fields of sand, littered with giant rocks. These great distances were covered by sturdy wagons, pulled by teams of oxen, fourteen, sixteen or even eighteen strong. At night the landscape was pinpricked by a constellation of campfires, as white traders, missionaries, Nama, Herero and San sought comfort from the cold of the desert night. The whole nation clustered around thousands of fires, telling ancient stories or dreaming of cattle, wealth or power.

The peace of this enormous landscape was regularly punctured by the thunder of gunfire as commando bands fought local wars, making and breaking treaties. At times they headed out on enormous hunting expeditions, often hundreds strong. The profits to be had selling hides and ivory in the markets of the Cape meant that the wildlife of the area was decimated, almost as ruthlessly as the buffalo of the American Great Plains would be two decades later. Elephants and rhinos completely disappeared from the south and centre of the territory.[11]

By the last decades of the nineteenth century the economies of the Nama and Herero were becoming coupled to the markets of the Cape. Large herds of cattle were marched south, and traders brought guns and powder in exchange. We know little of the lives of the traders, but they were often men on the fringes of society – prospectors, dreamers or conmen. Today, their abandoned wagons lie in the inaccessible parts of the southern deserts, and the bleached bones of oxen and men can be found beneath the sand.

The traders' inflated prices introduced a European blight to the land – debt. The potent Cape brandy they hauled north – literally by the barrel load – brought alcoholism. As society changed, the old knowledge that had guaranteed self-sufficiency, such as digging for wells, was increasingly set alongside newer skills: those of the gunsmith, blacksmith and sharpshooter. By the 1880s south-western Africa was on its way to becoming a fully functioning frontier capitalist society, and the Africans were as much capitalists as the white traders with whom they shared their campfires. It was a world that looked in many respects like that other frontier society, an ocean away in the United States. But in the south-west, the Africans – armed, mobile and fluent in the language of the whites – played the roles of both the cowboys and the Indians. The obsession with cattle was common to both the 'natives' and the whites, all of whom understood the significance of owning the land that could rear livestock. But since there were no railways and few harbours, there were still only a tiny number of white faces in the lands behind the Skeleton Coast. The region remained a backwater, one of those blank spaces on the map of Africa, outside the control of any European empire. To the people of London, or even Cape Town, life in the south-western interior of Africa was as mysterious as life in the deep oceans.[12]

2

The Iron Chancellor and the Guano King

It was claimed in the 1880s that there were three ways to build an empire: 'The English [way] which consists in making colonies with colonists; the German, which collects colonists without colonies; the French, which sets up colonies without colonists.'[1] There was much truth in this barbed comment. By 1887, the year the British celebrated Queen Victoria's Golden Jubilee, 'the greatest empire the world has ever seen' extended over 3½ million square miles of territory. Thousands of Britons had become the administrators and soldiers of the empire. Millions of others had settled in Canada, Australia, New Zealand and South Africa, creating dominion states that were umbilically linked to the mother country through trade, culture, language and government.

Germany, the new great power of Europe, had followed a different path. Millions of Germans had left their homeland and settled in all corners of the earth. Across North and South America German emigrants had come together to form highly productive and self-contained farming communities; elsewhere German traders and merchants wandered the globe staking a claim in new markets and seeking out a share of the riches of empire. They occupied remote trading posts on the banks of the Niger and the Congo rivers; they bought and sold from trading ships moored off the Gold Coast and Cameroon. In Germany the port towns of Hamburg and Bremen were growing rich on the back of colonial trade – but this meant trade with the colonies of Germany's European neighbours and competitors.

At the beginning of the 1880s, Germany still had no colonies and no frontiers of her own. Yet within the space of just one year she acquired the fourth-largest empire in Africa. This remarkable transformation began on 10 April 1883, the day the *Tilly*, a two-masted sailing brig, cruised silently into Angra Pequeña, the southernmost bay in south-western Africa. The passenger on board the *Tilly* was an unknown twenty-year-old trader named Heinrich Vogelsang, and the chain reaction he initiated embroiled Bismarck, Gladstone and the leaders of Portugal, France and Belgium. It mobilised and electrified the German public, and shaped the destinies of millions of Africans.

In 1883 Angra Pequeña looked almost exactly as it had done when the Portuguese had 'discovered' the Skeleton Coast in the 1480s. In the intervening centuries, it had occasionally harboured ships seeking shelter from Atlantic storms, and the Dutch had established a whaling station in the early years of the century. Since the 1850s, traders had arrived there from the Cape before heading inland to the settlements of the southern Nama clans, and from time to time the odd missionary had landed in the harbour.[2] If there was any sight likely to test a man's faith it was Angra Pequeña. It was almost completely without vegetation, a landscape of giant, half-buried boulders, their seaward faces pitted and sculpted by the South Atlantic winds. The bay itself was bitterly cold, refrigerated by Antarctic currents, while just over the stone hills loomed the burning-hot dunes of the Namib Desert. Yet this austere harbour was to become the first conquest of the German colonial empire. Few empires can have begun with such an inauspicious acquisition.

In 1883 the population of Angra Pequeña consisted of a handful of guano collectors and the English trader David Radford, the bay's only permanent resident. Radford had been living in Angra Pequeña for an unimaginable twenty-one years, making a living by hunting cat sharks and harvesting the precious oil from their livers, which was then used in the treatment of wounds. The shallow seas around Angra Pequeña swarmed with Radford's prey, especially off Shark Island, a long thin island that protected the bay from the full force of the South Atlantic. When Heinrich Vogelsang landed, David Radford's shack was the only permanent building in Angra Pequeña, but the young German quickly added his own feature to the landscape: a prefabricated hut brought down on the *Tilly* to which he gave the grandiose name 'Fort Vogelsang'.

His plan was to conduct a treaty with a local chief and thereby purchase this strange speck on the map in the name of Germany and his employer, Adolf Lüderitz. Vogelsang intended to set up a trading post in the harbour and then more inland, in the hope that they would eventually become the foundations for a future German colony. But first, Vogelsang had to reach the Nama settlement of Bethanie 120 miles inland.

Bethanie was home to one of the twelve Nama clans, the Bethanie Nama. The settlement had been named by members of the London Missionary Society after a neighbourhood of biblical Jerusalem. After the British missionaries abandoned Bethanie in 1828, it had been taken over by the Rhenish Missionary Society, and in 1883 the local German missionary in Bethanie was Johannes Bam. The Bethanie Nama were led by their *Kaptein*, Joseph Fredericks, then in his fifties. In the first decade of the nineteenth century, Fredericks's people had abandoned their lands in the Berg River area of the Cape Colony and moved to Bethanie. On his father's death Joseph Fredericks had inherited Bethanie and the burden of responsibility for his 1,200 people.

Vogelsang was a sallow youth from a far-off land, and with his long fleshy face and dark curly hair he must have looked an unimpressive sight as he arrived exhausted from his desert journey. But, despite his appearance and despite his years, he was experienced in the methods of colonial trade and, importantly, the duplicity of colonial treaties. Vogelsang had worked as a trader on the West African coast, where unfair treaties with Africans and their leaders were commonplace. Assisted in his task by Missionary Bam, who acted as interpreter and adviser, he entered into negotiations with Fredericks and applied all the lessons he had learned.

By 1 May a treaty had been agreed. Fredericks would receive two hundred rifles and £100 sterling – all trading near the Cape was carried out in the British currency. For this he agreed to sign away his rights to Angra Pequeña and the surrounding area to a radius of 5 miles. As Joseph Fredericks signed he could not possibly have realised that this sale of a small patch of desert around a desolate harbour would set in train the complete takeover of south-western Africa by European colonialists and disaster for his own people.

With Fredericks's signature on the contract, Heinrich Vogelsang trudged across the desert to 'Fort Vogelsang'. Back at the bay he dispatched a message to Germany reporting to his employer that the deal had been done; Angra Pequeña was his. On 12 May, Vogelsang raised the German flag over the empty harbour.

Vogelsang's employer, Adolf Lüderitz, was the son of a tobacco merchant, brought up in Bremen, a port city full of sailors, exotic goods and the whiff of adventure. Rather than follow his father and become an office-bound merchant, Lüderitz decided to trace the tropical goods that flowed into his hometown back to their source. He was twenty years old, the same age as Vogelsang in 1883, when he first left home. Between 1854 and 1859 Lüderitz lived and travelled in the United States and Mexico, where he became a rancher, breeding cattle and horses. One account claims that he was involved in armed confrontations with bandits, but little is known for sure. What is certain is that through his travels Lüderitz came to understand the scale of the wealth that was accumulated through colonial trade. He began to realise that, despite their efforts, German traders stood outside this mercantile revolution. The British civil servant Sir Eyre Crowe, writing decades later, captured exactly the awakening that inspired traders like Adolf Lüderitz:

> The young [German] empire found open to its energy a whole world outside Europe, of which it had previously hardly had the opportunity

to become more than dimly conscious. Sailing across the ocean in German ships, German merchants began for the first time to divine the true position of countries such as England, the United States, France and even the Netherlands, whose political influence extends to distant seas and continents. The colonies and foreign possessions of England especially were seen to give to that country a recognised and enviable status in a world where the name of Germany, if mentioned at all, excited no particular interest.[3]

In 1878 Lüderitz had inherited his father's company. He was forty-four years old and his travelling days should have been behind him. The settled life of a Bremen merchant might have suited his years but not his temperament. His company traded in guano and tobacco, but when the introduction of a tobacco tax threatened to ruin him, Lüderitz diversified. He began trading with West Africa, a tactic that had the added benefit of allowing him to indulge his seemingly undimmed lust for travel. By 1881 he owned a trading post in the British-run port of Lagos, in modern Nigeria.

Since the middle of the century German companies had been bartering European goods for palm oil, ivory and other tropical products all along the West African coast and down into the Congo. In 1881 the key port of Lagos was under British control, but of the 112 Europeans based there, forty-five were German nationals.[4] Just as the lone traders who travelled the deserts of south-western Africa inflated the value of the rifles, gunpowder, liquor and clothing that they exchanged for cattle, the trading houses of Hamburg and Bremen exaggerated the worth of the European goods they brought to the West African coast and undervalued the palm oil, ivory and ostrich feathers that the Africans gave them in exchange. West Africa also became a vast dumping ground for substandard European goods, often made especially for the trade. One of the most powerful trading houses, C. Woermann of Hamburg, specialised in exporting cheap alcohol to West Africa, and trade factories had sprung up around Hamburg specially to churn out hooch that was described to the Africans as 'rum' or 'liquor', but was in fact cheap potato spirit. In 1884, 64 percent of Hamburg's trade with Africa was paid for by alcohol exports.[5]

What Germany got from these treaties was merely the same exploitative advantages the British, French and Americans had already secured by similar means. The merchants of Hamburg and Bremen had begun to taste the exaggerated profits of colonial trade and were hooked. But while the trade with Africa was profitable, it was hardly secure, and the merchants were painfully aware that their continued wealth depended on access to the African coastal markets under the informal colonial rule of Britain or France. The fear that those powers might close the African coast to German ships led to calls for Germany to secure her own colonies and guarantee her access to the African markets.

Adolf Lüderitz found himself the victim of exactly the sort of restrictive tariff that the traders had long dreaded: in the 1880s, the British introduced an export tax and he was forced to close his West African trading station. It was around this time that he first learned of South-West Africa through the young Heinrich Vogelsang. Here was a place where he could trade with the local Africans free from the interfering reach of the British. In preparation for his new venture, Lüderitz bought 150,000 marks' worth of trading goods and sent Vogelsang to the south-west to find a bay that might become their foothold. Lüderitz knew that the Namib coast and the offshore islands were rich with guano and was in possession of a report that claimed that the region had deposits of copper. He hoped for more, perhaps gold or diamonds. After all, only a decade earlier diamonds had been found in Kimberley in South Africa.

The more Lüderitz invested his money and his hopes in South-West Africa, the more his ambition swelled. He imagined a network of trading posts and enormous mineral wealth ripped from the earth. He also dreamed (though perhaps less vividly) of a German colony of farms and German settlers. The first step in achieving this grand vision was to wrest ownership of the land from the local African leaders, which, as Vogelsang had shown, was the easy part. The greater challenge would be for Lüderitz to have his new territories recognised and offered consular protection by the German government. This would involve an encounter with the most formidable statesman in Europe: the Chancellor of the German Reich, Prince Otto von Bismarck.

Throughout the 1870s, Bismarck's view on colonies, in public at least, had been consistently negative. As long as German traders could sell their goods in British and French colonies, Bismarck saw little reason for Germany herself to claim colonies. He was acutely aware that Germany lacked a navy large enough to protect far-off territories, and to create such an armada would be an enormous expense. Moreover, if Germany were to become a colonial power, the administration of these foreign possessions would be another unwelcome cost. Bismarck had long been willing to send gunboats across oceans to intimidate and bombard Africans or Asians, or force them into unequal treaties. He was even open to the establishment of naval bases and coaling stations on foreign shores to make this sort of trans-global intimidation more efficient, but he remained resolutely opposed to formal colonies, stating, 'As long as I am *Reichkanzler*, we shall not pursue a colonial policy.'[6] So when in January 1883 Adolf Lüderitz came to Berlin to request consular protection for his planned trading post, he cannot have been too surprised that Bismarck responded, 'Sovereignty over this country now lies either with the Negro prince concerned, or with Lüderitz, but not the Reich.'[7]

Despite this apparently emphatic rebuttal, Bismarck was secretly biding his time to see if Lüderitz's acquisition became viable. Most importantly, he wanted to see how the British, with their possessions in the Cape Colony and at Walvis Bay on the Namib coast, would react to the presence of Germans in south-western Africa. Bismarck's customary anti-colonial stance was beginning to buckle under the weight of popular pressure.

Germany in the 1880s was in the grip of what became known as the 'colonial fever'.

Ever since unification in 1871, organisations had been formed to promote the idea that the young nation should acquire colonies. The earliest movements were created by merchants who wanted to secure new markets for German goods, and during the severe depression that followed unification, their economic arguments for colonial expansion gathered increasing levels of support. Then, on the eve of the 1880s, in the midst of an economic recession, a book was published that set in motion a full-scale national debate on the colonial question: *Does Germany Need Colonies?* by Friedrich Fabri, the inspector of the Barmen Rhine Mission. The immediate acquisition of overseas colonies, claimed Fabri, had become 'a matter of life or death for the development of Germany'. Despite Germany's military power – four times that of Great Britain in Fabri's estimation – without colonies she would remain a second-class nation. Although Fabri would never set foot in Africa, he set himself up as an African expert and in the 1880s helped found the *Westdeutsch Verein für Kolonialisation und Export* (West German Society for Colonisation and Export). Unlike earlier organisations, Fabri's society campaigned not for overseas markets, but for colonies to which German farmers might emigrate. In 1882 another movement was formed through the amalgamation of several smaller groups. The *Deutsche Kolonial Verein* (German Colonial Society) became the most influential pro-colonial movement.

In the Germany of the 1880s popular enthusiasm for empire, especially for empire in Africa, was stoked by the dramatic accounts of the great explorers and, despite having no colonies, Germany was at the forefront of tropical exploration. Long before unification, German explorers had proved their mettle by reaching lands bewilderingly distant and remote. Perhaps the greatest German explorer was Heinrich Barth, who had crossed the Sahara as a member of a three-man British-led expedition. After the deaths of both his colleagues, Barth had carried on alone, eventually reaching Timbuktu. By the time he left Africa he had travelled 12,000 miles during five years of unbroken exploration. The account of his journey, *Discoveries in North and Central Africa*, ran to five volumes and was published in English and German simultaneously. A decade later Friedrich Röhlfs became the first European to cross Africa from north to south, and in the 1870s Gustav Nachtigal added his name to this national roll of honour by exploring previously unknown parts of the central Sahara. During one expedition Nachtigal was given up for dead, only to escape the clutches of the jungle and dramatically reappear at Khartoum.

Germany could also claim a role in the most glamorous (and most stage-managed) African adventure of the age – Henry Morton Stanley's epic struggle to build an empire in the Congo for Leopold II, King of the Belgians. In Germany, some of the genuine excitement surrounding Stanley's exploration of the 'dark continent' stemmed from the fact that two German explorers were working alongside him. The German army lieutenant Hermann Wissmann had made his name exploring the Tushelango area, where he had 'virtually discovered' Lake Munkamba.[8] Another German, Curt von François, had worked alongside Wissmann until 1885, after which he had set off on his own to explore the Lulengo and Uruki tributaries of the Congo. Stanley later thanked von François for discovering 1,000 miles of navigable waterways that were added to Leopold's empire.[9]

By the time the 'colonial fever' was reaching its crescendo, German explorers had hacked their way through some of the continent's most impenetrable forests and trekked across its most desolate wastelands. They had endured appalling privations and encountered unimaginably exotic peoples, but for the ordinary millions caught up in the 'colonial fever' this was no longer enough. They longed to see Germany's representatives in Africa plant flags and claim new lands for the Reich – as Pierre de Brazza had done for France and Henry Morton Stanley had done for King Leopold. Writing on German public opinion at the end of 1884, a correspondent of the *London Globe* reported that, 'So deeply are the people imbued with a vague but nonetheless enticing vision of the wealth to be won in Africa that thousands of young men are longing and waiting for an opportunity to seek their fortune in the new El Dorado.'[10]

As the dream of a German colonial empire – once the fixation of a middle-class minority – spread across German society, it became increasingly intertwined with the issue of national prestige. If Leopold II of the Belgians, acting as a private citizen, could build a colony seventy-six times the size of his own realm, then surely Germany, fast becoming the greatest military power in Europe, had not only a right but a duty to take a slice of the colonial cake. The fear grew that if Germany continued to delay her arrival at the colonial feast she might find the door slammed in her face. By the middle of the decade 'colonial fever' was giving way to *Torschlusspanik* – 'door closing panic'. This national paranoia was stoked by the nationalist, conservative press and manipulated by the German Colonial Society. Bismarck himself acknowledged that 'public opinion in Germany so strongly emphasises colonial policy that the position of the German government essentially depends upon its success'.[11]

In March 1883, just a month before Heinrich Vogelsang landed in Angra Pequeña, Adolf Woermann, the owner of the Woermann trading house, wrote to Bismarck warning him that the British, French and Portuguese were combining to take control of much of Africa and push the German traders out. Just weeks later Bismarck received similar warnings from Heinrich von Kusserow of the Foreign Office, and in July the Hamburg traders added to the clamour for African colonies by again calling for the annexation of the coast of Cameroon. This time Woermann warned Bismarck that if Germany wanted colonies in Cameroon, 'now, so to speak, is the last moment to acquire them'.[12]

On 25 August 1883, as the pressure on Bismarck was increasing, Heinrich Vogelsang negotiated a second treaty with Joseph Fredericks of the Bethanie Nama. Even by the low standards of European colonialism, it was exploitative and one-sided. It is even suggested that Vogelsang may have plied Joseph Fredericks with liquor during the negotiations. Whatever his tactics, the substance of the deal was this: Fredericks would sell to Lüderitz a strip of coastal land stretching from the Orange River in the south up to a latitude of twenty-six degrees in the north. For this Joseph Fredericks and his people would receive £500 and sixty Wesley-Richards rifles. The treaty defined the coastal strip as a ribbon of land twenty 'geographical miles' in width. This 'geographical mile' was a German measurement that will have meant nothing to Fredericks, but is almost five times the distance of a normal (or English) mile. Fredericks had been tricked into selling off the bulk of his people's land. In a letter to Vogelsang, Lüderitz ordered his agent to 'Let Josef Fredericks believe for the time being that the reference is to 20 English miles'.[13] So outrageous was this second treaty that a later German administrator was dispatched to investigate it, but he died on his way back to Germany and the Bethanie Nama lost their land for ever.

At the beginning of 1884 Bismarck was still waiting to see how the British would react to Adolf Lüderitz's acquisition of Angra Pequeña. Despite several dispatches to the British government enquiring as to whether they had any historic claim on Lüderitz's land, the British had remained silent. Through high-handed inaction and a series of blunders, the British authorities gave the impression (to Bismarck at least) that they were attempting to strangle the new German colony at birth. In March 1884 news arrived that the British Cape government had, somewhat suspiciously, stumbled across a batch of previously lost documents that proved Britain had rights over Angra Pequeña. Bismarck was furious.

Three months later Heinrich von Kusserow, the pro-colonial official from the Foreign Office, sent Bismarck a memorandum that offered a positive assessment of Angra Pequeña as a potential trading post. Von Kusserow also took the opportunity to remind the Chancellor that the British – the very power that threatened to undermine German interests in Africa – had pioneered a colonial model offering Bismarck the possibility of acquiring colonies without the attendant financial burdens. Although much of the British Empire was made up of Crown Colonies, run by British administrators and garrisoned by British soldiers, other possessions were merely 'protectorates'. This was Britain's famous 'paper empire', in which the administration and development of vast areas was undertaken by private companies working under a Royal Charter and with only the nominal protection of the British flag. These companies recruited their own private armies and financed their own affairs.

There were already stretches of the African coast on which German traders were the dominant presence. If they could be persuaded to run those areas as colonies according to the British charter company model, then the declaration of an African empire would be a mere formalising of arrangements that already existed. Encouraged by von Kusserow, Bismarck began to regard the British model as a way of yielding to the public mood. Just weeks after receiving the von Kusserow memorandum, Bismarck made his final and irrevocable leap into the dark. 'Now let us act,' he told von Kusserow.[14]

In the spring of 1884 the highest levels of the German government were flung into action to secure the future empire. On 19 April, Bismarck informed Adolf Lüderitz that his private colony would receive full protection. Nine days later the Hamburg trader Adolf Woermann was summoned to Berlin and told that all German traders working on the West African coast were to be placed under the protection of the Reich.

Government and private business now began working together to give shape to the new empire. In May, Adolf Woermann supplied Bismarck with a set of guidelines that laid out in detail what would need to be done on the ground if Germany were to secure territory in West Africa. The guidelines told the government upon which shores the German flag should be planted and which African tribes would have to be coerced into signing trade agreements. Exactly a month after promising protection to Lüderitz, Bismarck telegrammed the man who was to have the honour of declaring the birth of Germany's African empire: the African explorer and long-time advocate of colonial expansion Gustav Nachtigal.

A Special Commissioner of the German government, Nachtigal was already on standby in Lisbon harbour on the German gunboat the *Möwe* (Gull). On receiving Bismarck's order, he set sail along the West African coast with orders to raise the German flag over the territories that were to become her new colonies. After this he was to make the long journey south, over the equator and along the Skeleton Coast, to Angra Pequeña. It would take him until July to reach West Africa, and in the intervening weeks Bismarck concentrated his attentions on diplomatic manoeuvres to convince the British that nothing untoward was taking place. Lulled into complacency by Bismarck and completely unaware of Nachtigal's mission, British administrators in London and at the Cape continued their leisurely debate as to the whether or not to annex the 900 miles of coastline between the Orange River and Portuguese Angola.

In July the *Möwe* finally arrived off the coast of Senegal, the first potential German colony. In 1884 Senegal was the site of a German trading post and German traders were highly active in the area, yet this first landing of the *Möwe* was an abject failure. Nachtigal came ashore, with his flags and declarations at hand, only to discover that the local African leader had just signed a protection treaty with the French. Hopes of a German colony in Senegal were dashed for ever.

Gustav Nachtigal's subsequent landings were more successful. At Togo he came ashore and claimed Little Popo in the name of the Kaiser. In August he raised the German flag at various trading posts along the Cameroon coast. At the mouth of the Cameroon River, Nachtigal was personally met by one of Woermann's younger brothers, and the *Möwe* was joined in convoy by two of the Woermann company's steamers. Woermann's representatives in Cameroon had even paved the way. When Nachtigal arrived at Douala he found the substantive details of the treaty had already been agreed between the local kings, the Woermann company and the agents of another German shipping line, Jantzen & Thormaehlen. By the time the British representative in the region arrived, the German flag fluttered over the bay and Germany had laid claim to 40 miles of impenetrable malarial mangroves – a coastline fatal not just to Europeans but to the Africans of the interior and even livestock, all of whom fell prey to the tsetse fly and the mosquito.

The final part of Nachtigal's secret mission had been to sail south and conduct friendship treaties with the people of south-western Africa on his way to Angra Pequeña, but given the accelerating pace of the 'scramble for Africa', Bismarck was unwilling to wait for Nachtigal and the *Möwe*. He dispatched two fast navy corvettes – the *Elizabeth* under Captain Schering and the *Leipzig* under Captain Herbig – that thundered into the silent bay on 7 August 1884. The next morning soldiers from both ships assembled in neat lines around the flagpole and were called to attention on the rocky waterfront. The German flag was slowly raised and a proclamation read out declaring that Adolf Lüderitz's private empire now enjoyed the protection and sovereignty of 'His Majesty Kaiser Wilhelm I'. Out in the harbour the two warships fired a twenty-one-gun salute and south-western Africa became the Protectorate of German South-West Africa.

To claim the rest of the Skeleton Coast, between the Orange River and the border with Angola to the far north, another German warship – the gunboat *Wolf* – was diverted to Africa en route to Singapore. In late 1884, in austere harbours and on windswept promontories all along the Namib shoreline, the crew of the *Wolf* repeated the same bizarre ceremony. Sailors in blue jackets raised their country's flag over empty land, their only witnesses the birds and the fur seals. One ceremony was held at Swakopmund at the mouth of the Swakop River, another at Cape Frio. A flag was also raised at Cape Cross in the shadow of the *padrão* hauled ashore by Diogo Cão four hundred years earlier. Unlike the fifteenth-century Portuguese, however, the Germans were to make real their claim of ownership.

There were few other episodes during the 'scramble for Africa' that illustrate so graphically the near-insanity that gripped the minds of otherwise reasonable men. From the comfort and splendour of London and Berlin, representatives of two of the world's greatest powers raced each other across oceans and fought a battle of wits to acquire one of the most desolate places on earth, a land virtually uninhabitable to outsiders and, ostensibly, worthless.

By the end of the 1884 almost 1 million square miles of Africa had been brought under nominal control of Germany and her charter companies. In addition, Germany had claimed possessions in Samoa and New Guinea. In October 1884 Germany's right to exploit her new empire in Africa was recognised by the powers of Europe and the United States at the Berlin Conference, held in Bismarck's own villa on Wilhelm Strasse. The African empire over which Germany claimed rights of protection at the conference was over five times the size of the Reich itself. Fourteen million Africans had (in theory at least) become the colonial subjects of Germany – although almost none of them had any idea that this seismic event had even taken place. At the start of her colonial odyssey, Germany found herself with considerable holdings, high aspirations but almost no experience in administering overseas possessions. Her few supposed colonial experts were quickly conscripted into the great enterprise. The explorer Gustav Nachtigal had already been made a Colonial Commissioner. Soldiers such as Curt von François and Hermann Wissmann made the leap from colonial mercenaries of King Leopold II to founders of the German army in Africa. Yet in the charter model of colonialism, it was the traders, not the servants of the crown, who were expected to shoulder the greatest burdens. Much of the pressure on Bismarck had come from the shipping companies and the merchants. Now they had their protectorates, it was up to them to make it pay, or so the theory went.

Bismarck's savvy diplomatic manoeuvres had captured the public mood and satisfied the popular call for colonies, but outside the trading houses of Hamburg and Bremen, the loudest of those calls had been for territories where ordinary Germans might settle and farm. Of the four African colonies, two were completely unsuitable for settlers. Togo and Cameroon would only ever be trading colonies, home to a skeleton staff of traders, agents, missionaries and increasingly soldiers – malaria and yellow fever made that a certainty. Of Germany's other two colonies, it was South-West Africa that seemed to offer the only real potential for settlement, although few could see it in 1884.

The process of transforming German South-West Africa into anything resembling a viable colony would take decades. In the first instance the Africans of the territory would have to be made to sign 'protection treaties' with Germany. And here again the trader was to lead the way; the flag would merely follow. Through his audacity, and the double dealing of his agent Heinrich Vogelsang, Adolf Lüderitz had won the right to exploit his possessions around Angra Pequeña, but he had also been burdened with the responsibility of administering the territory, a task that almost instantly proved too much for him.

In February 1885 the *Tilly*, the ship that had launched Lüderitz's empire, sank, taking with it much of his fortune. Further bad luck followed. Dreaming of diamonds, gold or at the very least copper, he funded a series of prospecting expeditions. They found nothing. Adolf Lüderitz would not live to realise the wonderful irony: these ruinously expensive expeditions, led by expert geologists and geographers imported at his own expense, had marched blindly across some of the richest deposits of surface diamonds on earth and come back empty-handed. With his funds dwindling, Lüderitz entered into discussions with a group of British financiers. Bismarck was horrified. To keep the British out of

Germany's newly won colony, the Chancellor quickly conjured into existence a German company ready to take over Lüderitz's remaining assets.

The German South-West African Colonial Company was a fragile concern from its inception. Most of its initial capital was spent buying out Adolf Lüderitz, and by the end of its first year of operation it had lost 45,159 marks.[15] The charter system of informal colonies led by traders had run aground. Short of capital and bereft of ideas, the company turned to the state for help. In order to keep hold of German South-West Africa and prevent the encroachment of British interests, Bismarck was forced to create the entity he had always sought to avoid: a state-financed colonial administration. With deep reluctance he appointed an Imperial Commissioner.

3

'This Is My Land'

On 2 September 1885 the newly appointed Imperial Commissioner of German South-West Africa, Dr Heinrich Ernst Göring, arrived in Walvis Bay aboard the British cruiser the *Namaqua*. Walvis Bay, by far the best anchorage on the south-west African coastline, had been seized by the British in 1878 and, along with the local African porters who unloaded ships arriving at the docks, the only residents were a handful of British officials.

Dr Göring, an overweight middle-aged provincial judge, was an unlikely Imperial Commissioner. He had no experience of Africa, but, by virtue of his birthplace on the German-Dutch border, he was fluent in Dutch, the language spoken across south-western Africa by the Nama and increasingly the Herero. His other key qualification was his knowledge of law: the first stage in the colonisation of South-West Africa was to be a legal rather than a military affair.[1]

It is a common misconception that the Berlin Conference simply 'divvied up' the African continent between the European powers. In fact, all the foreign ministers who assembled in Bismarck's Berlin villa had agreed was in which regions of Africa each European power had the right to 'pursue' the legal ownership of land, free from interference by any other. The land itself remained the legal property of the Africans. To begin to divest the peoples of the south-west of their property, Bismarck instructed Göring to negotiate a series of 'protection treaties and alliances between the German Reich and the autonomous rulers in South-Western Africa'.[2] In return for vague promises of 'protection and friendship', the Africans were to be bound to Germany.

He was given a staff of just two. The clerk Louis Nels was to help with administrative and legal matters, and the soldier Hugo Goldammer was given the grand title of Chief of Police, despite the fact that there was not a single policeman or soldier for him to command. In mid-September 1885 the three Germans left Walvis Bay and headed north towards the lands of the Herero. On 3 October their four covered wagons, each pulled by a team of eighteen oxen, reached the Herero capital at Okahandja. The town consisted of a hundred or so round huts, built from mud and branches and set along a bank of the Okahandja River, which, like all rivers in South-West Africa, flowed only briefly during the short rainy season. On a large bend in the river stood a row of brick houses belonging to Herero leaders. The most impressive, described by one German trader as 'resembling a villa', had its own stables and was the home of the foremost Herero chief, Maharero Tjamuaha.[3]

Being of the opinion that 'natives are easily impressed by appearance', Göring halted on the outskirts of Okahandja so that he, Nels and Goldammer could change their clothes. Göring, who had a particular penchant for dress uniforms, donned a navy-blue jacket with gold trim, a pith helmet, baggy trousers and riding boots. This attempt at a grand entry did not produce the anticipated response. Rather than being ushered into the presence of Chief Tjamuaha, Göring and his colleagues were directed to the local German mission station and told to wait. In late 1885 Chief Tjamuaha had more pressing concerns than the arrival of three overdressed German officials.[4]

Just as Göring and his colleagues reached Okahandja, the Witbooi, the most powerful of the Nama clans, had arrived en masse at the Herero settlement of Otjimbingwe just two days' ride away. In accordance with a peace treaty signed only a year earlier to end a decade-long war, they were seeking safe passage to fresh pastures in the fertile areas in the northern reaches of Hereroland. En route the Witbooi had been joined by several hundred Nama from other clans. They travelled in an enormous column made up of hundreds of wagons and thousands of cattle, stretching for over a mile. The Nama fighters were well armed and highly organised. Their leaders were unwilling to accept the Herero's traditional monopoly on the lush terrain of the central plateau.[5]

The threat posed by the Witbooi and their allies completely overshadowed the sudden appearance of Dr Göring and his entourage. But after a few days' wait, Chief Tjamuaha found time to grant Göring an audience. Old, tall and heavy-set, Tjamuaha was an impressive figure. In the Herero's praise poems he is described as 'so very black, black as the shadows by the mountains in the west'. As well as one of the most powerful men in South-West Africa, he was said to be one of the richest, owning more than thirty thousand head of cattle. Dressed in a thick cotton blazer, the chief greeted his German visitors warmly and settled down to talk. But while Göring was in mid-flow, he was hastily ushered out and the meeting abruptly terminated.

The next morning the leaders of the Witbooi arrived at Osona, a settlement just a few miles south-west of Okahandja. Wearing their distinctive white bandanas, tied in a knot around their broad-brimmed hats, the Witbooi headmen were flanked by armed fighters. As was the custom, Chief Tjamuaha welcomed the Witbooi *Kaptein*, Hendrik Witbooi, as if they were old friends, though the two men had only previously met on the battlefield. Tensions were high, but the negotiations began cordially enough. Suddenly, however, shots were fired and fighting broke out. Surrounded on all sides, the Witbooi managed to force their way out of what appeared to be an ambush, and the Herero suffered heavy casualties. From the safety of the Okahandja mission station only a few miles away Göring was able to hear the sound of battle.[6] As the wounded were brought back to their capital on the captured Witbooi wagons, he and Goldammer – both veterans of the Franco-Prussian War – attended to them as best they could. Göring later claimed to have extracted four bullets from the bodies of injured Herero fighters. The following day, the Germans attended the funeral of the fallen Herero, whose interment, Göring informs us, was accompanied by the 'howling of mourning women'.[7]

Almost seventy of Tjamuaha's men had been killed and over a hundred injured at the battle of Osona. The Witbooi had lost only twenty-four men but, forced into a retreat, they abandoned thousands of cattle and many of their wagons. As their battered and broken caravan headed south, Hendrik Witbooi, who had lost two of his adult sons, wrote to Chief Tjamuaha:

> Well you knew that I wanted peace, but you deceived me. You wanted to lure me into your kraal and then kill me without warning. I defended myself as best I might. You know how the day went. I had to withdraw because I ran out of ammunition . . . Now I am once again prepared for war and soon I will again meet you at the same place. So sit there and wait for me . . . truly, now the Lord shall judge between us.[8]

For Heinrich Göring the outbreak of war between the Herero and the Nama seemed, at least at first, like an incredible stroke of luck. He and Goldammer had garnered a great deal of good will by treating the Herero wounded. This may well have helped persuade Tjamuaha to agree to a second meeting at which Göring intimated that the 'protection treaty' he proposed was in fact some form of alliance between the German Kaiser and the Herero. After a week's consideration, Tjamuaha agreed. The treaty – drafted in German – was intentionally flattering, purporting to place the Kaiser and Tjamuaha on equal footing: 'His Majesty the German Emperor, King of Prussia . . . William I in the name of the German Reich, on the one hand, and Maharero KaTjamuaha [*sic*], Paramount Chieftain of the Hereros, on his own behalf and on that of his legitimate heirs, wish to conclude a protection and friendship treaty.'

Tjamuaha signed with his characteristic mark – an 'X' surrounded by a circle – and at a stroke Göring had secured a legal foothold for Germany in South-West Africa. Yet his success in bringing the Herero under German 'protection' placed him in an almost impossible position. Although he had fulfilled part of his mission, he was aware that when the war between the Herero and the Witbooi Nama intensified, the Herero would demand to see evidence of the 'protection' his treaty spoke of. Worse, by forming an alliance with the Herero, Germany had become the enemy of the Witbooi. An alliance with them or the other Nama clans now seemed highly unlikely. There was, however, a more substantial obstacle that would prevent Heinrich Göring from hoodwinking the Witbooi into a protection treaty.

Never was there a man less likely to be deceived by Göring than *Kaptein* Hendrik Witbooi, without question one of the most remarkable figures in the whole of African history. A later German governor believed he would undoubtedly have become 'an immortal in world history had not the fates decided him to be born to an insignificant African throne'.[9]

Despite standing only around five feet tall, Hendrik Witbooi was a feared military commander and the dominant force among the Nama peoples. He possessed a razor-sharp mind and, in stark contrast to the popular nineteenth-century European image of the African chief, he was extremely worldly. In 1885, he was fifty-five years old and had built up a body of knowledge and contacts that ranged far beyond the confines of his own people or the African south-west. He was well aware of events outside Africa and fully understood that the powers of Europe were seeking access to the continent and its people.

Like most Nama, Hendrik was a devout Christian. He could recite long passages from the Bible in Dutch, as well as in Khoekhoegowab, his native language. Despite his religious fervour, he held the missionaries in fairly low esteem, recognising them as agents of European colonialism. His distrust of the missionaries went hand in hand with a general distaste for Europeans. During his teenage years in the Cape, he had witnessed the devastation wrought upon the Nama peoples by the Boers as they fanned out across the Cape, forcing Africans off their land and into bondage. It had been the expansion of white settlement that had led Hendrik's father and grandfather to abandon the fertile Cape and move north into the desert wilderness of South-West Africa.

Perhaps most significantly of all – for historians in particular – Hendrik Witbooi was educated and literate. Due to an old war injury – a missing thumb on the right hand – he was no longer able to write his own letters. Instead, he dictated his correspondence to his friend and confidant Samuel Izaak, who also filled in the pages of his meticulously kept diary.

The history of imperialism in Africa is almost always written by the colonisers. Most African leaders left few written records. Furthermore, in most European accounts, both factual and fictional, Africans are mere ornamental details. They are either stereotypes or thin black figures, seen at a distance or through the sights of a rifle. The Sudanese, who die spluttering in the dust in the African memoirs of Winston Churchill, do so silently. Even Joseph Conrad, the European writer and traveller who came to see more clearly than most the true face of imperialism, conjured up in his masterpiece *Heart of Darkness* a nightmare vision of King Leopold's Congo in which black men and women speak few words of their own. Like the subsequent Herero leader Samuel Maharero – who plays an important part in this story – Hendrik Witbooi maintained a constant stream of correspondence with other leaders and his own lieutenants. He also sent letters to the German governors, commissioners and commanders of the local garrisons. Seeking to outmanoeuvre them, he wrote to the colonial newspapers and drafted appeals to the British officials in the neighbouring territories. What stands out about the Africans of the south-west, and leaders like Hendrik Witbooi in particular, is not just their ability to resist imperialism though military and diplomatic means, but the fact that they left us their own accounts of that long struggle – a rare glimpse of colonialism and colonial violence through African eyes.

Heinrich Göring's initial approach to Hendrik Witbooi took none of this into account. Unbearably pompous and arrogant, Göring subscribed firmly to the delusion that Africans responded best to threats and had to be addressed in stern tones, like mischievous children. What chance there was of a constructive dialogue between the two men evaporated the moment Göring put pen to paper. Seeking an end to the war between the Herero and the Witbooi, he wrote to Hendrik Witbooi,

> I have always heard, and read too, that you are a reasonable man. So act reasonably now; realise that the best course is to return home and live in peace with your old father and your tribe. To recapitulate: The German Government cannot permit chieftains, who have placed themselves under German protection, to support your enterprise of plunging a protected chiefdom into war . . . I trust you will attend my words.[10]

Witbooi simply ignored this letter. When eventually Göring's deputy, Louis Nels, wrote suggesting a conciliatory meeting, Hendrik Witbooi replied,

> I gather that you want to negotiate peace, you who call yourself a Representative. How shall I respond? You are someone else's representative and I am a free and autonomous man answering to none but God. So I have nothing further to say to you . . . a representative has less power than an autonomous man, I [see] no need to follow your summons at this point.[11]

Hendrik Witbooi's contempt for the Germans was matched only by his fury with the Herero. As the war escalated, Göring, Nels and Goldammer became mere spectators. Again and again, Witbooi's mounted fighters raided Chief Tjamuaha's cattle, each attack demonstrating the military prowess of the Herero's opponents and the worthlessness of their 'alliance' with the Germans.

Unable to influence events, in 1886 Göring trekked across the southern parts of the protectorate in an attempt to persuade the minor Nama chiefs to sign protection treaties. The journey to the south revealed how vast the Nama's territory was. Only about forty thousand strong, the Nama inhabited an area twice the size of Great Britain. To their east was the Kalahari Desert and in the west the Namib. Only in the middle of the territory did the dense grassland of the central plateau offer the Nama and their cattle some sustenance. The twelve Nama clans lived in scattered villages but were bound to each other through marriage and a strong political entity known as the *Wittkamskap*, a union of mutual protection and common purpose.

Göring's mission through Namaland was a wasted effort. Only a couple of the more minor chiefs agreed to sign. But Hendrik Witbooi, quick to re-establish his authority, scuppered even these small triumphs. When Chief Manasse of the Nama clan known as the Red Nation signed a treaty and accepted a German flag from Göring, Witbooi confiscated it. He then wrote to Göring: 'I captured the flag which you had presented to [Chief] Manasse. It is now in my keeping. I should like to know what to do with this flag; I ask because it is an alien thing to me.'[12]

In 1887, two years into his tenure as Imperial Commissioner, Göring was forced to report to Chancellor Bismarck that the situation in Namaland was 'not very encouraging'.[13] If the lack of progress was a disappointment for Bismarck, it was a disaster for the German South-West African Colonial Company. In 1885 it had bought out Adolf Lüderitz, who drowned the following year while exploring the Orange River. Angra Pequeña had subsequently been renamed Lüderitz Bay in his honour. But the minerals and riches that Adolf Lüderitz had dreamed of had never materialised, and the company's ambition to transform the protectorate into a flourishing mining colony had come to nothing. By the time of Lüderitz's death in late 1886, the company's funds were once more exhausted and new investors could not be induced to come forward. Financially and politically, German South-West Africa seemed a failed enterprise. Serious questions began to be asked in Berlin as to whether the protectorate was even worth keeping. However, at the very moment that Göring's mission seemed destined to fail, incredible news reached Berlin – gold had been discovered.

Remarkably, the precious metal had been found only a few hours' ride north of the headquarters Göring had set up in the Herero town of Otjimbingwe. The fortunate prospector was an Australian named Stevens, the owner of a small mine in a backwater called Anawood. Göring, in his role as Imperial Commissioner, had been the first on the scene and, having personally verified the find, he proudly transmitted the news to

Berlin. He even insisted on personally escorting the gold samples back to Germany, arriving in Berlin in early December 1887.

Only a year earlier, under almost identical circumstances, a gold strike in the Wittwatersrand Mountains of South Africa had led to the uncovering of one of the largest gold deposits on earth. The investors of the German South-West African Colonial Company held their breath in anticipation and Germany looked forward to her own colonial gold rush. All that remained was to determine the extent of the deposits.

A team of the nation's leading geologists and mineralogists was hastily assembled for an African expedition, but before they even reached South-West Africa, private mining companies and prospectors were rushing to invest. Germany's desert protectorate had become the jewel in the Kaiser's crown.

For the prospecting expeditions arriving in South-West Africa, the powerlessness of the German authorities was a profound shock. They were especially disturbed to discover that in order to prospect for minerals on land owned by the Nama they had to seek permission not from Imperial Commissioner Göring but from *Kaptein* Hendrik Witbooi. The expedition leader – a man as incapable of diplomacy as Göring – alienated Witbooi almost immediately. Perhaps imagining himself a character in a Wild West novel, he informed him that he came in peace. Unimpressed, Hendrik coldly responded, 'You come as friends? Well this is my land, and I don't want anything to do with the white man.'[14]

When the geologists and mineralogists arrived at Anawood, they made a sobering discovery. Although the gold samples that Göring had brought back to Germany were real enough, they had not come from Anawood, or anywhere else in South-West Africa. Small pieces of gold had been loaded into a musket and fired into the rock face. The gold find had been a hoax. The identity of the culprit remains a mystery, but the suspicion remains that it might have been a desperate, last-ditch attempt by Heinrich Göring to bring investment into the protectorate and save his mission.

If Göring was behind the hoax, it did him little good. Rumours of the Anawood find had spread fast, and one of the first to hear the exciting news was the English trader Robert Lewis. Lewis had lived among the Herero for several years, and had forged strong bonds of friendship and trust with several Herero chiefs. In addition to his trading activities, Lewis was a prospector and the holder of a decade-old contract with Chief Tjamuaha. This contract gave him exclusive rights to all prospecting and mining in northern Hereroland, but did not extend into southern Hereroland where the Anawood mine was located. To gain these mining rights Lewis set about exposing Göring's protection treaty as worthless.

Tjamuaha and his councillors were receptive to Lewis's claims. They were well aware that Göring's promises were empty and the treaty a meaningless document. Furthermore, they had turned against Göring and the Germans months earlier, due to the behaviour of the prospectors and mineralogists who had flooded into their territory. Under the terms of the protection treaty the Germans were expected to 'respect the customs and habits of the Hereros', but many of the prospectors, living among a people they considered inferior, were violent and abusive. Often drunk, some had taken 'liberties with the Herero women'. The chiefs were outraged. Yet it was Göring who transgressed the customs of the Herero most unforgivably.[15]

In 1885 Göring had purchased the old mission building in the Herero settlement of Otjimbingwe and had later decided to add an extension to the old building. Whether Göring was aware of it is not known, but the extension was built over a Herero graveyard, and the bones of the sacred ancestors were disturbed.[16]

When the news of this desecration reached Tjamuaha – probably through Lewis – he was enraged, and at the end of October 1888 he summoned Göring to Okahandja. Flanked by over a hundred of his people and Robert Lewis, he formally nullified the 'protection' treaty and dismissed Germany's Imperial Commissioner from his own protectorate. Göring left Okahandja fearing for his life. His nerves shattered, his last official act was to issue a general evacuation order instructing all Germans, including the missionaries, to abandon the protectorate. It was roundly ignored, even by his assistants, Goldammer and Nels. But the Imperial Commissioner had left, and German South-West Africa was German only on paper.

In Berlin, Göring's flight was viewed as a catastrophe. Bearded men in flannel suits held long meetings in the Colonial Department, trying to understand the causes of this fiasco. Few of Germany's colonial bureaucrats had ever left Europe, and they were baffled by Göring's failed mission. But they were unwilling to even consider the possibility that he had been outmanoeuvred by independent, literate and educated Africans.

Unable to come up with an acceptable explanation, they produced the next best thing: a scapegoat. The Colonial Department blamed Germany's abject failure on the British, the perennial enemy, who, they claimed, were conspiring to wrest South-West Africa away from the Reich. Given the role that Lewis had played in Göring's downfall, it was a vaguely plausible explanation and far more palatable than the truth. When this conspiracy theory was served up to Bismarck he immediately accepted its logic, stating, 'We are finding ourselves up against England rather than . . . the Hereros.' In this version of events, Göring had not been outmanoeuvred by so-called 'savages', but was the victim of 'Perfidious Albion'.[17]

Göring was largely forgiven, thanked for his loyal service and appointed German ambassador to Haiti – the only black republic in the western hemisphere. In January 1893, not long before leaving for Haiti, Göring's wife Franziska gave birth to a boy, whom she named Hermann.

Throughout the winter of 1888–9 the question of what do to with South-West Africa rumbled on in Berlin. In January Ludwig Bamberger, a liberal member of the Reichstag, publicly asked the question many officials had long debated in private: should

Germany finally abandon her claims to the protectorate? South-West Africa was running at a constant loss, and as long as the indigenous people resisted German rule and fought among themselves, there would be little prospect of the protectorate making a profit for the fatherland. Surely the sands and scrub of the Namib Desert, or even the grasslands of the central plateau, were not worth the effort of keeping them?

Only by deploying a full-scale military expedition could Germany truly take control, and this Bismarck refused to mount. 'There can be', he informed the Colonial Department, 'no question of applying force against the Hereros.' Bismarck's solution was in part a symbolic gesture, designed to appease nationalist and colonial lobby groups. He sent a tiny force to South-West Africa and gave their commander strict orders to avoid conflict with the Africans. However, to lead the expedition Bismarck appointed one of the very few German officers with any military experience in Africa, a man with very different ideas.[18]

4
Soldier of Darkness

Early on a June morning in 1889 a group of twenty-one German 'explorers' landed at the British port of Walvis Bay. Supposedly on a scientific expedition, each wore the standard uniform of the nineteenth-century explorer: khaki jacket and matching pith helmet. In the dark of the ship's cargo hold, chewing on bales of hay, stood two camels, procured during a stopover at the Canary Islands. For explorers they were suspiciously well armed, each man carrying a new Mauser 88 rifle, and their leader, Curt von François, was a captain of the Prussian army with a fearsome reputation. They were in fact a unit of German colonial soldiers.[1]

No one like Curt von François had ever before set foot on the sands of the Namib. Tall and with an elegant corkscrew moustache, he was the image of a nineteenth-century Prussian army officer. His family, descended from French Huguenots, had been in the service of the Prussian kings for over a century. Curt von François's reputation, however, had been made in the service of another monarch, Leopold II, King of the Belgians.

For three years von François had been a mercenary, paid by King Leopold to enforce and extend his rule over what had become a private slave state in the Congo. Armed with the rifle and the chicotte, a hippopotamus-hide whip that cut deep into human flesh, von François had raided villages and traded in slaves. In the forest of the Congo Basin, he had become a racial fanatic, with unshakeable views on how Africans should be treated. Von François took everything he had learned in Leopold's Congo to South-West Africa in 1889.

On landing, Captain von François was appalled to discover how little progress had been made in German South-West Africa.

The land remained in the hands of the local people. Worse still, the Africans remained unbowed, considering themselves equal to the whites. They were armed, owned property and would address German officers in a casual tone that no German soldier would dream of using. From the outset von François was determined to end Germany's difficulties through the application of 'force against the natives'. In a private letter he wrote: 'The Europeans [here] have failed to give the black man the right kind of treatment. They have made too many concessions, granting all [the black man's] wishes without bearing in mind that this is only interpreted as a sign of weakness.'[2]

Curt von François had received only one piece of advice from Heinrich Göring, 'Request reinforcements, stay in Walvis Bay and await the situation.' But in early July, von François marched straight to Otjimbingwe and attempted to reoccupy Göring's former headquarters. He and his men were refused access and were escorted by the Herero to a smaller building in the centre of the town belonging to the South-West African Colonial Company, a now partly British-owned enterprise. This was a deliberate policy of Chief Tjamuaha. Göring's abandoned mission station had thick brick walls and was located on a strategically important site. The new German base was far more vulnerable, and might easily be surrounded, should the Germans and Herero come to blows.

Thwarted and humiliated by this show of defiance, von François found it impossible to live alongside the Herero at Otjimbingwe. By early August tensions were running high. Louis Nels, Göring's former assistant who was in Otjimbingwe at the time, noted Captain von François's propensity to antagonise the Africans. Writing to Berlin, Nels warned officials at the Colonial Department that 'The Captain finds it difficult to subdue his anger about the Hereros and, as set out in the instructions, to avoid a war with the tribe.'[3]

In the early hours of 28 July, von François and his men rode out of Otjimbingwe without warning. They travelled for 22 miles, to the edge of the central plateau where the land drops to meet the fringes of the Namib Desert. At a location known as Tsaobis, von François ordered his troops to halt. There, they gathered supplies of limestone, sand and cow dung, and within a few weeks had constructed a small, rudimentary fortress that von François named Wilhelm's Fort, in honour of the newly crowned Kaiser Wilhelm II.

Von François had chosen Tsaobis for very specific reasons. It lay on the Bay Road, the trading route between Hereroland and Walvis Bay, and from Wilhelm's Fort he was able to disrupt the movement of guns and ammunition to the Herero and the Nama tribes. In accordance with his original orders, von François also impounded wagons belonging to the English trader Robert Lewis, who was still regarded as an enemy of the German Empire. In order to sustain his troops in such a barren location, von François permitted his men to confiscate supplies of food from passing traders. Even among the few Germans who had been drawn to South-West Africa, Wilhelm's Fort soon became known as 'The Den of Thieves'.

Von François's strategy at Wilhelm's Fort was to deliberately set himself on a collision course with the Herero and the Nama, both of whom relied heavily on trade from Walvis Bay. With a force of only twenty men, war with either nation would undoubtedly have meant the annihilation of the German garrison. By placing himself in such a precarious position, von François hoped to force Chancellor Bismarck into making a serious military commitment to South-West Africa. Either Bismarck would agree to his request for reinforcements or have to stand aside and allow the German garrison to be massacred – a politically unpalatable option.

It was a spectacular gamble, founded on von François's conviction that Bismarck's brand of cautious, penny-pinching imperialism had been a failure, and that the German people would demand strident military action in order to protect their precious colonies and develop them properly. Years later, defending his strategy, he wrote, 'Only serious, strong-minded and domineering actions against foreign nations, as well as quick diplomacy and battle successes, could excite the support of the German people. Negotiations, deviation, delay and deliberation were completely impossible and detested concepts.'[4]

Towards the end of 1889, after expressing his anger at von François's blatant disregard for his original orders, Bismarck reluctantly agreed to dispatch reinforcements to South-West Africa. It is perhaps Curt von François's greatest accolade that, from the sands of the Namib Desert, he was able politically to outmanoeuvre Otto von Bismarck, one of the shrewdest statesmen of the age. However, his victory over the Chancellor was not total. Bismarck sent him only forty-one troops, not the one hundred and fifty he had requested. The new 'Protection Army', as it eventually became known, was large enough to maintain and defend Wilhelm's Fort, but too small to stamp German authority over the peoples of South-West Africa. Two months after dispatching reinforcements to South-West Africa, Bismarck was removed from office by the young Kaiser Wilhelm II, and replaced by Count Leo von Caprivi. One of the criticisms levelled at Bismarck, at the time of his dismissal, was that he had lacked a true vision for Germany's colonies.

While von François awaited the arrival of reinforcements, a Herero council was assembled at Okahandja to debate whether to attack Wilhelm's Fort. Among those who favoured attack was Samuel Maharero, Chief Tjamuaha's increasingly influential son, and a long-time friend of Robert Lewis. Even before the council met, Samuel had sent a letter to von François warning him, 'If you come here with warlike intentions, then I ask you once again to pay heed to what I say, do not needlessly spend your money, but rather go home. If you do not want to listen to my words then please declare so openly and tell me directly that you are at war with us.'[5]

While many agreed with Samuel, Chief Tjamuaha, growing visibly old and frail, was opposed to attacking von François while his people were still at war with the Witbooi Nama. He concluded that, for the moment at least, the Germans were a lesser threat.

In January 1890, six months after he had established himself at Wilhelm's Fort, von François's reinforcements arrived, bringing the strength of the German garrison up to sixty-two men. With the Germans in a significantly more powerful position, the Herero council made a decision that would ultimately have a profound and permanent impact upon their people. They invited von François to Okahandja to negotiate a new protection treaty.

In May 1890, Curt von François and his men marched into Okahandja. Chief Tjamuaha invited von François and his officers to dine with him at his villa; at the meeting that followed, Tjamuaha, increasingly blinded by his fear of Hendrik Witbooi, agreed to sign a second protection treaty with Germany. Had Tjamuaha looked out of the window of his villa that evening he might never have signed. According to the traditional history of the Herero – stories related down through the generations – a terrible portent occurred that evening. One of the camels von François had imported into the colony chewed through its bridle and strayed into the town. Wandering around the inner sanctum, the hapless beast crossed between the chief's villa and the 'Holy Fire', the flame kept permanently alight to signify the life force of the Herero people. For a hornless animal to pass between the two was to break the strictest of Herero taboos and was viewed as an awful omen. In the traditional Herero calendar, in which each year is named after a significant event, the year the protection treaty was agreed became known as 'the year of the camel' and was regarded as a cursed year.[6]

For von François, the conclusion of a treaty with the Herero was vindication of his aggressive strategy and his personal mantra that when dealing with Africans, 'Nothing but relentless severity will lead to success.'[7] Like Göring, he had not the slightest intention of offering any military assistance to his new 'allies'. Rather, von François welcomed the continuance of the war between the Herero and the Witbooi.

In September 1890, the war reached a new level of intensity as the Witbooi launched a series of devastating attacks. The following month Chief Tjamuaha died. The passing of the old chief –

leader of his people for almost three decades – plunged the Herero nation into a deeply divisive succession crisis. Several minor chiefs laid claim to Tjamuaha's cattle and his power, among them Chief Tjamuaha's son Samuel Maharero.

Born in 1854, Samuel Maharero had been educated in the missionary school at Okahandja before being expelled for 'immoral behaviour'. The exact nature of his infraction remains unknown, but it was rumoured he was a heavy drinker. Much of Samuel Maharero's youth was spent in the shadow of his elder brother Wilhelm, but when Wilhelm was killed in a minor local dispute, Samuel Maharero became a leading contender for the Herero throne, despite being distrusted by sections of his own community, the traders and the missionaries.

On the death of Chief Tjamuaha, Samuel was challenged for the position of Paramount Chief by several uncles and a cousin, all of whom were well within their legal rights to pursue the chieftaincy. Lengthy meetings and bargaining turned into angry arguments and tussles. Divisions deepened and old enmities re-emerged. In past decades such disputes among the tribal elite might have had little consequence for the wider Herero nation, but during the decades of the 'scramble for Africa', internal divisions among African peoples were routinely exploited by European colonisers.

With the Herero focused on the succession crisis, von François was quick to act against their interests. In mid-October 1890, just days after Tjamuaha's death, he moved the German headquarters from Tsaobis in the Namib Desert to a valley nestled between the Auas Mountains in the east and the expansive Khomas Highlands to the west. The valley, known by its Dutch name of Windhoek, lay in the fertile heart of Hereroland. At the time the Herero, a semi-nomadic people, had temporarily abandoned the Windhoek valley in part because of its proximity to the land of the Witbooi. Two months earlier von François had requested permission to settle in the valley and been refused. With the Herero elite increasingly preoccupied, he occupied Windhoek, and ignored the Herero's complaints.[8]

The new location offered access to both Hereroland to the north and the territories of the various Nama tribes to the south. Windhoek also had a series of hot springs that provided ample, if slightly sulphurous, drinking water for the garrison. On a hilltop in the centre of the broad valley the Germans began to construct a large fortress. It was both a practical demonstration of their growing military power and a potent symbol of Germany's determination to entrench herself permanently in the south-west.

The new fort and the presence of an expanded garrison encouraged German farmers to settle around Windhoek. A South-West African Settlers' Company was founded and a postal service established between Windhoek and Walvis Bay. Moreover, a regular shipping service running between the colony and Germany was launched, operated by the shipping company of Adolf Woermann. By 1891 the white population of German South-West Africa stood at 139. South-West Africa was beginning to accumulate the trappings of a rudimentary colonial outpost.

Hendrik Witbooi's initial strategy for dealing with Curt von François had been to ignore him, as he had Heinrich Göring. However, as German farmers began to settle around Windhoek and Germany's presence in the territory took on an air of permanence, this strategy was rendered obsolete.

There seems to be no doubt that Hendrik Witbooi recognised, before the other chiefs and *Kapteins*, the dangers posed by German colonialism. He was certainly alarmed by May 1890. At that time the settlers concentrated around Windhoek were few, the German garrison was small compared to the fighting force of the Nama and the industrial weapons that would ultimately make the colonialists indomitable had yet to make their appearance. A lesser leader might easily have dismissed the whites as merely another tribe. Hendrik Witbooi, following events in the wider world, understood the true nature of German ambitions.

An avid reader of newspapers from the Cape, Witbooi had gradually pieced together an understanding of the colonial process. His letters reveal that by 1892 he had learned of the Berlin Conference, which he described as 'a large meeting to decide who should make Protection Treaties with the chiefs of which country in Africa'. He had also correctly deduced what rights to self-determination had been left in the hands of local Africans under the conference's infamous 'General Act'.[9]

In May 1890 Hendrik Witbooi concluded that von François and his men, along with the white settlers and traders, were the vanguard of a threat so great that it rendered his war against the Herero a parochial affair that could only strengthen the hand of a far more dangerous enemy. This epiphany is apparent in Witbooi's correspondence. In the spring of 1890 he abandoned his customary tone of confidence and authority and, in letters to other chiefs, including the leaders of the Herero, he became increasingly earnest and brotherly. He called repeatedly for reason and unity. At the end of May he wrote in exactly such terms to Chief Tjamuaha, urging him to reconsider the protection treaty he had signed with von François:

> This dry land is known by two names only: Hereroland and Namaland. Hereroland belongs to the Herero nations and is an autonomous realm. And Namaland belongs to all the Nama nations, and these too are autonomous realms, just as it is with the white man's countries: Germany, England and so on . . . Do you realise what you have done, or for whom you did what you have done? . . . My dear Kaptein [Tjamuaha], you will come to rue it bitterly. You will eternally regret that you have handed your land and your rights as a ruler to the white men. This war between us is not nearly as heavy a burden as you seem to have thought when you did this momentous thing.[10]

It was not until the summer of 1892 that serious discussions about peace between the Herero and Witbooi began. By this time Samuel Maharero had emerged as the successor to his father as Paramount Chief.

As the two sides inched towards peace, von François was confronted by an increasingly belligerent Samuel Maharero and, more worryingly, by the looming prospect of African unity. He responded by increasing his efforts to lure Hendrik Witbooi into a protection treaty and in early June 1892 he travelled to meet Hendrik at his mountain citadel of Hoornkrans.

A record of what was said at the meeting was made by one of Hendrik Witbooi's deputies. After the usual diplomatic pleasantries, von François spelled out Germany's future plans for the south-west, warning Kaptein Witbooi that 'large numbers of Europeans will be arriving by ship soon', and that these settlers 'must be protected'. He then assured him that 'German Protection' would be extended to those African nations willing to sign protection treaties. To which Hendrik Witbooi responded, 'What are we being protected against? From what danger or difficulty, or suffering can one chief be protected by another?' Aware that the 'protection treaty' was nothing more than a form of subjugation, Witbooi dismissed von François's overtures. 'I see no truth or sense', he told him, 'in the suggestion that a chief who has surrendered may keep his autonomy and do as he likes.' At his most eloquent, Hendrik warned his guest that although the Nama might appear to outsiders as separate nations, that might be divided and thus ruled, they were bound together by a deep and visceral kinship. 'This part of Africa is the realm of us Red chiefs . . . If danger threatens one of us which he feels he cannot meet on his own, then he can call on a brother among the Red chiefs . . . for we are one in colour and custom, and this Africa is ours.'[11]

When von François left Hoornkrans, Hendrik Witbooi surely understood that the Captain's visit was his final attempt to lure the Witbooi into a protection treaty by peaceful means. The threat of violence had been implicit but clear. Four weeks after the Hoornkrans meeting, Witbooi wrote to John Cleverly, the British Magistrate at Walvis Bay, appealing to the British for assistance:

> The Germans are encroaching on my land, and are now threatening to destroy me with war . . . some rulers surrendered to German Protection and are today bitterly sorry for they have not seen any of the beautiful

promises kept. The German told them he would protect them against mighty invaders threatening to take our land by force, without permission from the chiefs. But from what I hear and see of the man, it now appears the German himself is . . . doing exactly what he said we would be protected from . . . He has already executed men for owing money . . . German officials told my officials how they had beaten the men in a disgraceful and brutal manner, as the dumb and ignorant creatures they think us.[12]

Referring to the Conference of Berlin, which he erroneously believed had been held under British auspices, Hendrik made a remarkable plea to Cleverly:

I beg you kindly to be so good as to forward this letter to the Cape government, so British politicians may hear about this, and hold another conference and deliberate about these Germans, to recall them if possible, from our country, for they do not abide by the Agreement and conditions under which you allowed them to enter.[13]

Four months later the Witbooi and the Herero finally agreed peace terms, and for the first time since 1885 there was a realistic prospect of the two most powerful South-West African nations uniting in opposition to Germany's incursions. To counter this challenge, just three months after the peace had been signed, a force of over 250 German soldiers landed in South-West Africa. After numerous appeals for reinforcements, von François had been granted a force large enough to take offensive military action. As Hendrik Witbooi had repeatedly rejected the protection of the Germans, and it was he who best understood the danger the Germans posed, it was his people, the Witbooi Nama, who were the first targets of von François's expanded force.

Late on the night of 12 April 1893, Hendrik Witbooi, his son Klein Hendrik and adviser Samuel Izaak sat in deep conversation in Hoornkrans, the Witbooi's mountain encampment just 100 miles from Windhoek. It was autumn and the air in the Khomas Mountains was bitterly cold. Almost a thousand of Hendrik's people were scattered across the valley, huddled in groups, talking and singing around their fires. The flickering orange light fell on the round clay huts, where the Witbooi's children were sleeping. Beyond them, on the edge of the camp, large enclosures were filled with hundreds of cattle. Beyond these were the steep escarpments that surrounded Hoornkrans on three sides.

That night Captain von François and two hundred of his men were riding through the Khomas Mountains. The troops had been told they were on night manoeuvres. It was only when they reached the foot of the Hoornkrans escarpment that von François gathered his men around him and informed them of their real purpose. This was no exercise, von François explained: 'The object of this mission is to destroy the tribe of the Witboois.' Knowing that he stood little chance against the Witbooi in open battle, von François had decided to surround the tribe as they slept and exterminate them.[14]

Leaving their horses behind, the Germans stealthily climbed the steep slopes overlooking Hoornkrans. One by one the soldiers took up their positions. On the plain below, the Witbooi people were asleep in their huts. It was just before dawn. Smoke was rising from the dying fires and the only sounds were unruly horses and the stirring of cattle in the distant enclosure. As the sun began to rise von François got to his feet and gave the signal. A second later two hundred rifles fired simultaneously. The thunder of the volley gave way to the discordant metallic clanking of reloading, followed by re-aiming and firing. Over the next thirty minutes, more than sixteen thousand rounds of ammunition were fired.

In the settlement below, hundreds burst from their homes and ran in search of cover. Children screamed hysterically, and the cries of the wounded were audible above the thunder of the rifles. Bodies lay in the sand; the injured clutched at gaping wounds. The few Witbooi fighters who managed to load their guns began to return fire, but to little effect. Bullets poured down upon them, killing indiscriminately.

Hendrik Witbooi, shocked and confused, still managed to give an order. He commanded the Witbooi men to run towards the dry river on the far side of the valley, hoping that the Germans would give chase and leave the women and children unharmed.

As Hendrik was ushered away, he might have caught sight of his twelve-year-old son. The boy, who had spent his short life coping with a partial paralysis, had been shot while trying to escape. Wounded, he crawled towards the dry riverbed, where a German soldier killed him with a shot to the head.

Up in the hills, above the dust and the screaming, von François, sabre in hand, gave a second order and his men began to fumble for their bayonets. Seconds later they were charging down the slopes into Hoornkrans, firing as they went. To the horror of the Witbooi, rather than chasing the men to the riverbed, they began to butcher the women, children and the elderly. Hendrik Witbooi's eldest son Klein Hendrik described the fates of those who had remained in the camp:

[They] sat still as they thought their lives were safe, and that though they might be taken away for servants they would not be killed. So we all thought. We thought the men might be killed but not women . . . the women and children they shot in the houses, the wounded as well as the dead they did not bring out, but burned the houses over them . . . On the day of attack, the Germans captured an old man, a church elder, who was too old and infirm to run away, and who had hidden himself among the rocks. They tied him up and took him to their wagons and shot him the next morning with 3 bullets.[15]

Petrus Jafta, a Witbooi fighter, watched the massacre of his people from a nearby hilltop:

I and two other men got on a small Kopje [hilltop] and saw some women sitting a distance away. We called to them to get away, but they remained until the Germans passed. One of the soldiers shot one of these women. The others begged for their lives and asked the Germans to make slaves of them rather than kill them. The German soldiers took the women away, driving them before them . . . one woman was killed while her child clung to her screaming; a soldier shot the child through the head, blowing it to pieces. I saw the child shot. The soldier aimed at it. Houses were set on fire and burnt over the bodies of dead women and children . . . On another side of the werft [camp], all the women were killed except two of whom one was wounded. I did not count them, the bodies were decomposing when I went there [later] . . . Many children were killed in the houses . . .[16]

The slaughter at Hoornkrans was so indiscriminate that even some of von François's men were shocked. When one German soldier, knife in hand, cornered Hendrik Witbooi's sister, one of his comrades held back his arm and shouted for the woman to run.[17]

When the slaughter came to an end the sun had risen fully over the valley. Kurt Schwabe, a German soldier who had taken part in the attack and witnessed its immediate aftermath, wrote:

> On all sides terrible scenes were disclosed to us. Under and over the hanging rocks lay the corpses of seven Witbooi, who in their death agony, had crawled into the hollow, and their bodies lay pressed tightly together. In another place the body of a . . . woman obstructed the footpath, while two three-to-four-year-old children sat quietly playing beside their mother's corpse . . . [It] was a fearful sight; burning huts, human bodies and the remains of animals, scattered furniture, destroyed and useless rifles, that was the picture that presented itself to the eyes.[18]

Schwabe and his comrades did not spend long surveying the carnage. With von François's blessing, they looted the remains of the Witbooi camp. Even the church was raided. Amid the smoke and devastation the soldiers of the most powerful army on earth groped and rummaged through the ruins of mud huts and stripped the bodies of women in search of booty. They then carefully listed the treasure captured for Germany and for the Kaiser: 212 stirrups, 74 horseshoes, 12 coffee pots, 12 coffee-grinders, 122 pieces of cutlery, 44 bits and bridles, 3 violins and a pair of opera glasses.

Von François's men also seized eighty Witbooi women. They were brought to the new German fortress in Windhoek and distributed among the troops as house slaves. There is no record of their ultimate fate or how they suffered, but von François argued that their capture and abuse was 'an appropriate form of punishment'. One of the female captives, Witbooi's daughter, defiantly told her captors to 'hasten back to the big ships in which you came, for my father will return soon to drive all white men from this land'.[19]

At Hoornkrans von François and his men had killed eight old men, two young boys and seventy-eight women and children.[20] Only one German soldier had died; two were lightly wounded. In his report to the Colonial Department, von François claimed the attack had been so successful 'that any further resistance on the part of Witboois is out of the question'.[21]

5

'European Nations Do Not Make War in That Way'

The Hoornkrans massacre was unprecedented in the history of South-West Africa, a land shielded from European colonialism for so many centuries. But by the end of the nineteenth century the tactics employed by Curt von François had been used against innumerable peoples across the world. In Africa, Asia, Australia, and North and South America, soldiers like von François had unflinchingly ordered mass executions, driven millions from their land and taken part in what military strategists liked to describe as 'small wars'.

While colonial wars were undoubtedly small by European standards, they were almost always cataclysmic for the tribal peoples concerned. Very few of them were wars in the conventional sense; rarely were matters in the colonies settled by the clash of opposing armies on the battlefield. Grand set-piece encounters like the colonial battles of Omdurman or Isandlwana were rare events, and such battles account for only a tiny fraction of those who died confronting European colonisers. The majority were killed in massacres, ambushes and punitive raids, events identical in many respects to von François's attack on Hoornkrans.

Through much of the nineteenth century, empire-building was portrayed in Europe as a noble crusade, an act of charitable paternalism. The colonial massacre and the punitive raid clashed with this fiction and were hidden from the public gaze, little discussed outside military circles. Even today they remain relatively obscure in Europe. Those that are remembered tend to have involved the death of a notable European, or yielded an unusual quantity of booty.

What is also forgotten is how easily and how often conflicts in the colonies became genocidal. Accepted rules and conventions of warfare were widely regarded as inapplicable to wars against 'savages'. By the time of the 'scramble for Africa' in the 1880s, various indigenous peoples across the world had been forced to the brink of extinction; a handful had been pushed over that final precipice.

The pattern was the same on every continent. Settlers came in search of land and displaced native populations, leading to the loss of pastures and hunting grounds, and often to famine. Hunger sparked armed confrontations. The parity of military technology that existed between the colonised and colonisers in South-West Africa was a rare exception; elsewhere settlers and soldiers were equipped with far superior weapons to the native tribes who opposed them. Almost always, the musket and later the rifle overcame the spear of the indigenous warrior.

In Australia the convicts whom the British government had once considered settling on the Namib coast had decimated the Aboriginals. In Tasmania during the 1820s and 1830s settlers had exterminated almost the entire Aboriginal population; fumbling attempts to relocate the more remote tribes led to the near extinction of the entire people within just thirty years. Across North and South America the Indian nations had been swept from their lands by repeated waves of European settlement.

All of this was clear, even in the first half of the nineteenth century, yet across Europe, some searched for more palatable explanations as to why the indigenous peoples of the colonies seemed unable to survive contact with Europeans. Religious theorists suggested that the black races of Africa, Asia and the Americas had been simply holding their lands in trust for the whites in accordance with a divine plan. As the higher race was now ready to take possession of its inheritance, the blacks were no longer needed, and simply faded away. The nineteenth-century British theologian Frederick Farrar put it best: the 'irreclaimable savages', unable to embrace civilisation, were, he believed, destined to 'disappear from before the face of it as surely and as perceptibly as the snow retreats before the advancing line of sunbeams'.[1]

In the latter half of the century, as Africa became the focus for a renewed burst of colonial conquest, the destruction of indigenous peoples was increasingly explained using ideas drawn from science rather than scripture. While the advent of Darwinism represented a direct and powerful challenge to the Church, the religious scandal surrounding the publication of *On the Origin of Species* has tended to obscure the fact that, in many ways, Darwin's ideas were perfectly in keeping with his times. While the religious establishment was rocked to its foundations, much of the Victorian scientific elite, along with various economists, philosophers and politicians, welcomed 'Darwinism' wholeheartedly. It was a theory that advanced concepts that were already current and that allowed them to thrust open doors upon which they had already begun to knock.

The first group whose plight was taken as evidence that the 'struggle for life' was the key force shaping human society, as well as the natural world, was not the indigenous races of the colonies but the industrial poor of Europe's teeming cities. From the comfortable Georgian squares of West London and the garden suburbs of Berlin, the millions trapped in the slums were easily dismissed as men and women who had simply failed to adapt. They were the 'unfit' and had been consigned to the bottom strata of the society, a harsh world of crime, violence, alcoholism and destitution. 'Theirs is the life of savages', said the Victorian social investigator Charles Booth, when considering the fate of the nineteenth-century underclass.

In the colonies the fate of those other 'savages', the dark races of the world, seemed to be governed by the same laws of natural selection. Surely their disappearance was a result of their inability to adapt to the arrival of stronger, more capable races and the civilisation they brought with them? The annihilation of the Tasmanians, the Patagonians, the Native Americans and perhaps soon the Africans all testified to their innate weakness, their unfitness for the future.

While imperialism could be justified by a number of arguments – economic self-interest, European rivalry and the white man's duty to spread civilisation and the Gospels – the extermination of whole races was more difficult to explain. Yet Social Darwinism, along with a range of racial theories taken from the older Scientific Racism of the late eighteenth and early nineteenth centuries, was able to recast both historical and contemporary events, and in this capacity it took on the twisted logic of a witch trial.

The white races had claimed territory across the globe by right of strength and conquest. They had triumphed everywhere because they were the fittest; their triumphs were the proof of their fitness. Whole races, who had been annihilated long before Darwin had put pen to paper, were judged to have been unfit for life by the very fact that they had been exterminated. Living peoples across the world were categorised as 'doomed races'. The only responsibility science had to such races was to record their cultures and collect artefacts from them, before their inevitable extinction.

The spread of Europeans across the globe came to be regarded as an almost sacred enterprise, and was increasingly linked to that other holy crusade of the nineteenth century – the march of progress. Alongside the clearing of land, the coming of the railways and the settlement of white farmers, the eradication of indigenous tribes became a symbol of modernity. Social Darwinism thus cast death itself as an agent of progress. The notion that the strong were destined to overcome the weak in the struggle for life became almost a mantra, repeated thousands of times in memoirs, speeches, biographies and scientific tracts. Any last spasms of Christian morality or guilt could be allayed by the fact that all this was inevitable.

Of course there were those who strongly opposed every aspect of this form of colonialism. In the early nineteenth century, millions of people across Europe, including Charles Darwin's own family, had mobilised to confront the brutality and iniquity of slavery. When slavery was finally abolished, the same organisations turned their energy and compassion to the fight against imperialist violence. Liberals in Britain, France and Germany condemned the mistreatment of native peoples and spent decades writing reports, publishing pamphlets and holding public meetings to draw to public attention the aspects of imperialism that were otherwise little discussed. But by the time Africa was divided up at the Conference of Berlin, advocates of an unbridled colonialism had learned to harness a distorted version of Social Darwinism in order to dismiss the views of the humanitarians as hopelessly outdated and unscientific. After all, there was no humanitarianism, compassion or brotherhood in nature.

The British explorer William Winwood Reade, writing in the 1860s, captured the growing consensus of his age. The last chapter of his book *Savage Africa*, entitled 'The Redemption of Africa', concluded with a prophecy of the continent's future. Reade's vision was founded upon his unshakeable belief that Africa belonged to the white man.

> Africa shall be redeemed. Her children shall perform this mighty work. Her morasses shall be drained; her deserts shall be watered by canals; her forests shall be reduced to firewood. Her children shall do all this. They shall pour an elixir vitae into the veins of their mother, now withered and diseased. They shall restore her to youth and to immortal beauty.
>
> In this amenable task they may possibly become exterminated. We must learn to look on this result with composure. It illustrates the beneficent law of Nature, that the weak must be devoured by the strong.[2]

Reade fervently believed that in the not-too-distant future European noblemen would build their estates in Central Africa and 'young ladies on camp stools under palm-trees will read with tears "The Last of the Negroes", and the Niger will become as romantic a river as the Rhine.'[3]

Although Germany came late to the colonial table, her scientists had been among the first to accept the logic of Social Darwinism. In 1868, while working on *The Descent of Man*, Darwin, in a letter to Wilhelm Preyer, Professor of Physiology at the University of Jena, reported that 'The support I receive from Germany is my chief ground for hoping that our views will ultimately prevail.'[4]

Germany was particularly receptive to Darwin, partly because his ideas attracted the support of a number of well-respected German scientists. Chief among them was Ernst Haeckel, one of Germany's most esteemed intellectuals. Haeckel began to explore what very quickly became known as Darwinism soon after the publication of *On the Origin of Species*. Over the next forty years he wrote a stream of highly influential books on evolution, some of which became among the most popular works of non-fiction published in Germany during the age of the Kaisers. A generation of German scientists and intellectuals came to know Darwin partly through the filter of Ernst Haeckel, and one of the key characteristics of Haeckel's work was the way in which he applied Darwin's theories to human racial difference. The extreme caution that Darwin had exercised when making links between his central theories and the struggles between the human races was not practised by Haeckel.

While Germany's scientists stood at the forefront of the Darwinian revolution, in her African empire – particularly in South-West Africa – her colonialists were confronted with a situation that was at odds with the fundamental racial suppositions at the heart of imperialism. Germany's only African colony suitable for large-scale white settlement remained dominated by tribes of Africans who had, in almost every respect, failed to accord with colonial theory. The Nama and Herero had not retreated into the hinterland in the face of the white man, nor had they fallen prey to introduced disease. The continuing military and economic independence of the South-West Africans was profoundly unsettling to the German pro-colonial lobby, and by the 1890s a deep-seated frustration with German colonialism had taken hold. Before the Hoornkrans massacre, armchair imperialists in Berlin, and agitators in the Missionary and Colonial societies, had accused the Colonial Department of failing to apply military force properly in South-West Africa. Some interpreted the massacre at Hoornkrans and the removal of Bismarck from office as portents heralding a new era in the colonies. From now on, they hoped, the Nama and Herero would be put in their place by German military might. Yet, as events quickly demonstrated, all that von François had achieved at Hoornkrans was to start a war he was incapable of winning.

After fleeing Hoornkrans, Hendrik Witbooi and his people found refuge in the Khomas Mountains on the fringes of the Namib Desert. There, Kaptein Hendrik wrote letters to the leaders of the other Nama tribes, whom he beseeched to join him in an alliance against the Germans. In April 1893 he wrote again to John Cleverly, the British magistrate in Walvis Bay whom the Witbooi rightly deduced was a channel through which he could alert the outside world to the massacre at Hoornkrans. He hoped to outmanoeuvre the Germans by appealing directly to public opinion in Europe. After describing in detail the attack his people had suffered, Hendrik Witbooi concluded his letter to Cleverly:

> Please let these miserable and frightful events be quickly known to all the great people in England and Germany. I cannot think that such a war as the Germans have now made is done by such a mighty and civilised people – is it a straight forward or usual way of making war?[5]

To ensure Cleverly reported the massacre to his superiors Hendrik sent his own son, Klein Hendrik, and one of his most trusted lieutenants, Petrus Jafta, to deliver the letter personally. Since both had been at Hoornkrans when von François had attacked, they were also able to corroborate Witbooi's account. Five days later Cleverly replied: 'I cannot understand how there could have been a killing of women and children such as you tell me of. European nations do not make war in that way.'[6]

Cleverly's response was disingenuous. As an official of the British Empire he knew exactly how European nations made war against 'savages'. But he wrote a report based on Hendrik Witbooi's letter for the Under Secretary of Native Affairs in Cape Town, and took sworn affidavits from Petrus Jafta and Klein Hendrik.

Sometime later reports of the German 'exploits' at Hoornkrans began to appear in the British press, specifically stating that the victims had been mainly women and children, and intimating that what had taken place there was a massacre. They stood in stark contrast to earlier reports, published in the German press, that had hailed Hoornkrans as a victorious battle fought solely against the military forces of a savage tribe. The alternative version of events was reprinted in several German newspapers, directly challenging the veracity of the official account.[7]

As Berlin's political classes debated whether the destruction of the Witbooi Nama had been achieved with too much or too little ferocity, Hendrik Witbooi and three hundred of his men launched a series of raids against the Germans in Windhoek. In one, the Witbooi drove off around forty horses belonging to the German garrison. When von François arranged to purchase replacement animals from a local trader, the Witbooi captured the new horses before the Germans could take possession of them. With only seventy horses to the Witbooi's three hundred, von François's garrison was temporarily immobilised and the writ of German colonial power in South West Africa extended only to the limits of Windhoek. In June the Witbooi attacked again. Beyond the range of German rifles, they galloped their horses back and forth and waved their hats in full view, mocking their enemy's inability to give chase.

Hendrik Witbooi then turned his attention to the road between Windhoek and Walvis Bay, attacking a German convoy twenty wagons strong and effectively severing Windhoek's supply lines. Throughout the conflict, the Witbooi focused their attacks solely on von François and his garrison. The German farmers around Windhoek were left unharmed. When Gustav Voigts, an early settler who later became one of the colony's leading businessmen, made a trek through Namaland with about five hundred oxen, he turned to Hendrik Witbooi for permission, and later wrote:

> Witbooi knew full well that we were Germans with whom he was at war and that he might have captured the 500 oxen without a shot being fired; but we, for our part, knew just as well that Hendrik would keep his word whatever happened, and we were not disappointed.[8]

For seven months the Witbooi held von François's forces at bay. Young men of other Nama clans left their settlements and rode off to join them in avenging the Nama blood spilled at Hoornkrans. Yet throughout 1893 Curt von François, now promoted to the rank of major, sent a series of dispatches to Berlin that played down the seriousness of the military situation. While appealing for artillery and more soldiers, he repeatedly attempted to reassure his superiors that final victory was close at hand. But over the course of the year, officials in the Colonial Department pieced together the reality.

Following several unsuccessful offensives against the Witbooi, demands for the removal of Curt von François reached the floor of the Reichstag. One speaker summed up the situation: 'Major François is not the right man in the right place and must be replaced by someone else . . . [Hendrik] Witbooi is the real master of the country and François is no match for him.'[9]

In November 1893, apparently oblivious to the precariousness of his position, Curt von François sent a letter to the German Chancellor, Count Leo von Caprivi, confidently outlining the campaigns he was planning for 1894. In doing so he effectively brought his own career to an end. These ill-conceived and over-ambitious expeditions would almost certainly have brought Germany into conflict with three more of the South-West African tribes, including the Herero. The man who had been charged with making South-West Africa safe for German settlement had dragged the colony into a potentially disastrous era of permanent war and instability. At the end of 1893 a new commander was dispatched to save German South-West Africa from Curt von François.

Theodor Leutwein arrived in the newly founded port of Swakopmund, 20 miles north of Walvis Bay, on 1 January 1894. He was serious-minded, calculating, a realist – in many respects the antithesis of von François. German South-West Africa's third colonial master was the son of a pastor who had studied law before entering the army. At forty-four he was as much a diplomat as a soldier, and his overriding aim as governor was to draw a line under the first chaotic decade of German colonialism in South-West Africa.

Leutwein understood the limits of German power in the colony and the relative strength of the Africans. The inability of Dr Göring and Curt von François to grasp these basic realities stemmed, in large part, from their misconceptions of the Herero and Nama as backward or 'undiscovered'. Leutwein was unburdened by such stereotypes, and his ambitions in South-West Africa were limited, in the short term at least. In the first stage of his wider plan he merely sought for the Germans – both settlers and soldiers – to establish themselves permanently in the colony. To achieve this he was willing to use military force, but unlike von François he did not consider the garrison the only available option.

Theodor Leutwein had studied the British colonial experience in depth and sought to colonise German South-West Africa using the same principles. He set great store by the imperial maxim 'divide and rule', and his long-term strategy was to isolate and then confront each of the territory's ethnic groups, one by one. At the conclusion of each small war, Leutwein planned to foist upon the defeated Africans a treaty that would divest them of a little of their tribal land and strip them of a little of their independence. He planned to turn the Africans against each other whenever possible, to erode traditional clan unity and undermine the power of chiefs. Leutwein's first aim was to pressure the tribes who had refused to sign protection treaties under Heinrich Göring or Curt von François.

Just weeks after his arrival, Leutwein marched out of Windhoek with one hundred troops and headed for the settlement of the Khauas Nama, 100 miles to the south-east. In a surprise raid he captured Andreas Lambert, the chief of the Khauas, along with the bulk of his people's rifles and horses. When Lambert attempted to escape, Leutwein had him put on trial.

Acting as both prosecutor and judge he sentenced the chief to immediate execution. The next day he appointed a puppet ruler and forced the Khauas to sign a treaty accepting permanent German sovereignty.

He then turned to the Franzmann, one of the older Nama clans, who lived on the edge of the Kalahari to the south of the Khauas. When the Germans arrived at the Franzmann's camp, Leutwein ordered his troops to take up positions on a hill overlooking the settlement. The Franzmann chief, Simon Kopper, along with the elders, was then forced to sign a treaty under the barrels of the Germans' guns. Once again they were made to accept the Kaiser as their overlord.

Like most colonial treaties, those imposed upon the Khauas and Franzmann Nama were unwarranted and destructive interventions into sovereign societies. But what is most striking about these treaties is how relatively lenient they were. There was, for example, no attempt to seize their land. Although Leutwein had under his command a force stronger than that with which von François had attacked Hoornkrans, he sought merely to bind the various African nations closer to Germany, in economic, military and cultural terms. This is not to say that Leutwein was a benign imperialist: his policies were a measure of his pragmatism, not his liberalism. But they were also proof that his arrival had ushered in an age of more 'professional' colonialism.

After overwhelming the Khauas and Franzmann Nama, the new governor felt strong enough to move cautiously against the Witbooi, the only Nama clan still outside the 'protection' of the German Empire. In 1894 Hendrik Witbooi had gathered his people together in a new settlement high in the Naukluft Mountains. Appreciating the strength of the Witbooi and the considerable difficulties of fighting in the mountains, Leutwein did not launch an immediate attack, but instead attempted to encourage Hendrik Witbooi to accept German protection through negotiation.

Between May and August, Leutwein dispatched a remarkable series of letters to Hendrik Witbooi. Many are astonishingly frank and, in contrast to the bombastic edicts issued by Heinrich Göring, Leutwein's tone was measured and respectful. In a letter written on 9 April 1894 he attempted to describe the wider forces that had brought the Germans and the Witbooi to war with one another:

Developing events have brought about that His Majesty the German Emperor is now paramount sovereign of Namaqualand, and there is nothing to be done about it. All other Captains of the country have resigned themselves to it, you are the only one who has refused and must fight us to destruction . . .[10]

In another part of the letter he warned Hendrik Witbooi,

Should I succeed in killing you and all your men, the war would be at an end, but should you succeed in killing me and all my men, the war would be no means be at an end, for the Emperor of Germany would, from his vast army, send double or treble the numbers of men, and many more field-guns, and you would have to start over . . . His Majesty the German Emperor has sent me with specific orders to carry on the war to your destruction, unless you surrender. I do not know you and I have no personal enmity against you at all, but shall of course carry out my orders and fight you to the death . . .[11]

In one of his replies to Leutwein, Hendrik Witbooi defiantly wrote:

I have never met the Emperor [Kaiser] and therefore cannot have offended him by word or by deed. God has given us different realms on Earth, and through that I know and believe that it is neither a sin nor crime for me to want to remain the independent chief of my country and people. If you want to kill me for this without any fault of mine, there is no harm done, nor is it a disgrace: I shall die honestly for that which is my own.[12]

Still unwilling to attack, Leutwein informed Hendrik Witbooi on 20 May that he had not yet commanded his troops to storm the Naukluft as his 'conscience still whispers that you may one day accuse me of having allowed you too little time'. Three months later, in a remarkably candid letter, Leutwein told Hendrik Witbooi that if he were to allow the Witbooi to keep their autonomy, 'I should be blamed not only by my Lord the

German Emperor but by all the German people. You are more spoken about in Germany than you suppose . . . Incidentally, our letters are forwarded to Berlin, and are also communicated to my men.'[13]

Leutwein's decision to postpone the attack was not motivated exclusively by his desire to avoid bloodshed, nor his growing respect for Hendrik Witbooi. He was equally eager to avoid being defeated, and it was only after reinforcements had arrived from Germany that he finally, and perhaps reluctantly, launched his assault. It is, however, some measure of his determination to use diplomacy, and his appreciation of the Witbooi Nama as a military force, that the attack came on 27 August, almost four months after the Germans had first arrived in the Naukluft Mountains.

Despite his caution, Theodor Leutwein still underestimated the military skill and resolve of the Witbooi. The German attack began with a ponderous advance through the narrow gorges of the Naukluft during which they were ambushed by Witbooi fighters firing down on them from virtually invisible positions. Ludwig von Estorff, an officer who had recently arrived in the colony but who was to stay in South-West Africa for the next seventeen years, had his first encounter with the Witbooi in the Naukluft. Writing afterwards he admitted that the Witbooi were 'Far superior to us when it came to marching, enduring deprivation, and knowledge of and ability to use the terrain i.e. their agility. It was only in weaponry, courage, perseverance and discipline that the [German] troops surpassed the enemy.'[14]

Of these four factors it was their 'weaponry' that saved the Germans in the Naukluft. After suffering heavy casualties, Leutwein abandoned efforts to outfight the Witbooi and set about battering them into submission with artillery. Having fought against the Germans for a year and a half, and with his people on the verge of starvation, Hendrik Witbooi finally accepted German offers of a peace treaty on 9 September after an unrelenting artillery barrage.

For the Witbooi, the thirteen-day battle in the Naukluft Mountains was a salutary lesson in the power of German artillery. It was this, above all else, that convinced Hendrik that he had no choice but to come to terms with the Germans. For Theodor Leutwein, who had nearly been defeated, the battle was taken as dramatic confirmation of his conviction that South-West Africa could not be colonised by military means alone.

On 15 September 1894, a decade after Bismarck had first laid claim to South-West Africa, the Witbooi Nama signed a 'Protection and Friendship Treaty'. As the Witbooi remained a potent military force even in defeat, the terms of the treaty were relatively favourable. They were to abandon the Naukluft and settle permanently in their former base at Gibeon in the south of the colony. There, Leutwein would establish a military post and appoint a garrison commander. That commander, the treaty stated, would be instructed by Leutwein 'to maintain friendly and accommodating relations with the Captain [Witbooi] and his people'.[15]

Hendrik Witbooi's main obligation under the treaty was to 'maintain peace and order in his territory'.[16] In recognition of these services rendered to the German government, he was to be paid an annual stipend of 2,000 marks. Witbooi was to retain much of his traditional authority, and all whites living in his territory were 'obliged to adhere to the laws and customs of his land'.[17] Economically the war had cost the Witbooi much, but, under the terms of the treaty, they retained their land and were at liberty to rebuild their cattle herds.

The first signs of tension between the pragmatism of Leutwein's strategy and the aspirations of the colonial lobby in Berlin emerged over the protection treaty with the Witbooi. Although Leutwein had ended the war and brought about the peaceful conditions necessary for increased German settlement, he was lambasted by the colonial societies and by elements within the tiny Windhoek settler community. What particularly offended the governor's opponents was that he had failed to crush the Witbooi decisively in battle and then failed at the negotiating table by not imposing draconian terms upon them. The Kaiser himself became embroiled in the ensuing scandal. His advisers went as far as to suggest that he refuse to ratify the treaty with Witbooi as it was 'objectionable in several respects'.[18]

What particularly irked the colonial societies and large sections of the public was the slow pace of settlement. In the ten years since the Conference of Berlin, only 1,200 German settlers had migrated to South-West Africa. Although Leutwein's policies promised an eventual end to the independence and military power of the Africans and an increased rate of German settlement, a long-term, gradualist approach was increasingly out of step with the prevailing mood in Berlin at the end of Germany's first decade as a colonial power.

6

'A Piece of Natural Savagery'

Many of the eager young men who abandoned Europe for the colonies during the second half of the nineteenth century were attracted by the allure of life on the colonial frontier. Many others, however, including the millions of Germans who emigrated to the United States, were just ordinary men and women who wanted little more than a job and perhaps their own plot of land. Both poor and poorly educated, such people were not drawn from Europe by the prospect of adventure; rather, they were pushed out of the continent by powerful economic, social and even religious forces. It was the dramatic emergence of such pressures that convinced many Germans that the settlement of their overseas colonies, and in particular German South-West Africa, was a matter of grave national importance.

By the last quarter of the century the twin forces of industrialisation and urbanisation had begun to disrupt traditional modes of life profoundly. The industrial boom that followed unification had been accompanied by the concentration of huge swathes of farmland into the hands a tiny number of powerful landowners. Millions of rural families were displaced. Landless and destitute, they gravitated to the cities where they were conscripted into the new industries. This same pattern had, of course, taken place elsewhere in Europe, but in Germany the sheer velocity of the transformation was breathtaking and the social rupture caused by mass urbanisation was aggravated by an unprecedented population boom.

During the last quarter of the nineteenth century, Germany experienced a baby boom even greater than that which followed World War II. Between unification and 1914 the population more than doubled, reaching 68 million – a figure that neither

France nor Britain has yet to reach. This was welcomed by the new industrialists, who saw it as a guarantee that their factories would never run short of labour, and by the militarists, who longed for an ever-larger army. Others interpreted Germany's growing population as evidence of the essential vitality of the Germanic race. In the 1880s and 1890s, however, it was the engine for a social disaster.

As early as the 1870s Germany's cities were seriously overcrowded. At the time of unification, Berlin already had a higher population density than London. By the end of the 1890s, the majority of Berliners were either first- or second-generation immigrants from the countryside. City planners, such as they were, failed repeatedly (and understandably) to grasp the sheer enormity of the country's population boom. Numbers that forecasters believed would not be reached for decades were exceeded within years. Even the most forward-thinking municipalities found themselves completely incapable of housing the thousands who arrived each year from the countryside. Germany became a nation of enormous slums.

The poorest districts of Berlin were among the most overcrowded and unhealthy in Europe. Conditions in the capital were made worse by the construction of the *Hinterhöfe*, blocks of seven-storey red-brick tenements built around central courtyards. They had been conceived as the solution to the city's housing problem and instead became its emblem. Whole families were crowded into single rooms, several families into apartments designed for one. Poverty and overcrowding inexorably led to the familiar nineteenth-century urban cocktail of endemic and epidemic diseases – tuberculosis, typhus, cholera and influenza.

The masses trapped in these tiny single-roomed hovels eventually became known as the *Volk Ohne Raum* – people without space. Their plight became a national fixation and was taken by many in nationalist circles as evidence that what Germany needed, above all, was space. The search for space, new land for the excess population, became a key feature of *fin de siècle* German thinking and politics.

The widespread perception that the nation was incapable of finding space for its population was strengthened by an unrelenting stream of emigration. Over the course of the nineteenth century millions of Germans emigrated to the Americas. By the 1890s a fresh exodus of staggering proportions was under way. Within just ten years, 1,445,181 German immigrants arrived in New York alone, many of them quickly moving on to German agricultural settlements across the country or to the so-called 'German Triangle' around Cincinnati, Milwaukee and St Louis. Thousands gathered on Manhattan's Lower East Side, in what became known as Klein Deutschland – Little Germany. By 1900 the German population of New York was 324,224 – only Berlin and Vienna could boast larger German populations – making New York the third-largest 'German' city on earth.

While some argued that emigration was a necessary safety valve needed to maintain social order, others asked why Germany was incapable of offering succour to her own people. Conservatives worried that the loss of so many economically active citizens might undermine the economy, while militarists feared that it could rob the nation of the manpower needed to defend (or perhaps expand) the Reich. Yet what the nationalists found most disturbing, when they looked across the ocean to the German communities of the Eastern Seaboard and Midwest, was the enthusiasm with which the emigrants, known as the *Auswanderung*, abandoned their 'German-ness' and embraced America.

In certain circles, the loss of the *Auswanderung* was regarded as a form of racial haemorrhaging. Schemes by which German immigrants might be helped to maintain their cultural roots were discussed and plans were drafted for the establishment of German language schools abroad. To the right and the nationalist wings of German politics one solution was to redirect the flow of the *Auswanderung* away from the United States and towards Germany's African colonies. This would not only prevent German emigrants from being subsumed into an alien culture but transform the colonies themselves.

As a renewed enthusiasm for colonial settlement took hold in the 1890s, 'paper possession' of large parts of Africa was no longer enough. Successful and populated colonies came to be regarded as an essential feature of any powerful European state. Pragmatists like Theodor Leutwein, who warned that such colonies would take decades to establish, were condemned as backward-looking and eventually as unpatriotic. Looking back on the period from 1907, Sir Eyre Crowe of the British Foreign Office eloquently described the mood:

> The dream of a colonial empire had taken deep hold on the German imagination. Emperor, statesmen, journalists, geographers, economists, commercial shipping houses and the whole mass of educated and uneducated public opinion continued with one voice to declare: We must have real colonies, where German immigrants can settle and spread the national ideals of the Fatherland and we must have a fleet and coaling stations to keep together the colonies which we are bound to acquire . . .[1]

Underlying the new colonial enthusiasm of the 1890s were deeper and older ideas about the nature of the German people – the *Volk*. A generation of journalists, politicians and philosophers, repelled by the economic distress and materialism of their age, turned to mysticism for solutions. The German character itself, they believed, was essentially un-urban and un-industrial. Therefore what the nation's leaders might consider progress was really a social catastrophe that served to separate the people from their true essence.

At the very core of their thinking lay the belief that only through interaction with the soil could a German encounter his or her true sprit, and fully become part of the *Volk*. These *Volkisch* theorists argued that the true danger of mass emigration to America was not simply the loss of population, but specifically the loss of Germany's peasants and small farmers. No successful society, they claimed, could ever be founded upon industry and the city.

In order to preserve the German peasant from the forces of industrialisation, *Völkisch* theory undertook a remarkable feat of doublethink. As the bulk of the agricultural land in Germany itself had fallen into the hands of rich landowners, the true Germanic mode of life – that of the farmer peasant – was now permanently denied to millions of Germans. Without this bond to the land the nation would eventually face a spiritual calamity. But this precious connection, between *Volk* and soil, could be replicated in the African colonies. Even though the soil they would be tilling was that of another continent and not the sacred earth of Germany, life as a farmer in a distant colony was far preferable to an urban existence in Germany. In a strange leap of consciousness that contradicted many older *Völkisch* ideas, they claimed that only by leaving Germany could the *Auswanderung* become truly German.

If Germany were able to settle her colonies, they argued, the whole nation would be redeemed. Germany would have a new colonial population on which it could call for raw materials, export markets and military manpower in times of war. But more importantly, the children of the colonies, immersed from birth in a true Germanic life and bound to the soil, would become a living repository of the *Völkisch* spirit. Germany's colonies would become the incubators in which those values would be preserved, safe from the forces of modernity and industrialisation that would inevitably continue in Germany.

The organisation that promoted these arguments most vigorously was the Pan-Germanic League. Founded in 1894, the Pan-Germans espoused a virulent form of racial nationalism. While passionately advocating settler colonialism in Africa, the league, like other branches of the nationalist right, also claimed that Germany's population problems were so acute that they necessitated the colonisation of Germany herself. As old antipathies towards the ethnic Polish population of Prussia, the most eastern region of the German Reich, became increasingly racialised in the later nineteenth century, schemes to strengthen the 'German element' of the population and prevent the 'Polonisation' of Prussia were proposed. What became known as 'inner colonialism' promised to keep Prussia German and channel the *Auswanderung* away from the United States. Some schemes were even enacted and landless Germans, who otherwise might have washed up on Ellis Island, were given bank loans and encouraged to settle in eastern Prussia.

In addition to the idea of 'inner colonialism', the Pan-Germans also breathed new life into old concepts and began privately to debate the idea that Poland and the Baltic states might be 'acquired' by Germany and colonised. The expansionist dreams of the Pan-Germanic strain of German nationalism are best illustrated by a map issued by the league in 1899, outlining the borders of Germany as they dreamed they might be in the year 1950. On the Pan-German map most of Poland has been annexed by Germany, as well as the French province of Alsace-Lorraine and the area around the port of Dunkirk, parts of Belgium and the Netherlands. Also incorporated into the great Reich are southern Denmark, the German-speaking provinces of Switzerland, as well as Hungary, Bohemia, Slovakia, north-eastern Italy and parts of Lithuania.[2]

Extreme as their policies were, the men of the Pan-Germanic League were not figures of the lunatic fringe. The league was a highly respectable, even intellectual organisation. Its leading members held seats in the Reichstag; others were academics at the nation's most respected universities. An inordinately large number of German schoolteachers were members of the Pan-Germanic League. To the league and other advocates of German racial nationalism, their enthusiasm for the settlement of German South-West Africa went hand in hand with an enthusiasm for 'inner colonialism' in the 'Eastern Marches', and even for the future creation of a 'Greater Germany'.

Even for those who did not fret about the ethnic make-up of eastern Prussia, or harbour dreams of life on the frontier, the overseas colonies that Germany had grabbed in 1884 had an almost mesmerising appeal. Although, as Bismarck had predicted, Germany's colonies were of little economic consequence (the costs of garrisoning South-West Africa made that colony an active liability), they were a source of endless fascination and immeasurable national pride. In Berlin a Colonial Museum and a Museum of Ethnology were opened. Shops in the capital began to supply specialist clothing, designed for tropical conditions, and equipment for use in the colonies, much of it laughably impractical.[3]

The aspect of imperialism that perhaps most enthralled the European public during the last quarter of the nineteenth century was the discovery of strange tribes and exotic cultures. This was magnified enormously when it became possible for millions of Europeans to see these exotic races themselves. In the last years of the century, an age in which European cities vied with each other for status and entrepreneurs sought out new ways of entertaining vast captive urban audiences, individuals from the colonial world (and even the Arctic Circle) were brought to Europe to appear as living exhibits.

Supposedly untouched by science and unburdened by culture, such peoples clearly occupied positions lower down the chain of being, but they were pure and unpolluted, in a way that held enormous appeal to the populations of industrial London, Paris and Berlin. In Germany they were known as the *Naturvolk* – the natural people – and were viewed as fragile specimens of races very possibly doomed to extinction in the not too distant future. Just as Europe's ethnographers rushed to salvage the artefacts and record the cultures of the tribes unearthed by imperial expansion, the urban public clamoured to see representatives of the 'dying races'.

In Germany the people of the new *Weltstädte* (world cities) could encounter the *Naturvolk* in the popular *Völkerschauen* (people shows). Some took place in circuses or even zoos, others in the ever-popular *panopticons* (see-alls). Specialists like Carl Hagenbeck, who had made his fortune trapping and exporting exotic animals and is considered by many to be the father of the zoo, supplied living specimens of the exotic races to the *panopticons*. Human exhibits displayed in Germany in the late nineteenth century included people from Sudan, North America, the Pacific Islands, Somalia and Lapland. Today, when a stroll through most European or American cities involves encounters with members of most of the races of the earth, the appeal of the nineteenth-century *Völkerschauen* is difficult to understand, but in the racially monotone Europe of the nineteenth century they were a sensation.

The more established *Völkerschauen* sought to maintain a semblance of respectability and distinguished themselves from the backstreet freak shows by evoking the legitimacy of science. Before German race scientists began to travel to the colonies themselves, the *Völkerschauen* offered them access to a steady stream of human subjects, to examine and measure. The proprietors of the *Völkerschauen* could then assure their audiences that their living exhibits had been authenticated by men of science. They could even claim that their shows, in some small way, were contributing to scientific progress.

In the summer of 1896 an event took place that was to eclipse all the traditional German *Völkerschauen* and offer German race scientists an unprecedented opportunity to advance their studies. The Berlin Colonial Show was a joint venture between the government's Colonial Department and the Colonial Society, whose patron was Kaiser Wilhelm's close friend the Prince von Hohenlohe. With both royal patronage and state support, it was destined to be a spectacular affair, but what made it a true sensation was that more than one hundred colonial subjects from across the whole of the German colonial Empire were recruited for the event.[4]

It was envisaged as a human zoo placed in the very heart of the empire. There, all the races over whom the Kaiser claimed dominion could be viewed in their natural and primitive state. The 'exhibits' were to be housed with a series of specially built and ethnologically authentic native villages within an enclosure in Berlin's Treptow Park. According to an official report, the event 'transplanted a piece of natural savagery and raw culture to the centre of a proud and glamorous metropolis, with its refined morals and fashion-conscious people'.[5] It was both an official celebration of Germany's new empire and a chance for the Berlin bourgeoisie to revel in the sheer excitement of their nation's colonial adventure.

The men of the German Colonial Department had other motives. They had deliberately encouraged the local administrations in the colonies to recruit from the ruling elites of each territory. They considered the Colonial Show an opportunity to demonstrate the might of Germany to the human exhibits. The British had done much the same thing in the 1880s, when they organised a tour of Britain for Cetshwayo, the exiled King of the Zulus, whose forces had defeated a British army at the battle of Isandlwana. British colonial officials had taken Cetshwayo to the Woolwich Arsenal to see guns being forged and to the seaports of southern England where the ships of the Royal Navy stretched out to sea for miles. For the same reasons, the leaders and future leaders of Germany's potentially rebellious tribes were taken on specially arranged tours of Berlin, a city described by a visitor as one 'massive barrack' in which the air, said another, 'stinks of [gun] powder'.

But as the 'natives' brought to Berlin were from the local elites, they also tended to be from the most Westernised sections of the colonial populations. They were often from families who had been in contact with Europeans for decades, who had skilfully exploited those contacts to establish their position. Most had long been exposed to the missionaries and some were devout Christians who wore European dress. Many of them had little to do with the indigenous cultures they were now expected to enact in Treptow Park. At least one group had to be shown how to construct the traditional huts they were to live in. Another, that included members of the dominant family from the Dula peoples of Cameroon, were utterly unwilling to perform any of the supposedly traditional ceremonies that the organisers assured them were essential aspects of their own culture. It was, however, the contingent from German South-West Africa who challenged official expectations most profoundly.

Even before they had left the colony, a clash of wills between the German organisers and the South-West Africans had begun. The Herero and Witbooi Nama refused even to embark for Germany until a formal contract had been signed with Governor Theodor Leutwein. When they finally arrived at Hamburg, it was clear that the racial expectations of the German public and the proud independence of the South-West Africans were completely at odds. Most of the Herero and all of the Witbooi men wore European-style military uniforms, bandoliers and side arms. The Witbooi wore hats with the characteristic white bandanas. Those in civilian clothes wore European suits, revealing that they were just as 'fashion-conscious' as the people of Berlin. The women wore bodiced dresses with puffed sleeves and fashionable floral patterns. They were evidently not the 'pieces of natural savagery' described in the official report.

Friedrich Maharero, the son of Samuel Maharero and grandson of Chief Tjamuaha, was particularly well attired, in a fashionable black felt blazer, crisp white shirt and colourful silk bowtie. Like the other Herero he was tall, young and strikingly handsome. Yet it was not merely the clothes of the South-West Africans that shocked the organisers: the decision to recruit only from the local elites meant that the 'exhibits' were educated and accustomed to being treated with respect. Petrus Jod, the nephew of Hendrik Witbooi, was a particularly profound challenge to German racial expectations: he was a schoolteacher who spoke eloquent High Dutch and carried a copy of the Bible at all times.

When the Herero and Nama arrived in Berlin, officials demanded they abandon their Western clothes and dress in more 'genuine' attire. They were especially disturbed by the fact that the South-West Africans and many of the Cameroonian men wore trousers, which they believed would undermine the authenticity of the entire Colonial Show. When German ethnographers supplied them with 'authentic' African clothes, they refused to wear them. The devout Petrus Jod argued that it would be against his Christian beliefs to wear what he called 'heathen clothing'. As the spread of the Gospels was one of the supposed achievements of German colonialism, none of the organisers could come up with an effective counter argument, so Petrus and the others remained in neat Victorian suits – including the trousers. Similarly, the Herero kept their hats and Boer-style military uniforms.

Despite lacking in 'authenticity', the Herero and Witbooi were the high point of the exhibition when it opened. The official purpose of the show was to expose the unbridgeable gap between savage and cultured peoples, but Friedrich Maharero, Petrus Jod and their colleagues seemed living proof of how successfully the chasm had been bridged. The gentlemen and ladies of Berlin, whose notions of what Africans looked like and how they might behave had been gleaned from the turgid prose of the explorers, peered intently across a barrier at human exhibits who wore identical suits, starched white shirts and fashionable summer dresses. These 'savages' sat peacefully reading their Bibles or stared back at them. Some members of the South-West African delegation, such as the Herero Josephat Kamatoto, could not only speak Dutch but were also fluent in German and could converse, across the fence, with the visitors who had come to marvel at the primitive habits of their African subjects.

To the utter horror of the organisers, the dapper dress, good looks (and one presumes the conversational skills) of the young African men from the south-west began to attract attention from the women of Berlin. The twenty-two-year-old Friedrich Maharero, in particular, found himself the focus of much attention and began to flirt shamelessly. Worse still, the women flirted back. Years after the show, when Friedrich was back in South-West Africa, love letters from his Berlin admirers continued to arrive in the colony. They were intercepted and confiscated by the missionaries and Friedrich never received his fan mail.

The men behind the Berlin Colonial Show had been determined that the country's leading race scientists should take a key role in the event. In 1896 racial science in Germany was dominated by physical anthropology. In Berlin, perhaps the most distinguished anthropologist was the Deputy Director of the Berlin Museum of Ethnography, Professor Felix von Luschan.

Professor von Luschan was a leading proponent of the dubious anthropological 'science' of phrenology – the study of the human skull. Phrenology was widely believed to offer a means by which the characteristics and mental abilities of the individual could be determined by the examination and measurement of the external shape of their skull. Early phrenologists focused on criminals in an attempt to define the typical dimensions and appearance of the 'criminal type' – sometimes referred to as the 'criminal race'. Von Luschan used similar measurements to determine the abilities and characteristics of whole races. His studies had led him to acquire one of Germany's largest collections of human skulls.

The Colonial Show brought to Berlin 103 members of the various races of the empire. It was such a rare opportunity to advance his work that von Luschan willingly made do with living specimens, and with the full cooperation of the organising committee he was given permission to conduct anthropological examinations upon the 'exhibits'.

Each morning the professor, accompanied by his wife and a gaggle of eager students, left industrial, urban Berlin and embarked upon a daily anthropological safari, amid the fake African villages clustered around the fishponds in Treptow Park. The progress of von Luschan's urban safaris was not without obstacles, however. When working with living subjects, anthropologists and phrenologists measured various facial features ranging from the length of noses to the angles of the jaw line. For the subjects, these examinations were uncomfortable and degrading. Among the Africans and Pacific Islanders of the Colonial Show there was a palpable lack of enthusiasm and many outright refusals.

For a man whose normal contact with non-Europeans involved taking measurements of their skeletons, it was a shock for von Luschan to come face to face with Africans who were very much alive and often completely unwilling to submit to his demands. Several of the 'exhibits' refused to allow von Luschan and his students to strip them of their clothes, measure their bodies or even photograph them in the supposedly traditional costumes they had refused to wear.

The most disturbing aspect of his encounters with the human exhibits was that their demeanour, independence and level of education represented a profound challenge to the racial theories that underpinned the professor's work. When he met the representatives of the Herero and Witbooi peoples, von Luschan was extremely agitated by the experience. Rather than question his racial presumptions, von Luschan dismissed these particular Herero and Witbooi as exceptions. He stated in the official report, produced to commemorate the Colonial Show, 'I doubt that all Hereros make such a thoroughly distinguished impression and have such a gentleman-like appearance as those we have seen here in Treptow.'[6] Only when he was permitted to examine Vitje Bank, a thirty-year-old Witbooi woman, was normal service restored for Felix von Luschan. Clearly recovered from his earlier shocks he described her as a bushman-like dwarf of 'a not inconsiderable imbecility'.[7]

Back in Treptow Park, the behaviour of the Africans continued to diverge from the expectations of the organisers. The show was a farce. By day the organisers struggled to maintain an air of authenticity, cajoling the human exhibits to occupy themselves making supposedly traditional handicrafts or preparing authentic food. But by night those same Africans sat by fires, drinking and singing the German folk songs they had learned as youths, and as the temperature dropped they slipped back into their warm European clothing.[8] This scene of conviviality, hidden away in a closed park in the dead of night, was a far more accurate reflection of the way many of the peoples of Germany's empire lived than anything seen during opening hours. Yet each morning the European clothes and empty bottles were hidden away and, after von Luschan had negotiated for his callipers and slide rules to be fixed to a few more unwilling heads, the public were allowed back into the park, and the fantasy version of colonial life began once again.

The highlight of each day for the Berlin audiences (though clearly not for the 'exhibits') was the cultural performance. The exhibition organisers noted with pride that 'whenever dance routines were carried out by the blacks, the ring of spectators grew massively, so that the officials had difficulties keeping order'.[9] The South-West African delegation refused to take part in the cultural performances, just as they had refused to abandon their clothes or submit to anatomical examinations. The best the organisers were able to achieve was to persuade them to pose grudgingly in front of their makeshift village.

Had he attended the Berlin Colonial Show, Theodor Leutwein would not have been surprised by the refusal of Friedrich Maharero and his colleagues to submit to the demands of their German hosts. Leutwein's long-term strategy was rooted in his firm appreciation of their strident independence. Yet in the autumn of 1896, as the mock African villages in Treptow Park were dismantled and the Nama and Herero delegations steamed home, a plague was sweeping south across their continent. The pestilence was the first in a series of calamities to befall the Herero (and, to a lesser extent, the Nama), which allowed the Germans to slowly undermine the defiant independence of the Africans that had so impressed the Berlin crowds.

Rinderpest was the term the Boers had given to a highly infectious virus that was fatal to cattle. The British called the disease 'Steppe Muraine' or, more literally, 'cattle plague'. The most deadly strains of the *Rinderpest* are capable of entirely wiping out infected herds. The virus first arrived in Africa in the late 1880s, possibly carried by Indian cattle imported into Eritrea by the Italian colonialists. By the mid-1890s it had become a continental pandemic. First, the horn of Africa was devastated, then, as the pestilence swept down through Eastern and Central Africa, the Masai of Kenya suffered catastrophic losses. In 1895 reports from German East Africa indicated that some herds had been reduced to only 10 percent of their original number. Across Africa the missionaries evoked fiery passages from the Old Testament to explain the apocalypse. Some warned their congregations that the pestilence was the work of a wrathful God, angered by their continued devotion to heathen practices.

Throughout 1896 the *Rinderpest* inched its way towards the borders of South-West Africa, and in April 1897 news reached Windhoek of the first infections within the colony.[10] The Herero, owners of the largest herds, had the most to lose. There are no precise figures, but the German Commissioner for Settlement later estimated that half of the entire Herero herd, perhaps thirty thousand cattle, perished within the first six months. By the end of the epidemic the missionaries were reporting that some Herero communities had lost 95 percent of their livestock. The scene on the central plateau in the last months of 1897 was apocalyptical. Thousands of putrefying animal corpses were littered across the landscape. Unable to gather enough wood to build pyres, the Herero attempted to bury the carcasses. In some places the internment of such a vast number of decaying animal bodies led to the contamination of ground water and the poisoning of the precious wells.

With only a fraction of their animals still alive, thousands of ordinary Herero were suddenly destitute. As committed pastoralists they had few crops to fall back on and little experience of agriculture. Their traditional diet was based almost entirely upon milk and meat, and very quickly they began to suffer from malnutrition. In desperation whole communities were forced to abandon their settlements and ancestral lands. While still reeling from the calamity of the *Rinderpest*, the Herero were visited by a series of subsequent plagues. In the spring and summer of 1898 epidemics of both typhoid fever and malaria swept through their territories. Thousands who had been weakened by the effects of malnutrition now succumbed. The same year their lands were devastated by a plague of locusts that consumed the crops the Herero had desperately planted in the hope of sustaining themselves while their herds slowly recovered. The plague of locusts was followed by a severe drought that withered the remaining crops and killed off yet more of their cattle.

The first indication of how the calamities of the late 1890s were to change the relationship between the Herero and the Germans was the arrival of thousands of impoverished Herero at the European settlements and the mission stations, places they had until now avoided. In the immediate aftermath of the *Rinderpest*, the missionaries reported a sharp rise in conversions as traumatised Herero abandoned their culture, along with their homes. Huddled around the mission stations, they appealed to the charity of the German missionaries and called for the protection of a new god. Others, who believed their land to be cursed, took the last of their cattle and crossed into the British territory of Bechuanaland in search of new pastures and a chance to rebuild their stocks of cattle.

The Herero's cattle were not only a source of sustenance, but also an economic commodity. Cattle were the currency of the south-west and the engine of the Herero economy: the commodity with which they bartered for horses, rifles, ammunition and many of the luxuries and necessities of daily life. The herds that the Herero ushered across the central plateau had been an enormous reservoir of wealth, which had permitted the Herero to remain independent of the Germans and their colonial economy. Under Samuel Maharero's leadership the Herero had been forced into a series of compromising treaties with the Germans, and Governor Leutwein had managed to interfere egregiously in tribal affairs, but few Herero had submitted to working for the German administration or labouring on the farms of the white settlers. In late 1897, the unprecedented sight of Herero men and women doing precisely this sharply illustrated the enormity of their plight. In some of the worst-hit areas, Herero women went into service in the homes of settlers, while their men laboured for the *Schutztruppe*, helping to construct the network of forts and garrison houses the Germans were busy developing throughout the late 1890s.

Although many of the poorer Herero had no choice but to work for the Germans during the *Rinderpest* epidemic, most were able to return to their homes and their traditional ways of life as their herds began to recover. But the *Rinderpest* had given both the missionaries and the colonial authorities a tantalising glimpse of how the colony might be developed, if only the Herero could be induced to abandon their land altogether, sell off their cattle and become the labouring underclass of the whites. Moreover, the temporary poverty of the Herero permitted the Germans to alter the map of Hereroland permanently.

For centuries the Herero had owned their lands in common. Their chiefs had traditionally not considered their pastures a form of property that could be sold or bought. As the *Rinderpest* cut swathes through their herds, saddling the ruling elite with considerable debts, the chiefs were increasingly pressured by German traders to settle their accounts through the sale of land. Samuel Maharero had broken the taboo of selling land some years earlier, but the bulk of the land sold before the *Rinderpest* was south of Okahandja. Samuel had disposed of this land in the hope that the Germans who settled there would act as a buffer against the Witbooi, whose own territory lay to the south. The land sales conducted during the *Rinderpest* epidemic were of a different order. To pay their debts the chiefs sold tracts that were not only prime grazing land, but also in the heart of Hereroland. Although it was not apparent amid the turmoil and misery of the late 1890s, the sale of land was the most serious long-term consequence of the *Rinderpest*, as it allowed the Germans their first real foothold in Hereroland itself.

Although the amounts of land transferred to German ownership during the *Rinderpest* were relatively small, German ambition was great. Prevailing opinion, among both the settlers in Windhoek and the colonial societies in Berlin, considered the *Rinderpest* a unique opportunity for Germany to accelerate the settlement of German South-West Africa. Even Leutwein abandoned his caution and saw the *Rinderpest* as a chance to speed up the transfer of land from African to German hands.

However, the moment the epidemic subsided the Herero dashed the dreams of many settlers by abruptly ending the sale of their remaining cattle. Seeking to regenerate their herds, they rejected the offers of the traders, many of whom were in fact would-be settlers seeking to acquire enough livestock to establish a ranch. In their frustration the traders began to engage in unscrupulous practices: ludicrously exaggerating the value of their goods, demanding cattle in payment, and valuing the Herero and Nama's livestock at about half their real worth. Officially Theodor Leutwein condemned such practices, but he did little to stop them, accepting that the long-term settlement of South-West Africa was predicated on the transfer of cattle to the whites.

The colonial authorities themselves grasped the opportunities presented by the impoverishment of the Herero to try to establish themselves as the arbitrators of land in the colony. In the years immediately following the epidemic, the prospect of eventually forcing the Herero off the land and into native reserves was discussed as a realistic future prospect.

By the end of the 1890s the position of the Germans in South-West Africa was undoubtedly stronger than it had been in 1896, the year of the Berlin Colonial Show. Not only had the settlers established their presence in Hereroland, the *Schutztruppe* guarding them had been enormously strengthened. Of the 780 whites reported as residents of Windhoek in the colonial census of 1896, six hundred were soldiers. The army had also expanded its network of fortresses and garrison stations, establishing outposts across Hereroland and the Nama territories in the south.

Although the accelerated pace of German colonial penetration during the 1890s caused flashes of excitement in the settler bars of Windhoek and the colonial societies of Berlin, when examined from a distance progress was modest. Not only did the Herero withstand the *Rinderpest*, typhus and malaria epidemics, and hold the line against further German encroachments on their land, they were also able to rebuild their herds and their wealth. At the dawn of the twentieth century Windhoek and the other white settlements were like base-camps from which the colonisation of the territory might theoretically be attempted at some future date. South-West Africa remained largely in the hands of the Africans. What was questionable in the year 1900 was not the resilience of the Africans in the face of colonial encroachment, but Germany's long-term commitment to the task of forging a viable colony in the southern African deserts.

7
King of the Huns

By the start of the twentieth century the old vision of colonialism, built on the notion of the 'white man's burden' and a belief in the moral duty to spread the Gospel, had, in certain circles, come to be regarded as unscientific, sentimental and inexcusably old-fashioned. Although there had always been disagreement as to how far the dark races of the world might be 'raised up', most colonialists had agreed that as long as the 'natives' accepted their subordination passively, they had a critical role to play in the colonial project. This was a world view steeped in a form of eighteenth-century racial paternalism that had emerged from the latter stages of the great political struggle over transatlantic slavery. In opposing slavery the abolitionist movements had asserted that black Africans – and by implication all other natives races – were possessed of divine souls and were therefore both 'men and brothers'.

A palpable shift away from these views had begun in the 1850s, and by the time Africa was subdivided among the powers of Europe in the 1880s the old racism was being severely challenged by a biological view of race. The clinical clarity of the new 'biological racism' was used to explain away as inevitable (and even desirable) genocidal episodes – such as the extermination of the Tasmanian Aboriginals by British colonists in the 1820s and 1830s – that only decades earlier had been considered lamentable tragedies.

It was an event in Asia, rather than Africa, that most graphically demonstrated how deeply the notion of 'racial war' had seeped into the mindset of Wilhelmian Germany and the views of Kaiser Wilhelm II himself. In 1900 the Kaiser dispatched a force of German soldiers to China, as part of an eight-nation alliance whose mission was to put down the Boxer Rebellion. The vast majority of those killed by the rebels of the Society of the Righteous and Harmonious Fist – known to Europeans as the Boxers – were Chinese Christians. However, European newspapers focused on the violent deaths of a small number of Europeans. The German justification for joining the international coalition was that during the initial rebellion the German legation had been stormed and the envoy, Klemens von Ketterler, had been killed. The Kaiser interpreted von Ketterler's death as a personal affront, and in one of his characteristic fits of rage demanded, 'Peking must be razed to the ground.'[1]

On the morning of 27 July 1900 the German contingent of the international force was assembled in neat lines at the harbour side in Bremerhaven ready to embark for China. On a specially built podium the Kaiser, for once out of the reach of his minders and advisers, was free to speak his own mind. Possibly improvising or deviating from a prepared speech, Wilhelm issued a command to his troops which so shocked his advisers that they immediately arrested all reporters present and confiscated their notebooks. A lone correspondent, who had been sitting on a rooftop alongside his photographer, was able to slip away and report the Kaiser's speech.

Wilhelm began by warning his soldiers of the brutality of the Boxer rebels, but then went on to instruct them to ignore all the standard conventions of warfare: 'When you come before the enemy, let him be struck down; there will be no mercy, prisoners will not be taken. Just as the Huns one thousand years ago . . . made a name for themselves in which their greatness still resounds, so let the name of Germany be known in China in such a way that a Chinese will never dare even to look askance at a German.'[2]

When the German contingent under the command of Alfred von Waldersee (a close friend of the Kaiser) arrived in October 1900, the Chinese Empress Dowager had already been captured and a siege of the Forbidden City brought to an end. Undaunted and determined to grab the headlines, Waldersee organised a series of punitive expeditions. Although never seriously opposed, the Germans massacred thousands of innocent Chinese peasants. When the letters of soldiers serving in China were leaked to left-wing newspapers, the brutality of the German raids was reported in the German press. One soldier wrote to his family: 'You cannot imagine what is going on here [in China] . . . everything that stands in our way is destroyed: men, women, children. Oh, how the women scream. But, the Kaiser's orders were: no pardon will be granted. We have sworn to uphold our oath.'[3]

The reputation the German army acquired in China in 1900, and the Kaiser's ridiculous speech at Bremerhaven, gave rise to the derogatory term 'Hun' for the Germans during World War I.

In 1900 Kaiser Wilhelm clearly had little difficulty envisaging the conflict in China as a racial war in which the normal rules of war did not apply. Five years later, writing to US President Theodore Roosevelt, Wilhelm revealed his deep conviction that a Darwinian confrontation between Europeans and the Chinese race was inevitable: 'I foresee in the future a fight for life and death between the "White" and the Yellow for their sheer existence. The sooner therefore the Nations belonging to the "White Race" understand this and join in common defence against the coming danger, the better.'[4]

Wilhelm was not alone in allowing these sorts of overarching racial suppositions to influence his world view. Before World War I the German General Staff had begun to use the term 'yellow peril' in its official publications on China and Germany's small colonial possessions there. The term was also applied to the Japanese, a people whose rulers were extremely pro-German and whose political structures and sense of racial mission had been partly inspired by the example of Wilhelmian Germany. Wilhelm still despised them.

In expressing his views on the people of Asia to President Roosevelt in 1905, the Kaiser was preaching to the converted. Between 1889 and 1896, before he took office, Theodore Roosevelt had written an epic, four-volume history of the American frontier. *The Winning of the West* was, at the time, considered a major contribution to American history. Roosevelt argued that wars between the lower races and the white race, although characterised by extremes of violence, were ultimately necessary:

> The most ultimately righteous of all wars is a war with savages, though it is apt to be also the most terrible and inhuman. The rude, fierce settler who drives the savage from the land lays all civilized mankind under a debt to him. American and Indian, Boer and Zulu, Cossack and Tartar, New Zealander and Maori, – in each case the victor, horrible though many of his deeds are, has laid deep the foundations for the future greatness of a mighty people. The consequences of struggles for territory between civilized nations seem small by comparison. Looked at from the standpoint of the ages, it is of little moment whether Lorraine is part of Germany or of France, whether the northern Adriatic cities pay homage to Austrian Kaiser or Italian King; but it is of incalculable importance that America, Australia, and Siberia should pass out of the hands of their red, black, and yellow aboriginal owners, and become the heritage of the dominant world races.[5]

Theodore Roosevelt, like his friend the historian Frederick Jackson Turner, believed that the wars of the frontier had been part of a grand historical process that had created the American character. By the very act of becoming frontier people, the whites of America had evolved into a stronger, more virile and resourceful people. The American character, so different from that of Europeans, Roosevelt and Turner claimed, was essentially a product of the frontier, and the new freedoms it afforded those who settled there. Far from the constraints of authority and the taming influences of bourgeoisie society, life on the western edge of white dominion had created a race of rugged individualists. They were naturally distrustful of government, quick to violence and adapted in innumerable ways to an untrammelled life amid wide-open spaces.

Although the age of the American frontier had, by the 1890s, effectively come to an end, its myth still exerted enormous influence over the German imagination, in part thanks to German popular fiction.[6] The most successful author of German 'Western' novels was Karl May. May had been writing since the mid-1870s, but it was in the 1890s that his books began to attract a mass audience. Karl May, like his most of his readers, had never set foot on the American frontier, yet in a series of hugely popular pulp novels he portrayed an American frontier populated by German 'Westmen' who found within themselves an innate predisposition for life on the frontier. May's most successful hero, 'Old Shatterhand', although of average build and height and with no experience of the outdoor life, quickly became a master of the frontier and more than a match for the 'Yankees', the perpetual villains in May's books. May portrayed the American 'West' almost as if it were a German colony. His characters drink German beer and sing traditional German folk songs around their campfires.

Karl May's Western novels reflected and perhaps contributed to a growing fascination with notions of national and racial expansion and the frontier. May achieved what the colonial societies had been struggling to do since the 1870s, by convincing millions of ordinary Germans that they were naturally a frontier people.[7]

In seeing the answers to Germany's problems – both demographic and spiritual – as lying on the colonial frontier, May was not a lone voice. With the American experience as their example, a swathe of the nation's philosophers, geographers and politicians, along with the *Völkisch* mystics, promoted their firm belief not only that Germany's colonies could save the *Volk Ohne Raum* from the misery of the industrial cities, but that the colonial frontier might become a new arena in which the German spirit could undergo a revitalisation, in terms similar to those which they believed had forged the rugged character of white America.

Some of the most important of these ideas appeared in the writing of a now forgotten figure, Friedrich Ratzel. As a young journalist in the 1870s, Ratzel had travelled extensively around the United States writing articles for the *Kölnische Zeitung*. At that point in his career Ratzel had been particularly impressed by America's burgeoning cities and had managed to avoid romanticising life on the frontier, as so many later writers were prone to do. After returning to Germany he embarked on an academic career, and this led him to reassess the importance of the frontier in the development of culture.[8]

Although his early studies had been in zoology, Ratzel's later work was in the new discipline of geography, and by the 1880s he had emerged as one of Germany's foremost geographers. The theories that Ratzel developed as a geographer were heavily influenced by concepts drawn from his zoological background and the work of his original mentor, Ernst Haeckel. Ratzel's interest in the anatomical sciences remained strong for much of his life. One of his many friends, with whom he maintained a healthy correspondence, was the racial anthropologist Felix von Luschan.[9]

It was in the late 1890s that Ratzel began to fuse ideas inspired by Social Darwinism with the theories about space and migration being developed in geography. Specifically he applied the notion of the 'struggle for existence' to the study of migration, both animal and human. To Ratzel the invasion and colonisation of the world outside Europe by the white race, and the displacement of indigenous peoples, was all part of the 'struggle for existence', motivated above all by the search for 'living space'. Darwin had shown that when animals moved to new environments, over time they adapted and evolved to those new conditions. From this Ratzel concluded that when human races migrated they adapted their cultures to the new environment.

If a race was successful in adapting to the conditions of a different territory their culture advanced and their population increased. These two factors naturally motivated adaptable races to migrate. Human history, in Ratzel's view, was driven forward by a constant series of migrations, each inspiring new adaptations to new environments and each adaptation advancing the culture and increasing the population of the migrating race. Ratzel even speculated as to whether the drive to migrate was, in itself, a feature of a virile and vigorous race.

Migration, Ratzel argued, was essential for long-term survival of a race. Each people had no choice but to increase the amount of space it occupied. To stop migrating and adapting to new environments was, in Ratzel's conception, to stop advancing and risk being overtaken by other races better fitted for survival.

It was crude Social Darwinism, partly inspired by nationalism and colonialism and scribbled on a map. In 1897 Ratzel published his influential book *Politische Geographie* and named his new theory *Lebensraum* – living space. Friedrich Ratzel's academic theories were, at times, intertwined with his political support for colonialism. During the first wave of colonial enthusiasm that swept over Germany in the 1880s, he helped found the right-wing and expansionist German Colonial Society. He became committed to the idea that any colonies Germany was able to grab hold of during the 'scramble for Africa' needed to be settled by German farmers, rather than just exploited by industry or traders. Ratzel claimed that territories used only as a source of raw materials or as markets for trade goods were not true colonies. Colonisation took place only when a conquered territory was farmed, and even then, only if the land was placed in the hands of small peasant farmers rather than large land companies. When discussing Germany's empire, Ratzel specified German South-West Africa as one potential source of *Lebensraum* for the German people.

Lebensraum theory also dismissed the current notion that the races who came into contact with European colonialists suffered some form of inexplicable extinction. Ratzel felt no need to deny the true cause. Colonial peoples disappeared because they were persecuted, enslaved and exterminated. This was done by colonialists, traders and soldiers. There was little mystery. He hedged his bets somewhat by arguing that perhaps the inner cultural weakness of the native races of Africa, America and Asia made them passive, and therefore incapable of withstanding the European assault. However, he was clear that the means of their destruction was the gun and the gallows. All this was acceptable because the people Europeans were destroying were what he termed 'inferior races'.[10] Their land was required by a stronger race who quite naturally took it by force.

Importantly, given the role his ideas (and innumerable distortions of them) were to play in the story of German colonialism, Ratzel felt that wars of extermination were an inevitable aspect in the search for *Lebensraum*. To capture space, the vigorous nations of the earth would have no choice but to fight wars against the indigenous peoples in a 'struggle for space'. When looking for examples of the sorts of conflict that had been effective in 'quickly and completely' displacing indigenous races he listed those fought during the nineteenth century in North America, southern Brazil, Tasmania and New Zealand.[11] These wars, that Ratzel viewed as models for future colonialism, were wars of extermination; some were genocides.

The man who most forcefully promoted and distorted Social Darwinian theories such as *Lebensraum* in German South-West Africa was not Governor Theodor Leutwein – who disliked theoretical justifications for colonialism – but the Commissioner for Settlement, Dr Paul Rohrbach.

Rohrbach was sent to South-West Africa in 1903 by the Colonial Department, to evaluate the colony's potential for large-scale farming and mass settlement, and to carry out a comparative study of the colonial methods used by the British in South Africa and those deployed in German South-West Africa. Specifically, he aimed to determine if the system of forced expropriation of land, used successfully by the British, might be applied in the German colony.

Rohrbach's mission was part of a larger, government-backed scheme, aimed at increasing the pace of German settlement. Although by 1903 the pace of settlement was greater than it had ever been, migration to the German colonies was as nothing when compared with the continuing flood of emigrants to the United States. Even some of those who had migrated and settled in German South-West Africa clearly harboured ambitions to leave for America eventually, as they registered their new farms under names such as Dixie, Alabama and Georgia.

To help lure more settlers to the colony, Rohrbach had been granted a budget of 300,000 marks and given a special mandate. He was to report directly to the Colonial Department in Berlin, an arrangement that, in theory, made him the most senior official in the colony after Governor Leutwein.[12] Rohrbach was well suited to this role. He was highly able, and resilient enough to withstand the hardships of travel in the deserts; above all, he was utterly dedicated to the colonial mission and an advocate of the Social Darwinian and racial theories that underpinned it.

In his book *Der Deutsche Gedanke in der Welt* (German World Policies), written in 1912, Rohrbach described, with breathtaking frankness, the principles that he had come to believe should govern the colonisation of Africa:

> It is not right either among nations or among individuals that people who can create nothing should have a claim to preservation. No false philanthropy or race-theory can prove to reasonable people that the preservation of any tribe of nomadic South African Kaffirs . . . is more important for the future of mankind than the expansion of the great European nations, or the white race as a whole. Should the German people renounce the chance of growing stronger and of securing elbow room for their sons and daughters, because . . . some tribe of Negroes . . . has lived its useless existence on a strip of land where ten thousand German families may have a flourishing existence and thus strengthen the very sap of our people?[13]

In 1903 Rohrbach, like Governor Theodor Leutwein, understood that the Africans, once disinherited and pacified, could become a considerable economic resource. However, the experience he gained in South-West Africa later led him to conclude that whole African nations could be legitimately exterminated. In 1907, he published *Deutsche Kolonialwirtschaft* (German Colonial Commerce), in which he stated: 'In order to secure the peaceful White settlement against the bad, culturally inept and predatory native tribe, it is possible that its actual eradication may become necessary under certain conditions.'[14]

During his time in South West Africa, Paul Rohrbach was most preoccupied with what opportunities colonialism might offer his own people, not with what it would mean for the indigenous races. The destruction or enslavement of the lower races – whichever it had to be – was merely an effect of colonialism, rather than its aim. Pushing aside notions that had been used to justify colonialism in the early nineteenth century – racial paternalism, the spread of the Gospel and the suppression of the slave trade – Rohrbach saw its sole function as the spread and the advancement of the white race. This stood in marked contrast to the more pragmatic stance of Governor Leutwein, who saw his role as balancing the opposing interests of both black and white, until the Africans could be forced to accept their lowly position.

Rohrbach imagined that during the twentieth century Germany might settle 2 million of its sons and daughters on African soil. From those pioneers, subject as they would be to the unique conditions of a frontier society, would evolve a new variant of the German character. Rohrbach saw the colonies as the crucible from which a more virulent strain of 'German-ness' would emerge and slowly be transfused into the body of the Reich:

> The colonial type is . . . a source of great inner wealth for any nation which develops it successfully. It is not that the lazy and timid, but the active and determined men of a nation find their way across the seas, which explains much in the American character . . . In view of our very large numbers it is of no consequence if several thousand people leave home annually, even if they are ever so strong and capable. Across the ocean, however, the selection gradually produces a race of special qualities . . . It is . . . better accustomed to living on a big scale both without and within.[15]

With these notions at the forefront of his mind, Rohrbach surveyed the farmland of German South-West Africa and sought to determine by which methods it might be made most productive.

In the same years, Governor Leutwein set about constructing the infrastructure needed to realise large-scale settlement of German South-West Africa. While the principle of divide and rule, by which he had subdued the Nama and Herero, had been borrowed from the British, the governor and his allies in the Colonial Department now looked to the American West for inspiration. On the American frontier, white settlement had been accelerated by two critical policies: the rapid construction of the railways and the creation of native reserves. Angelo Golinelli, the official in charge of South-West African affairs at the German Colonial Department, wrote that railways in the colonies 'are built as a prelude to subjugation and pacification'.[16] As in the United States, the train would transport cattle to market, take supplies and labour to the white settlers and allow for the rapid deployment of the army, should the 'natives' resist the other element of Golinelli's policy – their gradual confinement in reserves. Governor Leutwein believed the development of the railways was so critical that in 1897 he travelled to Berlin and made a personal appeal to the Reichstag for the necessary funds.[17]

By 1902 a line connecting Windhoek with the rapidly developing port of Swakopmund had already been completed. In 1903 work commenced on a second railway project, linking Swakopmund to the copper mines at Otavi – the colony's only industrial venture of any real consequence. As the Otavi line began slowly to inch its way across the desert, the various ways the Africans might be forced to make way for German settlers were being debated among the missionaries and colonial administrators. In 1903 Leutwein agreed, albeit half-heartedly, to an official policy of reserves, and two were established, a Witbooi reserve in Rietmond and a Herero reserve at Otjimbingwe.

The Herero and Nama were perfectly able to see that the coming of the railways and the establishment of reserves were the first moves in the gradual annexation of South-West Africa. Above all, they feared being forced into areas that were too small or infertile for them to practise their traditional pastoral lifestyles. When the Herero chiefs were asked to agree to the establishment of a second reserve near Okahandja, they rejected the German proposals. But in 1903 neither the Herero nor the Nama leadership regarded any of these developments as cause to rise up and rebel against German rule.

For all their losses of land and independence, the Herero and Nama still had economic power over central and southern parts of the colony. They had sold land and cattle, the latter in vast quantities. Some had slipped into debt to the traders and others had lost land in unfair treaties, but most of the tribes remained masters of much of what they surveyed. According to Paul Rohrbach's own figures, by 1903 only 10 percent of the farmland owned by the Africans, which the settlers might be able to exploit profitably, had been purchased.[18] The situation was less favourable for some of the smaller southern Nama clans. The Bondelswarts and the Veldschoendragers had lost considerable amounts of their land to private settlers and land companies, but the largest tribes, including the Herero, had retained the greater part of their ancestral land.

The sale of land by Nama *Kapteins* had given the German settlers a firm foothold in the south of the colony, but it had also enriched the Nama elite. Hendrik Witbooi, now in his early seventies, rather than being disinherited by the colonial process, was growing steadily richer by selling plots of land. One farm sold to the settler Dr Kämpffer brought Witbooi seven annual payments of 1,000 Reichmarks – in itself a small fortune. Kämpffer, whose son became a celebrated writer of colonial fiction under the Nazis, was no doubt making a point when he named his farm *Deutsche Erde* – German Soil.[19] Other settlers, unable to persuade the chiefs to sell them a plot, were forced into an even more unpalatable relationship. In a deeply resented inversion of the customary colonial relationship, they were forced to lease land from the Nama or Herero.

While the land sales brought the chiefs large fortunes, they still counted their real wealth in cattle. Both the Herero and Nama had recovered from the disastrous *Rinderpest* epidemic of the late 1890s. By 1903 the Herero herd stood at around fifty thousand, while the Nama owned perhaps as many as twenty-five thousand cattle. As the average price of a head of cattle in southern Africa was around 150 Reichmarks, Samuel Maharero, who, like many of the other chiefs, owned thousands of cattle, was in effect a millionaire.

The prosperity of the African elite, relative to that of most white settlers, was taken as further proof that Leutwein's system of gradual colonialism had failed disastrously. The settlers dismissed South-West Africa as a colony in which the whites were beholden to the blacks in ways that ran counter to the very principles of colonialism. Viewing the colony through the prism of late nineteenth-century racism, they sought not merely the rapid advancement of their interests and prosperity, but the immediate and utter subjugation of the Africans.

In the summer of 1900, members of the white population in South-West Africa had used an upcoming Reichstag debate on the use of corporal punishment in the colonies as an opportunity to let their opinions of the Herero and Nama be known in Berlin. In their address, forwarded to the Colonial Department, they wrote:

> From Time immemorial our natives have been used to laziness, brutality and stupidity. The dirtier they are the more they feel at ease. Any white men who have lived among natives find it almost impossible to regard them as human beings at all in any European sense. They need centuries of training as human beings; with endless patience, strictness and justice.[20]

The centre of opposition to the governor and the cauldron in which the settlers' racial hatreds fermented was Windhoek. By 1903 the capital had become a European enclave into which few Africans ventured. Although by European standards it was more a large village than a small town, it was just big enough to become a fantasy-land. Beneath von François's fortress, the enormous disparities between the Africans and the settlers, in both numbers and military power, were rendered almost invisible. Convinced of their own strength and of the need to circumvent the governor, retired soldiers of the German *Schutztruppe* and the most extreme settlers came together in bars and taverns like the infamous Kasino Sylvester to vent their frustrations. There they condemned the supposed leniency of the governor, and denigrated the Africans as 'baboons' and the colony as 'Monkeyland'. Well aware of the discontent among the settlers, Theodor Leutwein described them as 'inclined, with the inborn feeling of belonging to a superior race, to appear as members of a conquering army, even though we had conquered nothing'.[21]

The racial contempt that both settlers and soldiers felt towards the Africans was compounded by their frustrations, impatience and greed. The result was a wave of violence and abuse, the records of which can be seen in the Namibian National Archives in Windhoek. Official reports of beatings, rapes and murders committed in the years up to 1904 speak of a colony slipping out of control, in which isolated settlers and *Schutztruppe* officers were able to act with almost complete impunity against ordinary Herero and Nama, and even members of the wealthy elite.

The most commonly reported incidents were beatings. Many of these attacks were viewed by their perpetrators as semi-official acts of corporal punishment. They were carried out with *sjamboks* – hippopotamus-skin whips – and were invoked by the smallest infraction or perceived lack of respect towards a white person. A mistake made while working for a settler, a minor theft, simple failure to respond to a question – all could be punished by whippings or beatings.

One case reported in 1902 involved a German baker named Schaeffer, who accused the ageing Herero under-chief, Assa Riarua, of insolence and attacked the old man. Dragging Riarua from his store and out into street, Schaeffer publicly flogged him 'until the blood ran'. The humiliating abuse of a prominent

Herero elder was such a serious – and potentially dangerous – event that Governor Leutwein personally intervened in the case, fearing the Herero might retaliate. Yet even this blatant case of abuse did not result in a custodial sentence. An out-of-court settlement was reached in which Schaeffer was ordered to pay a fine of 20 marks.[22]

The case that most deeply damaged Herero relations with the Germans took place in the middle of 1903. Barmenias Zeraua, the son of Herero Chief Zacharias Zeraua, later recounted the events that led up to the death of his wife:

> In 1903 my wife was expecting her first baby, so in accordance with the universal custom of the Hereros I sent her, by ox-wagon, to her mother's home . . . Before leaving Omaruru we met a German named Dietrich, who asked me whether he would be allowed to travel with us in my wagon to Karibib. I said I had no objection, so Dietrich came along with us . . . That evening we outspanned about 12 miles from Omaruru on the main road. We killed a sheep and had our evening meal which Dietrich shared with us. We gave him the fried sheep liver to eat [a delicacy]. Then two boys went to attend to the cattle and my wife went into the hood of the wagon with her baby to sleep . . . I said 'Good-night' to Dietrich and went to sleep . . . suddenly I was awakened by the report of a revolver. I jumped out of the tent of the wagon and saw Dietrich running away on the road to Omaruru . . . I went back to the wagon, the baby was crying and I shook my wife to wake her. As I touched her I felt something wet. I struck a match and saw that she was covered with blood and quite dead . . . I took up my baby and found that the bullet which killed my wife had gone through the fleshy part of its left leg just above the knee.[23]

Dietrich was charged with manslaughter, not murder, and was at first acquitted. He was finally sentenced to three years' imprisonment, but later released and made a non-commissioned officer in the *Schutztruppe*.

The outrage felt by the Africans at their treatment by settlers and soldiers was aggravated by a colonial legal system that made it nearly impossible for them to obtain justice under the law. Although the African elite had retained possession of their land, their legal rights had been silently stripped from them.

The courts were staffed by former soldiers or settlers, few of whom had even the most rudimentary legal training. In Leutwein's memoirs, *Elf Jahre Gouverneur* (Eleven Years as Governor), he noted that the evidence of one settler was deemed legally to outweigh that of up to seven Africans. When whites who had killed Africans were convicted, they were almost always sentenced to terms of imprisonment lasting just months. Africans found guilty of killing whites were hanged.

The racial bias of the German legal system was equally blatant in cases of rape. When accusations of rape by settlers were brought before the courts, it was not uncommon for the judges to rule against the victim and sentence them to be jailed or whipped for bearing 'false testimony'.

From Windhoek, Governor Leutwein was unable to dictate the verdicts of all the provincial courts, nor control the behaviour of the settlers. Out in the provinces, authority lay in the hands of the District Officers posted in a network of miniature fortresses and garrison houses with command over small units of soldiers. These officers, answerable to the governor, were responsible for maintaining the peace and upholding the terms of the protection treaties. As many *Schutztruppe* soldiers planned to settle in the colony at the end of their term of service, they were firm allies of the settlers and, like many of them, were dissatisfied with Leutwein's policies. Some were also prone to dealing with the Africans in an extremely aggressive and provocative manner. The excessive violence and even murders that characterised their responses to minor infractions or local disputes were in part a consequence of the very nature of the German forces in South-West Africa.

Unlike the other colonial powers, the Germans, upon staking claim to a colonial empire in 1884, had chosen not to form a regular colonial army. Instead they had formed small 'protective forces' – *Schutztruppe*. What marked out the *Schutztruppe* of South-West Africa from those stationed in Germany's other African colonies was that the entire force – both officers and men – were white. Black Africans were not conscripted into its ranks, as was the case elsewhere. Under the protection treaties signed by both the Herero and Nama, the Africans were obliged to send men to fight alongside the Germans when requested and, on those occasions, the African fighters were given the desert-brown *Schutztruppe* uniforms and placed under the command of German officers. Yet no Africans were ever formally recruited. The *Schutztruppe* was a white man's army, and in South-West Africa it became a hothouse of ultra-nationalism and racial fanaticism.

The *Schutztruppe*'s reputation for extremism was matched only by its record of indiscipline. They and the colonies in general were regarded by the regular army as a dumping ground into which disgraced officers could be placed. A disproportionate number of *Schutztruppe* officers in South-West Africa were men with a chequered past; some had only agreed to serve in the colonies in the hope of reviving their careers.

In the last years of the late 1890s and early years of the twentieth century, as levels of racial abuse in South-West Africa began to increase, a succession of junior *Schutztruppe* officers were implicated in murders, rapes and beatings of Africans. The tendency of such officers to adopt a disproportionately violent stance towards Africans was aggravated by the sheer isolation of their postings. Many units were stationed tens or even hundreds of miles from their commanding officers. From tiny garrison stations, they were responsible for vast areas but were for the most part unsupervised, unrestrained and often under-occupied. Those who committed the most grievous excesses were dismissed and their crimes explained away as cases of 'tropical frenzy'. Governor Leutwein's inability to exercise control over such officers provided the sparks that led to war and disaster in German South-West Africa.

In 1903 the young officer Lieutenant Walter Jobst was stationed in Warmbad, a remote Nama settlement on the border with the

Cape Colony and 200 miles from the nearest town of any significance. Jobst had been a member of the German contingent that had carried out punitive raids in China in the aftermath of the Boxer Rebellion. By 1903 he had come to value African life as cheaply as he had Chinese life three years earlier.

The people of Warmbad, a Nama clan known as the Bondelswarts, were only about one thousand strong. Since Jobst's arrival, they had come to regard him with a mixture of fear and repugnance. In late October 1903, a dispute erupted between Jan Christian, the chief of the Bondelswarts, and a Herero woman on her way to the copper mines of the Cape. It concerned, of all things, the price of a goat. Although this minor incident had already been resolved by the time Lieutenant Jobst became involved, he still chose to summon Jan Christian to appear before him. Under the terms of the protection treaty between the Germans and the Bondelswarts, Jobst had no jurisdiction over affairs between Africans, and the chief ignored the summons. Jobst's response was to gather a group of his men and confront Jan Christian. A series of interviews recently conducted among the elders of the Nama community in Warmbad reveal how the event is remembered in the Nama's traditional oral history:

> The two Germans went straight to the house of the Chief and entered his room where he was lying on the bed with a scarf on his head. The soldiers forced him out of the bedroom. In the meantime, the Lieutenant had also made his way to the Captain's house. He had a mongrel dog with him. When he saw the soldiers wrestling with the Chief, he shouted an order at his soldiers: 'Shoot him!' They pulled the trigger and shot the Chief dead. The only word that he could say before he collapsed was: 'Now the war starts.'[24]

Within seconds Lieutenant Jobst, his sergeant and another soldier were gunned down by the Bondelswarts just yards from the dead chief's house.

Although lives had been lost, what had happened at Warmbad posed no real threat to the colony. Yet the reaction in both Windhoek and Berlin escalated wildly. Governor Leutwein privately condemned the behaviour of Lieutenant Jobst, but his public response was to issue a blood-curdling declaration of war against the Bondelswarts. Anything less would have risked incurring the ire of the settlers, the German colonial societies and his superiors in the Colonial Department in Berlin. The Kaiser's reaction to a minor incident, in a one-horse town in the southern wastelands of an economically defunct colony, can only be described as hysterical. He demanded that military reinforcements be immediately dispatched, not just to South-West Africa, but to all German territories, 'lest we lose all our colonial possessions'.

In late November, a force of *Schutztruppe* began the long trek south from Windhoek to Warmbad, a journey of 500 miles. Governor Leutwein himself headed the column, personally taking command of the crushing of the Bondelswarts. He left much of northern Hereroland in the hands of Lieutenant Ralph Zürn, a young officer as belligerent and impetuous as the late Lieutenant Jobst.

8

'Rivers of Blood and Money'

By 1904, the European quarter of the town of Okahandja had developed into a thriving colonial outpost. A string of German stores and settler homesteads ran along the main street, and a fortress had been constructed to house the local garrison and defend German interests. Opposite the fortress stood the new railway station connecting Okahandja to Windhoek, just 50 miles to the south. Outside the town, in the fertile grasslands of Hereroland, large tracts of pasture had been bought up by settlers and Okahandja had become the central node in a network of German-owned farms.

The Herero section of Okahandja, just a few miles to the north, had grown into a large sprawling settlement, always teeming with life. Thousands of Herero also lived in the surrounding areas. They made a living from riverbed farming and, on the plains beyond the mountains, reared their prized long-horned cattle, coming to town for supplies, and to buy and sell their livestock. Other Herero travelled to Okahandja from all over Hereroland, as the town was home to their Paramount Chief, Samuel Maharero.

Samuel ran his court from a splendid villa, built in the fashion of the German settlers. With a vast personal fortune based on cattle and increasingly on the sale of land, his home, furnished with plush velvet sofas and heavy carpets, reflected his social position. Govenor Leutwein described Samuel Maharero as 'a true ruler', a proud man of 'impressive appearance' At home in Okahandja, among his own people, he was regarded as a 'family person', a ruler who devoted much of his time to his children and to grooming his son Friedrich Maharero for the Herero chieftaincy.[1]

For Samuel, and many Herero, Okahandja was also a holy place, the spiritual centre of the ruling Maharero clan, whose ancestors were buried in a family cemetery by the Rhenish mission. It was also at Okahandja that Samuel Maharero maintained the holy fire of his clan, through which the living generations kept in touch with their ancestors.

On the morning of Tuesday 12 January 1904 Okahandja was deathly silent. It was the height of summer, and the sweltering heat lay like a shroud over empty streets. The only activity in the German quarter was within the walls of the fortress. Three dozen soldiers and armed settlers huddled behind the parapet watching over their own homes and shops through the sights of their rifles.

The German population of Okahandja had abandoned those homes and shops because of a rumour. Two days earlier, while on his journey to Okahandja, Alex Niet, a local Boer trader, had passed a column of around three hundred armed Herero men, also heading for the town. When Niet had reached Okahandja, he had reported this news to Lieutenant Ralph Zürn, the local Station Commander.

Lieutenant Zürn, a junior officer still in his twenties, had been placed in charge of a large area in the very heart of Hereroland. His term of command coincided with negotiations for the establishment of a second Herero reserve. This offered Zürn ample opportunity to demonstrate his utter contempt for the Herero. His arrogance, and a series of abuses committed against the Herero of Okahandja, fuelled both the Herero's sense of injustice and Zürn's paranoia that they would eventually seek retribution. When Zürn heard from Alex Niet that three hundred Herero were on the move, he was convinced it was the prelude to some sort of uprising and ordered all whites in Okahandja to evacuate their homes and take shelter inside the fortress.[2]

For two days, soldiers and setters had remained on twenty-four-hour watch over the town, and for two days nothing happened. That morning two of the more senior settlers, Councillor Duft and Dr Maass, volunteered to leave the safety of the fortress and venture out into Okahandja to investigate. They headed through the empty streets towards the Herero camp and on their way they passed a Herero Church elder known as Old Johannes, who glanced ambiguously at them and mumbled a few incomprehensible sentences in the Herero language, Otjiherero. Although puzzled by the old man's behaviour, Duft and Maass continued towards the Herero settlement. As they approached they saw around a hundred Herero men saddling their horses. Overcome with fear, the two men ran back to the fortress convinced that the arrival of so many Herero was the preparation for an attack and that Johannes's 'facial expression' had been some sort of a warning.

Back inside the walls of the fort, Duft and Maass briefed Lieutenant Zürn, who again jumped to the worst conclusion. Without making any attempt to establish the facts, Zürn sent a telegram to the Colonial Department in Berlin reporting, not that the Herero were preparing to attack, but that the uprising had already begun.

It is not known who fired the first shot, but what is clear is that shortly after Duft and Maass arrived back at the fort, both soldiers and settlers had begun to fire from the battlements into the streets of Okahandja. In response, the Herero emerged from their homes and laid siege to the fortress. They also attacked the German quarter, raiding homes and stores, and killing two German couples who had decided not to take refuge in the fortress. To prevent the Germans sending reinforcements from Windhoek, the Herero tore up the railway tracks and managed to overturn a railway coach just outside the station.

The German missionaries of Okahandja, whose mission station stood just 300 yards south of the fort, were caught in the crossfire. When the firing started, Missionary Phillip Diehl was forced to rush for cover as bullets tore through the mission station. 'One bullet', he wrote afterwards, 'penetrated my study, embedding itself in the wall above my desk . . . If I had been sitting there, as I had at the same time the previous day, I would now be a dead man.'[3] One of few photographs of Okahandja, taken in January 1904, shows the steeple of Diehl's church pock-marked by rifle fire. Later Diehl was shocked to discover that the bullets that had been aimed at his home had come not from the rifles of the Herero, who had carefully avoided the mission compound, but from the German fortress.

The one hundred Herero men that Duft and Maass had seen saddling their horses that morning were not the harbingers of an impeding uprising. They were merely representatives of one of the northern Herero clans recently arrived in Okahandja in order to seek the arbitration of Paramount Chief Samuel Maharero in an inheritance dispute. They were some of the armed Herero riders that the trader Alex Niet had seen riding to Okahandja a few days before.

The Herero viewed the Germans' actions prior to 12 January as extremely hostile and provocative. Not only had the whole community and the entire garrison barricaded themselves in the fortress and ranged their guns over the town but – as Samuel Maharero had discovered – Zürn had also requested that reinforcements be urgently sent from Windhoek. Although the Herero had not been planning an attack, and Samuel Maharero had not even been in Okahandja on the morning of 12 January, the behaviour of Lieutenant Zürn and his men had raised tensions to such an extent that the Herero response, when it came, was bloody and emphatic.

The outbreak of hostilities, based as it was on false rumours and a misinterpretation of events, might otherwise have been limited to Okahandja and resolved through negotiations. However, by 1904, the Herero people had endured several years of abuse and provocation and events in Okahandja were the spark that set all of Hereroland ablaze.

In the following days, a wave of violence radiated out from Okahandja. Brandishing clubs, knives and guns, the Herero attacked German farms and isolated homesteads across the great central plateau. Settlers were killed in their beds, on occasion by their own Herero servants. Men who had murdered or raped Herero, whom the German authorities had failed to punish, were hunted down. Traders who had extorted cattle and exaggerated debts were also killed. The Herero seized (at times seized back) large numbers of cattle from the traders and the settlers.

The wave of violent anger that began in Okahandja was, in part, a furious reaction against Lieutenant Zürn himself. As the historian Jan-Bart Gewald has shown, it was Zürn more than anyone who had substantially deepened Herero grievances and pushed them to the point at which a relatively minor incident in one town could lead to a general uprising across the whole of their territory.

One episode that had exacerbated tensions occurred just five weeks before fighting in Okahandja broke out. It concerned the forging of a land treaty. At the end of 1903, Zürn had summoned a number of Herero leaders from northern Hereroland to a meeting at the German fort in Okahandja. He had demanded they sign a contract that transferred large tracts of their ancestral land to the German authorities and established a second Herero reservation. When the chiefs refused to sign the treaty, Zürn had them unceremoniously removed from his office. He then forged what he imagined were passable imitations of their signatures: a series of indistinct 'X's. In fact, several of the Herero chiefs were perfectly able to read, write and sign their own names. On 8 December 1903 Zürn announced that the boundaries of northern and central Hereroland had been formally agreed, irrespective of the chiefs' rejection of the necessary treaty.[4]

This transgression had infuriated the Herero, but even before this Zürn had established himself as a figure of hate. On at least one occasion in 1903 Zürn had ordered his men to exhume skulls from various Herero graves in Okahandja. By the early twentieth century, race scientists in Germany were paying increasing sums for the skulls of Africans and other 'native' peoples, and Ralph Zürn had probably come to regard the skulls of the Herero as an easy source of additional income. For the Herero, the desecration of their ancestors' remains, as Heinrich Göring had discovered two decades earlier, was regarded as an act so odious as to be utterly unforgivable.

In 1905, Ludwig Conradt, a German trader and close friend of Chief Samuel Maharero, claimed that the desecration of the graves at Okahandja had been one of the main reasons why the Herero had risen up.[5] Even among settlers who had little contact with the Herero leadership, it was fairly well known that Zürn had goaded them to the point of revolt and that he was at least partially responsible for the war. Samuel Maharero also singled out Zürn as the chief author of the conflict, writing to Leutwein on 6 March 1904, 'This is not my war . . . it is that of Zürn.'

It is reasonable to assume that Leutwein and the German authorities knew that Zürn was the immediate cause of the violence. But once the war had begun, concerted efforts were made to ensure that all blame was laid on the Herero, and Samuel Maharero in particular. In June 1904 Zürn was quietly relieved of his command and sent back to Germany. As a final insult to the people whose destruction he had set in train, he brought back to Germany a Herero skull looted from the graves at Okahandja. In Berlin he donated the skull to the collection of Felix von Luschan, the racial anthropologist who, eight years earlier, had attempted to carry out anthropological examinations on Herero and Witbooi – including Friedrich Maharero, Chief Samuel's son – during the Berlin Colonial Exhibition.[6]

Friedrich Maharero was probably by his father's side in January 1904 when they received news of the Germans' attack. They were at that time some distance from Okahandja, visiting a sick friend. As the violence spread from the town, the Paramount Chief issued a formal order to his people. In this open letter, Maharero accepted that the war could now not be stopped and set down the rules by which the Herero would fight. He specifically forbade violence against women and children and, apart from a few incidents in the early chaotic days of the conflict, this edict was obeyed. While German men were attacked and killed, only four women and one child were killed during the whole course of the war.[7]

What happened to the Lange family at the settlement of Barmen, 25 miles from Okahandja, was typical. On the evening of 12 January, farmer Lange was dragged from his house and beaten to death. In panic, his wife grabbed two of her three children and fled with them into the bush. Mrs Lange and her children were not pursued by her husband's killers. A day later she and her children were picked up by a Herero patrol and escorted to Okahandja, where they were handed over to the German authorities. Brunhilde, the family's youngest child, who had been abandoned in the family home, also survived unharmed. A sheepherder discovered the child and delivered her to a local mission station.[8]

Samuel Maharero's order also made it clear that the war was solely against the Germans and was not to become a general race war against all whites. Boers and Englishmen, traders as well as settlers, were not to be attacked. Nor were the mixed-race Baster people or the Herero's old enemy the Nama. Again, these instructions were strictly carried out.

By contrast, the settlers and their allies among the *Schutztruppe*, once they had recovered from the initial shock of the uprising, conducted a brutal war against the Herero. Herero working for German companies or farmers were arrested and imprisoned. There were cases of lynching, and isolated Herero communities who did not take part in the rising – and even declared their 'loyalty' to the Kaiser – were nonetheless attacked. Photographs taken by settlers in early 1904 depict the beaten bodies of Herero men hanging from trees. In late January three gallows were erected on a hilltop in Windhoek and the execution of captured Herero became a regular public spectacle. The corpses of hanged rebels were left for days, as a warning to others.[9] In one of the Cape Town newspapers, an anonymous correspondent, signing 'A German Settler', wrote: 'We have commenced to hang these black rascals instead of shooting them and I can assure you we hang them nicely.'[10]

Within days of the outbreak of war in German South-West Africa, news reached Berlin that German settlers, subjects of the Kaiser, had been killed. The deaths of whites and the publication of casualty lists – constantly updated, if often inaccurate – made it impossible for the Herero rising to be viewed as simply another native revolt. The conflict in South-West Africa came to be regarded, by both the public and the government, as a national emergency and a blow to German national pride.

From the start, the outburst of intense fury against the Herero was channelled and manipulated by an array of nationalist and pro-colonial societies. Along with the right-wing press, they set out to portray the Herero as savages, their uprising motivated by innate brutality. Ignoring the facts, they repeatedly claimed that the Herero had launched an indiscriminate racial war and that, as savages, they fought without restraint. Many newspapers also carried reports of atrocities – most exaggerated, some entirely fabricated – claiming that a number of German children had been killed, that white women had been raped and that some of the male settlers who had been killed had had their noses and testicles cut off.[11]

To amplify the impact of these stories, artists produced fantastic illustrations. One engraving showed a gang of marauding Herero holding down a defenceless German woman in a white dress.[12] As the artist had no knowledge of life in South-West Africa, he depicted the Herero wearing the overalls and hats common among black sharecroppers in the Deep South of the United States.

With large swathes of the German public increasingly transfixed by events in South-West Africa, few people dared to challenge the accuracy of the reports from the colony. In an atmosphere of 'war fever', investigation into what had sparked the rebellion was eclipsed by the larger issue of how Germany should respond. The dominant argument – which runs through much of the propaganda – was that the Herero had to be punished. A campaign launched by the German Colonial Society drummed up support for a large-scale military intervention. In a public statement, issued only days after fighting in Okahandja had started, the society warned that 'Europeans can assert themselves only by maintaining the supremacy of their race at all cost.'[13] Other newspapers and pro-colonial pamphlets denounced the Herero, claiming that as a 'savage race' they would respond only to overwhelming military force.

These racial assumptions tapped into the general atmosphere of militarism that pervaded the Germany of the Kaisers. While to large sections of the German public the uprising was seen as an affront to German national honour, the army saw it as a rare opportunity. With the exception of the German contingent who had taken part in the crushing of the Boxer Rebellion three years earlier, and the small colonial force that had recently fought a murderous war in German East Africa, few of the soldiers in Kaiser Wilhelm's enormous army had actually tasted battle. Germany had been at peace since 1871. The glorious battles fought against the French at the time of unification were now history. An entire generation, inculcated in the Prussian warrior cult, had been starved of the chance to fight. Thousands rushed to volunteer for the war against the 'Negro Chief' Maharero. When rumours of an expeditionary force began to circulate, and later when placards appeared across Germany calling for volunteers, young officers clamoured for places and their families called in favours from influential contacts.

Civilians were not immune to the jingoism. Otto Seifert, an ordinary citizen, was so incensed by the reports of Herero savagery that he wrote to his Kaiser suggesting tactics that might be employed against them. The Herero could easily be defeated, he informed Wilhelm, if Germany were to 'poison their water supplies'. Seifert continued,

> After all we are not fighting against an enemy respecting the rules of fairness, but against savages. Never must we allow the Negroes to

prevail. The consequences of such a victory would be dire indeed since even now the Negroes believe that Africa belongs to them rather than to the Lord above.[14]

The Kaiser was inclined to agree. Sixteen years into his reign and with an enormous army standing idle under his colours, the rising of the Herero offered Wilhelm II and Germany the rare opportunity to showcase her military might and underline her status as a colonial power. In February 1904 Wilhelm placed command of the war against the Herero in the hands of the highest military authority in the land, General Alfred von Schlieffen. Today von Schlieffen is best remembered as the tactician whose plans for a simultaneous attack on France and Russia were posthumously realised in the summer of 1914. In the late winter of 1904, he turned his attention from the dilemmas of Germany's strategic position in Europe and focused on an insignificant colonial conflict at the other end of the world. He promptly dispatched the largest colonial army ever assembled by Germany.

From the middle of February, and at regular intervals thereafter, steamers of the Woermann Line left for Swakopmund, now the main port of German South-West Africa. The latest industrial weaponry was stacked in the holds: light portable artillery, repeating-rifles and Maxim machine-guns. On the decks, hundreds of soldiers waved at the jubilant crowds as they slipped out of Bremen or Hamburg. Most were young volunteers, but a small number were seasoned colonial soldiers, veterans of the Boxer Rebellion and the war fought against the Wahehe people of German East Africa ten years earlier.

Among the contingent of volunteers sent to South-West Africa on the steamship *Lucie Woermann* was a Bavarian Senior Lieutenant, Franz Xavier von Epp. In the photograph of von Epp in colonial uniform, he stands tall, with a neatly trimmed moustache and deep-set, staring eyes. At thirty-six, he was an experienced, battle-hardened colonial officer, and a passionate advocate of racial and Social Darwinist theories. We know how von Epp viewed the coming war against the Herero, and what he thought of Germany's colonial mission, thanks to a diary that he kept throughout his time in South-West Africa. Much more than a military journal, the pages are peppered with his thoughts on race, space and German national destiny. While en route to South-West Africa he wrote, 'The world is being divided . . . With time we will inevitably need more space; only by the sword will we be able to get it. It will be up to our generation to achieve this. It is a matter of our existence.'[15]

Also aboard the *Lucie Woermann* was another German officer with his own vision of Germany's destiny in Africa. Captain Maximilian Bayer had volunteered for service against the Herero and, like von Epp, he believed that Germany was destined to expand her living space. Bayer regarded the recent history of the United States as a model of how Germany might transform her own colonial frontiers. German South-West Africa was to be Germany's 'Wild West', and the local Africans would ultimately go the way of the Native Americans. Believing the whole process to be ordained by God, Bayer wrote:

> Our Lord has made the laws of nature so that only the strong have a right to continue to exist in the world, and so that the weak and purposeless will perish in favour of the strong. This process is played out in a variety of ways, like, for example, the end of the American Indians, because they were without purpose in the continued development of a world that is striving towards a higher level of civilisation; in the same way the day will come when the Hottentot [Nama] will perish, [it will] not [be] any loss for humanity because they are after all only born thieves and robbers, nothing more.[16]

By 1 March, two thousand German troops had landed in South-West Africa. They were transported across the Namib Desert in the open carriages of the new narrow-gauge railway line and readied for action. It was then, as the new arrivals began to mix with *Alte Afrikaners* (Old Africans) – the troops and settlers who had lived in the colony for years – that rumours of the military prowess of the Herero began to diminish their confidence. While awaiting transport in Swakopmund, von Epp was appalled to learn that Samuel Maharero's men were armed with Mauser rifles, identical to those carried by his own men. 'The black swine know how to use them too,' he confided to his diary.[17]

While von Epp and Bayer and other German officers viewed the war as a racial crusade, their commander, Governor Leutwein, had a different view of how the uprising should be managed. It had taken Leutwein over a month to get back from the south after the suppression of the Bondelswarts Nama. He had travelled by sea, landing at Swakopmund on 11 February, finally reaching Okahandja on the 18th. It was perhaps only then that the full complexity of the situation in Hereroland became apparent to him. Whereas the defeat of the Bondelswarts had been merely another stage in the slow process of German expansion, the rising of the Herero nation risked becoming a fully fledged colonial war.

Since the outbreak of hostilities, the force under Samuel Maharero had swelled to around four thousand fighters. However, following the initial surge of bloodletting, the Herero had not sought to press home their advantage, nor attempted to assault the various fortifications in which much of the German population had taken refuge. Instead they had withdrawn to Okanjira, an area of low rugged mountains set amidst a maze of impassable gorges, two days' march from Okahandja. As the shooting war had in effect come to an end, Leutwein's instinctive approach was to open up negotiations with Samuel Maharero, whom he had known for a decade. But in the first week of April, Kaiser Wilhelm, acting through intermediaries in the General Staff, denounced any efforts to negotiate with the Herero. Wilhelm issued an order demanding that the Herero uprising be 'relentlessly suppressed', and von Schlieffen instructed Leutwein to march on Hereroland and deliver a decisive blow.

Publicly Leutwein did not oppose or criticise his orders, but privately he regarded von Schlieffen's strategy as doomed. Even with two thousand reinforcements, Leutwein had just over three thousand soldiers under his command. With this force he was expected to confront a Herero force of four thousand, while policing the rest of the colony.

It is remarkable that, even after two decades of contact with the peoples of South-West Africa, the military elite in Berlin were able to convince themselves that such a small and inexperienced force would be able to overwhelm a substantially larger Herero army. The generals were similarly unperturbed by the enormous logistical difficulties of supplying the force in the deserts of South-West Africa. Nor were they concerned by the fact that the Herero knew the territory in minute detail, whereas the Germans did not even have proper maps of Hereroland. Although some overconfidence can be explained by the inordinate faith they placed in artillery and the Maxim gun, their readiness to discount the military and strategic abilities of the Herero also points to deeply held racial suppositions.

Leutwein it seems was disturbed by the lust for vengeance that emanated from Berlin. As early as February 1904, he had come to suspect that Kaiser Wilhelm and some of his advisers within the General Staff were clamouring not merely for the defeat of the Herero, but for their annihilation. Writing to the Colonial Department, he openly counselled against a war of extermination, on grounds of pragmatism rather than humanity: 'I do not concur with those fanatics who want to see the Herero destroyed altogether. Apart from the fact that a people of 60,000 or 70,000 are not so easily annihilated I consider it a bad mistake from an economic point of view.'[18]

On 7 April 1904, reluctantly following von Schlieffen's orders, Theodor Leutwein led a force of just eight hundred men out of Okahandja. The remainder of the enlarged garrison was spread across the colony, protecting German settlers and maintaining a watchful presence in the south, among the Nama. Riding with Leutwein's *Schutztruppe* were one hundred African scouts, fifty of them from the Witbooi clan, compelled to fight alongside the Germans under the protection treaty Hendrik Witbooi had signed with Leutwein in 1894.

At the Herero encampment, near a waterhole at Okanjira, thirty thousand Herero, along with large numbers of cattle (estimates vary between twenty and forty thousand head), had come together under their Paramount Chief. They were protected by Samuel's four thousand men at arms, of whom two and a half thousand were armed with modern rifles, while the rest carried traditional weapons of clubs and knives. Okanjira offered commanding views over the surrounding scrub and the Herero dug a series of trenches along the escarpments to fortify their camp. On 9 April, Leutwein's columns approached, throwing a colossal plume of dust in their wake.

After a cautious advance along narrow valleys, the Witbooi scouts located the Herero encampment, giving Leutwein just enough time to move his artillery pieces into position. The initial ensuing bombardment failed to overwhelm the Herero fighters in their trenches. Rather than panicking, they held their fire until the German troops were in range in order to maximise the impact of their salvos. However, the battle turned when German shells and grenades began to overshoot the trenches and crash down among the women and children camped on the far side of the Okanjira escarpment.

Shocked by the impact of the German guns and the devastating force of new Pirkin grenades, Samuel Maharero disengaged from battle and ordered an evacuation. When Leutwein's men finally reached the site of the Herero camp, all that remained were thousands of empty huts and, as Emil Malzahn, an officer under Leutwein's command, put it, 'scattered Herero body parts caused by our grenades'.[19]

Despite forcing the Herero to retreat, only superior firepower had saved the Germans from defeat. A British correspondent, writing for the *South African Review* and *Daily News*, who had witnessed the battle, reported: 'The Hereros . . . are better armed, bolder in their attacks, and above all more clever in their tactics than was expected.'

Four days later Leutwein's now exhausted men followed the tracks of the Herero to the waterhole of Oviumbo, 12 miles north of Okanjira, and staggered into an ambush. Spread out on the hills above the riverbed, the Herero rained bullets down from concealed positions. When the Germans marked their own positions with red flags, to prevent their units firing upon each other, the Herero made their own flags, creating enormous confusion. For ten hours much of Leutwein's force was pinned down by rifle fire from several directions. Unable to distinguish friend from foe, and with three-quarters of their ammunition expended, the Germans were saved only by nightfall. That evening many of Leutwein's most senior and experienced officers pleaded with the governor to retreat. Convinced that if the battle were allowed to continue for another day his positions would be overrun, and in charge of a force that had patently lost its nerve, Leutwein ordered a night-time march back to Okahandja.

When details of the defeat at Oviumbo became known in Berlin, a storm of criticism was unleashed. Much of it was focused on the governor who, it was claimed, had brought shame on Germany by retreating in the face of racially inferior Africans. In a telegram to the General Staff, Leutwein was forced to defend his actions. With some justification be pointed out that, 'by ordering the night march from Oviumbo, I saved the military force from disaster'.[20]

What Okanjira and Oviumbo demonstrated was that raw conscripts, drawn from the slums of the industrial cities, were at a profound disadvantage when set against men whose entire lives had been spent in the saddle with rifle in hand. They were further hampered by having to fight across a terrain they did not understand and over which they found it extremely difficult to maintain their supply lines. The Herero were excellent marksmen and, like the Boers, highly skilled in the art of concealment. Rather than acknowledge this, the Kaiser and the High Command chose to pour their vitriol on the one man whose knowledge of the colony might have allowed them to bring the war quickly and cheaply to an end. On 9 May, after brief consultations with von Schlieffen and the Head of the Military Cabinet, Hülsen-Haeseler, Kaiser Wilhelm relieved Governor Theodor Leutwein of his military duties.

The man chosen to replace Theodor Leutwein as commander in South-West Africa was General Adrian Dietrich Lothar von Trotha, a ten-year veteran of the German colonial army. Between 1894 and 1897, von Trotha had been a commander in German East Africa and had forged a reputation for ruthlessness. During the Wahehe uprising, von Trotha had unflinchingly ordered mass hangings and the summary executions of prisoners of war. He had burned down entire villages, sometimes with their inhabitants still inside. Von Trotha's treatment of the local peoples was so extreme that it even drew opposition from Hermann Wissmann, the Governor of German East Africa. Wissmann had served alongside Curt von François in the Belgian Congo in the 1880s and had a reputation for cruelty and violence. Yet when he heard of von Trotha's appointment to South-West Africa, he warned the Colonial Department that von Trotha was 'a bad leader . . . and a bad comrade'.[21]

By the time von Trotha left German East Africa in 1897 he had become convinced that the rebellions he had helped crush were merely a prelude to a larger racial war that Germany and the white race in general were destined to fight against the 'lower races' across the world. Three years later von Trotha had been placed in command of the First East Asiatic Infantry Brigade. In the terrible aftermath of the Boxer Rebellion, he was in charge of a unit that attacked Chinese villages in a series of punitive raids. By 1904 von Trotha was considered a hardened colonial specialist. He was the favoured choice of both the army and the Kaiser, who instructed him to 'end the war by fair or foul means', adding, 'I entrust this command to you with the fullest confidence in your insight, energy and experience'.[22] Wilhelm Lorang, a soldier who served under von Trotha in South West Africa, described him as 'a human shark' and 'the most bloodthirsty animal in his [Kaiser Wilhelm's] war arsenal'.[23]

On taking up his new command General von Trotha was in no doubt as to how the Herero should be treated when they dared to oppose the will of their colonial masters. Writing in 1904, he stated:

I know enough tribes in Africa. They all have the same mentality insofar as they yield only to force. It was and remains my policy to apply this force by absolute terrorism and even cruelty. I shall destroy the rebellious tribes by shedding rivers of blood and money. Only then will it be possible to sow the seeds of something new that will endure.[24]

Von Trotha landed at Swakopmund on 11 June, his desert-brown colonial uniform draped in medals, including the Iron Cross. On arrival in Windhoek he held a meeting with Governor Leutwein. The two clashed instantly. Seeking assurance that the Herero were not to be annihilated, Leutwein again suggested that a place might still be found for them in the colony after their military defeat. Von Trotha dismissed Leutwein's ideas, claiming he did not take war seriously.

In order to prevent Leutwein from interfering with his plans, von Trotha declared a state of martial law, which made him supreme commander in both military and civil affairs. This manoeuvre marked the beginning of a period of effective military dictatorship in South-West Africa that was to last until November 1905.

Von Trotha's appointment also short-circuited the command structure in German South-West Africa. Although Leutwein was a soldier, as the governor he answered to the Colonial Department and the civilian government. Von Trotha answered only to the Chief of Staff and the Kaiser, a separate chain of command that bypassed the Reichstag and side-stepped civilian control. This disastrous duality in the command structure, which Imperial Germany had inherited from pre-unification Prussia, allowed von Trotha to sideline Leutwein and the Colonial Department. It was later severely to limit the ability of Chancellor Bernhard von Bülow to exercise control over von Trotha.

With additional troops and equipment arriving almost weekly, von Trotha set about planning war against the Herero, a people he described in his diary as *Unmenschen* – non-humans.[25] Since the battle at Oviumbo two months earlier there had been little fighting. Out of an estimated Herero population of sixty to eighty thousand, as many as fifty thousand had gathered around Samuel Maharero. This enormous body of people, along with tens of thousands of their cattle, had migrated north and made camp at the foot of a large plateau in north-central Hereroland known in the Dutch as the Waterberg – the Water Mountain.

The Waterberg was a place of deep cultural importance to the Herero, a people whose traditions and religion were woven into the landscape itself. On the slopes of the Waterberg plateau grew a forest of large fig trees, some hundreds of years old. According to the Herero creation myth, their ancestors had first descended from heaven by climbing down through the branches of fig trees. For generations the Herero chiefs had held their councils beneath the shade of their broad leaves. The mountain itself was of equal significance. It was the last major source of underground water within the borders of South-West Africa, before the acacia bushes of the scrub-deserts slowly gave way to the utter desolation of the Kalahari – a wilderness the Herero knew as the Omaheke. With its deep underground aquifers and many waterholes, the Waterberg was known to the Herero as Otjozondjupa, named after the calabash gourds in which they stored sour milk, a symbol of wealth.

In the shadow of the sheer red sandstone cliffs of the Waterberg, rising 650 feet above the desert, and amid the trees of their ancestors, the Herero nation built a city of *pontoks* – traditional huts made of branches and blankets or cow hide – that stretched along the 30 miles of the Waterberg. Each village housed one of the Herero clans, a wretched imitation of their home settlements. The great encampment at the Waterberg was, in effect, the Herero nation condensed, the vast distances between their settlements erased, and the bonds of kinship and culture heightened by shared hardship and the presence of an external foe.

Samuel Maharero himself camped near the waterhole of Ohamakari, on the southern side of the *pontok* city. Either here, or under the fig trees on the slopes of the Waterberg itself, he and his fellow chiefs held their councils and debated their strategy. According to German intelligence, the Herero chiefs had split into three camps of opinion. The first favoured negotiating with the Germans; the second were happy to settle matters on the battlefield; the third, led by Samuel Maharero, believed the Herero should abandon South-West Africa altogether and seek refuge in British-controlled Bechuanaland – modern-day Botswana. To reach Bechuanaland, the Herero would be forced to cross the Omaheke Desert. But such a crossing could only be attempted after the arrival of the summer rains in December, and even then with severe difficulty.[26]

In June 1904, from his headquarters in Windhoek, General von Trotha also considered the Herero's options. If they were to flee into British territory, Hereroland would be abandoned and the rich pastures that the German settlers had coveted for so many years would finally be theirs. The flight of the Herero would also bring the rebellion to an end and render unnecessary the enormously expensive and dangerous military expedition he was preparing against them. However, such an exodus would prevent von Trotha from bringing the retribution of Germany and the Kaiser down upon the heads of 'the rebellious tribes'. For this reason the strategy he devised was predicated on his determination to destroy the Herero utterly, and to strike before they were able to find refuge across the desert.

Adopting the concept of concentric deployment, as developed by Germany's great military strategist Helmuth von Moltke, von Trotha, as he said in his own account, planned to 'encircle the Herero masses around Waterberg and to annihilate them with an instantaneous blow'.[27] By early July he had assembled an army of six thousand men, by far the largest the colony had ever seen. In fact the number of soldiers under von Trotha's command in

August 1904 far exceeded the number of settlers they had ostensibly been sent to defend.

The abundance of men and equipment at von Trotha's disposal were the fruits of the 585 million marks raised in extraordinary loans by the Colonial Department to pay for the war. The colony itself – impoverished as ever – was able to contribute only 110 million towards its own defence.[28] Economically as well as militarily, the extent to which Germany was willing to stretch herself in order to punish the Herero – a people who had months earlier stopped attacking German settlers – was hugely disproportionate.

In early August, as his men began to assemble around the Waterberg, General von Trotha issued orders stating that it was imperative that all units avoid alarming or provoking the Herero, who were well aware of the build-up of German forces. Von Trotha could only contemplate the annihilation of fifty thousand people because they were concentrated in an area just 30 miles long and 20 wide. If the Herero were to disperse, not only would they slip the trap, but there was a risk that Germany would be dragged into a protracted and possibly un-winnable war fought over vast distances. One soldier wrote to his parents: 'We have been lying here for some time now. We will be here until the mousetrap closes if the Herero do us the favour of not escaping.'

Despite von Trotha's strict orders, there were a number of minor skirmishes. Just days before the attack, his own nephew, Lieutenant Thilo von Trotha, was involved in two conflicts that led to the shooting of seventy Herero. The younger von Trotha was reprimanded by his uncle, who warned that such premature actions 'have to be avoided if the aim of the war, annihilation of the whole lot, is to be achieved'.

The Herero simply allowed the Germans to assemble around them at the Waterberg. Samuel Maharero failed to launch a pre-emptive strike when the Germans were at their most vulnerable. Nor did he attempt to break through the encirclement. Maharero seems to have rejected the idea of attempting flight across the Omaheke in the dry month of August, possibly because the very old and very young would have found the journey nearly impossible and few of the Herero's precious cattle were likely to survive such an exodus. Furthermore, the Herero were tending a number of their people – including women and children – who had been wounded at the battle of Okanjira.

Samuel Maharero's inaction at the Waterberg was most probably a result of his belief that at any moment he could enter negotiations with the Germans and the war would come to an end. Indeed, ever since arriving at the Waterberg, the Herero had been expecting negotiations and had made repeated overtures to the Germans. While von Trotha sought to avoid clashes in order to keep the Herero concentrated at the Waterberg, Samuel Maharero kept his men at arm's length from the Germans in order to facilitate peace negotiations. He even allowed a German unit to inspect the Waterberg mission and police station, both sacked in the early days of the conflict and both well within the Herero's lines of defence.

From the Herero viewpoint, their victory at the battle of Oviumbo four months earlier had been a clear demonstration of their power and determination to fight for their land and traditions. They had not only defeated the Germans, despite their enemy's advanced weapons, but also inflicted significant casualties. According to all the conventions of warfare recognised by the peoples of South-West Africa, the logical next step was to enter into negotiations and avoid further bloodshed.

Samuel Maharero could not possibly have realised that his war against the Germans had – in the minds of the Kaiser and the military elite in Berlin – escalated to such a point it was no longer a colonial war in any recognisable sense. By the time of General von Trotha's appointment, it was clear that nothing but an overwhelming military victory would appease a German public who had been whipped into a frenzy by months of unbridled colonialist propaganda.

In his own accounts of the war, von Trotha says little of Herero attempts to open negotiations. The German Official

History of the campaign, written by the army's own historians, is equally evasive on the subject. According to surviving German records, some of the main Herero sub-chiefs, including the influential Salatiel Kambazembi, attempted to initiate negotiations in late July. At that time Major Ludwig von Estorff, one of the most experienced and respected officers in the *Schutztruppe*, strongly recommended that von Trotha enter into talks. Von Trotha refused. Discussing the peace feelers of the Herero chiefs in his diary, he dismissed their attempts to negotiate with the phrase 'fought together, caught together, hanged together'.[29]

On 4 August 1904 General von Trotha issued his 'Directives for the Attack on the Hereros'. The German force was to be divided into six detachments. Each would approach from a different direction and encircle the Herero encampment. Given the size of the battlefield, the encirclement would be far from watertight. However, the enemy the Germans were seeking to trap were mainly civilians: women, children and the elderly, together with their slow-moving cattle. Once contained, the Herero would be bombarded with artillery and grenades. When the Herero fighters, who still outnumbered the Germans, attempted to break through the encirclement, they would be forced back by the Maxim guns – capable of firing three hundred rounds per minute. The whole battle would be coordinated by a team of scouts who were to scale the sheer cliffs of the Waterberg. There they would track the movements of the Herero and signal their positions to their comrades below using heliographs.

In the early hours of 10 August 1904, two days shy of seven months since the Herero in Okahandja had risen up, von Trotha emerged from his tent for a final briefing with his most senior officers. They assembled before a large map of the Waterberg, on which the plan of battle had been marked. After the briefing they all posed for a photograph.

The next morning at six o'clock exactly the German guns burst into life. Most of the Herero were asleep in their huts when the first shells and grenades crashed down among them. People were blown apart by shrapnel and their *pontoks* incinerated. Led by their Nama guides, the Germans crept forward to tighten the noose. When the Herero counter-attacked, they were met by the twelve Maxim guns that had been strategically placed around the encirclement. Throughout the day, wave after wave of Herero fighters struggled to break the stranglehold. Those carrying guns formed lines of attack, and when they fell, a new line of fighters would take the rifles of the dead and launch a fresh assault. Behind the fighting men, the women collected the dead and tended to the wounded as best they could.[30]

At around three o'clock in the afternoon, after nine hours of constant fighting, the Herero finally managed to punch a hole in the German lines. The breakthrough came when Maharero's men overran a German position on the south-eastern side of the encirclement. Both contemporaries and historians have speculated as to whether von Trotha left the south-eastern flank of his force deliberately weak, in the hope that if the Herero did break through, they would be forced to retreat into the Omaheke Desert.

The German detachment on the south-eastern edge of the great encirclement, commanded by Major der Heyde, was small compared with the units placed at the disposal of the five other commanders, and General von Trotha had been warned of this disparity before the battle. Chancellor Bernhard von Bülow, writing in his memoirs (published posthumously in 1931), was in no doubt that this had been a deliberate strategy. He stated that, 'In order to be rid of the Hereros sooner, he [von Trotha] suggested that they be driven into the waterless desert with women and children.' Paul Leutwein, the son of the governor, also claimed that his father 'foresaw the breakthrough of the Herero and their resulting flight into the sandveld or across the border. He realised that in both cases the entire people would be lost.'[31] Perhaps this aspect of von Trotha's plan – if it was a deliberate tactic – was a tacit acknowledgement that, despite all the troops and war materials at his disposal, it was still impossible to annihilate fifty thousand people 'with an instantaneous blow'.

By nightfall on 11 August, the Herero nation, tens of thousands of people, were rushing headlong through the breach in the German lines, funnelled in the direction of the Omaheke. None of this was clear to General von Trotha in his field headquarters 10 miles away: the reports of the battle were confused and contradictory. It was only at dawn on 12 August that the events of the previous day finally became clear. By then most of the Herero had fled into the desert.

To his profound frustration, von Trotha was not able to pursue the Herero immediately on the 12th, due to the utter exhaustion of his men and horses. On the 13th, a small number of German units followed the trail of the Herero into the desert. Captain Maximilian Bayer described the scene that met them in the immediate aftermath of the battle:

> The route along which the enemy fled was totally trampled over a width of some 100 metres. Here, the entire people, with its wagons and thousands of animals, all women and children, old people and warriors, had moved in hasty flight. Everywhere there were signs of the desperate, panicky haste in which the Herero had fled intent only on saving their lives . . . Along the route there lay skins, empty water-bags, leather bags and all kinds of junk which the fleeing people had cast away so as to be able to run faster.[32]

Within just two weeks, most of the pursuing German units had exhausted their water supplies and were forced to turn back. Yet even by this point, the desert had taken its toll on the Herero. Adolf Fischer, a German private, wrote the following account of the plight of the Herero as they were pushed ever deeper into the Omaheke:

> The greater part of the Herero nation and their cattle lay dead in the bush, lining the path of their morbid march. Everyone among us realised what had happened here. To the right and left of us were putrid, swollen cattle carcasses. Vultures and jackals had already filled themselves to

their bellies' content. They had an infinite supply of meat, more than they could possibly consume. Whenever we wanted to wet our burning palates, we had to pull our tired horses by their bridles through the swollen animal carcasses to drink a forbidding, disgusting broth from the puddles of water. Whenever we dismounted, our feet would hit against the human bodies. There was a young woman with wilted breasts, her frozen face covered with flies and curled up next to her hip an aborted birth. There was also an old woman, who had great difficulty walking. Eight or ten leg rings made from rough iron pearls – the sign of her dignity and wealth – had eaten her flesh to the bone . . . There was a boy. He was still alive; staring into the night with a stupid grin from an empty mind . . . Whoever took part in the chase through the Sandveld lost his belief in righteousness on Earth.[33]

It was only after the battle of the Waterberg that the full genocidal scope of von Trotha's plans became clear. Accounts vary as to when the command was given, but at some point, probably before the battle itself, von Trotha issued orders that no Herero prisoners were to be taken. Although a written version of that command has never come to light, Major von Estorff, a firm critic of von Trotha's policies, recorded in his journal that orders banning the taking of prisoners were in place soon after the Waterberg. Major Stuhlman, who fought at the Waterberg, also recorded having received the order not to take prisoners. In a diary entry made before the battle, he wrote: 'We had been explicitly told beforehand that what we were dealing with was the extermination of the whole tribe, nothing living was to be spared.'[34]

It is clear from accounts given later by both German soldiers and African scouts fighting alongside them that from the start of their pursuit, the Germans began systematically to execute men, women and children. But as von Trotha was no doubt aware, the enormous logistical difficulties of pursuing the Herero into the wastelands of the Omaheke meant that his units were incapable of catching and killing the Herero in numbers that he deemed acceptable. On 16 August, and again on the 26th, he issued orders to his troops to cut off waterholes and set up patrols along the perimeter of the Omaheke in order to prevent parties of Herero from slipping westwards, back into the colony where they could find water and food.

Dehydration was the biggest killer. Herero who had been able to slip cattle through the gap in the German lines quenched their thirst by drinking cows' blood, leaving a trail of desiccated carcasses in their wake. Those without cattle bore holes, up to 30 feet deep, into the dry riverbeds of the Omaheke. When a little water appeared at the bottom, panic ensued. In the rush to drink, people were crushed, even buried alive, when the walls of these improvised wells collapsed. Katherine Zeraua, a survivor of what was later called 'the trail of tears', narrated her experiences to a German missionary:

> Like thousands of others, she had fled into the desert. She had lost track of her family members and was accompanied by three orphaned children. Now the misery began. There was nothing to eat and the thirst was even worse . . . she walked mostly during the nights. During the days she sought shelter by rocks or by thorny bushes. In the course of their journey they kept coming upon many dead bodies. One day they spotted a bushy shelter. They ran to it in the hope of finding anything edible for the children. But what they found were only dead or dying people. They also found a familiar face from Otjimbingwe. She greeted him. Then she said, 'Come we have to push on!' He said: 'Why should I continue? What reason is there for me to live now that I have lost everything, my family, my belongings?'[35]

The German Official History of the battle of the Waterberg described von Trotha's strategy as a stunning strategic success:

> The hasty exit of the Herero to the southeast, into the waterless Omaheke, would seal his fate; the environment of his own country was to bring about his extermination in a way that no German weapon, even in a most bloody or deadly battle, ever could . . . [their] death rattle and furious cry of insanity echoed in the exhalted silence of eternity. The Herero indictment had come to an end and they had ceased to exist as an independent people.[36]

9

'Death through Exhaustion'

Early in October 1904, six weeks after the battle of the Waterberg, the men of the German 1st Field Regiment– a unit of *Schutztruppe* commanded by General von Trotha – arrived at the last known waterhole deep inside the endless expanses of the Omaheke. Von Trotha's men were exhausted, their supplies almost at an end and their horses on the brink of collapse. They were patently in no condition to venture further into a desert that had not even been properly mapped.

The waterhole where von Trotha and his men halted stood in a small clearing by the dry bed of the Eiseb River. It was known to the Herero as Osombo zoWindimbe. In 1904, it was a desolate backwater, and today Osombo zoWindimbe is so remote that very few Namibians have even heard of it. Nevertheless, it is one of the most important sites in Namibian history and arguably a place of major significance in the wider history of the twentieth century.[1]

Just after sunrise on 3 October 1904[2] von Trotha's men were woken and assembled for the daily roll-call. Once they had been brought to attention, General von Trotha appeared, with several of his most senior officers: Paul von Lettow-Vorbeck, von Epp and most probably Maximilian Bayer. Turning towards his troops, the general read aloud the text of a proclamation that he had drafted the previous day. It was written in a bizarre form of pidgin that von Trotha, considering himself an expert in African affairs, believed was the appropriate language with which to intimidate the Herero:

I, the Great General of the German troops, send this letter to the Herero . . . The Herero people must leave the land. If they do not do this I will force them with the Groot Rohr [Cannon]. Within the German borders every Herero, with or without a gun, with or without cattle, will be shot. I will no longer accept women and children, I will drive them back to their people or I will let them be shot at. These are my words to the Herero people. Signed: The Great General of the Mighty Kaiser, von Trotha.[3]

At the end of his speech von Trotha turned his gaze towards thirty-five recently captured Herero, mainly old men, women and children. On the general's orders, two of their number, both men, were dragged towards a makeshift gallows where they became victims of what Captain von Epp described in his dairy as a 'theatrical hanging'.[4]

Copies of von Trotha's proclamation – translated into Otjiherero and written out on small folded pieces of paper – were attached around the necks of old men, women and children who were then driven into the desert by volleys of gunfire aimed over their heads. The Extermination Order – as the Osombo zoWindimbe proclamation has become known – was the explicit and official confirmation of the policies that most German units had followed ever since the battle of the Waterberg. It ended any pretence that the war was being fought to end the uprising. The aim of the conflict was to eradicate the Herero as an ethnic group from German South-West Africa, either by their extermination or by their wholesale expulsion from the colony. A single copy of the original Extermination Order has survived and is in the Botswana National Archives in Gaberone. It is an almost unique document: an explicit, written declaration of intent to commit genocide.

The day after issuing the Extermination Order, von Trotha wrote to the General Staff explaining the new policy to his superiors.

Since I neither can nor will come to terms with these people without express orders from His Majesty the Emperor and King, it is essential that all sections of the nation be subjected to rather stern treatment . . . My intimate knowledge of so many Central African tribes, Bantu and others, has made it abundantly clear to me that the Negroes will yield only to brute force, whereas negotiations are quite pointless . . . They will either meet their doom in the sandveld or try to cross into Bechuanaland.[5]

In the same report, von Trotha reiterated his belief that the extermination of the Herero was merely a phase in a wider racial war in Africa, a conflict he had long predicted was inevitable: 'This uprising is and remains the beginning of a racial struggle, which I foresaw as early as 1897 in my reports to the Imperial Chancellor.'[6]

The actual military plan surrounding the Extermination Order called for the abandonment of the pursuit into the Omaheke. Only one unit, Major von Estorff's, would continue to operate in the desert. The vast bulk of the army was to be distributed along the border between the Omaheke and the Waterberg itself, forming a cordon to prevent groups of Herero from returning to their former homelands. Any Herero caught on the border between the desert and Hereroland were to be shot on sight.

Von Trotha was aware from the beginning of the potential damage the Extermination Order represented to 'the good reputation that the German soldier has acquired'. In a supplementary order he stipulated that while he was in 'no doubt that as a result of this order no more male prisoners will be taken', he was equally confident that 'neither will it give rise to atrocities committed on women and children. These will surely run away after two rounds of shots have been fired over their heads.'[7] Driven back into the desert, these women and children would simply die of thirst and malnutrition or be forced out of the colony.

All units not required for the operations on the border of the Omaheke were to be sent east, back into Hereroland, to execute the second half of von Trotha's plan. Once resupplied, these troops were formed into what became known as *Aufklaerungspatrouillen* – Cleansing Patrols. Their task was to sweep across Hereroland and 'clean up the entire district of broken groups of Hereros'.

As von Trotha was well aware, there were several thousand Herero still within Hereroland. They fell into two categories. The first were escapees from the battle of the Waterberg, who had managed to avoid German patrols and move back towards their homelands. The second were Herero who had not been at the Waterberg and, in many cases, had taken no part in the rebellion. Although at least fifty thousand Herero had gathered at the Waterberg under their Paramount Chief Samuel Maharero, there were still perhaps twenty to thirty thousand Herero who had stayed in their villages throughout the uprising. Many lived in isolated settlements in the northern and western parts of the colony, far from the areas of white settlement. Not only had some of these communities not taken part in the uprising, they may well have known very little about the war at all. Such communities spent 1904 living in their traditional villages preoccupied with the daily difficulties of keeping themselves and their cattle alive. On von Trotha's orders, these people were to be shot on sight.[8]

They proved easy targets for the German patrols. Time and again the diaries of commanders in the Cleansing Patrols reveal that their attacks were focused upon ordinary Herero villages, rather than upon anything resembling a military force. This fact is borne out by the low rates of casualties (from action rather than disease) among the men of the German units.

There are very few descriptive passages in the diaries and dispatches of the soldiers involved in the Cleansing Patrol, but there are a few unguarded phrases that hint at the slaughter that took place across Hereroland in 1904 and 1905. Wilhelm Lorang, a soldier in von Epp's company, later explained that, as he understood it, the Extermination Order permitted the Germans to 'shoot, kill, hang. Whatever you liked. Old or young. Men, women, children.' According to Pastor Elger, a missionary based in the Herero town of Karibib, the motto of the Patrols became 'Clean out, hang up, shoot down till they are all gone.'[9]

From Africans working for the *Schutztruppe*, there is another set of accounts that describe in more detail the actions of the Cleansing Patrols. In late 1904 Hendrik Campbell, a member of the mixed-race Baster people from the town of Rehoboth, was in command of a contingent of Baster men compelled to fight for the Germans under the terms of their protection treaty. Campbell and his men witnessed the actions of one of the Cleansing Patrols in the last weeks of 1904:

At Katjura we had a fight with the Herero, and drove them from their position. After the fight was over, we discovered eight or nine sick Herero women who had been left behind. Some of them were blind. Water and food had been left with them. The German soldiers burnt them alive in the hut in which they were laying . . . Afterwards at Otjimbende we [the Basters] captured 70 Hereros. I handed them over to Ober-Leutenants Völkmann and Zelow. I then went on patrol, and returned two days later, to find the Hereros all lying dead in a kraal. My men reported to me that they had all been shot and bayoneted by the German soldiers.[10]

The area over which the Cleansing Patrols operated was 100,000 square miles in size. Although the Germans considered the entire region 'Hereroland', it was also home to communities of Damara, Owambo and San. Most soldiers had only been in the colony a few months and could not distinguish these different African peoples. Many of those killed by the Cleansing Patrols were almost certainly non-Herero. Hundreds of miles from their senior commanders, operating on the fringes of an endless desert and under orders to shoot Herero on sight, it may well have been a very small step for exhausted men to reinterpret their orders as a licence to kill all Africans.

On occasion, the Cleansing Patrols were unable to reach bands of Herero in the desert and instead sent lone messengers out into the bush in the hope of luring them into ambushes with false promises. In the most famous case, a group of some three hundred Herero, who had made camp on the western perimeter of the Omaheke Desert, were located by a German patrol. On 29 October the Germans sent a messenger to the Herero camp to assure them that if they reported to the waterhole of Ombakaha, 20 miles to the east, they would be allowed to surrender and their lives would be spared.[11]

The next day, their leader Joel Kavezeri and eighty of his men set out for Ombakaha to accept the German offer. When they arrived they were offered some tobacco and – as it was noon – were permitted to sit in the shade of a tree. They then entered into negotiations with the local German commander, Lieutenant von Beesten, who, in the middle of their conversation, suddenly ran for cover, shouting orders for his troops to open fire. One of the few survivors, Gerard Kamaheke later described what had happened:

> I sat there waiting, when suddenly the Germans opened fire on us. We were nearly surrounded, and my people tried to make their escape. I tried to fight my way through, but was shot in the right shoulder and fell to the ground, and I lay quite still and pretended to be dead. I was covered with blood. The German soldiers came along bayoneting the wounded; and as I did not move they thought I was dead already and left me. The chiefs Saul and Joel and all the other headmen were killed. I got up in the night and fled back to our camp, where I found our women and children still safe and also some survivors of my 70 men. We then fled away towards the Sandveld and scattered in all directions.[12]

In the Official German History of the campaign in South-West Africa, Ombakaha is described as a battle, yet not a single German soldier was killed or wounded. In his own report, Lieutenant von Beesten noted that 'all enemy fighters were shot at distances between 10 and 300 metres' – the optimum range of the Maxim gun.[13]

Ombakaha was not an isolated event. Across Hereroland, bands of Herero were tricked into believing it was safe to return from the bush, and then killed. Such massacres encouraged the Herero to move into the more remote parts of their territory or enter the Omaheke.

Despite its brutality, it was evident as early as November 1904 that the Extermination Order and its agents were failing to ethnically cleanse South-West Africa of the Herero. Furthermore, extended operations even in the more fertile areas of Hereroland had pushed von Trotha's men to the very limit of their endurance. About half of the soldiers involved in operations against the Herero were suffering from the effects of typhoid, dehydration or chronic dysentery. On 25 October Senior Lieutenant Haak (who was to die in action a month later in one of his first active engagements) described the state of a group of *Schutztruppe* recently arrived in Windhoek from the bush:

Herero Chief Tjamuaha KaMaharero and his council in the pre-colonial era.

The Bondelswarts Nama leadership photographed in 1876 in their home town of Warmbad.

Chief Samuel Maharero, who led the Herero nation in their war against the German colonisers.
Germany's nemesis, Hendrik Witbooi, Kaptein of the Witbooi Nama, photographed in the 1890s.
Heinrich Ernst Göring, father of Hitler's deputy Hermann Göring and the first Imperial Commissioner of German South-West Africa.
Curt von François, the ruthless 'soldier of darkness' who led the first colonial force to German South-West Africa.

Friedrich von Lindequist, the young Deputy Governor photographed here in the 1890s in a Windhoek beer garden (seated, right with a beer tankard). Popular among the settlers, Lindequist was an early advocate of *Lebensraum* theory.

Cattle and ox-drawn wagons traversing the long trade route to the Cape, through the vast, arid interior of South-West Africa.

Governor Theodor Leutwein's first meeting with his successor, General von Trotha, Windhoek June 1904.

In October 1904, Hendrik Witbooi and his mounted Nama fighters joined the war against the Germans.

German volunteers are cheered as they march off to war against the 'Negro King' Maharero, amid the feverish atmosphere of Berlin in late January 1904.

A reprisal against the Herero. Hangings were common both during and after the anti-colonial wars. Several postcards were printed depicting similar public executions.

Von Trotha's army preparing to march on the Herero encampment at the Waterberg on the edge of the Kalahari Desert.

A German reconnaissance patrol guided through the Waterberg escarpments by a Witbooi Nama scout. The Nama fought alongside the Germans at the Waterberg, but after witnessing the brutal aftermath, they decided to rise up as well.

General Lothar von Trotha who ordered the extermination of the Herero nation.

The work of the 'collection patrols'. Starving Herero were captured in the bush and sent to the newly opened concentration camps.

Herero prisoners being transported to the Swakopmund concentration camp in cattle trucks.

The largest of the concentration camps, beside the German fort in the capital Windhoek. At its height, this camp held 7,000 prisoners.

A group of Nama women and children, captured by a German patrol and forced to pose for the camera.

Herero women in the Swakopmund camp used to pull railcars loaded with ammunition and provisions. The majority of prisoners in all the camps were women and children.

> These are the troops who have been in the field the longest. It is impossible for me to really describe their appearance and the condition of their horses as they arrived in town yesterday. The uniforms were hanging like rags off emaciated human shapes, whose faces were burnt beyond recognition, with stubbly beards and long hair; some had replaced missing boots with cloth that was wrapped from their feet to the knees. The poor horses looked pathetic.[14]

It seems that Theodor Leutwein became fully aware of the Extermination Order only some weeks after it had been proclaimed at Osombo zoWindimbe. Still nominally Governor of South-West Africa, Leutwein was horrified by von Trotha's policy, more on economic than humanitarian grounds. On 23 October he wrote to the Colonial Department informing them that Chief Salatiel Kambazembi – one of the key Herero chiefs under Samuel Maharero – had requested negotiations to end the war. Leutwein also requested formal confirmation that as civilian governor he had the authority to accept a Herero surrender.

During the tussle for power that followed, von Trotha wrote to Leutwein admitting that the battle of the Waterberg had failed to exterminate the Herero and explaining how his new policy would lead to their ultimate annihilation, no matter what obstacles Leutwein might put in his way: 'the eastern border of the colony will remain sealed off and terrorism will be employed against the Herero showing up. That nation must vanish from the face of the earth. Having failed to destroy them with guns, I will have to achieve my end in that way.'[15]

Von Trotha sought support for his extermination policy from the army, and again, the civilian branches of government were pushed aside. Leutwein effectively resigned and was given leave. After eleven years as governor, he left the colony. The military rule that von Trotha had declared on his arrival in Windhoek in June 1904 was now unchallenged.

It is a mark of the brutality of German colonialism in South-West Africa that Governor Theodor Leutwein and Major von Estorff – of whom we shall hear more later – are almost heroes in this sorry history. The *Alte Afrikaners* (Old Africans), as von Trotha called men like Erstorff and Leutwein, had few moral qualms over disinheriting Africans of their land and property. They set out systematically to undermine their social structures and adopted a culturally corrosive policy of divide and rule. But their conception of colonialism still had a role for the Africans, if only a subservient one. The gulf between the policies and attitudes of Leutwein and Erstorff, and those of Lothar von Trotha, was symptomatic of the great shift from the old paternalist racism of the eighteenth and nineteenth centuries, and to the new biological racism of the twentieth century.

Although Theodor Leutwein's policies resulted in his removal from office, he had nonetheless been completely correct in concluding that von Trotha's plan to exterminate the Herero was logistically and militarily impractical. By November 1904 the appalling conditions of von Trotha's men and the impossibility of their task had become apparent to the military authorities in Berlin. On 23 November General von Schlieffen, still in overall command of the strategy of the war, wrote to Chancellor von Bülow that 'while von Trotha's intentions are commendable, he is powerless to carry them out'.[16] Chancellor von Bülow and the civilian officials of the Colonial Department did not share von Schlieffen's admiration for von Trotha's intention. In the early stages of the war von Bülow's coalition government, swept along by an overwhelming popular support for the war, had supported the generals' hard line. However, when Chancellor von Bülow received the text of the Extermination Order, he was horrified.

Von Bülow feared that Germany's international reputation, already tarnished by her actions in East Africa and China, would be further damaged should the Extermination Order become widely known. In the same year that Germany sent von Trotha to crush the Herero, the international campaign against the horrors in the Congo Free State reached its apex. Under Leopold's regime, millions of Congolese women had been kidnapped and their men forced to collect increasingly unrealistic quotas of wild rubber. When quotas were not met or resistance offered, the mercenaries of the King's *Force Publique* had inflicted barbaric punishments and unleashed murderous raids against innocent villagers. During the autumn of 1904, the newspapers of Europe and America carried almost daily reports cataloguing the barbarity of Leopold's colony and condemning the King himself in the harshest terms. With details of the war in South-West Africa beginning to appear in the foreign press, Von Bülow feared that von Trotha's policies, in particular the Extermination Order, might be seen in the same light and had the potential to 'demolish Germany's reputation among civilised nations and indulge foreign agitation'.[17]

It is perhaps unsurprising that Kaiser Wilhelm, the man who did more to undermine Germany's reputation than any of his contemporaries, was blind to the dangers of the Extermination Order and von Trotha's brutality. Wilhelm continued to applaud von Trotha's 'vigorous action' and energy, long after the Extermination Order had become a matter of grave concern to German politicians. Untroubled by the potential scandal the Kaiser wrote to the general: 'You have entirely fulfilled my expectations when I named you commander of the colonial troops, and I take pleasure in expressing, once again, my utter gratitude for your accomplishments so far.'[18]

In late November 1904, Wilhelm was confronted by both his Chancellor, von Bülow, and his Chief of the General Staff, von Schlieffen. Von Bülow complained that German policy in South-West Africa was barbaric and potentially scandalous, while von Schlieffen considered von Trotha's strategy commendable but utterly impractical. What followed was a battle of wills between the Kaiser and von Bülow.

Von Bülow's office requested that Wilhelm rescind the Extermination Order with immediate effect. Rather than responding, the Kaiser and his entourage left Berlin on a five-day hunting trip to his Hohenlohe estate in eastern Prussia. Only on 8 December – five days after receiving the Chancellor's request – did Wilhelm finally agree that von Trotha should also 'treat mercifully those Herero who voluntarily surrender'.[19] When von Bülow asked the Kaiser to agree to a specific text explicitly withdrawing the Extermination Order, Wilhelm took another eight days to reply. Meanwhile the killing in Hereroland continued.

When General von Trotha received the telegraph of his new orders, he was reportedly enraged and instantly offered his resignation, which was refused. In an attempt to appease him, von Schlieffen reassured von Trotha that 'His Majesty has not forbidden you to shoot the Hereros', rather that 'the possibility of showing mercy is to be restored'.

Just four days after agreeing to rescind von Trotha's Extermination Order, Kaiser Wilhelm received a report he had secretly commissioned some weeks earlier. On 10 November 1904, the Kaiser had personally instructed Count Georg von Stillfried und Rattonitz, an officer in von Trotha's army on sick leave in Germany, to report 'on his views on the native question and military conditions in South-West Africa, in the past two years'. He had not informed Chancellor von Bülow, the Reichstag or General von Schlieffen, circumventing all official channels of civilian and military authority.

Although he only held the rank of Lieutenant, Count von Stillfried was an aristocrat and as such was trusted by the Kaiser. Stillfried had first arrived in South-West Africa in 1900 and been placed in command of a small unit of troops. By all accounts, he was admired by his men and fellow officers alike. He had fought at the Waterberg, and had a genuine understanding of the colony and German operations therein. On 12 December, exactly eleven months after the start of the war, Stillfried's report – fifty-five pages long and painstakingly handwritten in neat gothic calligraphy – was presented to the Kaiser. Stillfried recommended that in order to ensure the Herero would pose no future threat to German colonialism, 'The surviving natives have to be disarmed all and one, and anyone in possession of a rifle should be punished with death.' The chiefs, the dynasties around which the Herero nation was built, were to be eradicated, to ensure the docility of the Herero. Stillfried recommended that 'All chiefs should be executed and their families – even if they are innocent – should be deported to another colony so that they will never again gain influence among their people.'[20]

What distinguishes Stillfried's recommendations from the policies of General von Trotha is that they took into account the economic realities of the colony. Stillfried understood that the war to annihilate the Herero had generated a compelling argument for their continued survival, in the short term at least. During the conflict the demand for cheap labour had become so acute that it enormously increased the value of the Herero as an economic asset. However, the means by which Stillfried proposed the labour of the Herero be exploited was profoundly different from anything Theodor Leutwein had ever suggested. He recommended that 'All natives from the warring tribes, apart from those who work for the Government, should be leased out either in large or small numbers to private persons, farmers and merchants and so forth. Here they should perform labour for food.'[21] He went on,

> All native prisoners will have to carry a numbered identification tag made from brass and if away from their homes will be entitled to produce a pass. All natives who have been sentenced to captivity shall be placed in confined areas nearby the place where they will work. They shall be supervised by one of their compatriots but not by a chief. [The supervisor] will provide the police with a continuous flow of information.[22]

'Confined Areas' – *Geschlossenen Niederlassungen* – was the critical phrase in the Stillfried Report. It alluded to a device that had been disastrously deployed only three years earlier during the Boer War. There the British commander-in-chief, Lord Herbert Kitchener, had forced around thirty thousand Boer women and children, and over one hundred thousand black and coloured Africans, into large enclosures of barbed wire, several layers thick. Poorly run, insanitary, and badly provisioned, these enclosures saw over twenty-five thousand Boer civilians, and perhaps as many as fourteen thousand Africans die, most from disease and the effects of malnutrition. In the British Parliament, the Liberal MPs C. P. Scott and John Ellis had condemned the practice and described the enclosures as 'concentration camps'.[23]

The military rationale for the British use of concentration camps in the Boer War had been to separate a guerrilla army from a local civilian population from whom they received sustenance and among whom they took refuge. Four years earlier, the Spanish rulers of Cuba had forced civilians into similar camps during the revolt of 1896. The concentration camp was therefore not a new concept, but the way in which Count Stillfried recommended it should be applied was entirely novel. When Kitchener had launched his clearance campaign and set up the camps, British intelligence believed that there were twenty thousand Boer guerrillas still in the field. In South-West Africa, the Herero were already a defeated and scattered people. They were not engaged in a guerrilla war and, following the battle of the Waterberg and the disintegration of Herero leadership, they had not been able to field anything resembling a military force.

Stillfried's 'confined areas' were to be both concentration camps and work camps. It was this addition of forced labour that was to make the concentration camps of German South-West Africa so disastrous for the thousands of people imprisoned within them.

A copy of the Stillfried Report, full of marginal notes written by the Kaiser, was sent to the Reich Chancellery around Christmas 1904. Stillfried's recommendations for forced labour appealed to Chancellor von Bülow and others who feared for Germany's reputation the longer the war dragged on. Work camps suggested that the Herero nation would be permitted to survive, albeit as virtual slaves. As it was widely believed that Africans were inherently lazy, forced labour was even considered a means of moral and cultural 'upliftment'.

On 14 January 1905, the dispute over policy in South-West Africa was resolved when revised orders, incorporating many of Count Stillfried's proposals, were wired to von Trotha. The general was directly ordered to establish a number of what the orders termed *Konzentrationslager* – a literal translation of the English 'concentration camp'. Enshrining Stillfried's ideas into official policy, Chancellor von Bülow specifically stated that 'the surrendering Herero should be . . . put under guard and required to work'.[24]

The new orders were intentionally vague, so as not to preclude field executions or halt the actions of the Cleansing Patrols. In the orders that von Trotha sent to his officers in the field, he made it clear that the continuation of military operations against the Herero was to take precedence over the administration of the camps or the feeding of surrendering Herero in the concentration camps.

In order to bring the Herero into the camps, the Cleansing Patrols were permitted to take prisoners. However, many officers and soldiers followed General von Trotha's lead and interpreted their new orders as narrowly as possible. Several units continued to hunt and kill Herero, and Herero were still attacked while attempting to surrender. Many were lured out of hiding by the assurances of African messengers sent into the bush. Even in the face of this continued violence, thousands were induced to surrender, and as early as February 1905 it was apparent that many more Herero had been able to survive than the Germans had imagined possible. Perhaps as many as thirty thousand had lived by foraging for wild onions and roots, and hunting small game. By the end of 1904, over four months after the battle of the Waterberg, what little food there was to be found in Hereroland had been consumed. According to the Herero's own oral histories, their malnourishment was so severe that they had taken to eating scorpions. By February and

March 1905, their suffering was such that thousands began to surrender, independent of the collection patrols.[25]

They emerged like ghosts from the Omaheke and the distant corners of Hereroland. They dragged themselves into the German towns of Omaruru, Karibib, Windhoek and Okahandja. Most were women and children, and all were in an appalling state of advanced malnutrition. Pastor Elger, a missionary in Karibib, a small town in western Hereroland, described the Herero who arrived there as being 'mere skeletons covered by a thin film of skin'.[26] Unsure how to deal with the influx, most settlers stood aside and watched as malnourished Herero died on their streets. When the District Commander of Omaruru made the mistake of expressing some concern for their plight, he was compelled to apologise publicly in a newspaper and reassure the local settlers that he was not guilty of 'dizzy humanitarianism'.[27]

As early as February 1905, the Herero who had surrendered in the German towns, along with those collected directly from the bush, were loaded in open cattle-trucks or marched in human caravans by soldiers into the hastily constructed concentration camps.

There were five main camps. Each had been located in or near a site of German settlement, as it was there that the need for African labour was most pressing. The largest camp – with a capacity of seven thousand – was in the capital, Windhoek, on the steep slopes that led down from the walls of the German fortress. Two smaller camps were set up in the former Herero homelands at Karibib and Okahandja, where the Germans planned to expand their farming operations and would need a steady supply of free labour. The last two camps were established in the coastal towns of Swakopmund and Lüderitz – the colony's two ports.[28]

Most of the records, both military and civilian, for the concentration camps of German South-West Africa have been lost or were deliberately destroyed to prevent them falling into the hands of the South Africans in 1915. However, a surprising amount of official documentation from the camp at Swakopmund has survived. Historians know relatively more about the Swakopmund camp thanks, in large part, to the work of two remarkable local figures. The first was the civilian District Commissioner for the town of Swakopmund, Dr Fuchs. An efficient and punctilious civil servant, Fuchs carried out an investigation into conditions in the camp that reveals a wealth of detail and demonstrates that knowledge of the suffering of the prisoners extended far up the chains of command, in both Windhoek and Berlin.[29] The other resident of Swakopmund whose testimony is critical is the local Rhenish Missionary, Heinrich Vedder.

Missionaries like Vedder were the only non-military personnel permitted to enter the camps. They were allowed to take Sunday services and conduct funerals. Some were even given permission to set up small hospices inside the camps, where they tended the dying and administered the last rights. They also supplied books, most commonly the Bible, and in some camps they struggled to keep up with demand.[30]

Heinrich Vedder had only recently arrived in the colony when he was given the task of setting up a mission among the prisoners in Swakopmund in early 1905. Young and energetic, Vedder became one of the most vocal of the missionaries. His letters – and the responses from missionaries working in other camps – tell us not only about the Swakopmund camp but about the whole concentration-camp system. In an entry in the *Swakopmund Missionary Chronicle* of December 1905, Vedder painted a vivid picture of the conditions in the Swakopmund camp. He tells us that the Herero

> were placed behind a double row of barbed wire . . . and housed in pathetic structures constructed out of simple sacking and planks, in such a manner that in one structure 30–50 people were forced to stay without distinction to age or sex. From early morning until late at night, on weekends as well as on Sundays and holidays, they had to work under the clubs of the raw overseers until they broke down. Added to this

food was extremely scarce. Rice without any necessary additions was not enough to support their bodies, already weakened by life in the field and used to the hot sun of the interior, from the cold and restless exertion of all their powers in the prison conditions in Swakopmund. Like cattle, hundreds were driven to death and like cattle they were buried. This opinion may seem harsh or exaggerated . . . but then I cannot suppress in these chronicles the wanton brutality, the lusty lack of morality [or] the brutish sense of supremacy that is found among the troops and civilians here. A full account is almost not possible.[31]

The appalling suffering of the Herero in the Swakopmund concentration camp was directly linked to the success of Swakopmund's economy. The town had become German South-West Africa's main port. Despite the fact that it had no natural harbour and was an extremely poor anchorage, it had overtaken Walvis Bay in both size and importance. Twice a week, a steamer from the Woermann Company arrived offshore, bringing supplies and reinforcements, along with goods and new settlers seeking refuge from Germany's overcrowded cities.

The desperate need for labour in Swakopmund was a direct consequence of its lack of a natural harbour. Unable to dock, the Woermann ocean liners were forced to anchor offshore and unload their cargoes into flat-bottomed transport boats that ferried both goods and passengers to the shore. In 1905, the inmates of the concentration camps were used to unload these transport ferries and carry the goods up to depots inland. Others were used to build an extension to a wooden jetty. Others again were formed into work gangs and made to labour on the construction of government buildings and even private residences.

The main concentration camp in Swakopmund was administered by the army and was located somewhere near the northern entrance of the town, near the coastline. A number of concentration camps came into existence, at various times. The largest of them was the military camp, which often held more than 1,000 prisoners at a time. It was located near the waterfront, where the labour of the inmates was required.[32]

Prisoners in Swakopmund, like those in the other camps across the colony, were given utterly inadequate food rations. In von Trotha's initial orders of 16 January he had specifically instructed military commanders in charge of the camps to keep rations to an absolute minimum. The *Portionsliste*, the army's ration list, placed concentration-camp prisoners just above mules and horses in order of priorities. The official camp ration was 500 grams of rice or flour per day, calculated on the presumption that prisoners of war were male. Women and children – who made up the vast majority of the camp's population – were often given half rations. As neither rice nor flour was known to the Herero, they had no knowledge of how to cook it. In many cases, the prisoners were not even provided with pots or pans with which to prepare their food. The prisoners ate these unfamiliar rations raw, unaware that uncooked they caused diarrhoea. As early as 1 March 1905, in a letter to the Mission Headquarters in Wupperthal, Missionary Vedder complained that the 'people suffer their daily meal of rice, which due to the lack of pots is very difficult to prepare . . . hundreds are breaking down due to the lack of nutrition and are dying'.[33]

In Swakopmund, as in the other coastal camp in the southern port of Lüderitz, the deleterious effects of insufficient and inappropriate food were considerably augmented by the cold maritime climate. The coastal strip of the Namib Desert has its own distinct microclimate. When the skies are clear and there are no winds, temperatures on the coast can be almost as high as those in the desert itself, but such conditions are rare. On most days a thick bank of sea-fog shrouds the coastline, blocking out the sun. Even on clear days, the warmth of the sun is often counteracted by icy winds that rush inland from the South Atlantic.

To help them acclimatise to the conditions at Swakopmund, the missionaries and the local army commanders issued some of the prisoners with second-hand clothing, but in February 1905 von Trotha personally intervened to stop this. Instead prisoners were issued with rough hessian sacks, with holes cut out for their arms and heads. These were almost entirely ineffective against the ocean winds. The predictable result of exposing an already weakened population to malnutrition and freezing temperatures was the rapid spread of disease: influenza, dysentery and scurvy – believed by the Germans to be infectious – as well as pneumonia, smallpox, syphilis and other sexually transmitted diseases. As in all the concentration camps, there was no sanitation at Swakopmund and the sick were left untended, lying for days or weeks in their own excrement. The camp quickly became infested with flies and maggots, which spread infection further.[34]

The awful decline in the health of prisoners, caused by conditions in the Swakopmund camp, was not permitted to stand in the way of their exploitation as forced labour. In all the concentration camps Herero prisoners were placed under the jurisdiction of the army's Military Supply Division, known as the *Etappenkommando*. The civilian administration was able to requisition Herero prisoners from the army free of cost. The regulations under which labour was distributed specifically stated that prisoners were to receive food 'but no payment'. Private individuals and companies were also able to hire Herero labourers from the *Etappenkommando* for a *Kopfsteuer* – 'Head Tax', of fifty pfennig per day, or ten Reichsmarks per month. All profits were siphoned directly into the coffers of the colonial government.[35]

The method by which the army kept track of the thousands of Herero in the camp system had been suggested in the Stillfried Report. In early 1905, tens of thousands of oval-shaped metal tags stamped with the Kaiser's crown were produced in Dresden and shipped out to the colony. Dissatisfied with this arrangement, von Trotha proposed that prisoners be permanently marked with their identification numbers. Whether he imagined branding or tattooing is not clear.[36]

Due to the lack of male prisoners, it was mainly women and children as young as twelve who were rented out to private individuals. Girls and younger women were in particularly high demand as domestic servants. On 29 March the colonial government under von Trotha introduced formal regulations for the renting out of the prisoners. The local civilian administration was made responsible for collating all requests for Herero labour. These requests were then transmitted to the *Etappenkommando*.

The distribution of Herero prisoners to private settlers and soldiers became so widespread that the colonial government eventually passed an ordinance forbidding officers from taking their Herero servants home to Germany at the end of their terms of service. One of those caught flouting this regulation was Count Stillfried himself, recently promoted to the rank of captain. When Stillfried returned to South-West Africa in April 1906 he brought with him his wife and child, for whom he acquired a Herero man named Franz as a servant. When he finally came home in 1908 Stillfried attempted to 'export' Franz and, despite his rank and status, was arrested and court-martialled for the offence. In spite of overwhelming evidence against him, the Count was acquitted, his letter of acquittal signed by the Kaiser personally.[37]

The Herero recruited by private individuals as farmhands or servants were arguably more fortunate than those hired out to private companies. Each morning, the overseers employed by various German firms assembled thousands of Herero and marched them from the camps, through the streets or across deserts, to public construction sites. Women, men and sometimes children were forced to build roads, construct buildings, lay rails or stack heavy bags of food or ammunition. In Swakopmund, Herero women were formed into teams of eight and – in lieu of oxen or horses – made to pull the wagons on the narrow-gauge railway.

As surviving photographs show, at Swakopmund, the Woermann Shipping Line employed so many concentration-camp prisoners that they were permitted to open their own 'enclosure'. In this private concentration camp, the prisoners – described at times as 'stock' or 'head', as if they were cattle – lived in conditions almost identical to those in the main military camps, although there seems to have been a slightly better supply of pots to cook with.

In an affidavit submitted to the Governor of the British Cape Colony in August 1906, three coloured workers from Cape Town, who had the previous year passed through Swakopmund, described the conditions under which the female prisoners were made to labour in an indeterminant Swakopmund camp:

> These unfortunate women are daily compelled to carry heavy iron for construction work, also big stacks of compressed fodder. I have often noticed cases where women have fallen under the load and have been made to go on by being thrashed and kicked by the soldiers and conductors. The rations supplied to the women are insufficient and they are made to cook the food themselves. They are always hungry, and we, labourers from the Cape Colony, have frequently thrown food into their camp. The women in many cases are not properly clothed . . . old women are made to work and are constantly kicked and thrashed by soldiers.[38]

It is hard to determine the number of lives lost in the camps. The only camp that kept records of mortality in 1905 was the Swakopmund camp. According to their statistics approximately 40 percent of the prisoners in Swakopmund died during their first four months of captivity, and any prisoner who entered the camp was likely to be dead within ten months. And this was almost certainly an underestimation of the true death rate at Swakopmund.

A photograph smuggled out of the camp – probably in mid-1905 – shows the withered body of a young Herero boy. It is not clear if he is dead or alive. Each rib is visible and around his waist is a tightly bound leather strap worn by most prisoners, possibly to subdue the pain of hunger. Otherwise, he is naked, clutching in his right hand his only possession – a hessian sack.

It has been suggested that the extremely high mortality rates in the camps were the result of accidental neglect, disorganisation within the army or simply the ignorance of those tasked with administering the camp system.[39] However, a report written by Dr Fuchs – the civilian District Commissioner of Swakopmund – demonstrates that both the colonial administration in Windhoek and the most senior officials in the Colonial Department in

Berlin were fully aware of what took place in the camps, and chose not to act.[40]

In early 1905, two months after the opening of the camps, the missionary Heinrich Vedder brought the death rates in Swakopmund and the other concentration camps to the attention of his superiors at the Rhenish Mission's headquarters in the German town of Wupperthal. At a meeting with the Colonial Department in Berlin, the missionaries confronted officials with Vedder's reports. In response, a muted and carefully worded order for the immediate drafting of a report into conditions in the Swakopmund camp was issued by the Colonial Department. The order was sent initially to the Deputy Governor of South-West Africa, Hans Tecklenburg, who passed it on to District Commissioner Fuchs.

Dr Fuchs was given full access to the camp, and his report, although hastily written, was damning in its conclusions. According to Fuchs's calculations, around 10 percent of the entire population of the Swakopmund camp had died in the last two weeks of May 1905.[41] In his opinion, corroborated by the local government doctor, the Herero in the Swakopmund camp were dying at an alarming rate due to 'inadequate facilities'. The poor conditions were made worse by the 'raw, uncommon ocean climes and the weakened state in which they [the prisoners] arrived'.[42]

Dr Fuchs also compared the death rates of the prisoners in the concentration camp with that of a number of Damara and Owambo migrant labourers living in Swakopmund at the time and working 'in the service of the local government'. Fuchs informed his superiors that not one of them had died since he had taken command on 15 September 1903. In fact, among all groups in Swakopmund, German and African, civilian and military, and even those held in the local prison, mortality rates had remained 'constant'.

In conclusion, Dr Fuchs stated that in order to reduce the mortality rate, 'It is necessary to provide [the prisoners] with accommodation that is sheltered from the wind, properly ventilated rooms, warm clothes (coats, trousers, blankets, shoes) and some variation in the food (rice, flour and, where possible, also some meat, onions or lard) as well as medical attention'.[43]

Fuchs's report was intended to be secret. Copies were sent only to Hans Tecklenburg in Windhoek, Oskar Stuebel, Director of the Colonial Department in Berlin, General von Trotha and Colonel Dame, the head of the *Etappenkommando*. In response, von Trotha, Tecklenburg and Dame all argued that despite the horrendous death rate, the flow of Herero prisoners to Swakopmund and the other coastal camps at Lüderitz had to continue in order to meet the pressing need for labour. Colonel Dame noted that while it might be unfortunate that women prisoners were made to work at the Swakopmund and Lüderitz camps, the need for labour was so acute that 'there is no alternative'.[44] Oskar Stuebel accepted Fuchs's claim that better food might improve conditions at Swakopmund, but then proceeded to denounce the rationale behind Fuchs's report. Not only did he fail to implement Fuchs's recommendations for better conditions, he rejected his suggestion that prisoners who were already sick should be sent inland, away from the freezing conditions at the coast.

There is even evidence that – at least in the mind of Deputy Governor Tecklenburg – the camps were intended to weed out the weak and leave only the stronger Herero. In a letter written to the Colonial Department in June 1905, Tecklenburg argued that the high death rates were in Germany's long-term interests. The concentration camps would leave the Herero culturally broken and decimated. Any Herero who survived the hardships would become the slaves of the German colonisers and they would necessarily be the strongest and fittest. He noted that,

> The more the Herero people now feel the consequences of the uprising on their own bodies, the less the coming generations will feel inclined to rebel. Sure, the death of so many natives has a negative commercial impact, but the natural life-force of the Hereros will soon allow them to recover their numbers; the future generations, which could possibly be mixed with a bit of Damara blood, would thus have been bottle-fed with [an understanding of] their inferiority to the white race.[45]

Wilhelm Eich, the Rhenish Missionary in Okahandja, where 1,500 Herero had been divided between three small concentration camps, claimed on 19 June 1905 that 'The overseer of Camp I [the military camp] told me recently that he was under orders only to seek out the strong for His Majesty [Wilhelm II].'[46]

The most damning evidence suggesting that the mass deaths of prisoners in the concentration camps was known of and approved by the German authorities is found in the National Archives of Namibia. In the vaults of the archives is a *Totenregister* – a death register – for the Swakopmund camp.[47] It records the deaths of some of the thousands of Herero prisoners who perished in between January 1905 and 1908. Similar *Totenregister* may have existed for the other camps but have since been lost, or were deliberately destroyed.

The pages of the Swakopmund *Totenregister* are divided into columns in which the military clerk or camp officer entered the names, genders and ages of deceased prisoners. However, officiating clerks had no need to enter details in the column indicating the 'cause of death'. That came pre-printed – 'death through exhaustion, bronchitis, heart disease or scurvy'.

10

'Peace Will Spell Death for Me and My Nation'

In the last days of September 1904, six weeks after the battle of the Waterberg, nineteen Witbooi Nama soldiers galloped through the Auas Mountains of southern Hereroland. They wore armbands in the German colours and desert-brown German uniforms, ripped and torn by thorn bushes. They were part of a contingent of one hundred Witbooi men, sent north earlier in the year, to fight alongside von Trotha's men, in accordance with the treaty of protection Hendrik Witbooi had signed with Governor Leutwein back in 1894. In the aftermath of the battle of the Waterberg, they had slipped away from their German commanding officers and rushed south.[1]

At the Waterberg, the Witbooi had watched as the Germans bombarded and machine-gunned Herero women and children. As part of the patrols sent out towards the Omaheke, they had been ordered to execute captured Herero and had come to understand that the ultimate aim of von Trotha's army was not the defeat of the Herero, but their annihilation.[2] Although supposedly the allies of the Germans, they had been routinely abused and threatened. German officers had pointed to Herero corpses and told them that they were next.[3]

After a week in the saddle and a journey of almost 200 miles, the nineteen Witbooi finally reached the small village of Rietmont in the Urigab Highlands. It was here, during the summer months, that Hendrik Witbooi and his key lieutenants resided. By coincidence Carl Berger, a German missionary from the nearby town of Gibeon, the Witbooi's main settlement, was with Hendrik Witbooi in Rietmont when they arrived. According to Berger, the nineteen men were unusually reserved and insisted on speaking with their leader in private. After their meeting, Hendrik Witbooi called a council of the Witbooi elders, who gathered on wooden stools under a tree by their *Kaptein*'s house. Berger was allowed to attend and later wrote an account of the meeting,

> Kaptein Hendrik Witbooi, who was seated on his usual little field chair . . . looked a lot older. His posture was slouched and one could hear from his words that his soul had suffered greatly. He told us what his people had said. We told him that it was all unthinkable. He himself knew the Germans for many years and therefore was aware that what his people had told could not possibly be true. To this, he simply shrugged his shoulders and said in muted tone, 'Who can I believe if not my own people?'[4]

Despite Berger's protestations, Hendrik Witbooi had good reasons to believe the reports from the Waterberg. Since the start of the Herero-German War, many settlers in the southern Nama lands had begun to call openly for the disarmament of the Witbooi and the other Nama clans. Dark mumblings that had once been restricted to the bars and clubs were now flowing freely from the mouths of soldiers and farmers. Some suggested that the position of *Kaptein* should be forcibly dissolved. In a letter of August 1904 Lieutenant Schmidt, the German District Commissioner in charge of the southern town of Keetmanshoop, warned Governor Leutwein that 'Even the least observant among the natives have a feeling that once the Government has finished with the Herero, they will come down on the people of Namaland.'[5]

Not only did settlers make such remarks openly, often directly to the Nama; some of their most inflammatory utterances were printed in the newspapers. On 14 December 1904 Georg Wasserfall, the editor of German South-West Africa's largest newspaper, the *Deutsch Suedwestafrikanische Zeitung*, wrote an editorial in which he openly stated, 'The Herero should not be exterminated – the Nama, yes – the reason being that the Herero are needed as labourers, and the Nama are an insignificant tribe.'[6] In May, Baron von Nettelbladt, a South African regarded as an expert on events north of the Orange River, penned an article for the *South African News* in which he claimed that while the Herero 'belong to the industrious and healthy Bantu races', the Nama 'appear to be no good for any kind of labour, and . . . belong to the dying nations'.[7]

Hendrik Witbooi, the other leaders of the smaller Nama tribes, and a significant number of their people, were fully literate and able to read these articles. They were left in no doubt that the mood in the south was darkening. Throughout 1904 there had been other portents: in April, for example, the German garrison in the south had doubled and the implementation of a previously agreed land settlement was repeatedly postponed. It was in this climate that Hendrik Witbooi received news of the battle of the Waterberg and the massacre of Herero prisoners.

On 2 October, the day before von Trotha issued the Extermination Order at Osombo zoWindimbe, Hendrik Witbooi dictated a series of letters to the leaders of the other Nama clans declaring his intention to rise up against the Germans. One of the greatest tragedies in the story of Germany's rule over South-West Africa is that the letters to the Nama chiefs were written only after the Herero had been defeated and driven into the Omaheke. In January 1904, when the Herero War had begun, Samuel Maharero had attempted to forge a grand anti-colonial alliance with his former Nama enemies. He had written to Hendrik Witbooi asking him to join the fight. In what must be Samuel's most elegant and passionate letter, he wrote:

> I appeal to you, my brother, do not shy away from this uprising, but make your voice heard so that all Africa may take up arms against the Germans. Let us die fighting rather than die of maltreatment, imprisonment or some other tragedy. Tell the kapteins down there to rise and do battle.[8]

Samuel Maharero's letter never reached Hendrik Witbooi. His messengers were intercepted south of Windhoek by Hermanus van Wyk, leader of the Rehoboth Basters, who confiscated the letter and handed it over to Governor Leutwein. When Hendrik did call upon the Nama *Kapteins* 'to rise and do battle', all hope of a grand African alliance had been lost, and with it any realistic chance of some sort of victory.

A leader of almost irresistible charisma, Hendrik Witbooi was revered as a holy man by many of the Nama. By 1904 he was in his seventies and had come to believe that his last mission in life, as ordained by God, was to expel the Europeans from the African continent. Despite the seeming impossibility of this endeavour, Hendrik was able to draw much of the Nama nation to him. Within a month the Witbooi were joined by Chief Manasse Noreseb of the so-called Red Nation, Simon Kopper of the Franzmann Nama and the Veldschoendragers under Kaptein Hans Hendrik. The Bethanie Nama were split down the middle. Half sought to remain neutral, but the rest joined the Witbooi under the leadership of Cornelius Fredericks, the nephew of Joseph Fredericks, the chief who had been duped by Heinrich Vogelsang into signing Adolf Lüderitz's fraudulent treaty twenty years earlier. Some of the Nama clans rejected Witbooi's call to arms. The Tsain Nama of Keetmanshoop, the Hai Khauan of Berseba and the Baster people of Rehoboth chose not to fight, seeking to save their people from the horrors of war. The Topnaar Nama from around Walvis Bay and the Swartsboois who lived among the Herero in the north-east were all taken prisoner by units of von Trotha's army before they had the opportunity to join Hendrik Witbooi's alliance.

Despite everything he had heard of German treatment of the Herero at the Waterberg, and in the Omaheke Desert, Hendrik Witbooi and his allies were determined that the war in the south would be fought according to the rules and conventions that were a central part of Nama tradition. Hendrik's declaration of war reveals that his aim was to drive the Germans out of Nama territory and not to annihilate them. The declaration was personally delivered by Hendrik's deputy

Samuel Izaak and addressed to Sergeant Beck, the District Commissioners of Gibeon and the representative of German power in the Witbooi's own territory. It read: 'I leave it at your discretion to transport all women and children to Lüderitz Bay in ox wagons so that they may return to Germany . . . Men without weapons . . . are also free to join them. They will not be molested.'[9]

The Nama uprising, like that of the Herero nine months earlier, began with a wave of attacks against the centres of German settlement and isolated farms. Despite having spent the previous months demanding the army be let loose against the Nama, most German settlers were completely taken by surprise when the war arrived on their doorsteps.

The first casualties of the war were the Gibeon District Commissioner von Burgsdorff – killed while trying to accost Hendrik Witbooi – and Ludwig Holzapfel, one of the settlers who had most vocally demanded the total disarmament of the Nama, even suggesting to the colonial government that they be 'punished for their sins'. On the orders of Hendrik Witbooi, both Ludwig Holzapfel and District Commissioner von Burgsdorff were given proper Christian burials. Holzapfel's wife and children, who were with him when he was intercepted by Witbooi fighters, were left unharmed.[10]

The sparing of Frau Holzapfel and her children was in fact quite normal throughout the German-Nama War. While around forty male German settlers and soldiers were killed in the initial weeks, Hendrik Witbooi went to extraordinary lengths to ensure the safety of women and children. It was so widely understood that the Witbooi and other Nama would not attack women and children that, in the town of Gibeon, only German men took refuge in the local fortress, leaving the women and children in their homes. On 8 October, the same day that the Germans blew up Hendrik Witbooi's family church, a column of Witbooi soldiers escorted a group of German women and children from the surrounding towns through the war-ravaged county and delivered them safely to Gibeon.[11]

While Hendrik Witbooi was willing to have his men escort German women and children to safety, he harboured no illusions as to what treatment his own people might expect from General von Trotha. As the Nama men prepared for war, many of the women were sent across the borders to the British Cape Colony or Bechuanaland. Hundreds of others, along with their children and even the elderly, had no choice but to stay with their men. In October 1904 whole Nama clans abandoned their settlements and travelled into the deep desert. There they set up remote encampments to house the women and children, while the men rode off to attack the Germans.[12]

For all their sabre-rattling, the colonial authorities, like the German settlers of the south, were shocked by the sudden rising of the Nama. When General von Trotha was informed of the uprising, he used it as an opportunity to call for further reinforcements, but with the vast bulk of his army on the fringes of the Omaheke or protecting the settlers around Okahandja and Windhoek, only around two hundred German soldiers could be mustered in the south.[13]

Only when his forces had reached the settlement of Otjimanangombe on the Bechuanaland border on 9 October, completing the cordoning-off of the Omaheke, did von Trotha turn his attentions to the situation in Namaland. On 24 October, the general arrived back in Windhoek. He then placed Colonel Berthold von Deimling in command of the campaign against the Nama.

Like Franz von Epp and Maximilian Bayer, Colonel von Deimling had been among the first officers to arrive in South-West Africa in the winter of 1904. Unlike his comrades, Deimling was not a veteran of the Boxer Rebellion, having spent the year 1900 frustrated behind a desk in the General Staff. Command of the southern army was an enormous opportunity for a man already in his fifties to prove his mettle. Deimling was another advocate of von Moltke's principles of concentric encirclement, upon which the battle of the Waterberg had been fought. While officers like Ludwig von Estorff had openly criticised von Trotha's strategies, Deimling had been in full agreement. Confident that 'war is not a matter of knowledge, but of talent', he set out to apply the same principles against the Nama.

It was not until the first week of December 1904 that Deimling began offensive operations. His first action was to march on the Witbooi who were then encamped in Rietmont. Although the Witbooi did not make a stand at Rietmont, they were forced into a hasty evacuation of the settlement, and it was during the attack on Rietmont that Hendrik Witbooi's diaries – invaluable to later historians – were captured.

A few days later Deimling's men, having had their first taste of the difficulties of marching through the southern deserts, attempted to surround the Witbooi in the Auob Valley, 60 miles north-east of Rietmont. It was here that the only real battle of the war took place. When they reached Auob, the Germans were pinned down by the withering Nama rifle fire, which led to fifty-nine German casualties, killed or wounded.[14] However, the real significance of Deimling's attacks at Rietmond and Auob was that they encouraged the Witbooi to adopt exactly the form of guerrilla warfare that von Trotha and von Schlieffen had desperately sought to avoid in their war with the Herero.

From the moment the war began, Hendrik Witbooi and the other Nama commanders recognised that a mass battle with the Germans would be near-suicidal. As the Witbooi and other Nama tribes had fought both against and crucially alongside the Germans, they were familiar with their tactics and fully understood the power of modern artillery and machine-guns. They were therefore determined to fight strictly according to their own military traditions.

During their wars against the Herero in the 1870s and 1880s, the Nama had operated in small, highly mobile bands known as commandos. Originally conceived as a cattle-raiding tactic, the commando system was easily adapted to guerrilla warfare and was to prove devastating against the unwieldy German columns. In each ambush or raid on a German convoy or isolated farm, the Nama would capture all available weapons, ammunition, horses and cattle. They kept the weapons and took cattle and horses into South Africa to sell to British traders, providing the Nama with the funds needed to purchase ammunition and continue the war.

The Nama knew the locations of the hundreds of waterholes scattered across the south. This allowed them to conduct offensive operations over a vast range and to seek refuge where the Germans would not dare to venture. Water, more than any other commodity, determined the nature of the German-Nama War. As often as not, the Germans were forced to abandon their patrols or turn back in mid-pursuit when their water bottles ran dry.

Many of the German troops who had been dispatched to German South-West Africa, and who now found themselves confronting the Nama, were ill-equipped for combat in the south. Large numbers had arrived in June and July, deep winter in the southern hemisphere. New to Africa, they were totally unprepared for the excruciating heat of high summer – November to February – during which temperatures regularly exceeded 40 degrees Celsius. As operations in the south got under way, large numbers of troops quickly began to suffer from dehydration. When water was available, the Germans struggled to locate or confront the Nama commando units. Mounted pursuits were known to last for weeks. Under certain conditions both pursuers and pursued could see each other across the desert, but to the utter frustration of the Germans, the Nama always remained out of rifle range. At times the Nama lured the Germans through ever-changing landscapes into regions of the desert they did not know. Drawing them into the mountains, or into narrow gorges, the Nama would suddenly turn and ambush their pursuers.

At night the Germans sat huddled around campfires, their sentries peering into the darkness, fearing night-time raids. As temperatures fell to just 3 or 4 degrees above freezing, they were forced to wrap themselves in their saddle blankets, foul-smelling and soaked with horse sweat. One soldier described how the men of his units would 'huddle together to beat the cold . . . In this way, I have spent many a night with open eyes, kept company by my most trusted companion, my rifle, while looking up into the star-speckled night sky.'[15]

Many mornings the Germans would wake to discover that the trails left by the Nama's horses had been blown away by the strong winds that always seemed to accompany sunset. During the campaign against the Herero, the Germans had had African scouts, skilled trackers capable of picking up a half-obscured trail in the desert. Now at war with almost the entire indigenous population of the colony, they were on their own. Young German volunteers, with only a few months' experience and almost no knowledge of bush craft, were completely incapable of determining in which direction the Nama had escaped.

The result was a war of over two hundred minor engagements but, with the possible exception of the attack on the Auob Valley, no formal battles. In this respect it was like most colonial conflicts, except that now it was the colonised rather than the coloniser who dictated the tactics. In many of the two hundred known encounters, the Germans were attacked by an unseen enemy. Industrial weaponry – light field artillery and the Maxim machine-gun – that across the colonial world had allowed small European armies to crush much larger forces, became liabilities rather than assets. Soldiers weighed down by the very weapons that were supposed to win them the war became easy targets for Nama riflemen, or found themselves too slow to pursue their opponents effectively.

Even when they were able to give chase, unaccustomed to the landscape, unfamiliar with the complex network of waterholes and with their energy sapped by the heat, the German soldiers were always unable to engage the Nama on terms advantageous to their weapons and tactics. In his memoirs Constantin Jitschin, a cavalryman who was fighting the Nama near the Auob Valley in January 1905, described the war against the Nama as he experienced it:

Our soldiers gradually became tired of the fighting. But then, this guerrilla war was also uncommonly strenuous. Every time we thought we were about to engage them in battle, we were too late. The enemy no longer presented himself for open battle, he always avoided it. We were in a very bad state. Everyone had burned faces and stubble-beards. Many mothers would not have been able to recognise their own sons in these wild southwest men. The physical and emotional strain that we had to endure could be read from the faces of everyone.[16]

One of the German commanders who best adapted to the demands of Nama guerrilla warfare was Paul von Lettow-Vorbeck, adjutant of the *Schutztruppe* and another veteran of the Boxer Rebellion. Sometime around May 1905, Lettow-Vorbeck was placed in command of a ragtag force sent out to hunt down the Bethanie Nama and their leader, Cornelius Fredericks. Lettow-Vorbeck's account brings to life the challenges facing the officers and men of the southern army and the dire state of the *Schutztruppe* in 1905:

Since we did not have a force ready to take on Cornelius, one comprising of helpers, typists, orderlies and a few other zealots was put together and placed under my command. It took a while before we picked up Cornelius' trail. We wanted to surprise him in his camp at night, but someone warned him and he fled in the last minute. Now, I followed him breathlessly – three hours' march, two hours' rest, day and night. Then, at a steep black ridge, the chase went vertical. He had to cut loose the women, children, the old and those that that would be spared by us. Finally, we caught up with the fighters and our front took fire. Flanking them on the left we galloped over the rocky ground. The enemy rode as fast as they could, we were right behind them. But our troops were at the end of their abilities, and we could go no further. The opportunity appeared to ride to nearby Chamis [a German supply post] and to continue with a fresh company. With them, the enemy was once again found, and it came to a small battle. But it was without results: Cornelius escaped.[17]

Lettow-Vorbeck never caught up with Cornelius Fredericks. In January 1906 he was wounded and after recuperating left the colony bound for Germany. He later became the dominant force in the *Schutztruppe* of Cameroon and then German East Africa.

He was merely one of the more fortunate (and later more famous) of the many German casualties of the war.

Of the twenty-one thousand troops who served in South West Africa between 1904 and 1907, around ten thousand eventually left the colony due to their wounds or as a result of sickness. As in the war against the Herero, disease more than combat decimated the German ranks. To cope with the numbers of soldiers who succumbed to typhus and other conditions in the south, a string of field hospitals was established along the road between the town of Keetmanshoop and the port of Lüderitz.

In December 1904, just three months into the war against the Nama and with fifteen thousand troops now under his command, General von Trotha considered the situation so desperate that he wrote to Berlin requesting that operations be suspended. He also reiterated his belief – first expressed at the outbreak of the Nama War – that a railway should be constructed from Lüderitz to the interior to allow military operations to be conducted in the south. Understandably, Oskar Stuebel, the Director of the Colonial Department, interpreted these requests as 'a declaration of bankruptcy on the part of General von Trotha', who after all was confronting a Nama force of just two thousand fighters.[18]

General von Trotha's problems in the south were not all of Hendrik Witbooi's making. Since October 1903 Jacob Morenga, another highly able and well-regarded Nama leader, had been fighting his own guerrilla war against the Germans. Morenga was perhaps the greatest exponent of guerrilla warfare in the whole history of South-West Africa. His tactics were based around the incredible horsemanship of his men and an understanding of the landscape that came from a lifetime's experience. He lived almost entirely off his enemies' supplies, launching repeated raids on German farms and outposts. When German patrols pursued him, Morenga would lure them ever deeper into the mountains, until, exhausted, lost and running out of water, they were forced to abandon the pursuit.

In May 1906, Morenga was interviewed by a South African journalist for the *Cape Times*. When asked if he was aware that 'Germany was one of the mightiest military powers in the world', he replied: 'Yes, I am aware of it, but . . . [Germans] cannot fight in our country. They do not know where to get water and do not understand guerrilla warfare.'[19]

Other than his tactical genius, Morenga's greatest strength was his ability to draw men to him. When he first launched his war against the Germans, he had only eleven followers. By September 1904 his band had grown to 150. By November the following year, the Germans claimed that around three hundred armed and mounted men rode under Morenga's banner.

Born to a Herero father and a Nama mother, Morenga understood how to forge alliances across cultural barriers in a way that the older chiefs were unable to do. Hendrik Witbooi never fully forgave the Herero for the deaths of his sons at the battle of Osona in 1885 and was at times limited by the deep bonds and divisions of ethnicity. Morenga was free of such constraints and gathered around him a cadre of men who shared his anti-colonial vision. Among his followers were a senior Bondelswarts leader, several Herero and even a white Australian named E. L. Presgrave, of whom little is known.[20]

During the Nama War, Jacob Morenga became a legendary figure among the black peoples of southern Africa, known as 'The Black Napoleon'. His status was boosted by tales of his cunning and audacity. When he and his men stole the horses of a German patrol – who were sleeping around a campfire only yards away – he left a letter addressed to the German commander, thanking him for the horses and asking if the Germans might consider feeding their horses better in future as he had 'no use for emaciated nags like these'.[21] Despite the humiliation they suffered at his hands, some German officers were willing to admit that Morenga was a formidable opponent. In *Im Kampfe gegen die Hereros* (The War Against the Hereros), Captain Maximilian

Bayer described Morenga as a 'towering personality . . . an astute soldier' and 'an enemy who deserved our respect'.[22]

Morenga showed the power of the Africans when they fought according to their own military traditions and put aside ethnic divisions. These were lessons that, by the start of 1905, were being learned more widely. Although Hendrik Witbooi's declaration of war came too late to save the Herero, there was a brief phase in the war during which Herero and Nama forces fought together against their colonisers. After the battle of the Waterberg, several hundred Herero fighters had ridden south, seeking to join the forces of Hendrik Witbooi. Among them was Samuel Maharero's son Friedrich, who found the Witbooi camped near the Auob Valley, on the southern fringes of Hereroland, preparing for battle. They included Hendrik Witbooi's nephew Petrus Jod, the pious Witbooi schoolteacher with whom Friedrich had spent the summer of 1896, when both had been displayed as human exhibits at the Berlin Colonial Show. For a brief moment, both men fought together against the nation that had invaded their land and had regarded them as objects to be put on display. Records show that a month later Friedrich Maharero had reached Bechuanaland, where his father and the remains of his community had found exile. Petrus Jod is believed to have died fighting the Germans sometime in October 1905.[23]

In April 1905, seven months after hostilities had begun, von Trotha decided to base himself in the south and take personal command over the campaign. Constrained by his narrow imagination and devoted to his simplistic view of Africans, von Trotha merely replicated the approach he had used against the Herero, issuing the Nama with an edict not dissimilar to the Extermination Order of 1904. Issued on 23 April 1905, von Trotha's declaration, describing the Nama using the pejorative 'Hottentot' and written in the same bizarre pidgin as the Extermination Order, warned Hendrik Witbooi and his people that they would suffer a similar fate to the Herero should they continue to fight:

> The Great and mighty German Emperor is prepared to pardon the Hottentot people and has ordered that all those who surrender voluntarily will be spared . . . I announce this to you and add that those few refusing to surrender will suffer the same fate suffered by the Herero people who, in their blindness, believed that they could successfully wage war against the mighty German Emperor and the great German People. I ask you: Where are the Herero people today? Where are their chiefs today?[24]

Von Trotha also placed a price in the head of the Nama leaders, offering thousands of marks 'to whoever delivers these murderers, dead or alive'. Neither this financial inducement nor the proclamation itself had any effect on the course of the war; they were an indication of von Trotha's growing desperation.

By the middle of 1905, the number of Nama conducting operations in the field was no more than around 1,500, and von Trotha's inability to defeat or capture such a small force of African insurgents was becoming increasingly embarrassing to the German Chief of Staff and the Colonial Department. The settlers – once von Trotha's greatest admirers – began to turn against him. With thousands of Herero still unaccounted for in the north and the entire south consumed by the Nama insurgency, the decisive blow that von Trotha promised would crush the 'rebellious Africans' had clearly failed to materialise. By the summer of 1905, the hero of 1904 had come to be seen as an inflexible militarist whose policies were a threat to the colonial economy. At the very moment that his stature and reputation were under attack, General von Trotha suffered two personal calamities. In June 1905 Lieutenant Thilo von Trotha, the General's nephew to whom he was particularly close, was killed in a clash with the Bethanie Nama.[25] Soon afterwards von Trotha's wife died in Germany. The assurance and confidence that had marked von Trotha's first months in command now began to escape him. In late September 1905 he wrote to the Kaiser requesting that he be relieved of his command, once an appropriate successor was found.[26]

At the beginning of July 1905, General von Trotha and his commanders were consumed with their own dilemmas and had no idea that Hendrik Witbooi and his men were in a desperate state. Despite all their military successes, they had been forced to take refuge at Tsoachaib, a dry and desolate riverbed about 30 miles west of Gibeon, where at least a hundred Witbooi men, women and children were struggling to survive.[27] It was winter and freezing winds blew down the Naukluft Mountains 25 miles away. They had little food and no tobacco to numb the pain of their injuries. Hendrik's deputy Samuel Izaak was particularly ill, weakened by malnutrition and half poisoned by bad water. As his condition worsened, he pleaded with Hendrik Witbooi to enter into peace negotiations with the Germans. Exhausted by almost a year at war, Hendrik's brother Peter and many of the elder men agreed. The prospect of surrender was strongly opposed by the younger men who had witnessed the battle of the Waterberg and the massacres of Herero that followed. They were championed by Hendrik Witbooi's son Isaak. In mid-July, in the midst of their internal debate, a messenger arrived at Tsoachaib with a letter from the German military authorities that urged Hendrik to surrender. On 27 July, addressing the German District Commissioner for the southern district of Keetmanshoop, Hendrik responded as follows:

> Peace will spell death for me and my nation, for I know that there is no place for me in your midst. As regards your offers of peace, what else are you doing than lecturing me as you would a schoolchild? You know only too well that I have rendered you many a service in times of peace, but in your peace I can see nothing but a desire to destroy us to the last men.[28]

A month later and just over a year into the war, Hendrik Witbooi and his men, having recovered some of their strength, were on the offensive again, attacking German convoys and raiding farms across the south. On 29 October 1905 they launched an attack on a German supply convoy near the town of Fahlgras in central-eastern Namaland. During the attack Hendrik Witbooi was hit in the thigh by a shard of shrapnel. The German soldiers who watched through binoculars later described Hendrik staggering to his horse and fleeing the battlefield, accompanied by his men.

With their leader seriously wounded and bleeding profusely, the Witbooi made a dash for the border with British Bechuanaland, but after three days in the saddle, Hendrik collapsed east of Khoes and just 30 miles from British territory. His last words were reported to have been, 'It is enough now, the children shall have peace.' Hendrik Witbooi's body was wrapped in a blanket. A Bible was placed on his chest and he was lowered into an unmarked grave. Fearing that the body would be exhumed by German soldiers, his men drove their cattle over the grave to conceal it.[29]

The death of Hendrik Witbooi marked the beginning of the slow disintegration of the Nama alliance. A few days after his burial, the Witbooi fighters, along with the members of other Nama clans who had joined them, held a meeting in the desert to debate their next course of action. On his father's death, leadership of the Witbooi fell to Hendrik's eldest son Isaak. He and many of the younger Witbooi men wanted to continue the fight. However, Samuel Izaak, for three decades Hendrik's under-*Kaptein* and a highly respected elder, favoured negotiations. At dawn the next morning, the young men under Isaak Witbooi rode off to continue the war, alongside Jacob Morenga and the other Nama bands. Samuel Izaak and the majority of the Witbooi clan, along with their allies the Veldschoendragers, set out for the small town of Berseba some 60 miles away. Home to the Khari-Khauan, a community of Nama who had remained loyal to the Germans throughout the war, Berseba was neutral territory.[30]

On 20 November, having first written to the German authorities to discuss the possibility of surrender, Samuel Izaak and his men handed themselves over to the German Station Commander at Berseba, Lieutenant von Westernhagen. On the date of their capitulation, the Nama force under Samuel Izaak consisted of seventy-four men and sixty-five women and children. Lieutenant von Westernhagen – a junior officer without the authority to accept the Witbooi surrender – telegrammed his superior, Major Ludwig von Estorff. On 21 November von Estorff eagerly accepted Samuel Izaak's terms, without qualification or delay. To ensure his actions were acceptable to his superiors, von Estorff sent a telegram to his commander, Colonel Dame, who promptly approved.

The undignified haste with which von Estorff and Dame accepted Samuel Izaak's surrender is an indication of the terrible state of the German army in the south. By November 1905, many of the army's depots stood practically empty, supplies of ammunition were running low and much of the war material the Germans needed to maintain their force in the field was in transit from Germany. The death of Hendrik Witbooi and the surrender of Samuel Izaak suddenly and unexpectedly offered the Germans a glimmer of hope. It held out the prospect that the Nama alliance might dissolve and that the remaining Nama bands might surrender, bringing the war finally to an end.[31]

The news of Hendrik Witbooi's death came too late for von Trotha. On 2 November, the Kaiser had finally approved his request and the general had been relieved of his command. As he arrived in the port of Lüderitz, to board a ship back to Germany, von Trotha received a telegram announcing the death of Hendrik Witbooi. He claimed to have thanked the messenger who brought the telegram with the words, 'This is the best news you could have brought me.'[32]

On 19 November 1905, a guard of honour assembled on the Lüderitz harbour and almost the entire white population gathered to say farewell to General von Trotha. In a speech to the assembled crowd, the man who had promised he would vanquish rebellious African tribes with 'rivers of blood and money' told the people of Lüderitz, 'In this land I have lost everything that was dear to me in life.'

On his return to Germany von Trotha was awarded the Pour le Mérite, the highest military order of the day, and was thanked personally and wholeheartedly by the Kaiser for his loyal service. The German High Command, in its Official History of the Herero War, stated that the 'devoted service and self-sacrifice that Lieutenant General von Trotha rendered for Kaiser and Reich deserves the warmest gratitude of the fatherland'.[33]

11

'You Yourselves Carry the Blame for Your Misery'

Just after noon on 22 November 1905, the twin funnels of a Woermann Line steamer appeared on the horizon, near the port of Swakopmund. On board was German South-West Africa's first civilian governor, Friedrich von Lindequist. When the ship dropped anchor, the upper echelons of Swakopmund society assembled expectantly at the harbour side. The men wore top hats and black frock-coats, the women pristine ankle-length dresses.[1]

As von Lindequist stepped onto the rickety wooden jetty, a staccato click from the boot-heels of the senior army officers who lined his path in full dress uniform echoed over the cheers of the small crowd. After a few words of welcome and a brief address by the leading members of Swakopmund's Jewish community, barely audible above the roar of the waves, the new governor was whisked away.

Friedrich von Lindequist was to rule over German South-West Africa for just one and a half years. In that time he brought peace (of a sort), oversaw rapid economic development, helped increase rates of settlement and captained an enormous programme of public works. Von Lindequist achieved all this while continuing the extermination of the Herero and Nama peoples begun by General von Trotha. To understand why and how this was possible, it is necessary to know something of the man himself.

Von Lindequist was a product of the German Colonial Department. He had served his apprenticeship in German South-West Africa itself. In 1894 – the year after the Hoornkrans massacre – von Lindequist's uncle, a chief aide to Kaiser Wilhelm, had helped ease his nephew into the position of Deputy

Governor. For four years, von Lindequist had served under Governor Leutwein in Windhoek, forging many lasting friendships with the settlers. Photographs from the period show him side by side with the settlers, drinking beer from ornate Bavarian mugs in Windhoek's many improvised *Biergärten*. He was, as one historian observed, 'a settler favourite'.

Despite his image as a man of the people, von Lindequist was a deeply ambitious man. In June 1899, his determination was rewarded when he was appointed Imperial Consul to the Cape Colony, an extremely auspicious promotion for a young man of only thirty-eight. Just months after arriving in Cape Town, the potential of von Lindequist's posting increased exponentially. On 12 October 1899, the army of the Boer Republic attacked a British armoured train at a small station north of the Kimberley diamond mines, beginning the Boer War. The German government's official position was that the war was an unfortunate conflict fought 'between two Christian and white races, that were of the same Germanic stock'.[2] Among the German public, however, there was considerable, often vocal support for the Boers, a small republic confronting the army of the mightiest empire on earth. For the next three years, Cape Town became the best possible posting for a young, ambitious German diplomat, and von Lindequist thrust himself into the centre of the diplomatic maelstrom, travelling across frontlines and holding meetings with key British officers, including Lord Kitchener.

Despite the importance of his position and the arduous nature of his schedule, von Lindequist maintained close ties with his friends in German South-West Africa throughout his time in Cape Town. He also used his growing influence in Berlin to lobby in support of their interests. In April 1904, for example, he threw his weight behind settlers' demands for a pre-emptive military strike against the Nama, despite the fact that the Nama had honoured their military treaties and had not shown any inclination to rise up against German rule. Von Lindequist's uncompromising attitude towards the Africans, on this and other occasions, won him yet more admirers in both Windhoek and

Berlin. When the Colonial Department began its search for a civilian governor to take over from von Trotha, Friedrich von Lindequist was the obvious choice.[3]

Von Lindequist's arrival in Swakopmund in November 1905 marked the end of what had been effectively a military dictatorship under General von Trotha. For a year and a half, ever since he had sidelined former Governor Leutwein, the general's writ had run unchallenged. His narrow-minded, militaristic strategies – although supported at first by the settlers – had left German South-West Africa in a chaotic state. While the war had allowed certain sectors of the economy to expand out of all proportion, others had stagnated.

The central fertile areas of Hereroland, where hundreds of Germans had built their farms, were almost empty of both Herero and settlers. After two years of war many farmers had not dared return to the land they had abandoned in January 1904, let alone establish new farms. Most had remained in the larger towns, where the garrisons afforded them some sense of security. With the farms empty and the Herero decimated, cattle-rearing – the economic raison d'être of the colony – had essentially collapsed. The revival of the civil economy was high on von Lindequist's list of priorities in 1905. However, neither this nor any of his other ambitions could be realised until the wars against the Herero and the Nama were brought to a final conclusion.[4]

As von Lindequist took command, around thirteen thousand Herero were in German captivity. Of these, 8,478 were held in the concentration camps; the rest had been put to work on various projects around the colony, the construction of the railways absorbing the bulk of them.[5] Thousands more remained in the bush, hiding in the semi-desert areas on the fringes of the Omaheke. There they avoided German patrols and, against all expectations, continued to survive by foraging for roots.

In the south, General von Trotha had left an even more serious and seemingly intractable crisis in his wake. Although Hendrik Witbooi lay in an unmarked grave somewhere in the southern

Kalahari, the Nama War was far from over. Those Witbooi who had yielded to the leadership of sub-Kaptein Samuel Izaak had surrendered, but the rest of the Witbooi clan, along with the militias of the other rebellious Nama nations, had not. The Bethanie Nama of Cornelius Fredericks, the Franzmann Nama of Simon Kopper, the Bondelswarts of Johannes Christian and the band of men who rode with Jacob Morenga all continued to wage a war of ambushes and lightning commando raids.

Ranged against them were ten thousand German troops. Ill equipped and inexperienced, they struggled to maintain their own vulnerable supply lines, let alone suppress the Nama insurgency. Although the Witbooi had lost their most inspirational leader, their tactics were so effective and the landscape so inhospitable that, by the time von Lindequist took charge, many of his most senior commanders had come to the conclusion that the war was un-winnable.

Von Lindequist first turned his attention to the Herero and the north. In December 1905, just a month after von Lindequist arrived, Kaiser Wilhelm signed an Imperial Decree expropriating all land previously owned by the Herero. Vast tracts of Herero pasture were now available to current and future settlers, and the funds needed to expand and develop the colony's infrastructure were in place. On the day of his arrival in Swakopmund, von Lindequist began the task of inducing the last of the Herero in the bush to surrender.

In one of his first tasks as governor, von Lindequist visited the Swakopmund concentration camp. Escorted by the camp's military staff and members of the press, he was ushered through the barbed-wire fencing and onto a podium. From there von Lindequist surveyed the eight hundred Herero, most of them women. Despite having only a day's warning, Missionary Vedder had done his best to disguise the true state of the prisoners by distributing some second-hand clothing. Looking down through a pair of tiny rimless glasses that sat precariously on the ridge of his nose, von Lindequist delivered a speech to the Herero:

> Hereros! The great German Kaiser has sent me as the replacement of Governor Leutwein to take over the government of the land. I was filled with a deep pain when I heard about your uprising; you had no reason to do this . . . That the majority of your chiefs and leaders are now dead or exiled in another country; that your entire nation has been destroyed and that you are now held in captivity; that is entirely your own fault. But you will be free again, except for those who took part in the killing of farmers and traders – they will get their just deserts. I will not be able to lighten your burden until your compatriots, who are still in the bush, desist and report to us . . . The sooner they present themselves, the sooner your captivity will come to an end. I cannot at this moment make any particular promises for the future; this however I say to you: anyone who behaves well will also be treated well.[6]

When trying to understand Friedrich von Lindequist's policies as Governor of German South-West Africa it is difficult not to speculate whether his time in South Africa during the Boer War had had an impact upon his ideas and methods. As German Consul in Cape Town, von Lindequist had a unique insight into the British conduct of the war and Kitchener's disastrous concentration-camp policy.

The rationale behind the British decision to intern Boer civilians had been, in part at least, to deny the Boer riflemen the support and succour of the civilian population and thereby undermine their insurgency. Kitchener also hoped that the imprisonment of their families would induce the Boers to surrender, and the British went as far as to give smaller rations to the families of men still in the field.

Von Lindequist's promise to the Herero – that their suffering in the concentration camps might come to an end if their 'compatriots, who are still in the bush' surrendered – bears the hallmarks of Kitchener's earlier strategy. Yet there was one crucial difference. In the Boer War the concentration camps had been part of a strategy aimed at ending an ongoing insurgency. In

German South-West Africa, the Herero were defeated when von Lindequist took command. As he admitted in mid-1906, they had no ability and no desire to fight. The concentration camps were not part of a military strategy.

Furthermore, von Lindequist had absolutely no intention of releasing the Herero inmates of the concentration camps, no matter how many of their 'compatriots' surrendered. Perhaps von Lindequist hoped that this false promise would seep back to the Herero in the bush, carried by the Damara men employed as guards or by Herero escapees. Another possibility is that by holding out the vague promise of freedom, von Lindequist believed he might induce the Herero in the camps to work harder or suffer their privations without complaint. Whatever his motives, von Lindequist's speech at Swakopmund was the first in a series of deceptions.

The Swakopmund speech also marked the beginning of von Lindequist's attempt to rewrite history. After promising the Herero better treatment if their compatriots surrendered, he went on to demand that the Herero accept blame for the war and supplicate themselves before his authority and that of the Kaiser. 'Do you admit', he asked them, 'that you started this war without reason and that you yourselves carry the blame for your misery?' To this the assembled prisoners were made to reply in unison, possibly by the missionaries, 'Yes we know it.' Von Lindequist then asked, 'Do you trust that I will govern you justly and benignly from now on?' The Herero were encouraged to reply, 'Yes, we trust you.' Then, von Lindequist concluded, 'I greet you all in the name of the Kaiser; behave well and your future will be favourable.'[7]

Von Lindequist, the career diplomat, understood what von Trotha, the blinkered soldier, had not. He was acutely aware that Germany's international standing was at a particularly low ebb in the first years of the twentieth century due, in part, to persistent accusations of militarism and 'excesses' in the colonies. In such a climate, the overt brutality of the Extermination Order and the continuing horrors of the concentration-camp system risked damaging Germany's reputation further. Von Lindequist set about creating an alternative history, to conceal both his own policies and the past excesses of General von Trotha.

Von Lindequist's speech to the Herero at Swakopmund was the beginning of a much larger process of distortion, which concealed the reality of the wars fought against the Herero and Nama. Under von Lindequist, distortions and falsehoods that had initially emerged in the pro-colonialist propaganda of early 1904 were set down as historical fact. In von Lindequist's version of recent events, the wars Germany had waged against the Herero and Nama had been fought in self-defence. The German army had simply rushed to the defence of a desperate settler population. In this way von Lindequist became the first architect of South-West Africa's Official History, a fictional account of the colony's past that proved so resilient that many aspects of it outlived the German Empire by over seventy years.

In February 1907, thirteen months into his tenure as governor, von Lindequist was able to boast in a dispatch to Berlin that 'the northern and central parts of the territory are practically void of Hereros'. Von Lindequist completed the ethnic cleansing of Hereroland with the support of a group General von Trotha had repeatedly marginalised – the missionaries.

In Windhoek, von Lindequist held a meeting with Friedrich Eich, the head of the mission in Hereroland, and suggested that the missionaries might try to convince the last Herero, still hiding in the bush, to surrender. Von Lindequist was careful to portray the task as peacemaking. After some consultation, Eich and the missionaries agreed.[8]

From von Lindequist's standpoint, the missionaries were ideally suited to the task in hand. The most senior had been in Hereroland for more than three decades, most understood the terrain and some even spoke Otjiherero. They had nurtured personal friendships with various Herero communities, bonds that might now be re-established. The missionaries for their part were eager to play a wider role in the colony and regain their congregations. For the eighteen months of von Trotha's rule, the mission had stood on the brink of collapse. The war had separated the missionaries from their congregations and after the Waterberg they had become a virtual irrelevance in the north.

In the second week of December, von Lindequist announced that his administration would provide funds for the restoration of two abandoned mission stations in Hereroland: one at Otjihaënena some 60 miles east of Windhoek, the other in western Hereroland at Omburo. These would be the stations from which the missionaries would begin 'collecting' the last of the Herero still at large. To help the missionaries entice them out of the bush, von Lindequist supplied the two collection stations with blankets, food and tobacco. More importantly, he agreed that no soldiers would patrol the bush or appear at the collection points. By leaving the operation entirely in the hands of the missionaries, von Lindequist was able to move more of the army south to fight in the war against Nama.

The Omburo collection station in western Hereroland was the first to be opened. To run it, the mission appointed the experienced and highly respected missionary August Kuhlmann, who, along with his family and a few Herero faithful, arrived at Omburo on 21 December 1905. The actual task of trekking through the bush, locating and persuading bands of Herero to surrender was not to be carried out by the missionaries themselves, but by Herero specially recruited from the thousands of prisoners working on the railways. The twenty Herero recruited by Kuhlmann were organised into what were called 'Peace Patrols'. They were equipped with horses, given supplies of food and even issued rifles. Their role was to locate their compatriots hiding in the bush and explain to them that the Germans were now willing to accept their surrender. In the bush the Peace Patrols assured the terrified Herero they encountered that at the collection sites there were no soldiers and that there would be no ambushes or tricks, only food and the chance of reuniting with the missionaries and their faith. To add authority, the Peace Patrols were also issued with copies of a lengthy proclamation, written by Governor von Lindequist, offering food, shelter and security:

> Hereros . . . General von Trotha, who conducted the German war against you, left for Germany a few days ago. His departure means that the war will come to an end . . . I call upon all Hereros who move about in the bush and on the mountains and who have to sustain themselves on meagre bush foods and theft: come and put down your weapons. Hereros, thousands of your compatriots have already surrendered and are now being fed and clothed by the government. I have made every precaution that they will be treated well. The same I guarantee you . . . Come to Otjihaënena and Omburo . . . Come soon Hereros before it is too late.[9]

Only four days after setting up camp at the Omburo collection station, the first of the Peace Patrols disappeared through the heat haze into the bush. Four days later they returned with a human haul of twenty-two emaciated Herero. Over the next months thousands of ghost-like figures staggered out of the bush and, true to von Lindequist's promise, they were issued with food, blankets, tobacco and a great deal of proselytising by Kuhlmann and the other missionaries.

In the initial stages of the collection campaign, the food consisted mainly of standard government rations: flour, rice and canned beef. But as the rainy season set in during February, Kuhlman's garden by the adjacent River Omaruru began to yield crops of vegetables. Rested and fed, the Herero started to show signs of recovery. It seemed their torment had come to an end. By February, Kuhlmann reported that there were 1,700 Herero at Omburo; by June there were more than four thousand. Such was the success of the missionaries at Omburo and Otjihaënena that two additional collection stations were established, at Otjozongombe near the the Waterberg and Okomitombe near the eastern border with Bechuanaland.

By April 1906 thousands of Herero were in the collection camps, slowly recovering from their ordeal. However, under the pretext that supplies were running low, they were gradually ushered out of the camps, probably by the Peace Patrols. Many were marched into the main German towns and from there they were transported to the concentration camps or directly to the railway works. The Herero at Omburo were transported to a concentration camp at Omaruru, 30 miles away; those at Otjihaënena were sent directly to the Windhoek concentration camp.[10]

The missionaries continued to cooperate with von Lindequist's government long after it had become clear that Herero collected by the Peace Patrols were destined for the concentration camps or to become forced labour on the railways. While some were privately appalled, there were only muted murmurs of discontent. Publicly the joint venture between the mission and colonial government was lauded as a huge success. In its official newsletter of 1906, the mission expressed its desire to 'extend our heartfelt thanks to the Lord for employing our mission to bring peace and orderliness in South West Africa.' Missionary Director Spiecker, who toured South-West Africa at the height of the collection campaign, gave a more honest assessment. During a visit to the Otjihaënena collection station, he wrote, 'I enjoyed myself in so many ways with these Herero; but again and again my heart was rendered heavy when I thought about what awaited them.'[11]

Governor von Lindequist had arrived in South-West Africa the day after Samuel Izaak had surrendered at Berseba and Major von Estorff had formally accepted his surrender terms. Just hours after landing in Swakopmund, von Lindequist had sent an urgent telegram to von Estorff ordering him to withdraw the guarantees he had made to Samuel Izaak and the Witbooi. When von Estorff ignored von Lindequist's orders, the governor was forced to accept that the terms of surrender were a fait accompli. He agreed that 'The Nama will be allowed to set up free settlements with directions from the local military authority', but to appease Berlin he demanded that their 'settlements will be guarded night and day by the military'.[12]

The dispute between von Estorff and von Lindequist over the Witbooi's surrender revealed that, under the new governor, it was the army who were now the restraining influence over the civilian administration. It also forced von Lindequist, who had promised the Kaiser a complete victory over the Nama nation, to devise an alternative strategy by which the remainder might be induced to surrender, and then broken. In the first week of December 1905 Samuel Izaak and 134 women, old men and children arrived in Gibeon, their former hometown and the location of the 'free settlement' in which they were to be permitted to live under the terms of surrender. They were instructed to make camp on a rocky hill opposite the German fortress, in which the white men of Gibeon had taken refuge from Hendrik Witbooi the previous year. Although the occasional German guard stalked their camp, they were largely left alone. No barbed wire surrounded their settlement; they were well treated by the German garrison and even allowed to keep some livestock. Slowly they began to recover from the privations of the war. The children were sent to a local mission school and, to the delight of the local missionary, Christian Spellmeyer, the entire community began to attend Sunday mass at the mission church.[13]

After two weeks in Gibeon, Samuel Izaak visited the German fortress, where he met the local officers. The mood was cordial, and men who only weeks earlier had been sworn enemies shared their war stories. To the amazement of the local commander, Major von Maercker, Samuel Izaak was able to read the German war maps, and even pointed out the places where he and Hendrik Witbooi had taken refuge and eluded their pursuers.

The treatment the Witbooi received at Gibeon, in stark contrast to the sufferings of the Herero in the concentration camps, was not proof that Governor von Lindequist planned to forgive them for rising up or wished to re-establish the German-Witbooi alliance. What motivated the governor's apparent generosity was the inability of the army to defeat the Nama militarily. Von Lindequist, it appears, planned to use Samuel Izaak and the Witbooi as a lure, with which he might persuade the other

Nama clans to surrender. On 7 December, he made the point clearly to Berlin, promising that 'the Witbooi will not be granted freedom, but they will, for a period, be treated as prisoners of war'.[14]

Samuel Izaak was convinced that the Germans were genuine in their desire to bring the war to an amicable conclusion, and that the good treatment his people had enjoyed at Gibeon would be extended to the whole of the Nama nation. Samuel agreed to send messages to the other Nama *Kapteins*, urging them to give up the fight and surrender at Gibeon. He assured them they would receive generous surrender terms and humane treatment. The first Nama leader who agreed to surrender was the Witbooi chief Sebulon, another of Hendrik Witbooi's former lieutenants. As he and a group of around two hundred of his people nervously approached Gibeon, Samuel Izaak rode out to meet them and allay their fears. During the next three months, over a thousand Nama followed suit. In February 1906, the last of the Witbooi, the men who had followed Isaak Witbooi and chosen to fight on after Hendrik Witbooi's death, surrendered to the Germans. A month later Cornelius Fredericks, leader of the Bethanie Nama, swayed by the encouraging reports from Gibeon, also came in.[15]

As the Nama clans surrendered in Gibeon, Governor von Lindequist was already preparing to renege on the terms of their surrender. In January, he and Colonel Dame ordered senior officers in Gibeon to inform the Nama that they were to be sent north to Windhoek. An order issued on 13 January to Major Pierer in Gibeon instructed him to

> Inform Samuel Izaak and the senior leaders that the transfer [to Windhoek] is required for reasons related to provision of food and furthermore that the promises made by Major von Estorff will remain uninfluenced by this move. Samuel Izaak will also be informed that the esteemed Governor wishes to meet up with him later on, to speak about the future of his people.[16]

In early February 1906, confident that the reasons for their transfer north were benign, almost two thousand Nama began the 200-mile journey to Windhoek, completely unaware that they were being marched to a concentration camp. An unknown photographer took a single image of the Nama's trek. It shows a long train of people stretched across the horizon. There are more women than men and, while a few of the elders are on horseback, most are walking, their mouths covered by scarves to protect them against the clouds of dust churned up by their feet. No German guards are visible.[17]

In the third week of February (the records do not give an exact date), the Nama arrived at the Windhoek concentration camp. It was located on the slopes of the hill on which the old German fortress stood. In place of barbed wire, the perimeter fencing consisted of a thick layer of felled camel-thorn trees, whose thorns grow several centimetres long and are easily capable of slicing through flesh. Inside the fence of thorns were several rows of closely packed, makeshift huts, formed from the branches of trees and covered with cloth. At the northern entrance of the camp stood a number of large, canvas army tents, which accommodated the hundreds of prisoners unable to find a place within the huts. The whole camp was dirt-ridden and foul-smelling. At that time around four thousand Herero prisoners were housed there.[18]

From February 1906 onwards, a steady stream of Nama prisoners flowed into the camp. The Witbooi were among the first to arrive; soon they were joined in captivity by members of the other smaller Nama clans, who one by one surrendered in the south and were marched north. The arriving Nama were housed in a separate part of the camp to the Herero, and just few days after their arrival, Governor von Lindequist came to address them.

Accompanied by a retinue of journalists, prominent settlers and government functionaries, the governor delivered a speech, blaming the Nama for the war and claiming that they had behaved in a barbaric fashion:

> Your uprising cannot be described as an actual war, but rather as an attack on unsuspecting and defenceless people. This is what is called premeditated murder . . . Kaptein Hendrik Witbooi is dead and he can therefore no longer be held accountable; but everyone standing here

today shares the guilt because you did not have to follow his orders. According to your treaty with the German Government, your principal leader was not Hendrik Witbooi, but the German Kaiser. You have broken this pact without reason and thereby made yourselves guilty of murder. The punishment for this crime is death and you all deserve to be executed. That justice will not take its proper course in this instance, is only due to the assumption that you were not aware of the extent of your actions and because [I] expect that you will try to atone for your crimes . . . I have confidence that you Samuel Izaak and you Hans Hendrik have enough influence over your people to prevent any further reckless deeds.[19]

Von Lindequist informed the Nama that they would suffer the same fate as the Herero, as punishment for the 'crimes'. 'You will be sent to work,' he warned them, 'and I advise you: work hard and follow the instructions of those who give them to you in my name.'[20]

With thousands of Herero and Nama in captivity, von Lindequist's civilian administration set about exploiting the labour of the Africans more intensely than had ever been attempted by von Trotha. Under von Lindequist, forced labour became the defining feature of the concentration-camp system and the main cause of its pathology. Von Lindequist's regime was so calamitous for the Herero and Nama that it can be considered a continuation of their extermination, by non-military means.

In Windhoek, the four thousand Herero already in the camps had been deployed in the construction of new government buildings, private homes, and even a villa for Deputy Governor Oskar Hintrager. However, it was the construction of the railways, by far the biggest public-works project attempted in the colony, that became the engine driving the whole concentration-camp system.

By 1906 two railway projects were well under way. The first ran between Swakopmund and the mines at Otavi in the north, the second between Lüderitz and the inland settlement of Aus in the south. Seven thousand Herero, spread across the colony, were already working outside the formal concentration camps, most of them on the railways. Many were housed in special mobile pens that moved along with the progress of the tracks, deeper into the desert or further into the bush.

The constant need for new labour on the railways encouraged the Germans to raid the Herero collection stations. So pressing was the demand for labour that the Germans even refused to allow the Herero enough time to recover from the effects of malnutrition. In early 1906, when work began on the Lüderitz to Aus railway, the colonial authorities ordered Missionary Kuhlmann at Omburo to send prisoners directly to the railways. He was specifically ordered to send as many as possible, the sick as well as the healthy, the old as well as the young.[21]

The work, especially the laying of the heavy steel rails and prefabricated steel sleepers, was extremely hard labour. Like the prisoners in the concentration camps, the forced labourers on the railways were inadequately fed and poorly housed. They were also routinely abused by their guards. Traugott Tjienda, a Herero man working on the Otavi railway, gave this statement describing the conditions:

> We were not paid for our work, we were regarded as prisoners. I worked for two years without pay . . . The soldiers guarded us at night in big compounds made of thorn bushes . . . women were compounded with the men. They were made to do manual labour as well. They did not carry the heavy rails, but they had to load and unload wagons and trucks and to work with picks and shovels . . . [Our women] were compelled to cohabit with soldiers and white railway labourers. The fact that a woman was married was no protection. Young girls were raped and very badly used. They were taken out of the compounds into the bush and there assaulted. I don't think any of them escaped this, except the older ones.[22]

The railway's voracious appetite for labour was, in part, due to the extremely high death rates suffered by the prisoners. According to statistics compiled by Firma Lenz, the company charged with construction of the embankments for the southern Lüderitz to Aus railroad, 2,014 Herero prisoners were employed on the line between January 1906 and June 1907.[23] In a report to the colonial authorities, Firma Lenz openly admitted that

1,359 of the prisoners had died over the course of those eighteen months.[24] The company's clerk even calculated the exact proportion of casualties: 67.48 percent.

In early 1906 the Nama in the Windhoek camp were prepared for forced labour. They were divided into two categories: the *Arbeitsfähige* ('work-able') and the *Arbeitsunfähige* ('work-unable'). The 'unable' were left to their fate in the Windhoek concentration camp, but those deemed able – men, women or children – were moved out to one of the many government construction projects around the colony; like the Herero, most were sent to the railways. Those who arrived on the Swakopmund to Otavi line worked alongside the Herero who had been forced out of Missionary Kuhlmann's collection point at Omburo.

The Nama, comparatively small in stature, found the labour regime on the railways perhaps even harder than the Herero. By 1906 it was being reported that they were ill suited to railway work and made poor labourers in general. Long before the Nama War, letters and editorials in the colonial newspapers had claimed that the Nama were an innately martial and untameable people who, when the time came, would be unable to adapt to the loss of their freedom and take on the role of landless, subservient labourers. Now it was claimed that this prediction had been borne out by experience and the Nama's future hung in the balance.

As an increasingly Darwinian world view took hold in German South-West Africa, attitudes towards the Nama darkened. The German anthropologist Leonard Schultze, who in 1905 had carried out field research among Nama prisoners, suggested that it was of vital importance for the success of the German colonial project that those races unfit for labour should be allowed to disappear. 'The struggle for our own existence allows no other solution,' he claimed. 'We, who build our houses on the graves of these races, have a responsibility to safeguard [our] civilisation, sparing no means.'[25]

The Nama, like the Indians of North America and the aboriginals of Tasmania, were a people whose labour was deemed to be of little value. Their reputation as warriors also worked against them. By the middle of 1906, the presence of Nama prisoners, especially the Witbooi, in the Windhoek concentration camps had begun to disturb the local settlers. An article published in the settler newspaper *Der Deutsche* on 1 August 1906 claimed that the population of Windhoek, both soldiers and settlers, were angry that the Witbooi were housed so close to German homes. Although by this point many of the Nama in the Windhoek camp were women, children and those unfit for labour, they were still deemed an unacceptable threat to the 2,500 white residents of Windhoek. The escape of a small number of Witbooi from the camp at the beginning of August put further pressure on von Lindequist to remove them from the capital.[26]

Having discounted them as labourers, von Lindequist looked for a solution to the Nama problem. His initial plan was to deport them to the German colony of Samoa, in the South Pacific, but this was hastily rejected by the Colonial Department due to 'the cost of transportation'. Von Lindequist's final solution was to dispatch the Nama to the concentration camp on Shark Island, in Lüderitz harbour.

12

The Island of Death

The town of Lüderitz had originally been envisaged as the gateway to the south of the colony. With Walvis Bay claimed by the British, the harbour at Lüderitz was by far the best remaining natural harbour between the border with Portuguese Angola and the Orange River. However, it was Swakopmund that established itself as German South-West Africa's main seaport while Lüderitz stagnated.

Each year a few more settlers came and went. They were fishermen, minor colonial officials or workers bound for the guano islands offshore. Lüderitz at the turn of the century had the appearance of a base-camp from which the colonial pioneers had intended to launch some great expedition that had somehow never come about. A British military doctor who visited the town struggled to understand how such a place could have been brought into existence:

> I don't suppose there is a more desolate, dreary, God-forsaken site for a town in the whole world than this, and nobody except extreme optimists like the Germans would ever have dreamed of trying to establish one here. There is not a drop of fresh water anywhere near, nor a plant nor tree of any description except seaweed.[1]

Yet within just two years, starting in 1904, two decades of stagnation were wiped away. Lüderitz was transformed into a thriving port town, not by the discovery of natural resources or a sudden wave of settlement, but by the German-Nama War.

In early 1905, the town became a major port for the arrival of troops and supplies, and the site of an important hospital. A Rhenish mission was founded, new hotels opened and houses built. Rows of military tents and hastily constructed depots began to appear. In 1907 the town even acquired its own generator, although the electricity supply was at first reserved for military installations and lighting the main street. Before 1904 Lüderitz had had just twenty permanent white residents; by the middle of 1905 the German population stood at a little more than eight hundred.

The conflict that was the unmaking of the Nama was the making of Lüderitz. War became the sole business. The town was dominated by soldiers constantly arriving on the transport ships from Germany, or amusing themselves while waiting to be shipped home, at the end of their term of service. Three 'waitress hotels' opened, the Fust Bismarck, Hotel National and the Central Hotel, attracting prostitutes and adding to Lüderitz's growing fame.

The soldiers were not the only new arrivals in Lüderitz in 1905. Opportunists, adventurers, drifters and thugs from across the world heard the rumours and made for the town. The record of criminal cases for those years hint at a frontier town driven by money, plagued by street violence and alcohol, and buoyed by an unreal wartime economy. Those arrested in Lüderitz during 1905 include men from as far afield as Argentina, Sweden and Ireland. This was a legendary period in Namibia's history: the years of the 'Wild South-West'.

For German soldiers and white adventurers, Lüderitz was a frontier boomtown, but the war that fuelled the boom also brought Lüderitz thousands of African prisoners. For them, as for all the black peoples of German South-West Africa, Lüderitz became the most feared place on earth.[2]

At its height, there were three German concentration camps in Lüderitz. The most dreaded stood on Shark Island, one of the three small islets that shielded Lüderitz harbour from the South Atlantic. Just 1,300 yards from north to south and 300 yards wide at its broadest, Shark Island was linked to the mainland by a narrow causeway.

As military operations in the south began to escalate, the colonial authorities built a large quarantine station on the island in which German troops arriving from the hinterland were held for about a week, before being allowed into town. Sometime in early 1905, another use for Shark Island was identified.

With only one, easily policed route on or off Shark Island, it was chosen as a site for a concentration camp. The camp was situated on the farthest tip of the island, where the winds of the South Atlantic crashed down from three sides. In its earliest form, it consisted of a few corrugated iron shacks, in which the guards sheltered from the wind and cold, and a line of barbed-wire fencing sealed it off from the rest of the island.

The main source of information we have about the early days of the Shark Island camp comes (again) from the letters of the missionaries. Although there are records that show that Herero prisoners were sent to Shark Island as early as June 1904, the camp properly got under way in early 1905, when a group of Herero were placed there. In late May 1905 Heinrich Vedder, the Swakopmund missionary, got hold of a military report from Lüderitz in which some of the first deaths on Shark Island were recorded. Writing to Wilhelm Eich, his colleague in Okahandja, Vedder reported that fifty-nine men, fifty-nine women and seventy-three children had died in the Shark Island camp. As the population of the camp at this time is unknown, a death rate cannot be deduced, but Vedder described it as being 'incredibly high'. A week after receiving Vedder's letter, Missionary Eich replied, 'Lüderitz lies heavy on my heart.'[3]

Later in the year, Eich noted that the Herero in the Okahandja concentration camp had heard of Shark Island and feared being sent there. On one occasion he was refused permission by the military authorities to inform a group of Herero in Okahandja that they were being sent to Lüderitz. 'I would have liked to have spoken with them before they left,' Eich wrote to Vedder, 'but they are not to know where they are going and therefore I was not allowed to speak with them.'[4]

Even Herero prisoners in the Swakopmund camp, which itself had extremely high death rates, lived in dread of being transferred to the Lüderitz camp. One account from Swakopmund in

1905 tells of a group of Herero assembled on the waterfront. Shortly after they had been informed that they were to be sent to Lüderitz, one prisoner fell to the ground, bleeding profusely, having drilled his fingers into his own neck in a desperate attempt to commit suicide.[5]

Officials of the Arthur Koppel Company, the German engineering company contracted by the Otavi railway concession to build the line between Swakopmund and the Otavi copper mines, reported in 1907 that a group of Herero prisoners working for them had escaped, 'solely out of fear that they might be sent to the south'.[6]

Those Herero who managed to escape the Swakopmund camp, or Koppel's railway camps in the desert, attempted to make the journey of 20 miles to the British enclave of Walvis Bay. From there they either went to work in the South African gold mines or simply lived on the streets of the British settlement. A German reporter encountering them wrote, 'Most lived off fishing or by begging from the Nama. Their mood is subdued; in spite of this they would not consider going back into German territory; they declared rather wanting to starve to death.'[7]

There are several eyewitness accounts that explain why the Shark Island camp was so deeply feared by the Herero. The Rhenish missionary August Kuhlmann was among the first civilians to visit the camp. What he saw in September 1905 shocked him profoundly: 'A woman, who was so weak from illness that she could not stand, crawled to some of the other prisoners to beg for water. The overseer fired five shots at her. Two shots hit her: one in the thigh, the other smashing her forearm . . . In the night she died.'[8]

Similar scenes were recorded by a group of South African transport riders – men hired to drive the ox wagons that ferried supplies from Lüderitz Bay to the hinterland in the years before the southern railway was constructed. According to the testimonies of several transport riders, the German overseers on Shark Island and the other Lüderitz camps used *sjamboks* indiscriminately and routinely to beat prisoners and force them to work. Percival Griffith, an accountant fallen on hard times, worked in Lüderitz unloading cargo during 1904. In an interview conducted at the beginning of 1905 for the South African newspaper the *Cape Argus*, Griffith described the scenes he had witnessed in Lüderitz:

On one occasion I saw a woman carrying a child of under a year old slung at her back, and with a heavy sack of grain on her head. The sand was very steep and the sun was baking. She fell down forward on her face, and the heavy sack fell partly across her and partly on the baby. The corporal sjamboked her for certainly more than four minutes and sjamboked the baby as well.

Are you ready to swear that you saw a white man sjamboking a baby, as well as its mother?

I am; I am ready to make an affidavit if it is required. I saw it with my own eyes. The woman, when the sjamboking had gone on for over five minutes, struggled slowly to her feet, and went on with her load. She did not utter a sound the whole time, but the baby cried very hard.[9]

In 1905 the same South African newspaper ran a whole series of reports on 'The German Operations' in Lüderitz using the accounts of transport riders. In an article published on 28 September 1905, a transport rider, who wished to remain anonymous for fear of retribution, described the punishment regime in a Lüderitz concentration camp:

I have seen women and children with my own eyes at Angra Pequeña [Lüderitz], dying of starvation and overwork, nothing but skin and bone, getting flogged every time they fell under their heavy loads. I have seen them picking up bits of bread and refuse food thrown away outside our tents . . . most of the prisoners, who compose the working gangs at Angra Pequeña, are sent up from Swakopmund. There are hundreds of them, mostly women and children and a few old men . . . When they fall they are sjamboked by the soldier in charge of the gang, with his full force, until they get up. Across the face was the favourite place for the sjamboking, and I have often seen the blood flowing down the faces of the women and children and from their bodies, from the cuts of the weapon . . . The women had to carry the corpses and dig the hole into which they were placed. They had no burial ceremony of any kind . . . The corpse would be wrapped in a blanket and carried on a rough stretcher . . . I have never heard one cry, even when their flesh was being cut to pieces with the sjambok. All feeling seemed to have gone out of them . . . This is only a sample of what is going on at Angra Pequeña.[10]

The most important witness to come to the Shark Island camp during 1905 was Lieutenant Düring, a German officer serving in the south. Evidently a relatively wealthy man, Düring brought one of the latest roll-film box cameras to South-West Africa. By 1905 the unwieldy dry-plate cameras of the nineteenth century were slowly being replaced by multiple-exposure roll-film cameras. These box cameras, pioneered by the American Kodak Company, were easy to use, highly portable and, most importantly, had short exposure times. They ushered in the age of the informal snapshot – a major departure from the formal posed styles of Victorian photographic portraiture. Lieutenant Düring and the other German officers who owned cameras created a scattered but invaluable catalogue of images from the war. While many of the photographs taken by German officers in South-West Africa were highly orchestrated portraits, Lieutenant Düring's were true 'snapshots', taken as mementos or *aide-mémoires*.[11]

In 1905 Düring was posted in the Nama town of Bethanie, a few day's ride from Lüderitz. Many of the photographs in his collection are of daily life, showing German soldiers and settlers going about their business in a backwater colonial town. But sometime in January 1906, presumably on his way back home to Germany, Düring arrived in Lüderitz. Like all soldiers arriving from the hinterland, he and a travelling companion, Dr Gühne, reported to the quarantine station on Shark Island. There Düring decided to visit the concentration camp and take photographs of the Herero prisoners, inadvertently leaving by far the best visual record of the camp.

Only five of Düring's photographs of Shark Island are known to have survived. The first, taken at some distance, reveals the general layout of the camp. The shelters the Herero had managed to construct – ragtag huts made from blankets and cloth – are strewn like garbage heaps across the rocks. Above these hovels, the German imperial flag flutters over a corrugated iron shack, most likely an improvised shelter for the handful of soldiers tasked with guarding the prisoners. Huddled together among the rocks are the prisoners themselves.

In one of Düring's snapshots a boy of about five years, his stomach bloated from malnutrition, his only clothing a torn sleeveless vest, stares at the ground. In another, even more disturbing image, Düring's companion, Dr Gühne, poses among the prisoners. Wearing his military tunic, he stands rigid and poised, walking cane in hand, a group of ragged, frightened Herero women at his feet.

Many photographs taken by German officers during the war contain images of African prisoners or servants being humiliated. Some were published as postcards and were often captioned with sarcastic comments, a visual form of *Schadenfreude* – the 'malicious delight in the misfortunes of others'.[12] In the colonial context, such photographs were a symbol of German power and African submission. The last image Düring took on Shark Island shows a naked, adolescent Herero girl standing in a tiny shack, probably the interior of the guards' shelter shown in the earlier image. Squeezed between the girl's thighs, in an unconscious effort to retain some semblance of dignity, are the torn remains of her dress that had been ripped from her body.

As in all the camps, rape was common on Shark Island, and the sexual exploitation of Herero women was not merely accepted – it was actively celebrated. Lieutenant Düring's photograph was one of many pornographic and semi-pornographic images taken of African women by German soldiers during the war. Some were made into postcards and sent to Germany or otherwise distributed in the colony.[13] One officer, Georg Auer, took several pictures of naked African women which he later published along with his diary.[14]

These postcards celebrating the extermination of the Herero and Nama or revelling in their powerlessness were in wide circulation. The British diamond prospector Fred Cornell recalled encountering some during his time in Lüderitz and on his travels across southern Namaland during 1905 and 1906:

I had seen . . . [a] whole series of illustrated postcards, depicting wholesale executions and similar gruesome doings to death of these poor natives. One of these, that enjoyed great vogue at the time, showed a line of ten Hottentots [Nama] dangling from a single gallows, some still standing on the packing-cases with a noose round their necks, waiting for the soldiers to kick their last standing-place away; some kicking and writhing in the death struggle, for the short drop did not break their necks, but only strangled them slowly, and one having a German soldier hanging on to his legs to finish the work more quickly.[15]

On the morning of 9 September 1906, after three days in the dark, fetid hold of a Woermann Line steamer, almost two thousand Nama prisoners were offloaded at Lüderitz harbour. They were marched in single file along the shore, towards the narrow causeway leading to Shark Island. Two-thirds were women and children.

It was only as they crested the highest peak of Shark Island by the lighthouse that they saw their destination. Over a thousand Herero prisoners crouched among the rocks behind three layers of barbed wire. They were emaciated, traumatised and – as the Nama arrived – struggling as best they could to warm themselves in the sunlight.

With the arrival of the Nama from the north, the population of Shark Island outnumbered the white population of Lüderitz, then only about twelve hundred strong. Already weakened by six months of captivity and hard labour in the north, the Nama suffered a rapid deterioration in their health within just weeks of their arrival. On 5 October 1906, less than a month after they had arrived, Missionary Laaf wrote: 'Large numbers of the people are sick, mostly from scurvy, and every week around 15 to 20 [Nama] die . . . of the Herero just as many are dying, so that a weekly average of 50 is counted.'[16]

In another letter, written just two and a half months later, Laaf reported that death rates had dramatically escalated: 'The dying among the Nama is frighteningly high. There are often days where as many as 18 people die. Today Samuel Izaak told Brother Nyhof:[17] "The community is doomed." If it continues like this, it will not be long before the entire people has completely died out.'[18]

As in the camps at Swakopmund, the health of the prisoners was severely undermined by the cold coastal climate. Lüderitz lies 450 miles further south and has an even colder climate. In the Shark Island camp, exposed on three sides to the South Atlantic winds, night-time temperatures plummeted to little above freezing. With only makeshift huts of rags and sacking for shelter, the prisoners struggled to keep themselves from freezing. One survivor described 'the night air on the sea' as 'bitterly cold'; 'the damp sea fogs drenched us and made our teeth chatter'.[19]

The health of the Nama on Shark Island was further undermined by malnutrition. As in the other camps, their rations consisted mainly of uncooked rice and flour; occasionally they received a little meat from horses or oxen that had died of disease or exhaustion. Cornell reported that food was so scarce on Shark Island that when rations were distributed the prisoners 'fought like wild animals and killed each other' to secure a share. With so many prisoners on Shark Island, the few alternative sources of food – oysters, sea urchins, seaweed and limpets – were quickly exhausted as prisoners scavenged at the water's edge hunting for anything vaguely edible.[20]

From the very start, the plight of the Nama was brought to the attention of the colonial authorities in Windhoek. Just a week after they arrived, Colonel von Deimling, the Commander of Military Operations in South-West Africa, wrote a secret letter to Governor von Lindequist imploring him to have the Nama evacuated from Shark Island: 'Since the Colonial Department had ruled out deportations the only feasible option is to place them in a reservation, because they cannot possibly stay in permanent captivity on Shark Island.' Von Deimling's request was refused.[21]

The Nama were not simply left to die on Shark Island. They were systematically worked to death. The records show that by October 1906, only weeks after their arrival, the Nama prisoners had been deployed as forced labour in the construction of a new quay in Lüderitz harbour. The German harbour engineer,

Richard Müller, who supervised the project, kept a meticulous diary of the works and sent numerous progress reports to his employers in Swakopmund.[22] According to Müller's records, he had at his disposal around three hundred Nama labourers at any given time. It seems that all available Nama labour on Shark Island was mobilised, regardless of gender. Only young children were spared work.

The labourers were made to haul large stones across the island and drag them into the freezing waters of the bay to form the foundations of the quay. All work was done by hand, and prisoners were forced to stand knee-high in the freezing waters for much of the day. Possibly out of principle, the women were not made to work in the water. Eyewitnesses describe how each evening the women would receive their men, half-frozen and exhausted, and massage their limbs back to life.

As early as 30 November 1906, Engineer Müller's reports to the Harbour Division reveal that the number of *Arbeitsfähige* – 'work-able' – Nama had shrunk to around a hundred prisoners, and that the majority were sick or dying. Between November 1906 and January 1907, the situation worsened. More prisoners fell ill and Müller became increasingly frustrated and concerned that the reduction in his allotted supply of labour would undermine the whole project. On Christmas Eve 1906, Müller submitted the following status report:

> Contrary to the Imperial Harbour Department's memo of 6 October 1906 . . . in which it is expressly said that 1,600 Nama prisoners will be set at [our] disposal, I now have only 30–40 people. The desired outcome is therefore not achievable . . . On the 7th of this month as many as 17 died in one night. If measures are not actively taken to acquire [new] labourers, I fear the work will not be completed.[23]

In mid-February 1907 the Harbour Division abandoned the project altogether, as 70 percent of the Nama on Shark Island were dead. Of those still alive, a third were so sick that the camp commander believed that they were likely to 'die in the near future'.[24]

There can be no question that the colonial authorities in South-West Africa knew that the Nama recently sent to Shark Island were dying in large numbers. In the files of the colonial government relating to the Witbooi Nama, there are copies of letters sent by the Lüderitz-based Missionary Emil Laaf and his colleague at Keetmanshoop, Missionary Fenschel, to the Rhenish Mission Society headquarters in Germany. These letters were, it appears, subsequently forwarded to the Colonial Department. Officials made copies, which they marked *Vertraulich* – confidential – and sent to their colleagues in the colonial administration of South-West Africa. The missionaries' correspondence was clearly read in both Berlin and Windhoek. Officials in both capitals were informed, in no uncertain terms, that within weeks of their arrival the Nama had begun to die and that the entire people were doomed if they were not evacuated or conditions in the camp ameliorated.

What the surviving records also reveal is that not only were Governor von Lindequist, and his deputy Oskar Hintrager, aware of the death rate on Shark Island, but when attempts were made by the missionaries and military commanders to have the Nama evacuated, they repeatedly and deliberately obstructed them.

In December 1906 Heinrich Fenschel, a Rhenish missionary based in the southern town of Keetmanshoop, 200 miles from Lüderitz, approached Colonel von Deimling, Head of the *Schutztruppe*, about the fate of the Nama on Shark Island. Von Deimling was, it seems, surprised by what Fenschel told him about the make-up of the prisoners on Shark Island. During their meeting, he admitted that 'It had never dawned on me that there are more women than men there'. Fenschel asked von Deimling to move the prisoners, especially the women and children, off the island, and the colonel promised to 'make arrangements immediately'.[25]

Yet by January, Colonel von Deimling appeared to have changed his mind and had taken no action. Undeterred, the two Lüderitz-based missionaries, Brothers Emil Laaf and Hermann Nyhof, turned their attentions to Commander von Zülow, head of the *Etappenkommando* in Lüderitz, in the hope that he might lobby Colonel von Deimling for the relocation of Nama to a more benign environment. According to Nyhof, von Deimling told Commander von Zülow, 'As long as I am in power, the Nama will not be removed from the island.'[26] In the *Missionary Chronicles* for Lüderitz for 1907, Colonel von Deimling was blamed for the continued suffering of the Shark Island prisoners. However, unknown to the missionaries, von Deimling had already attempted to have some prisoners removed from Shark Island.

In February 1907, following his meeting with Heinrich Fenschel, von Deimling had ordered 230 Nama women and children off the island and into a sheltered valley at the entrance to the town, used mostly by the many South African transport riders. From there, he hoped to have them shipped back to the inland concentration camps at Okahandja and Karibib.[27] Von Deimling waited until the last moment before informing the civilian colonial authorities, and on 19 February 1907 he sent a letter asking for final approval for this plan.[28] As Governor von Lindequist was in Berlin, supporting the passage of a new colonial budget through the Reichstag, his Deputy Governor Oskar Hintrager received von Deimling's communiqué. He replied: 'I sincerely ask that the relocation of Nama women and children to Damaraland [Hereroland] be cancelled and also that the women and children removed from Shark Island be taken back.'[29]

A fanatic advocate of German settler colonialism, Hintrager believed the security of white settlers and the reputation of German colonialism would be jeopardised if prisoners who had experienced the horrors of Shark Island were allowed to 'spread their stories of hate and mistrust against us'.[30] On these grounds, they were effectively sentenced to death.

Hintrager's determination to keep the Nama on Shark Island is all the more remarkable for the fact that he had seen at first hand the horrors of concentration camps. In 1900, Hintrager had fought against the British in the Transvaal during the Boer War and knew what Lord Kitchener's concentration camps had done to Boer civilians. Yet he took measures intended to ensure that the slow extermination of the Nama prisoners on Shark Island continued, despite the pleas of the missionaries and the requests of army officers.

When Hintrager rejected von Deimling's appeal, it seems that Governor von Lindequist still harboured hopes that what remained of the Nama might eventually be shipped abroad, completely eradicating them from German South-West Africa. In a Memorandum to Government on 12 December 1906, he personally insisted that the regime of exposure, malnutrition and forced labour continue unabated on Shark Island in order to reduce the numbers who might eventually be sent into exile:

> Since the Nama are at present safely confined to Shark Island where they are performing very useful work, I feel that their deportation may still be postponed somewhat. Perhaps one should wait and see first how the situation will develop and whether the numbers to be deported might be reduced somewhat so as to cut down the cost incurred.[31]

Von Lindequist was no doubt aware that the deportation of the Nama to any of Germany's tropical colonies would probably result in their extinction. In January 1904, eighty Witbooi, who had been fighting for the Germans against the Herero in the north, were arrested when Hendrik Witbooi declared war. They were deported to the German colony of Togo, where half of them died of tropical disease and forced labour. Their suffering was so extreme that the German authorities in Togo refused to take responsibility for the deaths and eventually returned forty-two of them to South-West Africa.

The slow extermination of the Nama on Shark Island was not the result of poor coordination, inadequate logistics, accidental neglect or administrative incompetence. When von Lindequist transferred the Nama to Shark Island in September 1906, the concentration-camp system had been in operation for twenty months. It was eighteen months since District Commissioner Dr Fuchs had written an official report that unequivocally stated that the death rate at Swakopmund was a result of overwork, and the lack of blankets, food, shelter and basic medical care. The fatal effects of the camps could be seen in Windhoek and on Shark Island itself. It could not have come as any surprise to von Lindequist that when the same system was unleashed upon the Nama, the effects were similarly lethal.

The majority of prisoners in the other concentration camps and working on the railways eventually became victims of their captivity, with mortality rates ranging between 40 and 60 percent. From the time of its inception under von Trotha to the eventual closing of the camp in April 1907, mortality on Shark Island consistently exceeded the other camps. Prisoners sent to Shark Island could only have been expected to die. The German garrison in Lüderitz called the camp 'Death Island'. This phrase was even used in an official report by Commander von Zülow of the *Etappenkommando*.[32]

Although the Nama on Shark Island were used as slave labour, the equanimity with which this resource was squandered strongly suggests that forced labour was a secondary function of the Shark Island camp. The camp's main focus from September 1906 onwards was the extermination of Nama prisoners. Nama deaths were the 'product' of the Shark Island camp; forced labour was merely one of the means by which those deaths were brought about. Shark Island was a death camp, perhaps the world's first.

The British Military Attaché to South-West Africa, Colonel Frederick Trench, independently came to the conclusion that the function of Shark Island was to liquidate as many of the Nama as possible, and perhaps even exterminate them as a race. Between 1905 and 1907 Colonel Trench was in regular contact with the chief administrators of German South-West Africa, including von Lindequist and Oskar Hintrager. In a report sent to the British embassy in Berlin on 21 November 1906 Trench claimed that the Germans' ultimate aim was the eradication of the Nama, in order to make the colony safe for white settlement:

> If I read correctly between the lines, the following are the principles accepted for the present and future administration of the Protectorate . . . The Hottentots [Nama] are to be 'permitted' to die out, but the Hereros and Damaras, who are good labourers and herdsmen, are to be retained, in a semi-servile state, as farm labourers etc. Steps are to be taken however to make the country a white man's country and above all an all-German one.[33]

While there is no doubt that von Lindequist and much of the colonial administration in Windhoek were complicit in the liquidation of the Nama on Shark Island, how much was known in the national government in Berlin? Again there can be little question that news of what was happening on Shark Island had reached leading members of the Colonial Department and Chancellor von Bülow's government.

The letters of Missionary Laaf, sent in October and December 1906, outlining conditions at Shark Island, were read by the new Head of the Colonial Department, Bernhardt Dernburg, and by November 1906 rumours of the conditions on Shark Island were known to have been circulating in Berlin. In December, while the missionaries were lobbying Colonel von Deimling to bring the Nama women and children off Shark Island, Georg Lebedour, a deputy of the Social Democratic party, raised the issue in the Reichstag. An anonymous correspondent described only as a 'concerned citizen in Lüderitz' had written to the socialist newspaper the *Koenigsberger Volkszeitung* reporting that 'Around 2,000 [Nama] are presently under German imprisonment. They surrendered against the guarantee of life, but were nevertheless transferred to Shark Island in Lüderitz, where, as a doctor ensured me, they will all die within two years due to the climate.'[34]

Lebedour read passages from the *Koenigsberger Volkszeitung* article to the collected deputies. Chancellor von Bülow and Dernburg, the Head of the Colonial Department, were present in the chamber, and Lebedour directly challenged them to inform the Reichstag of 'the extent of mortality rates on Shark Island and in other camps'. Thanks to Lebedour, it was impossible for either to claim ignorance on the matter after December 1906.[35]

Georg Lebedour was not a lone voice in the Reichstag. His ambush of Chancellor von Bülow's government was part of a concerted campaign by the left and centre parties to block the passage of a colonial budget that sanctioned additional funds for German South-West Africa. In the same debate, Lebedour claimed that the government, influenced by the settlers and their supporters in Berlin, was exploiting the war in order to increase the colonial budgets and seize 'native' land. 'The farmer lobby', he warned the chamber, 'are wishing, hoping and working towards the continuation of the war in the hope that the land of the natives will ultimately be confiscated.' He continued: 'It is tantamount to recklessness that the Government allows such people to drag it around by the nose and that it complies with these incomprehensible policies that will, inevitably, lead to the annihilation of some of the natives and the total slavery of others.'[36]

The Reichstag debates of November and December 1906 led to a bitter impasse and finally the defeat of the colonial budget. This in turn forced Chancellor von Bülow's government to seek re-election the following year, in what became known as the Hottentot election. Not only did the horrors of Shark Island become well known in Germany, but the parties of the left and their millions of supporters were genuinely horrified by the activities of their government and the army in South-West Africa. Despite the influence of the colonial lobby and their potent propaganda campaign, support for the settlers and von Bülow's government was far from universal. On the issue of colonialism, as in much else, Wilhelmian Germany was a deeply divided nation. The leader of the Social Democrats, August Bebel, spoke for many on the left when he stated that 'under some circumstances' colonialism was 'a great cultural mission', in which Europeans could 'come to foreign peoples as liberators, as friends and educators'. In late 1906 he and his party, along with the Socialists, were convinced that what Germany was engaged in on Shark Island was not the cultural mission of colonialism but a war of extermination.

While the colonial authorities in Windhoek and their supporters in Berlin did everything they could to deny that Shark Island was a place of extermination, the officers who ran the camp did surprisingly little to disguise it – or to conceal the bodies of its victims. The concentration camp was clearly visible from the town. German settlers looking from the windows of their homes and passengers on ships arriving and departing Lüderitz harbour would have been able to see the figures of the Nama and Herero scrambling on the rocks. Likewise the prisoners could see the lights of Lüderitz and hear the sounds of normal life just across the harbour, as they sat frozen in their shelters at night. The prisoners working on the new quay did so in full view of the public. So Governor von Lindequist's administration could not have been surprised when news of their suffering leaked to the German and eventually the foreign press.

Even more remarkable was the fact that the camp authorities made only half-hearted efforts to dispose of the bodies of those who died. An estimated eight to seventeen prisoners were dying on Shark Island each day. The accumulation of so many bodies, from a small camp situated not far from the centre of a town of only twelve hundred white residents, was not easy to overlook. Many were simply dumped into the sea. Leslie Cruikshank Bartlet, another of the South African transport riders who passed through the bay, came to Lüderitz in mid-1905 and witnessed the consequences:

> I have seen corpses of women prisoners washed up on the beach between Lüderitzbucht and the cemetery. One corpse, I remember, was that of a young woman with practically fleshless limbs whose breasts had been eaten by jackals. This I reported at the German Police Station, but on passing the same way three or four days later the body was still where I saw it first.[37]

Other bodies were buried in shallow graves around Lüderitz and in the deserts beyond. Some of these mass graves have recently come to light. However, anticipating the concentration camps of the Third Reich, some of the dead of Shark Island became a resource exploited in the name of medical and racial science.

In the course of the war, an industry had developed around the supply of body parts. In the Swakopmund concentration camp in 1905, female prisoners were forced to boil the severed heads of their own people and scrape the flesh, sinews and ligaments off the skulls with shards of broken glass. The victims may have been people they had known or even relatives. The skulls were then placed into crates by the German soldiers and shipped to museums, collections and universities in Germany. This practice was so widespread and accepted in South-West Africa that in 1905 it was depicted on a postcard. Clearly a retouched photograph, it shows five soldiers leaning over a line of skulls packed neatly in a wooden crate. One is carefully placing the final skull into the crate while his comrades pose with their pipes or smile at the camera.[38]

In June 1905 the German racial anthropologist Felix von Luschan had begun a correspondence with Ralph Zürn, the lieutenant in Okahandja whose aggression towards the Herero had helped spark the outbreak of war. Disappointed with the Herero skull Zürn had donated to him following his removal from the colony in 1904, von Luschan enquired about the possibility of acquiring further specimens. Zürn made some enquires of his own before assuring von Luschan that 'in the concentration camps taking and preserving the skulls of Herero prisoners of war will be more readily possible than in the country, where there is always the danger of offending the ritual feelings of the natives'.[39]

By the time the Nama were incarcerated on Shark Island, the dissecting and exportation of prisoners' bodies was no longer the prerogative of corrupt soldiers like Ralph Zürn. The process had become more professional and scientifically rigorous. Towards the end of 1906 the bodies of seventeen Nama prisoners, including that of a one-year-old girl, were carefully decapitated by the camp physician at Shark Island, Dr Bofinger. After breaking open the skulls, Bofinger removed and weighed the brains, before placing each head in preserving alcohol and sealing them in tins for export to the Institute of Pathology at the University of Berlin. There they were used by the aspiring racial scientist Christian Fetzer, then still a medical student, in a series of experiments designed to demonstrate the anatomical similarities between the Nama and the anthropoid ape.[40]

As well as preparing human remains for scientists in Germany, Dr Bofinger used the inmates of Shark Island for his own research. His area of study was scurvy, a fatal disease, the precise cause of which – an acute deficiency of vitamin C – had yet to be discovered in the early years of the twentieth century. The British had long known they could prevent the condition among the sailors of the Royal Navy by compelling them to eat sauerkraut and drink lemon juice. Outside the British Empire these practices had yet to catch on, and a lingering belief that scurvy was associated with bad hygiene or perhaps tainted meat had led doctors to look elsewhere for a cure. As many of the prisoners in Lüderitz suffered from bleeding gums and aching joints – classic symptoms of the condition – and were dying at an appalling rate, Dr Bofinger concluded that 'the Herero and Nama prisoners handed over to me for treatment in Lüderitzbucht offered plenty of opportunity to observe several hundred cases of scurvy'.[41]

But Bofinger's research was founded on the entirely false premise that scurvy was a contagious condition, spread through some form of bacterial transmission. Convinced that the disease was a major cause of death among the prisoners on Shark Island and that the squalor of the camp was helping to spread the disease, Dr Bofinger initiated a series of medical trials in which a range of substances, including arsenic and opium, were injected into living prisoners. He then determined the effects of these substances 'by opening up the dead bodies' in medical autopsies.

In his rush to find evidence to support his contention that an epidemic of scurvy was ravaging the population of Shark Island,

Dr Bofinger overlooked the more obvious explanation for the incredibly high death rate: the prisoners were living, half starved, on the edge of the South Atlantic in huts made of rags and being forced to carry out manual labour in ice-cold water. They were dying of malnutrition, exposure and exhaustion, rather than scurvy. Ironically, one of the substances Dr Bofinger tested on the Shark Island prisoners was crystallised lemon juice; if the cause of their suffering had been scurvy, Bofinger might have stumbled on a cure.

According to Missionary Laaf, Dr Bofinger was deeply feared by the prisoners. Writing in the *Missionary Chronicles* of 1906, Laaf reported that prisoners he had spoken to claimed that anyone who entered Bofinger's field hospital 'will not come out alive'. Laaf noted that it 'was never the case that even a single person recovered in the Lazarett [Field Hospital]'.[42] Dr Bofinger was somehow unable to understand why he was so feared and complained that 'the natives, especially the Nama, were only with difficulty persuaded to go the communal tent clinic that had been set up for them, and, in the course of the night, they would crawl back [and hide] in their own quarters'.

The death camp on Shark Island was finally closed in April 1907, over a year and a half after the Nama had surrendered and nearly three years since the battle of the Waterberg. What brought about the decommissioning of the camp was not a rejection of the policy of extermination, but a temporary shift in the balance of power that saw influence slip away from Governor von Lindequist and Oskar Hintrager, and fall into the hands of Major Ludwig von Estorff.

Von Estorff was the commander who had promised Samuel Izaak peace and freedom in return for his surrender in 1905, and had opposed von Trotha's policies in the Omaheke. For this he had been dismissed by the general as an *Alte Afrikaner* – an old-fashioned colonialist whose judgement was clouded by an unhealthy preoccupation with the continued existence of the African peoples of German South-West Africa. In April 1907 von Estorff was appointed Commander of the South-West African *Schutztruppe*. By chance the promotion was approved while he was on a visit to Lüderitz, during which he had seen at first hand the fate of the Nama on Shark Island. On taking up his new post, von Estorff immediately signalled his unwillingness to permit officers and men under his command to be deployed in the administration of the Shark Island camp, calling it 'a hangman's duty'. Against the express wishes of von Lindequist's office, he ordered the camp closed.[43]

On 8 April 151 men, 279 women and 143 children staggered across the narrow causeway between Shark Island and the mainland. They were taken through the town of Lüderitz itself, in full view of the local population. Some, including Samuel Izaak, were too weak to walk and had to be carried. Their destination was a sheltered bay on the other side of the harbour in which they were provided with blankets and food. Of the 573 Nama evacuated from Shark Island, 123 were so sick that von Estorff and Zülow believed that they were likely to die in the near future.

Estorff vented his disgust at what had taken place on Shark Island in a furious telegram to Oskar Hintrager. He warned, 'I am not prepared to accept the responsibility [for their deaths], since they were brought here in contravention of the promise I gave them in Gibeon in 1905, with the explicit support of the Command.'[44]

Von Estorff also dispatched an emphatic protest to the Colonial Department in Berlin, and it was this that ultimately forced Lindequist and Hintrager to accept the closure of a facility they had fought so hard to keep open. Von Lindequist was in Berlin when the camp's closure was authorised, lobbying the Reichstag for an increased colonial budget. Had he been in Windhoek, von Estorff might not have been successful.

Von Estorff's telegrams to the Colonial Department initiated a ridiculous exchange of communications between the administration in Windhoek and the Colonial Department in Berlin. The

Head of the Colonial Department, Bernhardt Dernburg, feigned shock at the fact that almost all the Nama prisoners had died on Shark Island, although he had been aware of it for months and had been directly challenged on the subject in the Reichstag only four months earlier.[45] Under pressure, Governor von Lindequist sent a melodramatic telegram to Hintrager demanding, in unusually imperious language, that his deputy 'Send, immediately, an official report outlining what the government knew about the conditions on Shark Island and also why nothing was done and why it was not reported to Berlin.'[46] Von Lindequist, who had just been promised the post of Deputy Head of the Colonial Department, surely feared that the revelations about Shark Island might wreck his career. Yet the Shark Island scandal was in the end a short-lived and rather half-hearted affair.

The official report was compiled and edited by Oskar Hintrager, despite the fact that he was one of the main architects of Shark Island. It absolved the colonial government of all blame and claimed that they had done everything, 'to improve the plight of the natives [on Shark Island]'. Hintrager maintained that the prisoners had had 'enough foodstuffs' and 'as much as possible the needs of the natives were met'.[47] Not only was Hintrager's investigation a whitewash, but the Acting Head of the Colonial Department responsible for accessing it was von Lindequist, who had been temporarily promoted while his superior, Bernhardt Dernburg, made an official tour of South-West Africa – which included an inspection of the now defunct camp on Shark Island.

Although von Lindequist, Hintrager, Dernburg and the politicians in Berlin explained away what had happened on Shark Island, Ludwig von Estorff was unable to forget. Shortly before he died on 5 October 1943, he wrote in his memoirs: 'Lindequist had seen the horrible effects of the concentration camps on the Boer families in South Africa. The same happened here . . . Trotha had begun the evil work and Lindequist had finished it. I could only stand aside, sad but powerless to do anything about it.'[48]

The exact number of those who died on Shark Island will

never be known. Throughout the concentration camps, the system of reporting deaths was haphazard and at times anecdotal. Indeed the recording of deaths on Shark Island began only in April 1906, and the deaths of many hundreds, perhaps more than a thousand, Herero prisoners who had been on the island before that date were not included in the official statistics.

According to the records that do exist, by March 1907 at least 1,203 Nama prisoners had died on the island. Of these 460 were women and 274 children.[49] In the month of December 1906 alone, 263 prisoners died, an average of 8.5 per day. In late October 1907, Major von Estorff estimated that more than 1,900 Nama had died on Shark Island.[50] These figures do not include the deaths of the Herero prisoners who were on Shark Island long before the arrival of the Nama. Missionary Laaf claimed they died in similar numbers.

The Africans who met their deaths on Shark Island were not the only victims of the Lüderitz camp system. Another concentration camp, run by the railway company Firma Lenz, also reported extremely high death rates. In total, perhaps as many as three or four thousand Africans died in the Lüderitz camps, a figure four times the German population of Lüderitz in 1907.[51]

According to a census carried out by Deputy Governor Hintrager in 1908, there were a total of thirteen thousand Nama alive in the colony at the beginning of that year; the pre-war Nama population had been around twenty thousand. Of the Nama who rose up against the Germans in 1904 – estimated at anywhere between five and ten thousand people – around 2,400 were sent into the concentration camp system; only around five hundred of them were alive when the camps were closed down. By 1909, only 248, just over 10 percent of those who had been imprisoned, remained alive.[52]

For some Nama communities, the extermination had been almost total. In October 1907 Major von Estorff reported that 'there are no longer any Veldschoendragers left'. The Witbooi had been nearly wiped out, and of the Bethanie Nama who joined the Witbooi against the Germans, less than a hundred were alive by 1909.[53]

The Herero, whose pre-war population had been estimated at around eighty thousand, had been similarly decimated. Those who survived the concentration camps were formally released by the Kaiser on his birthday in January 1908, a little over four years since the beginning of the uprising. Despite the Kaiser's orders, many Herero were not released immediately. Some camps were kept open until April 1908 to allow the authorities access to Herero labour in order that the Lüderitz to Keetmanshoop railway – the last major infrastructure project for which forced Herero labour was required – could be almost completed. According to the colonial census, only 16,363 Herero remained in the colony in 1908; 5,373 of them were children, many of whom had been born in the concentration camps, some as a result of rape. Eighty percent of the Herero nation had been killed or driven out of the colony.

Around a thousand Herero, including Samuel Maharero, had managed to escape into British Bechuanaland. Exiled from their homelands, they eked out a meagre existence. Although some were allowed to settle in a reserve at the eastern edge of the Kalahari, poverty forced many to seek work in the gold mines of the Transvaal. An unknown number found refuge in the Owambo lands to the north.

13

'Our New Germany on African Soil'

The morning of 27 January 1912 found the town of Windhoek abuzz with excitement. The red, white and black of the German tricolour hung from beneath windows and fluttered from masts erected along the main streets. It was the Kaiser's birthday, an occasion always celebrated with a degree of patriotic fervour in German South-West Africa, but in 1912 the celebrations were particularly memorable. Around seven o'clock in the morning, before the summer heat rendered even the most gentle physical activity almost intolerable, the citizens of Windhoek began to make their way up the steep hill upon which the German fortress stood. Their journeys took them through the centre of Windhoek, a town that had been transformed by war and by the slave labour of the defeated Nama and Herero. Along Kaiser Wilhelm Strasse, they passed the window displays of the new shops that sold imported luxuries. Along Garten Strasse, they passed the hot water springs that fed the city's new swimming pool. Those who cut through the Memorial Gardens walked over manicured lawns and between duck ponds. What had once been the home of the Herero was now a European city in miniature.[1]

That morning, the men of Windhoek wore their best white linen suits, and the ladies who accompanied them dressed in long ornate frocks of white lace. The new colonial elite were prosperous, proud, and acutely aware of rank and status. To emphasise their position, many had added the prefix 'von' to their surnames, implying a lost aristocratic heritage.

In front of the fortress, a 16-foot tall bronze statue of a mounted *Schutztruppe* towered above the growing crowds. The *Rider Statue*, as it became known, had been paid for by private donations raised in Germany. It was the work of the sculptor

Adolf Kürle, and was intended as a memorial to the soldiers and settlers who had lost their lives in the wars against the Herero and the Nama.[2]

Stern and austere, with a rifle in his hand, the rider was also a dramatic representation of the rugged 'colonial type' that the colonial societies and German nationalists had always claimed would emerge from the hardships and struggles of the colonial frontier. The unveiling of the *Rider Statue* on the Kaiser's birthday in 1912 was the moment that German South-West Africa came of age.

The men of the Windhoek garrison, dressed in the same *Schutztruppe* uniform as the rider, stood nearest the statue on the morning of the inauguration ceremony. After both soldiers and civilians had placed wreaths at the foot of the plinth, local notables addressed the crowd from a specially built podium draped in the national flag. The keynote speaker was Theodor Seitz, the new governor. Seitz began by reminding the assembled crowd of the many sacrifices that had been made by the colonial army in the name of the Fatherland during the wars begun in 1904, but he ended with a simple statement of fact:

> The principle behind this monument is to honour the dead and to encourage the living to propagate and build up what was achieved in a hard war, fought selflessly for the love of the Fatherland . . . The venerated colonial soldier that looks out over the land from here announces to the world that we are the masters of this place, now and for ever.[3]

The Germans were masters not only of South-West Africa's future, but of its past. Their version of the war had been set in stone and was now cast in bronze. The inauguration of the *Rider Statue* was the culmination of the process of historical denial and distortion begun by Friedrich von Lindequist. The brutality of the settlers in the years leading up to the war, General von Trotha's Extermination Order and the concentration-camp system were expunged from official history.

Part of the motivation behind the commissioning of the *Rider Statue* had been a determination to remember the Germans who had died in the war. Yet its location, on the lawns outside the old fortress, represented an equally determined effort to forget the suffering of the Herero and Nama. The statue had been erected on the site of Windhoek's main concentration camp, where only four years earlier perhaps as many as four thousand Herero, mainly women and children, had been starved, beaten and worked to death.

By 1912 nothing remained of the camp. The mud huts and thorn-bush fences were gone, and the bodies of the victims had been interred in mass graves scattered across the town. But no one who attended the inauguration ceremony could have possibly misinterpreted the significance of the location. The site of the former camp was now the centrepiece of the German version of the war, a history in which a genocide was transformed into a heroic struggle for civilisation and progress.

From his granite plinth, the *Rider* gazed out far beyond the city limits into hills that surround the town, once dotted with Herero villages. The Herero who had survived the war no longer lived in Windhoek Valley. When the concentration camps had been closed in 1908, the survivors had been distributed among the settlers and made to work virtually as slaves, raising cattle on land that had once been theirs. They lived in small, isolated groups. Under restrictions imposed by the colonial administration, all Africans over the age of seven were prohibited from travelling without their employers' permission and were made to carry passes, similar to those that had already been adopted in the British parts of South Africa (formerly the Cape Colony). Cut off from what remained of their families and communities, their culture almost atrophied.

In 1908 Matthias Erzberger, a Reichstag member for the Zentrum party spoke out and condemned the treatment of Africans in the colony. In the Reichstag itself he asked if they had not in fact been reduced to the status of slaves. Erzberger was loudly scorned by his fellow deputies and later referred to as a 'nigger lover'.[4] Three years later, when Major Ludwig von Estorff complained that the Herero on the farms 'are treated no different than slaves', he was simply ignored.[5]

The few Nama rebels who had survived the concentration camps were treated differently. Although the war had ended and the concentration camps had been decommissioned, the survivors of Shark Island were still incarcerated in 1912. They were held by the German army in a converted military stables in central Hereroland. Out of sight, Samuel Izaak, his sons and around a hundred of his people were being permitted slowly to die off. A headcount of the Nama held at Okawayo, conducted by the Germans in July 1909, revealed that of the Witbooi there were only thirty-nine men, sixty-five women and fifty-two children, some of whom had been born in captivity at Okawayo. Of the Bethanie Nama who had joined the Witbooi in rebellion, only thirty men, forty women and twenty-two children remained alive.[6]

The Nama clans who had rejected Hendrik Witbooi's appeals to rise up in 1904 had survived the war but had later been confined to small reserves. The Berseba Nama, some of the Bethanie Nama and the mixed-race Basters of Rehoboth all found that their territories had become islands of indigenously owned land in a sea of German farms. With so little land, many were forced to abandon their traditional lifestyles and seek employment as farm labourers.

In 1909 it had been suggested that the colony should make use of the Nama being held at Okawayo, by distributing them among the German farms in the south. However, the colonial authorities quickly discovered that although the colony was suffering an acute shortage of labour, the farmers had no interest in taking a people they regarded as inferior labourers, even as slaves. In March 1909, Major von Maercker, an officer of the *Etappenkommando*, wrote that 'giving the natives to the farmers as workers etc. will only cause problems, because, as we have experienced already, the Nama, who are on average small and weak, are poorly suited as farm labourers and are therefore not very popular with the farmers'.[7]

In the same year, the colonial government in Windhoek again toyed with the idea of deporting the Nama, this time to German

A scene from inside Shark Island, probably the first death camp in world history. Its mortality rates were over 70 per cent.

A German officer, Dr Gühne, poses among prisoners in the Shark Island concentration camp, *c.* June 1905.

German South-West Africa's first civilian governor, Friedrich von Lindequist, was the man responsible for the final solution to the Nama problem: Shark Island.

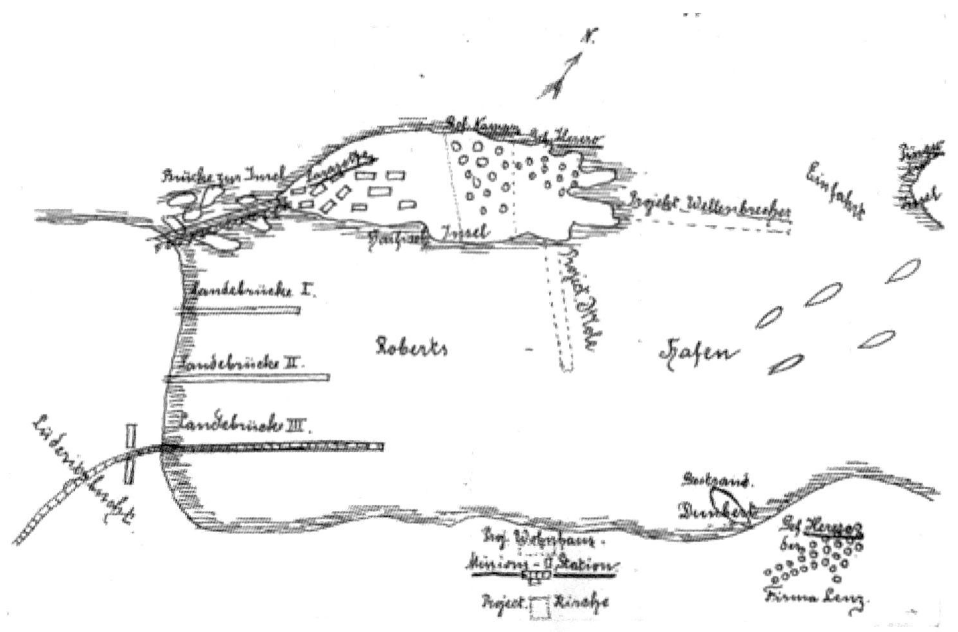

A hand-drawn map, produced by the local missionary, shows the location of the concentration camps on Shark Island and around Lüderitz bay. The main camp was divided into Nama and Herero sections while another camp, run by the railway company Lenz, is situated across the harbour.

An extremely rare photograph of the Shark Island concentration camp taken through the barbed wire fence. By October 1906, more than 2,000 prisoners had been driven onto the island.

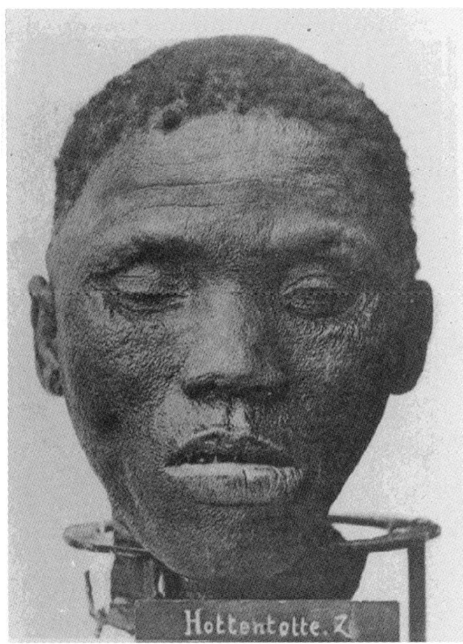

A postcard shows German soldiers packing skulls into crates, for export to university collections and race scientists in Germany.
The severed head of a Nama man – labelled 'Hottentotte 2'. Preserved in alcohol by camp physician Dr Bofinger, human heads were sent from the Shark Island camp to race scientists in Berlin.
Dr Eugen Fischer, whose study of the Rehoboth people of South-West Africa made him Germany's foremost race scientist.

The white residents of Windhoek gather on the site of the Windhoek concentration camp in 1912 for the inauguration of the Rider Statue, in honour of Germans who had died in the wars to exterminate the Herero and Nama.

'A people without space': German settlers in Windhoek, *c.*1912.

Veterans of the German colonial army carry the flags of the lost German empire through Vienna in 1939.

'For Justice and Honour': a Nazi propaganda poster demanding the return of the former German colonies in Africa.

Dr Eugen Fischer, Nazi Germany's leading race scientist. A late but enthusiastic convert to the Nazi cause.

Lindequist Street in Lüderitz in the 1930s. Nazism was enthusiastically embraced by much of the German settler community.

Members of the Hitler Youth and the Pathfinder movement parade in Lüderitz in the 1930s.

Ritter von Epp, as a young infantry lieutenant in colonial uniform.

Von Epp and Hitler greet Mussolini, Bavaria, September 1937.

Von Epp (front row, second from left) reunited with his old friend Hermann Göring (front row, centre), while in American custody at Mondorf-les-Bains in 1946. Epp, awaiting trial, died shortly after this picture was taken.

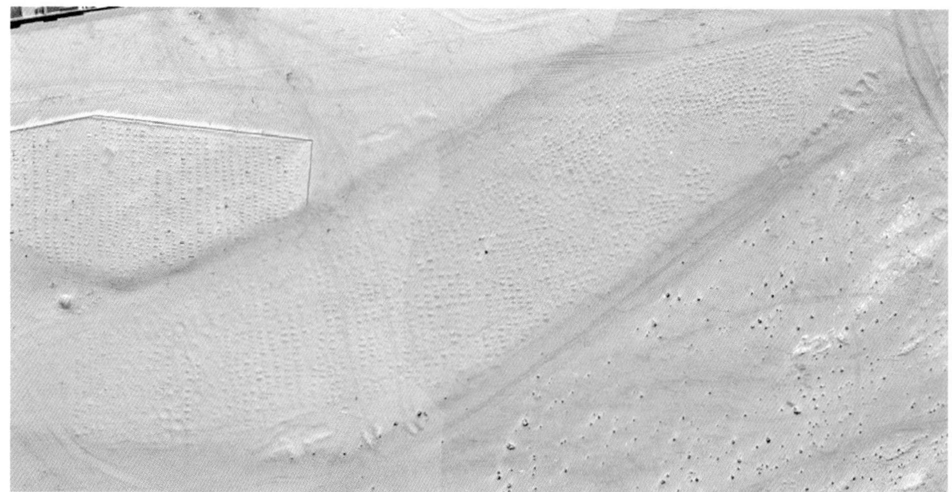

Aerial photography reveals the enormous graveyard of the concentration camps' victims, on the outskirts of the Namibian seaside resort of Swakopmund.

The remains of a victim of the Shark Island camp, in an unmarked mass grave in the southern Namib desert, photographed by the authors in 2006.

The bones of the dead emerging from the sand.

East Africa. Well aware of the Nama's reputation as guerrilla warriors, Freiherr von Rechenberg, the Governor of East Africa, vetoed the plan, fearing that the Nama might 'spread their dangerous influence among the people here'.[8]

In the years before World War I, with the Herero and Nama decimated and the survivors reduced to virtual slaves, German South-West Africa truly belonged to the Germans. While the Herero and Nama had been incarcerated in the concentration camps, Governor von Lindequist and Deputy Governor Hintrager had confiscated their former homelands. In December 1905, Kaiser Wilhelm had formally expropriated all Herero land, and in 1906, von Lindequist and Hintrager issued instructions for the Land Surveyors' Department to draft a new map of South-West Africa, subdividing much of the prime farmland of the Herero and Nama into hundreds of farm plots. On 8 May 1907, just weeks after Shark Island camp had finally been closed, the Kaiser completed the land grab, issuing a decree expropriating all Nama lands, apart from Berseba and the land of the Bondelswarts at Warmbad.[9]

By 1908 the German government had acquired a total of 46 million hectares of land that had once been the property of Nama, Damara, Herero and San peoples. The German settlers, some of whom had previously leased their land from the Africans or owed outstanding payments, were notified by the German colonial newspaper *Deutsche Kolonialzeitung* that each farmer would be able to submit a claim for his 'possession' to the Fiscal Department of the colonial government.

In 1913 there were 1,331 German farms; before the Herero and Nama wars there had been just 480. By the same year there were almost fifteen thousand settlers in the territory – in 1904 there had been only around five thousand, and in 1891 only three hundred. Many of those who had settled after the war were former soldiers, men who had chosen to stay behind and claim a plot of the land they had conquered. To cater for the farming boom, a host of new businesses had emerged. In Windhoek alone there were ninety-eight registered businesses in 1913; ten years earlier there had been just fifteen.[10]

The colony's Deputy Governor, Oskar Hintrager, who also acted as Secretary for Immigration and Settlement, was particularly dedicated to turning German South-West Africa into a model agricultural colony. Hintrager had spent years studying the example of the United States, and had marvelled at the endless wheat fields of the Midwest and the great profits made by the cattle ranchers of the western prairies. 'Agriculture', he explained to his superiors, 'is the backbone of all other vocations.'[11] To ensure that agriculture became the engine of the colonial economy, Hintrager and his colleagues set about providing aspiring farmers with interest-free loans. The average loan was six thousand Reichmarks, enough to buy basic tools and a farmhouse. In addition to the loans, new farmers were sold the cattle that had been confiscated from the Nama and Herero at drastically reduced prices.

Not all settlers, however, qualified for these loans. Governor von Lindequist, along with Hintrager, set down a number of criteria that aspiring farmers had to meet to be considered. They were expected to prove their 'German citizenship', demonstrate that they were of 'good repute' and had 'knowledge of an orderly agricultural enterprise' to be awarded loans.[12] By these means, von Lindequist could control who was able to own land in the colony. Such regulations were part of a programme of social engineering to ensure that the expanding white population would constitute a new colonial *Volk*. The popular colonial magazine *Kolonie und Heimat* (In the Colonies and at Home) described the type of German settler that was needed in South-West Africa:

> The man who is easily disheartened, who is afraid and used to leading a good social life, who needs spiritual replenishment and cannot bear loneliness or exertion in great heat, he should stay at home with his mother. But, the man who is not afraid of work and who carries a little bit of the devil in him, he is the right man for our Southwest.[13]

Völkisch fantasists and colonial fanatics like Paul Rohrbach had predicted that the hardships confronting new settlers in Germany's colonies would transform them into a rugged frontier people. Reconnected to the soil, united by race and culture and away from the moral pollution of Germany's cities, they would reject the superficiality and materialism of modernity, in favour of traditional modes of life. In reality, however, many of the settlers who came to South-West Africa did their best to replicate the materialism and decadence of modern Germany.

Life in Windhoek, for many of its residents, was far removed from the frontier fantasy. By 1912 the town offered most of the vices and indulgences that *Völkisch* and Pan-German agitators believed settlers would be better off without. Alongside its farm provision stores, Windhoek boasted several lawyers' practices, a notary, a bookstore, a tailor, two bakeries, eight hotels and two stores selling women's clothing. In 1912, Clara Brockmann, a famous female settler, enthused, 'In the large stores of Windhoek one can obtain everything that moves the heart; luxury and extravagance is cultivated even in the elegant, small towns. One lives like in Germany. The social activity is blooming.' The social life of the German population, now known as the *Süedwester*, had once been limited to campfire gatherings and improvised *Bierkellers*. By 1912 the colony had its own racecourse, bowling alleys and a movie theatre – although most social events were still lubricated by the produce of the colony's nine breweries and eighty-two bars. The march of progress was by no means restricted to the capital. Swakopmund had been founded in 1892 as a coastal outpost, manned by just nineteen Europeans. By 1909, it had a total of 112 businesses, including barbershops, beauty salons, laundries, a watchmaker and its own newspaper, the *Deutsch Südwestafrikanische Zeitung*.[14]

In the years before World War I, German South-West Africa was so alluring that even the sight of the Namib Desert and the Skeleton Coast, which had once struck dread into the hearts of hardened sailors, no longer seemed forbidding to prospective settlers. In her popular memoir, *Was Afrika Mir Gab und Nahm*

(What Africa Gave To Me and What It Took Away) published in 1909, Margarethe von Eckenbrecher described her first sight of her new homeland, glimpsed from the rails of a steamer en route to Swakopmund:

> The Namib offered the most glorious view, veiled in a blue haze, above which rested, rosy in the gleam of the sun, the enormous mass of the Brandberg [Mountain]. It is among the most beautiful things I have ever glimpsed in my life, so splendidly exalted and yet so desolate and lonely.[15]

Another settler, Lydia Höpker, who came to South-West Africa in 1910, described the colony as a paradise. Arriving just two years after the end of the war that had depopulated much of the colony, she was particularly taken by the emptiness of the landscape: 'Everything was so dewy fresh and untouched, roundabout loneliness [*sic*] and quiet; only from afar did the call of a bird resound now and again. We hiked silently through this beautiful morning. A dreamlike feeling enveloped me, and I felt enchanted, as if in another world.'[16]

As the number of settlers increased, supporters of colonialism in Germany were able to claim that German South-West Africa was a fully grown colony. Not only had it attracted thousands of settlers, in 1912 exports exceeded imports for the first time. In the context of the German economy as a whole, the figures were almost insignificant, yet even the British Consul, in his report of 1913, reluctantly had to accept that the colony was thriving. Clara Brockmann proudly announced in 1910 that the colony had become 'Our new Germany on African soil'.[17]

As enthusiasm for the colonies reached new levels, Germany set out to exploit South-West Africa and her other colonies fully, by establishing of a network of colonial colleges and research institutions. A German Colonial School was founded in Witzenhausen and three-quarters of its graduates went on to apply their skills in Germany's overseas possessions.[18] In Hamburg, the Colonial

Institute taught 'Ethnology of the German Protectorates' and 'Tropical Hygiene', while the prestigious Berlin School of Commerce offered a course in 'Colonial Economics', taught by Dr Paul Rohrbach.

At many institutions, the teaching of undergraduates existed alongside extensive research programmes, many devoted to maximising the productivity of the colonies. To help students from less fortunate backgrounds access careers in the empire, scholarships were established by German companies such as Deutsche Bank and Krupp Steel – both beneficiaries of increased colonial trade and government investment in the new colonial infrastructure.

Graduates of the colonial schools were drawn to the fertile north of German South-West Africa, the territories once owned by the Herero. There, new land could be broken and new methods applied. In the south, however, thousands of new settlers with little interest in farming were attracted by the thought of treasure and prospect of instant wealth.

In 1908 a coloured worker from Cape Town, Zacharius Lewala, had stumbled across a peculiar-looking stone while working on the rail line near Lüderitz. Zacharius, who had previously spent years labouring in the mines of Kimberley in South Africa, immediately recognised it as a raw diamond. Just miles from Lüderitz, in the sands that Adolf Lüderitz had scoured for minerals thirty years earlier, the Germans had uncovered one of the world's largest deposits of alluvial diamonds.

The discovery of diamonds came at a critical moment for the town of Lüderitz. As the war against the Herero and the Nama had drawn to an end, the army drifted away. The hotels were left empty and the bars fallen silent. 'It seemed', wrote a settler, 'as if Lüderitz was falling back into hibernation.'[19] When rumours of diamonds reached Lüderitz, people had run into the streets to rejoice. Within a year, each of the desert hills surrounding the bay had been claimed by competing diamond companies. Hundreds of men groped through the sand or shovelled it into the spinning wire drums of the clarification machines that separated the gems from the worthless rock.

Like all rushes, whether for diamonds, gold or oil, the Lüderitz diamond rush gave birth to folklore. The most enduring legend is that in certain sites it was not even necessary to dig, as the diamonds lay on the surface of the sand. There are stories of one diamond field, located just a few miles north of Lüderitz, in which prospectors would gather at nightfall and wait for the moonlight to pick out the twinkling diamonds that could be grabbed from the sand in handfuls.

The reality of diamond prospecting was not so romantic. The vast bulk of the work was done by black workers imported from the Owambo Kingdoms in the far north. Chained together at the legs, the Owambo were made to crawl across the desert on all fours, fumbling in the burning hot sand for diamonds. They were reduced to this miserable existence by drought and famine in their homelands that forced them to seek work from the Germans. The hardships of the labour itself were aggravated by the brutality of the overseers and their meagre rations. Many of the workers died.

As they criss-crossed the deserts, the Owambo may have discovered more than diamonds. In late 1904 and early 1905, when the death toll on Shark Island began to rise, many bodies had been disposed of in the desert outside Lüderitz. They had been interred in mass graves dug in what the German authorities must have presumed would always be uninhabited wasteland. That wasteland was now diamond fields, and the Owambo labourers were searching for diamonds in areas that contained the remains of Shark Island prisoners. Today two such mass graves have emerged from the sands just outside Lüderitz. Hidden in the still restricted diamond zone, the bones of what are almost certainly victims of the camps lie bleached and exposed in the sun. Abandoned diamond-excavating machines stand a few hundred yards away, half engulfed by the yellow sands of the Namib.

At the height of the diamond rush, the white population of Lüderitz was unconcerned by grim discoveries in the desert. As money began to flow into Lüderitz again, the old boomtown mentality swiftly returned. The bars reopened and the excesses of the war years were quickly surpassed. For a brief moment Lüderitz became one of the most dynamic places on earth.

Between 1908 and 1913, 52 million marks' worth of diamonds were discovered in South-West Africa.[20] With each find, the excitement mounted and the population of the south swelled. Just a few miles inland from Lüderitz, an entirely new town sprang up in the desert. Kolmanskuppe had a casino, a bowling alley and a spacious meeting hall in which regular vaudeville performers played to a full house. Those who had already made their fortunes built extravagant villas on the edge of the new town, overlooking the diamond fields.

During the diamond rush, the south of the colony was undoubtedly a man's world. There were tales of hard-living prospectors who made a fortune in an instant, and squandered it in just weeks in the bars and brothels of Lüderitz. Yet while the south did much to revive the wartime legend of the 'Wild South-West', the colonial societies and Germany's foremost colonial experts were struggling to erase that image. In the years leading up to World War I, the economic progress of the colony became inextricably linked with the issue of gender and those responsible for its future sought to remake South-West Africa into a colony that would attract German women. To be a fully productive, 'racially healthy' settler society, the south-west needed not just farmers, but farmers' wives.

The first campaign to encourage women to emigrate to South-West Africa had been launched in 1896, when the German Colonial Society offered free passage to the wives and fiancées of men serving in the colony. In a more overt attempt at social engineering, unmarried women were given free passage and employed as domestic servants. This was regarded as a way for the young women usefully to expend their energies until they found husbands. Clara Brockmann believed that a settler with a wife worked ten times better than one without, and H. Ladeburg, author of *Die Koloniale Frauenfrage* (The Question of Women in the Colonies), suggested that through 'marriage with a racial comrade [a male settler will] raise himself not only ethically, but also economically.'[21]

By 1913 there were three thousand white women in the colony, around a quarter of the total white population. Twenty years earlier there had been fifty-five. However, the campaign to encourage white women to settle in the colony had less to do with increasing agricultural productivity than with demands for *Rassenreinheit* – German racial purity.

German settlers in the south-west, like white settlers across the continent, had for decades taken African and mixed-race women as their concubines. Many had had mixed-race children. A small number had married their African or mixed-race partners and settled down to care for their children; others returned to Germany and abandoned their African families.

The first attempt to stamp out racial mixing was made by Curt von François in 1892. To discourage soldiers in the German garrison from taking up with African women, von François threatened to withhold their rights to a free plot of land in the colony at the end of their service. Despite these sanctions, a number of Germans, both among the settlers and von François's garrison, continued to live with and marry Africans, particularly women from the mixed-race Rehoboth Baster people.[22]

Even after German women had begun to arrive in the colony in larger numbers, sexual unions between white settlers and black or mixed-race women continued. The colonial economist Moritz Bonn claimed that 'the main cause of bastardisation in Africa was not the absence of white women but the presence of black ones'. Yet what truly disturbed Leutwein, and later governors, was not mixed-race couples but mixed-race children. Under German law, the children of German fathers automatically inherited their citizenship. Whether or not the normal rights of citizenship applied to mixed-race offspring became the subject of a complex and protracted legal dispute. Believing it was impossible to prevent white settlers marrying, cohabiting with or raping African women, Leutwein and his successors tried to prevent their mixed-race offspring being legally defined as Germans.

As scientific racial theories began to shape attitudes in the colonies, the debate about racial mixing focused on fears that black blood would seep into the white population itself. Racial purity became an issue that weighed heavily upon the shoulders of the officials of South-West Africa and colonialist agitators back in Germany. The magazine *Kolonie und Heimat* argued that the imperative task facing the captains of the colonial project was that of 'keeping our races abroad clean'.

The fight against racial pollution in South-West Africa was enthusiastically led by Deputy Governor Oskar Hintrager, a fanatical white supremacist. In September 1905 Hintrager, working closely with Hans Tecklenburg, the former Deputy Governor under von Trotha, passed an edict banning the colony's marriage registry officials from officiating at mixed marriages. In 1907 the High Court in Windhoek nullified all existing marriages between Whites and Africans. The presiding judge also ruled that that once a bloodline had been 'contaminated' with black blood, nothing could change the status of subsequent generations. African blood was regarded as such a powerful pollutant that those infected by it were permanently excluded from the white race.

When left-leaning deputies in the Reichstag complained about the racial laws in German South-West Africa, the colonists openly compared themselves to the former Confederate States of the US and to the Boers, who had rebelled against British attempts to impose liberal racial laws on them.

In March 1907 Dr Angelo Golinelli of the Colonial Department redrafted Paragraph 17f of the Colonial Home Rule Act, allowing men who maintained relationships with Africans to be disenfranchised. Settlers with black or mixed-race wives were also officially barred from receiving government allowances, or loans to help them buy and equip new farms or make improvements to existing plots.

Irrespective of how many years a couple had been married, the number of children they had, or the past record of the settler in civic life or military service, men with mixed-race families were expected to abandon them in the name of racial purity. Those who refused were banished socially and economically from white colonial society.

In May 1912, in the tradition of his predecessor, Governor Seitz passed his own Race Law. Seitz's decree required the registration of all mixed-race children at birth. It also provided the legal foundations for the forcible break-up of mixed-race families. The decree stated that 'If the cohabitation of a non-native man with a native woman becomes a source of public annoyance, the police may require the parties to separate and, if this does not happen within a specified time, may compel such a separation.'[23]

The racial laws pioneered in German South-West Africa became the model for racial legislation in other German colonies. Similar laws were passed in German East Africa in 1906 and Togo in 1908. In Germany's colony in Samoa, Secretary of State Wilhelm Solf personally intervened to ban interracial marriage in 1912, despite generations of racial mixing. In Berlin in 1905 there was even talk of a ban on interracial marriage, based on the German South-West African laws, being introduced in Germany itself. Although the law was not passed, the few mixed-race people who lived or had been born in Wilhelmian Germany were not permitted the status of citizenship.

The racial legislation pioneered in German South-West Africa propelled the issue of racial mixing out of the colonies and into Germany itself. A series of colonial debates held in the Reichstag between 1905 and 1912 were reported in the newspapers and discussed at length in the publications of the various colonial societies, and an entire lexicon of quasi-legal and pseudo-scientific terminology, much of it used in German South-West Africa, was introduced. Terms such as *Rassenmischung* (race mixing), *Rassenreinheit* (racial purity), *Rassenschande* (racial shame), *Mischlinge* (people of mixed-race) and *die Mischlingefrage* (the mixed-race question) seeped into the language. This terminology created the foundations of an increasingly biological understanding of race and racial mixing. It flowed into the much older discourse on the place of the Jews in German society and their supposed inferiority to ethnic Germans.

Not only was German South-West Africa the colony in which racial laws and new racial categories were pioneered, it also became the field-laboratory of German racial scientists. In the years after the Herero and Nama wars, they set out on expeditions to prove scientifically the danger that racial mixing posed to the settler population.

By the beginning of the twentieth century, it was commonly asserted by both scientists and colonial enthusiasts that racial mixing led to some form of 'degeneration' – a decline in the health and intellect of mixed-race offspring. Over generations, it was believed, mixed-race people would continue to produce children marked by a range of physical and mental inferiorities, even if they bred only with 'pure' whites. Various theories had been put forward to explain 'racial degeneration', and much evidence to the contrary had been ignored. Felix von Luschan, Director of the Berlin Museum of Ethnology, and formerly of the Berlin Colonial Show, believed that in mixed-race populations negative traits inherited from the lower race would dominate to the extent that, after several generations of *Blutsmischung* (blood mixing), such populations would eventually produce offspring who were pure-blooded members of that lower race. Von Luschan claimed to have personally studied this effect, known as *Entmischung* (de-mixing), in 'Hottentots'.

Despite von Luschan's claims and the preponderance of competing theories, the process of degeneration remained scientifically unproven and unobserved. Among the many scientists who set out to prove the theory was the young German anthropologist Eugen Fischer.

In 1906 Eugen Fischer was a rising academic star. His first major study, on the skull-width of Papuans, had won the prestigious Broca Award from the Parisian Anthropological Society. Buoyed by this success and the recent rediscovery of Mendelian genetics, Fischer, like many of his contemporaries, began to scour the globe for a mixed-race community whose physical traits and genealogical history would permit him to demo strate how racial degeneration actually worked.[24]

He required a community with an extremely specific racial heritage. The perfect case study would be an isolated, mixed-race people, who could trace their ancestry back to a single moment in history, when their forefathers – two peoples of 'pure' blood – had come together in sexual union. That moment of union, ideally between black and white, had to have taken place several generations earlier and, in the intervening decades or centuries, the mixed-race offspring needed to have eschewed interbreeding with all other peoples.

Scrutinising existing work on 'the bastardisation of the races', Fischer at first looked to the mixed-race populations of the southern United States, but in 1907 a colleague handed him a booklet titled *The Nation of the Bastards*. It had been written by Captain Maximilian Bayer, the German officer who had fought at the Waterberg alongside General von Trotha. After taking part in the pursuit of the Herero into the Omaheke in 1904, Bayer became a member of the German force sent to confront the commando units of Hendrik Witbooi. On his journey south, he encountered the town of Rehoboth, 50 miles south of Windhoek. Rehoboth was home to a small community of mixed-descent people known as the Basters, who traced their ancestry back to intermixing between white men and Nama women of the Cape centuries earlier.

The Basters had moved into the south-west in 1869, having been pushed out of the Cape by the Boers. In 1870, they had settled in Rehoboth, naming their new home after the town on the Euphrates mentioned in the Bible. The term 'Basters' dated back to the 1700s and was not considered offensive by the people of Rehoboth, or their descendants, who still live in Rehoboth and remain fiercely proud of their ancestry, their history and the name 'Basters'.

Although they had lived in South-West Africa for well over half a century and had been in constant contact with the twelve Nama tribes and the Herero, they had remained a tightly knit community, with few marriages between them and other local peoples. When Rehobothers married outside their community, it was normally a case of a Baster woman marrying a white man. Devoutly Christian, the Basters had also kept meticulous birth and baptism records, and most families could trace their lineage back several generations through church records. They were the ideal people for Eugen Fischer to test his theories on.

In 1904 the leaders of the Basters had rejected Hendrik Witbooi's call to arms and upheld the terms of their protection treaty with the Germans, supplying men to fight with the *Schutztruppe* against the Herero. It is partly through the accounts of Baster soldiers, shocked by the behaviour of their 'allies', that the true brutality of the war in the Omaheke later emerged. Having avoided becoming the targets of von Trotha, the Basters had survived the war with few casualties, and in 1908 they were two thousand strong.

Like any mixed community, their physical features varied from one individual to the next. Some looked distinctly Nama, while others clearly had European features; most were a mixture of both. The Baster women were particularly striking, with fair, afro hair and green or bright blue eyes, set above the high cheekbones common among the Nama. In an academic paper of 1910, Fischer wrote: 'Among the hideous, yellow-skinned stumpy Hottentot population, and also among the needy, skinny, dark Damaras, the Baster makes a good impression.'[25]

While Fischer fixated on their physical appearance, the Baster people, like most religious, conservative nineteenth-century communities, placed much greater emphasis on matters of spirituality, propriety and decency. They were immaculately and modestly dressed. Many of the men wore bushy Victorian moustaches; the women tied their hair in tight buns behind their heads and wore ankle-length, high-necked dresses.

Unlike the Nama, the Basters spoke only Afrikaans and had adopted most of the cultural traits of the Boers. Their family names were (and remain) a matter of pride, reflecting their determination to celebrate their mixed heritage. Eugen Fischer's notes contain his descriptions of members of the van Wyk and Cloete families, the Beukes, the Steenkamps and the McNabbs. These last were descendants of a Scottish sailor who had married a Baster woman. The current *Kaptein* of the Rehoboth Basters, John McNabb, is the grandson of the McNabbs whose photographs and anatomical measurements can still be found in Eugen Fischer's original files, held by the Namibian Scientific Society in Windhoek.

Within days of his arrival Eugen Fischer, aided by the local missionaries, began to force his scientific attentions upon the Baster community. Despite reassurances from the missionaries that his intentions were purely benign, the Basters were not easily persuaded to subject themselves to Fischer's programme of anatomical measurements. One elder reminded Fischer that 'the Basters were not savages', and asked him why he did not also carry out examinations of the white residents of Rehoboth, 'the missionary and the Oberleutnant [District Chief]'.[26]

Several of the Basters refused to submit themselves to Fischer's examinations; others only permitted him to carry out procedures that allowed them to retain their dignity. Fischer was especially disappointed that he was refused permission to measure genitals and pubic bones. He later complained, 'I tried several times to frisk around this area but it could not be done, especially with the women.'

In the face of determined resistance, Fischer was forced to reduce the scope of his examinations to measurements of arms, hands, legs and heads, and to resort to a more extensive use of photographs. In total, he examined and/or photographed 310 members of the Rehoboth community.

Throughout his time in Rehoboth, Fischer's work was characterised by a series of striking methodological lapses. Due to the refusal of the Baster people to be measured naked, many of Fischer's measurements were taken over heavy clothing and were extremely inaccurate. Even more worrying, a series of sample measurements from the two racial groups from which the Basters were descended, Nama and White Europeans, were also highly inaccurate. The measurements representing the average dimensions of 'pure-blood' Nama were based on examinations of just eight Nama individuals, whose body measurements were taken to represent their entire people.

After two months' fieldwork Fischer had completed his research. Before leaving Rehoboth, he briefly toyed with the idea of robbing the graves of his Basters' ancestors in Rehoboth's Christian cemetery. Unable to satisfy his 'ardent desire to encounter the dead of this small community', Fischer exhumed a number of Nama skeletons from a set of graves in the desert between Swakopmund and Walvis Bay.

After this 'encounter with the dead', Fischer left German South-West Africa and never returned. In many ways, Fischer's work and the conclusions it drew him towards were typical of racial studies of the era. His study was detailed and enormously complicated, while at the same time deeply flawed at a methodological level. Fischer's files contain hundreds of anthropological photographs of Rehoboth people. Many of his subjects have been photographed from several angles to illustrate specific cranial and facial features. As well as the photographic material, there are a number of charts mapping the complex genealogy of various Rehobother families. The files are well ordered, neatly catalogued and beautifully presented. The rigour belies the fact that the measurements were at times almost meaningless, and that Fischer's conclusions were merely the substantiation of preconceived racist assumptions, given legitimacy by the apparent application of scientific methods.

Nevertheless, in 1913 Eugen Fischer published the results of his study in a book entitled *Die Rehobother Bastards und das Bastardierungsproblem beim Menschen* (The Rehoboth Bastards and the Bastardisation problem in Man). Fischer claimed that his examinations of the people of Rehoboth showed that racial features and characteristics found in the Basters and inherited from their Nama ancestors had, with each succeeding generation, become dominant over the traits inherited from their white forebears. The process of racial degeneration was stamped on their bodies and the story of the Rehoboth Basters demonstrated the universal truth that 'every European people that has adopted the blood of inferior races – and that Negroes, Nama and many others are inferior only mad people would deny – has, without exception, atoned for the adoption of these inferior elements with their mental and cultural downfall'.[27]

Even before the publication of his book, Fischer had begun to tour and lecture on his findings. On publication, *Die Rehobother Bastards* helped Fischer establish himself quickly as Germany's foremost expert on racial mixing. It was regarded as a breakthrough study, the first successful application of modern Mendelian genetics to human anthropology. The book was still in print in 1961.

Fischer was emerging as a front-rank German racial scientist at the moment the pseudo-science of eugenics, the invention of Charles Darwin's cousin Francis Galton, was achieving an important place in German scientific discourse. The man chiefly responsible for the establishment of German eugenics was Alfred Ploetz, a passionate believer in the supremacy of the Aryan race. In the mid-1880s, Ploetz fused his ideas of Aryan supremacy with eugenics and began a crusade to preserve the purity of the Germanic people. In one of his books, he stated that the love of humanity 'is nothing more than love for its Aryan part'.[28]

As Ploetz had begun his studies before Francis Galton had devised the term 'eugenics', he called his science *Rassenhygiene* – race hygiene. Although Ploetz's term lacks the elegance of Galton's Greek etymology, it more accurately conveys the ideas of purity and pollution inherent in the eugenics movement. In 1895 Ploetz published his key book, *The Foundations of Racial Hygiene*, and in 1904 he helped found the periodical *Archiv für Rassen- und Gesellschaftsbiologie* (Archives of Race Science and Social Biology) and opened the Society for Racial Hygiene. In 1909 Galton agreed to become its honorary chairman. Eugen

Fischer, who had been involved in eugenics even before his time in German South-West Africa, was ideally placed to take up a leading position in the German eugenics revolution.

By 1910 Fischer was arguing that *Rassenhygiene* was the first step in 'saving our wonderful German nation', and that it was the duty of race scientists to convince the public of the intrinsic merit and importance of racial hygiene. Yet what allowed ideas like *Rassenhygiene* to gain ground in German society was not the proselytising of scientists like Eugen Fischer but the trauma of Germany's defeat and humiliation in World War I. The disaster of the war and the ensuing chaos helped radicalise Germany's race scientists and made German society more receptive to racial theories than ever before.[29]

14
Things Fall Apart

The Great War came to German South-West Africa in the early hours of 18 September 1914 when, under the cover of darkness, a flotilla of British and South African warships rounded the tip of Shark Island and quietly slipped into Lüderitz harbour. When the sun crested the rocky hills to the east of the town, revealing the harbour crowded with warships, panic caught hold of the local population. Men, still in their pyjamas, were seen running from their homes. A government official scurried through the streets carrying a box of official documents, and, with somewhat undignified haste, a white sheet was raised on a flagpole over the main jetty.[1]

The commanders of the colony's *Schutztruppe*, expecting an overland invasion by the army of the Union of South Africa, had dispatched the bulk of their forces in the south to their border on banks of the Orange River. Lüderitz, her people and her diamond fields had been left almost completely undefended. With the guns of the invasion fleet now ranged against the town, the mayor of Lüderitz Emil Kreplin, the resident judge Dr Dommer and the editor of the *Lüderitzbuchter* newspaper sailed out to the South African flagship. There, Mayor Kreplin formally surrendered Lüderitz to Colonel Beves of the Union army. By noon the next day the British Union flag had replaced the white sheet on the flagpole in Lüderitz harbour, and an invasion force of almost two thousand men had begun to come ashore and unload their equipment.

Six days later the *Armadale Castle*, an ocean liner belonging to the British-owned Union Castle Shipping Line and recently refitted as a warship, suddenly appeared off the coast of Swakopmund. Once in range she began to bombard the town, aiming her fire at the only two facilities of any strategic importance: the long wooden jetty and the mast of Swakopmund's long-range radio transmitter. Over the course of several raids, both were destroyed, and stray shells also landed on the Customs House and the offices of the Woermann Brock Company, a subsidiary arm of the Woermann Shipping Line. The day after the naval bombardment began, the German colonial authorities started to evacuate the civilian population inland. By 30 September, Swakopmund was effectively a ghost town. Tendrils of sand began to creep onto the wooden walkways and loiter in the doorways of shops and homes.

On Christmas Day 1914, a large force of South African soldiers landed at Walvis Bay, and two weeks later marched on Swakopmund. The only resistance the South Africans encountered came from a handful of German snipers, who fired a few volleys from the nearby sand dunes and remotely detonated a series of large mines, before making a hasty retreat. With the capture of both Lüderitz and Swakopmund, German South-West Africa was effectively sealed off from the 'Fatherland' and in the same months, similar fates befell Germany's other colonies in Africa.

In August 1914, as 1 million German troops had swept through Belgium following the grand battle plan of the late Alfred von Schlieffen, Germany's West African colony of Togo had also been invaded by French forces from Dahomey to the east and by British units from the Gold Coast (modern Ghana) to the west. The small German colonial police force had surrendered at the end of the month, giving the Western Allies the sort of quick victory that was good for morale and seemed to support the widespread conviction that the war in Europe would last only a few months. The invasion of German Cameroon was also well under way by the time Swakopmund fell to the South Africans. While the Belgian forces defending their homeland were being routed, their colonial units based in the Congo had marched into German territory from the south. French columns had also invaded German Cameroon from Chad and a British force of four thousand West Africans, led by 350 British officers, had launched a simultaneous invasion from Nigeria to the west. The British struggled against strong resistance from a German force made up predominantly of local African soldiers, but with the help of the Royal Navy the capital Douala fell at the end of September and the German garrison was forced to seek refuge in the neutral territory of Spanish Guinea.

Only in German East Africa had the German *Schuztruppe* taken the initiative. There a large force of African Askaris, led by German officers, came under the command of the inspirational Paul Emil von Lettow-Vorbeck. A veteran of the battle of the Waterberg, von Lettow-Vorbeck had witnessed the declaration of the Extermination Order at Osombo zoWindimbe, and in 1905 had been dispatched south to fight the Nama. By the end of 1914 von Lettow-Vorbeck had launched attacks against Belgian forces in the Congo and British positions in Kenya and Uganda, and had repelled a landing in East Africa by a large force of the British Indian Army at the battle of Tanga, the defining battle of a campaign that was to drag on until 1918.

In German South-West Africa, despite the dramatic landing at Lüderitz and the capture of Swakopmund, little was achieved in 1914. In stark contrast to the tactics of von Lettow-Vorbeck, Major Victor Franke, another veteran of the Herero and Nama wars and a recipient of the Pour le Mérite, made little attempt to confront the invading forces on the landing grounds. Enormously outnumbered, he had withdrawn his men inland, to positions behind the great shield of the Namib Desert. There they concentrated their efforts on maintaining control of the all-important railway hubs, in the south and centre of the colony, and defending the heartland of German settlement in the former Herero pasturelands around Windhoek. Before the Union army was able to launch an assault across the Namib to confront Franke's *Schutztruppe*, General Louis Botha, the South African Prime Minister and commander of the Union forces in Swakopmund and Walvis Bay, was forced to return to Cape Town to deal with a rebellion among Boer soldiers.

With Botha out of the picture for several months, the South African expeditionary force in Swakopmund, Lüderitz and Walvis Bay were left with nothing to do but settle into their billets and wait. For the officers in the Union army's logistics corps, the hold-up was an unalloyed blessing, allowing them and the thirty thousand black labourers they had brought with them to stockpile supplies and grapple with the enormous difficulties of fighting in the Namib Desert.

With so much time on their hands, some South African soldiers amused themselves by exploring the nearby deserts. In Swakopmund this led a handful of officers to stumble upon the last visible relic of the concentration camps that had been in operation in the town only six years earlier.

In February 1915 Eric Moore Ritchie, a lieutenant in Botha's personal bodyguard, came across an enormous cemetery on the southern edge of Swakopmund. It was situated near the European graveyard, but stretched out into the desert. While the European graves were well tended and shaded by exotic trees, those in the desert were merely rough mounds of sand, a sign of hastily dug, shallow graves. They had been dug in neat rows but had neither headstones nor crosses. Writing later, Lieutenant Ritchie described being particularly struck by the size of Swakopmund's cemetery. Not only was the desert graveyard several times the size of the European cemetery, it was hugely out of proportion to a town the size of Swakopmund.[2] Another South African soldier, the medical officer Dr Henry Walker, also happened upon the desert graveyard in early 1915. In *A Doctor's Diary in Damaraland*, Walker's war memoirs, he recalled his confusion as to why so many bodies, presumably those of 'natives', lay interred on the fringes of such a small town:

> Beyond the European cemetery is what is said to be the native burial-place. Rows and rows of little heaps of sand occupy about a thousand yards of desert. Some of these heaps have crude little crosses of sticks placed on them. It was very puzzling to explain why so many natives were buried near Swakopmund, in a place that was not even enclosed.[3]

The thousands of 'little heaps of sand' in Swakopmund's desert graveyard, the last resting places of the thousands of Herero who had died in the town's concentration camps, are still clearly visible today. Eroded by the wind and constantly shifting sands, they are less pronounced than they were in 1914, when Lieutenant Ritchie and Dr Walker encountered them, yet almost a century later the graveyard remains a shocking sight. Its scale is only truly apparent from the air, or on summer evenings when the low southern sun casts long shadows that pick out each individual grave. Swakopmund's graveyard, like the history of Shark Island or the Extermination Order, is well known to locals, and yet for a century the graveyard has been the town's unspoken secret. It is now sealed off from Swakopmund by a row of expensive modern villas, and many of the graves have been almost obliterated by the tyres of dune-buggies rented to tourists who used the graveyard as part of their desert race track. In 2007 a low wall was built to enclose the graves, and a plaque erected by Namibia's Herero community marks the site.

Thirty years to the month after the Conference of Berlin had ratified Germany's claim to South-West Africa, the South Africans finally started their advance across the Namib and Kalahari deserts. The South-West African campaign lasted just five months. As the main German settlements were captured one by one by the South Africans, the true horror of the fate that had befallen the Herero and Nama began to come to light. When South African units fighting in the north captured the fertile central plateau, they discovered a land largely depopulated and filled with horrific stories of recent events. In early May 1915, Dr Walker, the medic who had discovered the Swakopmund graveyard, arrived in the town of Otjimbingwe, in the wake of the fleeing *Schutztruppe*. Walker was struck by the profound fear that the German settlers felt at the prospect of life without the protection of their troops. 'Here, as elsewhere,' he noted, 'the

German farmer and villager are living in constant dread of natives, both Hottentot and Herero; and if an evil conscience makes people afraid, they have every reason to be so.' Walker, who was by now beginning to piece together the story of the Herero and Nama genocides, had come to understand why the German farmers feared retribution, and had grasped the relationship between the Swakopmund graveyard and the strikingly low numbers of Herero and Nama remaining in the colony. The German settlers of Otjimbingwe, Walker reported, are

> reticent as to what has become of the natives in these parts, for although a large Herero reserve is shown on the map, none are to be seen except a few . . . servant-girls, all very subdued and tame, and given to the singing of German hymns. Ugly rumour has it that most of them were driven into the desert to die of hunger or thirst.[4]

On 5 May 1915, after marching uncontested into the town of Karibib, the South Africans uncovered the most shocking evidence of the recent genocides. Not far from Karibib, advancing South African units came across the stables and supply station at Okawayo. There they discovered the last survivors of the Shark Island concentration camp, still interned six years after the camp had been closed down.

In 1909 the *Etappenkommando*, the rear supply division of the *Schutztruppe* under the command of Major Ludwig Maercker, had reported that 240 Nama prisoners remained alive at Okawayo. Most of them were Witbooi or Bethanie Nama. The South Africans failed to record how many were still alive in 1915, but among the survivors was Samuel Izaak, the leader of the Witbooi Nama. A decade after he had surrendered to the Germans on his own terms, Izaak was finally released. The Nama from Okawayo were eventually returned to their former hometowns of Bethanie and Gibeon, where the few who remained subsisted as landless labourers on German farms built on their tribal lands. Samuel Izaak was fifty-nine years old and terminally ill when the South Africans arrived. He died in June before reaching his hometown, Gibeon. Okawayo was later converted by the South Africans into an internment camp for captured *Schutztruppe* officers.

A week after the South Africans had reached Okawayo, General Botha's troops marched into Windhoek and by the beginning of July, the bulk of Major Franke's *Schutztruppe* had been forced into an area of scrub around Otavi and Tsumeb, two mining settlements in the north. After an indecisive encounter with South African units, Franke rather meekly surrendered. The next day, Governor Theodor Seitz, who just two years earlier had assured the crowds at the inauguration of the *Rider Statue* that the Germans would be 'the masters of this place, now and for ever', issued an order of surrender.

On 21 October 1915 German South-West Africa became the British Protectorate of South-West Africa, and a week later the Union army general, E. Howard Gorges, was appointed its first administrator. With the *Schutztruppe* defeated, General Botha's policy for the occupation of South-West Africa was to maintain 'the standing of the white race'.[5] The relationship between whites and the African majority was one of the many aspects of German colonial rule that remained almost untouched by the transfer of power from Berlin to Pretoria. Hence the surrender terms agreed between General Botha and Governor Sietz were unusually generous: German civilian administrators were permitted to remain in their posts, German schools were reopened, and men who had served as reservists were allowed to return to their homes and farms and carry on with their businesses. Only the *Schutztruppe* themselves were interned as prisoners of war.

The Herero and Nama who had survived the genocide revelled in the defeat of the Germans and had done everything in their power to assist the advance of the Union forces, but few believed that the South Africans would liberate them, restore their rights or return their homelands. The Herero, and even more so the

Nama, were well aware of the dire treatment of black Africans south of the Orange River. They did, however, hope that the end of German rule might usher in a more lenient administration in which they might regain a little of their cultural (if not economic) independence.

The South Africans, who just four years earlier had passed the Native Land Act, the foundation stone on which the Apartheid system was later to rest, had no interest in seeing the recent history of the colony reversed. There were those, however, in both Cape Town and London, who saw enormous benefits in having that history publicly exhumed.

In the aftermath of the German surrender, General Botha ordered the seizure and translation of all official German documents. Although the *Schutztruppe* had had the foresight to burn their own archives, the records of the central colonial administration in Windhoek and the files of several District Government Offices had been seized intact. As the South African garrison in Windhoek set up camp on the site of the former concentration camp, beneath the shadow of the *Rider Statue*, the mammoth task of translating three decades' worth of documents began. Through this process, the first detailed history of the Herero and Nama genocides began to emerge.

Even before the South African victory, the British press had tried to rekindle memories of the 'miserable war of extermination' the Germans had fought against the Herero. The final German surrender inspired a new intensity in this propaganda campaign. On 10 July 1915 *The Times* ran an article under the headline 'German Frightfulness' that reminded its readers that the war against the Herero had tarnished Germany as with 'lasting disgrace'.[6]

The subtext behind these condemnations was the hope that evidence of 'German Frightfulness' might ultimately be used to prepare a case for the confiscation of South-West Africa, and possibly all of Germany's colonies. Just over a week after the article appeared in *The Times*, Andrew Bonar Law, the British Colonial Secretary, pompously declared in the House of Commons that 'Nothing has done more to make the African natives appreciate the value of British rule than the experience they have had of German rule in Africa.'[7] Of the eleven Members of Parliament who spoke in the Commons alongside Bonar Law in the July 1915 debate on the German colonies, seven openly advocated annexation; four had no practical suggestions on the matter. None were opposed.

It was not until America entered the war in the spring of 1917, and the prospect of a final victory over Germany re-emerged, that the British and South Africans felt able to focus their attention on the fate of her former colonial possessions. On 28 April 1917, just three weeks after President Woodrow Wilson issued his declaration of war, the British Imperial War Cabinet met to discuss the matter of the German colonies. The meeting brought together General Botha, Jan Smuts and John X. Merriman, who officially concluded that South Africa would do all in her power to ensure that South-West Africa was not returned to Germany in the following peace settlement.[8]

The cataloguing and publicising of the atrocities committed in the German colony would be, in Merriman's phrase, the 'strong point' of a case for permanent confiscation. Compelling evidence of German colonial atrocities was needed, not only to condemn Germany, but to unify the Allies behind the Anglo-South Africa policy. Evidence of 'German Frightfulness', it was argued, might prove particularly valuable in convincing anti-imperialists in the American public that the confiscation of German colonies was not merely a pretext for the expansion of the British Empire.

British and South African condemnation of Germany's treatment of the Herero and Nama in 1917 was belated and disingenuous. Britain's own record of colonial and even genocidal violence laid her open to charges of hypocrisy. Moreover, during the Herero and Nama wars the British government had raised no official objections to Germany's treatment of her imperial subjects. Even when warned by their own military attaché, Colonel Trench, of the Germans' intentions to exterminate the Nama on Shark Island, London had lodged no complaints.

Britain's humanitarians had focused only a fraction of their energy on the crimes committed in South-West Africa under the Germans. They had reserved their most vocal denunciations for the Belgians and Portuguese, whom they regarded as the most cruel and inhumane of the colonial powers. The British press had similarly failed to fault German policy in South-West Africa. Throughout the Herero and Nama wars British newspapers had vacillated between their general enthusiasm for the great white colonial mission, and a barely disguised tone of condescension at the ineptitude and inexperience of the Germans. While they had dutifully reported the deaths of whites, they had often overlooked the killings and even massacres of Africans. When it had suited their purposes, they had lionised figures like Curt von François.

In the Cape Colony, the *Cape Argus* newspaper had repeatedly reported the German treatment of Herero and Nama prisoners in the concentration camps. Yet the Cape government had lodged no official complaints nor investigated claims that just across its border a system of concentration camps was in operation. On occasion, the South Africans had actively assisted the Germans. It was South African soldiers who finally captured and executed the Nama guerrilla leader Jacob Morenga, inside the Cape Colony in September 1907.

There can be little doubt that in September 1917, when the South Africans commissioned an official investigation into the treatment of the Herero and Nama under German rule, they were motivated primarily (perhaps exclusively) by self-interest and opportunism. Yet the investigation and the resulting report were characterised by a remarkable dedication to factual precision. Howard Gorges, John X. Merriman, Louis Botha and Jan Smuts were all astute enough to realise that their report needed to reflect recent events accurately, as any exaggerations or fabrications would be easily discredited by the German government and press. But the South Africans, who by this time had processed and translated thousands of captured German documents, also understood that Germany's crimes against the Herero and Nama had been so terrible that there was no need for exaggeration.

The officer commissioned to run the investigation was Major Thomas Leslie O'Reilly, of whom surprisingly little is known. He was a lawyer by profession, and an officer in the reserve of the Active Citizen Force. The records indicate he had joined General Botha's army just before the push inland from Swakopmund in February 1915, but after the German surrender, he had returned to South Africa on a year-long leave of absence. In 1916 he came back to South-West Africa and was appointed magistrate of the town of Omaruru in western Hereroland. There he encountered a Herero community who were not only willing to recount the story of their recent persecution, but who lived, even in 1917, under the lash of the local farmers whose taste for casual violence continued long after the surrender of the *Schutztruppe*. Having served on the Special Criminal Court, O'Reilly had adjudicated in cases of maltreatment and even murder of Africans by their German and Boer employers. In September 1917, when O'Reilly received a telegram from Howard Gorges asking if he would be interested in drafting a report on German abuses, he replied, 'I am as keen as mustard on it – I have been doing quite a lot of graft locally in that direction and even if they [Pretoria] change their minds, I intend going into the matter privately . . . It is quite enough to make one's hair stiffen.'[9]

He was given just three months to carry out his research and produce an initial draft of the report. The completed draft would then be submitted to the Administrator's Office in Windhoek and edited by Howard Gorges, before finally being published as a 'Blue Book', the term given to all British Parliamentary Reports. The foundation for much of O'Reilly's work was the mountain of translated German documents that had been assembled in Windhoek. They included orders and letters drafted by

Curt von François, the very first 'protection treaties' bearing the signature of Heinrich Göring, and the papers of Theodor Leutwein, General von Trotha and Friedrich von Lindequist. In addition to the captured documents, O'Reilly punctuated his report with passages written by the former Commissioner for Settlement in South-West Africa, now political journalist, Dr Paul Rohrbach.

The completed report made dramatic use of photographic evidence. Photographs of the lynching and hangings of Herero men, originally taken by German settlers and soldiers as souvenirs of the war, were collected as evidence. Many of the most horrific were reproduced in a special appendix to the Blue Book. Even the implements of what had been called 'paternal chastisement' – the beatings and corporal punishment meted out to the Africans – were catalogued and photographed. Leg irons, manacles, handcuffs and whips were all carefully numbered and annotations added, listing their various purposes and the intensity of physical pain each device was capable of inducing.

The aspect of O'Reilly's work that makes the Blue Book an almost unique document was the gathering of sworn statements. After the German surrender in 1915, hundreds of Herero and Nama had returned from exile in the Owambo Kingdoms, Angola and Bechuanaland. This allowed O'Reilly the opportunity to locate survivors whose collective experience covered every aspect of German rule. His interviewees included Herero who had been pushed into the Omaheke after the battle of the Waterberg and people who had evaded the Cleansing Patrols, as well as prisoners from the concentration camps. He also spoke to members of the Nama tribes who, as former allies of the *Schutztruppe*, had witnessed the atrocities they had committed against the Herero at the Waterberg and its aftermath. Other Nama were able to give accounts of their own persecution following Hendrik Witbooi's failed rebellion. The first of these interviews was conducted among members of the Herero community at Omaruru, where O'Reilly was based and well respected.

The way the Blue Book deployed the testimony of living

witnesses and the rigour with which O'Reilly appropriated the German documents foreshadowed the preparations for the case for the prosecution at the Nuremberg Trials thirty years later. In the history of colonialism in Africa, however, the Blue Book stands almost entirely alone as a reliable and comprehensive exploration of the disinheritance and destruction of indigenous peoples.

15

'To Fight the World for Ever'

While America's entry into the war in 1917 had emboldened the British and South Africans to prepare their case against German colonialism in Africa, equally seismic events on the Eastern Front persuaded the German High Command that it was they who would win and they who would dictate the peace terms. With both Germany and the Western Allies committed to their own contradictory visions of the future, diplomats in Berlin, London and Pretoria spent the last few months of the war redrafting the borders, and parcelling out the land and peoples of their own imagined Africas. While Major O'Reilly's Blue Book was being edited by Howard Gorges and debated by the leaders of Britain and South Africa, thousands of miles away in the offices of the German Colonial Department, far more radical plans for the long-term exploitation of Germany's African empire were being readied and refined.

The shift in Germany's fortunes that convinced millions of her citizens and soldiers that victory would finally be theirs began in the summer of 1917. When Russia's last great offensive collapsed, the Bolsheviks took power in St Petersburg. Lenin called for the socialisation of the country and an armistice with Germany. Russia's peasant soldiers responded by abandoning the trenches and literally walking home. Under the Treaty of Brest-Litovsk, Russia lost over a quarter of her population, almost 90 percent of her coal reserves and a third of her agricultural output. The Germans and their allies became the overlords of an area three times the size of the Reich itself.

The Western Allies were stunned by the terms of the Brest-Litovsk Treaty. Both the French and British governments looked on in horror at the strength Germany could draw from the enormous empire she had forged in the East. An official at the British Foreign Office feared the conquered territories might revive Germany, mollify the effects of the naval blockade and allow her 'to fight the world for ever and be unconquerable'.

To the German High Command, the immediate significance of Brest-Litovsk and the defeat of the Russians was that it tipped the scales of military power dramatically in Germany's favour. In order to secure her position as master of the East and force the Allies to return her colonies, the generals committed themselves to one final offensive that would defeat the French and British before the United States was able to bring her almost limitless military and industrial might into play on the Western Front.

Over the winter of 1917–18, the German divisions released from the Eastern Front – fifty in total – were ferried across Germany with thousands of artillery pieces, machine-guns and all the paraphernalia of industrial warfare. Like an enormous blood transfusion, the eastern divisions revived the army on the Western Front. The great Spring Offensive of 1918 was launched in the early hours of 21 March. The bombardment that heralded the attack was the most destructive in history, greater even than the titanic artillery duels fought between the armies of Hitler and Stalin a quarter of a century later. A million shells were assembled for a bombardment lasting just five hours. Whole British and French battalions were obliterated. Men were atomised in a maelstrom of shells, others spluttered to their deaths in clouds of lachrymatory, chlorine and phosgene gas. In the wake of the bombardment, through the smoke, gas and early morning spring fog, came the gas-masked storm troopers, the spearhead of a German force seventy-six divisions strong. On a front 50 miles wide they pushed the British Fifth Army aside and by the end of the first day they had burst through into open country.

The speed with which the storm troopers raced through the British lines, towards the old battlefield of the Somme, was rivalled only by the pace at which the German High Command and civilian leadership embraced the prospect of imminent victory. Buoyed up on a wave of jubilation, the Kaiser awarded the children of Germany a 'Victory Day' holiday and informed his entourage that should 'a British parliamentarian come to sue for peace, he must kneel before the imperial standard, for this is a victory of monarchy over democracy'.[1]

In March and April 1918, a German scheme for the annexation of territory in Africa, originally drafted in the first weeks of the war, was revived. In August 1914, the Foreign Secretary, Gottlieb von Jagow, had invited Wilhelm Solf, Secretary of the Colonial Department, to draft formal proposals for the expansion of Germany's empire in Africa. Solf, the former Governor of German Samoa and successor to Friedrich von Lindequist at the Colonial Department, duly submitted a memorandum complete with annotated maps. He proposed an adapted version of an old plan put forward at various times by colonialist movements and advocates for the creation of *Mittelafrika* – an enormous 'German Central African Empire' spanning the entire width of the continent, linking Germany's four pre-war colonies. At its centre was the Congo, a region that Belgium would be forced to surrender. The Congo was to be linked to German South-West Africa by the annexation of the Portuguese colony of Angola. While Portugal and Belgium were to be entirely ejected from the continent, the British and French would be permitted some minor role in the post-war exploitation of Africa, a continent that Germany was to dominate.

By 1918 the only land on the African continent still occupied by Germany was that under the feet of Paul von Lettow-Vorbeck and his ragtag army of Askaris. Yet the loss of her colonies had done little to dim calls for the establishment of *Mittelafrika*. Throughout the war, the colonial societies, the Pan-Germans and a host of other right-wing nationalist movements and intellectuals had maintained a constant clamour for colonial expansion in Africa. Six days after the launch of the Spring Offensive, Wilhelm Solf received a letter from a German industrialist that perfectly captures how the mirage of impending victory on the Western Front breathed new life into even the most radical of Germany's colonial war aims:

> In all human expectation our troops will be occupying the French channel ports in the next few weeks and will, it is hoped, stay there for ever. Therewith the final hour of England's world power and England's world empire will have struck. In the course of the centuries North America and Australia were Anglicised, South America Latinised. The time is at hand when Germany will be granted the power to Germanise virgin Africa.[2]

Solf became swept up by events, instructing officials in the Colonial Department to determine, in discussion with their colleagues in the Naval Office, where Germany might site naval bases and coaling stations to defend *Mittelafrika*. For advice they turned to representatives of the Woermann Shipping Line, whose predecessors had advised Bismarck which stretches of the African coastline might be claimed as German protectorates back in 1884. Together the navy, civilian government and private business speculated, as if composing a shopping list, over the suitability of the continent's various anchorages. While Solf favoured the annexation of the British port of Bathurst in the Gambia, the more military-minded thought Dakar in French Senegal would be easier to defend.

German colonial ambitions in the last months of the war were not limited to Africa. In 1915 those whose paramount concern was the annexation of enemy territory had turned their gaze away from Africa and towards the one arena of the war in which the army had been capable of making spectacular advances. In the same months that the *Schutztruppe* of Major Franke had retreated across the Namib Desert, the German armies on the Eastern Front, under the dual command of Generals Paul von Hindenburg and Erich Ludendorff, had battled their way across the expanses of western Russia in one of the most successful offensives of the whole war.

The 'Great Advance' of 1915 had driven the Russian frontline back by 250 miles and captured Congress Poland, the Baltic and much of European Russia, an area about equal in size and scope to that seized by the Nazis in 1941. This dramatic success allowed Germany to take control of the region's industrial resources and redirect her harvests towards Berlin and away from Moscow. It also presented her with an opportunity to realise a colonial fantasy of living space in the East that had existed side by side with her colonial aspirations in Africa since the last decades of the nineteenth century.

Over the course of the occupation, parts of the European East came to be seen by the occupiers as a *terra nullius*, an empty space under-cultivated and under-utilised by a people who had neither the technology nor the drive to shape the land to their will. One soldier described the East as 'a colonial land, which lies unexplored before its owner'.[3] Some in the army and among the nationalist right suggested that Germany had a 'mission in the East' to reshape the landscape, and to uplift the Slavic and Jewish peoples of the region by exposing them to the benefits of German *Kultur* and the fruits of German industry.

By 1917, new possibilities in the East had emerged. German officers, like the *Schutztruppe* of South-West Africa, began to imagine that they might never leave. They dreamed of land and farms, of possibilities as limitless as the landscape itself. General von Ludendorff spoke of the East as space in which the veterans of his army might become soldier-farmers, pioneers on the eastern fringes of German *Kultur*. Following an advance in the Crimea in 1917, Ludendorff began to discuss the possibility of creating permanent colonies for ethnic Germans there. The man tasked with devising the initial plans for the establishment of large-scale German colonies in the Ukraine was Friedrich von Lindequist, now retired from the Colonial Department.[4]

German settlement in Eastern Europe was imagined as a task that would follow Germany's final victory. However, the short-term needs of 'total war' – and the German army's propensity for bureaucratic cruelty and inhumane treatment – contradicted the nation's long-term and more paternal aspirations. The forced-labour regimes they instituted were brutal and poorly managed.

The army introduced a ludicrous number of rules and regulations. Punishments for even minor infractions were excessive, exemplary and often collective. Most damaging of all, the requisitioning of food left whole communities malnourished.

Yet for all its brutality, the German occupation of Eastern Europe during World War I is striking in how little it resembles German military policy in South-West Africa or Nazi occupation of Eastern Europe in the 1940s. The *Ostjuden*, the Eastern Jews who were the main translators for Ludendorff's army, were the same communities who were systematically murdered in their villages and town squares by the Nazi *Einzatzgruppen* twenty-six years later. Between 1915 and 1918, there was talk among the Germans in the East of settlement and colonisation but not of 'dying races' or concentration camps.

The euphoria that followed the initial successes of the 1918 Spring Offensive lingered far longer in Berlin and Potsdam than at the front. Just two weeks after the initial assault, the offensive had ground to a halt. A second attack, Operation George, was launched to maintain forward momentum. This too failed. The most famous casualty of Operation George was Manfred von Richthofen, the Red Baron, whose death opened the way for the young Hermann Göring to succeed him as leader of the famous 'Flying Circus' Squadron. A third offensive took the German army back to the River Marne where they had their first bruising encounter with the Americans, 318,000 of whom were now available for action. A million more were in training or crossing the Atlantic. A fourth attack pushed the Germans further towards Paris, a fifth took them across the Marne itself, and brought the French capital within the range of a special long-range Howitzer that crashed shells down on the terrified populace. But on the night of 18 July the Germans were halted and the tide of the war turned decisively and permanently against them. Within a month Bulgaria, Turkey and Austria-Hungary, one by one, fell out of the war.

As Germany's armies disintegrated and von Ludendorff lost his grip on the lands in the East that his army had held for three years, the British and South African propaganda campaign to seize her empire in Africa reached its climax. In early September 1918 *The Times* reported the publication of Thomas O'Reilly's Blue Book, claiming it would place 'before the world the ripe fruits of German "militarism Kultur" and "enable mankind to judge, on German official evidence, the claim of Germany to the restoration of her colonies" '.

In his memoirs, the British Prime Minister Lloyd George admitted that, had Germany agreed to peace in January 1917 rather than been defeated in November 1918, the British would not have sought the confiscation of even 'one of her overseas possessions'. As it was, in 1918 and at the Paris Peace Conference of 1919 the British and South Africans maintained a stream of propaganda, much of it focusing on Germany's mistreatment of the 'natives' in her colonies. They were careful to differentiate between the sorts of crimes committed in German South-West Africa and atrocities visited on the people of Africa in their own colonial histories, arguing that the extermination of the Herero had been executed according to a German plan. This, *The Times* believed, marked it out 'from the offences committed against natives which no care can altogether prevent'.[5]

Despite the blatant hypocrisy, the way in which the memory of the Herero genocide (the extermination of the Nama was almost completely ignored by the British press) became the focus of enormous attention in 1918–19 was truly remarkable. Not only was a colonial war acknowledged as an atrocity, the voices of its victims appeared in European and American newspapers and their testimonies were presented to the leaders of the world's thirty most powerful nations, as they gathered for the Paris Peace Conference of 1919.

The Paris Peace Conference took place in the Hall of Mirrors of the French Royal Palace of Versailles. There, forty-eight years earlier, with the Prussian army occupying Paris following their victory in the Franco-Prussian War, King Wilhelm I of Prussia had been pronounced the first Kaiser of Germany and the Second Reich had been born. By January 1919, the third and final German Kaiser was an exile in Holland and the Second Reich had collapsed under the weight of defeat, revolution and ultimately civil war. Germany remained, however, a nominal colonial power.

The case for the confiscation of German South-West Africa was prepared and coordinated by General Botha and Jan Smuts. In 1917 Smuts had become a member of the British War Cabinet, and his ideas for future world cooperation had grabbed the attention of American President Woodrow Wilson. The South-West African case was the centrepiece of a wider effort to convince Wilson, who was opposed to 'an annexationist peace', that all of Germany's colonies should be placed under the administration of the victorious powers.

During the Berlin Conference of 1884–5, at which Africa had been notionally carved up by the European powers, not a single African had been present. When the German portions of the continent were redistributed at Versailles, there were at least a handful of black faces. Blaise Diagne, the Senegalese deputy of the French Parliament, the man who had inspired so many francophone Africans to fight for France in the trenches, attended the conference, as did W. E. B. Dubois, the black American Pan-Africanist. There was also a delegation from the African National Congress, seeking to draw attention to South Africa's mistreatment of its own black populations, just six years after the passing of the infamous Native Land Act. However, there were no representatives of the Herero or Nama – the views of the 'natives' of Germany's colonies were presented to the conference second-hand, by missionaries and colonial 'experts'. Major Thomas O'Reilly was not there either. After completing the Blue Book, he had set himself up in legal practice, but quickly fell ill. He died in Cape Town in September 1919, exactly two years after he had accepted the commission to write the Blue Book, a victim of the Spanish Flu pandemic that claimed tens of millions of lives between 1918 and 1920.

The testimony held within the Blue Book was therefore particularly valuable. It allowed Hendrik Witbooi and others to speak from the grave, directly to those in whose hands the futures of their peoples rested. Yet what is most remarkable about the Blue Book and the propaganda barrage that supported it was that, in both the press and at the conference itself, the atrocities committed in South-West Africa were openly compared to those the German army had committed in Europe.

In 1914, during their advance through Belgium, the German army had reacted to supposed attacks by snipers and resistance fighters with a ferocity that had genuinely shocked Europe. The town of Louvain had been razed to the ground and over six thousand Belgian civilians had been murdered in a series of orchestrated mass executions and random killings, ignoring the distinction between combatants and civilians that Europeans imagined was the hallmark of civilised warfare. At the time the *Kölnische Zeitung* had falsely claimed that Belgian civilians had tortured wounded German soldiers and mutilated the bodies of their fallen comrades. The *Kölnische Zeitung* had exhaustively reported the Herero and Nama wars a decade earlier and considered the Belgian atrocities akin to those perpetrated by the 'Negroes in South-West Africa'.[6]

An investigation into the 'rape of Belgium' by the Germans in 1914 had been initiated by the Allies during the war and another Blue Book produced. This was distributed at Versailles alongside the South-West African report. Although both British and French propaganda energetically exploited the German atrocities in Belgium (and indeed those committed against the population of the occupied regions of northern France) for their own interests, they had not fabricated the events outlined in the report. The outrage felt across Europe and in America at the massacres at Liège and destruction of Louvain – described by the *Daily Mail* as the 'Holocaust of Louvain' – was genuine.[7]

In 1919, the genocides committed against the Herero and Nama were set alongside the massacres of Belgian civilians. At

Versailles, if only momentarily, the lives of black Africans were regarded as comparable to those of white Europeans.

As the history of German brutality in South-West Africa was unveiled, the massacres in the Omaheke and the mass deaths in the German concentration camps came to be seen as having anticipated the devastation of Louvain and the mass executions of Belgian civilians. Both events, taken together, were proof that the 'civilised world', united in victory, was duty bound to shackle the monster of German 'militarism'. An editorial in *The Times* of September 1918 stated:

> It had been widely supposed that in the oppression of Belgium the German capacity for wickedness had reached its limit. That was a foolish delusion. The inhuman outrages committed in Europe are insignificant compared to the savage abominations which were the foundation of German rule in Africa. Here we see the 'blonde beast' untrammelled. Here he gluts his appetite for blood, for plunder and for his bestial lusts.[8]

By the time Lloyd George opened the debate on the future of the German colonies at Versailles on 24 January 1919, the extermination of the Herero and Nama had been dragged from the shadows of colonial history and presented to a world audience. The South-West African genocides were as infamous in 1919 as they are forgotten today.

When the issue of the German colonies was debated by the presiding 'Council of Ten', Lloyd George almost immediately raised the policy of extermination the Germans had pursued in South-West Africa.[9] While President Wilson remained deeply suspicious of British imperialism, he needed little persuasion as to the nature of German colonial rule and, in the first debate, he agreed that the colonies should not be returned to Germany under any circumstances. Although at one point wrangling over the final status of South-West Africa threatened to derail the conference, the colony was finally declared a 'Class C Mandate' and placed under the control of the Union of South Africa. Each of Germany's other colonies in Africa and Asia were similarly assigned as mandates and distributed among the other victorious powers.

On Valentine's Day 1919 President Wilson gave a speech that suggested how much his views on Germany's colonial empire had been shaped by what the world had learned of events in South-West Africa. Announcing his intention to preside over a final reckoning with Germany, Wilson remarked:

> It has been one of the many distressing revelations of recent years that the great Power which has just been happily defeated put intolerable burdens and injustices upon the helpless people of some of the colonies which it annexed to itself; that its interest was rather their extermination than their development . . . Now, the world, expressing its conscience in law, says there is an end of that.[10]

16

A Passing Corporal

Germany's reckoning began the moment her armies returned. The force that most Germans had earnestly believed would be home for the Christmas of 1914 stumbled across the Rhine for the meagre festivities of 1918. They streamed home in their millions, from the blackened wastelands of the Western Front, and later from the lost empire in the East. The nation's roads became rivers of grey and steel as endless columns of soldiers fanned out across the nation, heading home. In Berlin, as they passed through the specially decorated arches of the Brandenburg Gate and beneath the thin wintry trees of Unter Den Linden, large crowds gathered to cheer. Even in defeat Germany's army, once the mightiest in Europe, looked nothing like a vanquished force. But the Germany they marched through in November and December 1918 bore only a vague resemblance to the dynamic, jubilant state that had waved them off to war four years earlier.

The unprecedented and unnatural effort of total war, particularly during the last two years, had taken an appalling toll. Germany was exhausted, shabby, run-down and, above all, hungry. In proud defiance of the Allied blockade, the wealthier classes had attempted to maintain some semblance of normality in their everyday lives; but it was paper-thin. The elegantly dressed gentlemen of Berlin still made an ostentatious show of smoking, but by 1918 their cigars were made from cabbage leaves and potato skins. They still drank coffee on café terraces, but it was brewed from acorns, the milk in it a watery imitation of the real thing.[1] The word *ersatz* (substitute) had taken on a new and central position within the wartime lexicon of the home front.

For the poor – the bulk of the people – war and hunger had become synonymous. There was no famine, as such, in Germany, but by November 1918 millions were suffering from the effects of long-term malnutrition. For a quarter of a million German civilians, the cost of total war had been total.[2] While politicians of the far right had delivered speeches demanding annexations and colonial expansion, the poor had rioted in the streets demanding nothing more than bread. These recent traumas were etched on the faces of the crowds who gathered to cheer, as best they could, the returning German army of 1918. Those civilians, who had witnessed the gradual collapse of morale, health and calorific intake, had slowly become accustomed to the appearance and feel of this new Reich. The returning soldiers, some of whom had hardly seen their nation during the war years, were profoundly shocked.

The troops were, in a way, refugees from another land. The fronts themselves had become almost a different country, a subterranean state of dugouts, ditches and trenches stretching for hundreds of miles across the continent. The soldiers who flooded back into Germany in 1918 found themselves abruptly ejected from the only adult existence many had known. Suddenly they were free of the inscrutable logic of survival, and the discipline and fanatical camaraderie of their units. Most worryingly for Germany, they were also bitterly divided.

Even before the final defeat, the German army had begun to come apart at the seams. Each stalled offensive and each broken promise had widened the gulf between officers and men, but by 1918 the critical division was between those who still believed in the war and their comrades who considered the whole thing to have been an enormous swindle. During the bleak, tense winter of 1918–19, demobilised soldiers began to take their places on the barricades and in the death squads of both the left and right. Some were genuinely dedicated to Communism or its demise, others were merely addicted to fighting. The army that left the trenches as brothers-in-arms were quick to turn their guns on one another, as Germany toppled into anarchy, revolution and counter-revolution. By the end of the year, talk of grand annexations in the East and the creation of a vast empire in Africa seemed to belong to another world.

No city was more ravaged by the German revolution of 1918–19 than Munich. It was there that the disintegration of the Second Reich began and from there that the Third Reich later emerged. The birth of the early Nazi movement in Munich is a story that brings together the movements and societies of Germany's *Völkisch* right wing – the very men who had campaigned most vociferously for her colonial empire – and the soldiers who had fought in those now occupied colonies. These two groups played critical roles in making Munich in the early 1920s a sanctuary for ultra-nationalist, anti-republican, anti-Marxist and anti-Semitic extremists.

The city's slide into chaos began on 7 November, four days before the Armistice. That day, a crowd eighty thousand strong took to the streets and effectively brought down the government of Bavaria, the German state of which Munich is the capital. The crowd raided the city's barracks, brushed aside the exhausted garrison and distributed hundreds of rifles to the workers and former soldiers turned revolutionaries. Congregating in the Theresienwiese, Munich's great public square, the jubilant masses found themselves a leader. Kurt Eisner was a Jewish poet and a socialist intellectual from Berlin, who had only just been released from prison. Still dishevelled, he stood before the enormous crowd and demanded the creation of a new Bavaria run by the people. That evening King Ludwig III of the ancient Wittelsbach dynasty, rulers of Bavaria since the fourteenth century, fled his palace never to return. The next day, the people of Munich woke to discover they were citizens of a new state, 'The Democratic and Social Republic of Bavaria'.

Just a week after the Kaiser's abdication, Kurt Eisner and his flimsy administration gathered in Munich's National Theatre to celebrate their revolution and proclaim the birth of their new and idealistic nation. Eisner spoke of justice and brotherhood and of making Munich an example to the whole world. Yet as the strains of Handel's *Messiah* rang out across Munich, in the half-light of the city's beer halls the forces of the right were planning the destruction of Eisner and the new Bavarian government.

Munich's right wing was numerous, fanatical and well funded. The city had long been at the forefront of *Völkisch* and nationalist politics. During the war years, the Pan-Germanic League and an array of smaller movements had worked hard in Bavaria to whip up support for annexation in the East and the creation of a German *Mittelafrika*. In the last desperate months of the conflict, their calls for harsher annexations and ever-larger swathes of Africa had grown louder and more fevered.

The movement had grown so large in Bavaria before the war that the league's national leaders had decided that the organisation's annual meetings were to be held in Munich. One of the driving forces behind the success of Pan-Germanism in the city was the wealthy publisher Julius Lehman, a founder member and a powerful financial backer. The Lehman family were owners of a leading publishing house, Lehmans Verlag, and under Julius Lehman's leadership they had come to specialise in the production of medical textbooks. Lehman also used his press to produce pamphlets for the Pan-Germanic cause and propaganda for various colonialist, racist or expansionist policies. In early 1918, he had been behind a war fund aiming to raise money to 'strengthen Germandom on our language borders and abroad, to support German settlers, students, libraries and economic enterprises, and [to help establish] colonies throughout the world'.[3]

As well as a passionate advocate of German imperialism, Julius Lehman was a fanatical believer in eugenics and a member of Alfred Ploetz's German Society for Racial Hygiene. Lehmans Verlag published Ploetz's eugenics journal, *Archiv für Rassen- und Gesellschaftsbiologie*, as well as an array of other race hygiene titles. At one point Lehman had even attempted to persuade Houston Stewart Chamberlain, the 'high priest of Aryan supremacy', to publish through Lehmans Verlag.[4]

Sometime in 1918, Julius Lehman became deeply involved in another of Munich's ultra right-wing societies, the Thule-Gesellschaft (Thule Society). Founded by a fraudster named Adam Glauer, who had renamed himself Freiherr von Sebottendorff, it was ostensibly a gentlemen's club for the study of Germanic culture and antiquity. Its small membership was drawn from Munich's elite: university professors, the aristocracy, the judiciary and wealthy business interests. Well heeled and influential, they held their meetings within a private suite of rooms in Munich's Four Seasons Hotel. These chambers had been specially decorated with symbols and runes drawn from the occult world of Aryan mysticism; one of those symbols was the swastika. At some point in 1918 the society's members adopted the greeting *Heil*. However, the members of the Thule Society were not primarily motivated by Aryan mysticism. These hard-headed men were much more interested in using their wealth and influence to promote the traditional policies of the *Völkisch* far right – the spread of German power and settlers beyond the Reich's borders and the maintenance of racial purity within. In July 1918, in an effort to spread this message beyond their exclusive membership, they purchased a Munich newspaper, the *Münchener Beobachter* (Munich Observer).

In November 1918 the members of the Thule Society, like most Munichers, were stunned by the speed and ease with which Kurt Eisner's socialist government took charge of their city and the Germany of the Kaisers disintegrated. Within forty-eight hours, the Second Reich and most of its institutions had simply ceased to exist. On 10 November, the day before the Armistice, Julius Lehman proposed that the Thule Society found an armed wing of the movement, the Kampfbund Thule (Fighting Thule League). With links to high-level commanders in the army sympathetic to their cause, Lehman and his co-conspirators quickly amassed a stockpile of weapons which they hid in his offices. Among those who followed Lehman into the Kampfbund Thule were several men destined to become powerful figures in the Nazi party. They included Alfred Rossenberg, the 'Philosopher' of National Socialism, and Hans Frank, the murderous governor of occupied Poland – both were to be hanged at Nuremberg. The most famous member of Kampfbund Thule, however, was Rudolf Hess, Hitler's deputy.

Despite all their careful preparations, Lehman's plot was uncovered, and when the stash of rifles was discovered, Lehman was arrested and imprisoned. Despite this setback, the Thule Society played a part in the destruction of Eisner's new republic, but in a way no one had imagined.

In early 1919, with the Kampfbund Thule in ruins, a young cavalry officer applied to join the Thule Society. Like all prospective members, Count Anton von Arco-Valley was asked to prove that he was of pure Germanic racial stock. When it was revealed that, despite his aristocratic title and dashing appearance, von Arco-Valley was half Jewish, he was immediately barred. Infuriated by this rejection, embittered by the loss of his status, rank and insignia at the hands of the socialist state, he set out to prove himself.[5] With one direct and surgical blow, he would confront his enemies on the left, and demonstrate to his detractors on the right that his dedication to German nationalism was unwavering – despite his Jewish blood.

On the morning of 21 February 1919 the young count loitered in a doorway near the offices of Kurt Eisner. When Eisner and his bodyguards passed, he rushed up from behind and shot him in the head. Count von Arco-Valley was also shot on the spot, but survived. Over the course of his protracted recuperation, he was able to witness Munich's slide into anarchy, as it had been Kurt Eisner who had held back the extremist forces of both the left and the right. Eisner's death began a chain reaction which ended in civil war.[6]

Almost immediately after Eisner's murder, an epidemic of political assassinations swept across the city. Workers and groups of revolutionary soldiers turned on the middle classes, making random arrests and raiding private homes, and the more moderate members of Eisner's coalition abandoned the city and formed an alternative government in the provincial town of Bamberg. By the middle of April 1919, this alternative government had amassed a small army of volunteers who blockaded the city. The ensuing crisis in Munich led to the formation of a new government, most of whom were of German-Russian background; one was Lenin's former press secretary. Their leader, Eugen Leviné, was a veteran of the failed Russian Revolution of 1905.

The first real confrontation between the Army of Bavaria's government-in-exile and Munich's 'Red Army' militia took place (ironically enough given what was to emerge from Munich) at a little town north of Munich called Dachau. When the Reds won that encounter, the Bamberg government turned to Berlin for help. The force that was then dispatched to crush Red Munich included units of the *Freikorps* – the Free Army.

The *Freikorps* were veterans of the regular army, who in the immediate aftermath of the war had bonded together in volunteer militias. Many fought with the devout aim of saving their nation from the forces of socialism. Others were merely unwilling to accept their nation's defeat and psychologically unable to find a way back to civilian life. Robbed of their youth, they were men whose closest bonds were to each other and to the unit. In their private war against the socialists and revolutionaries, they sought to recreate the camaraderie they had known at the front.

While the soldiers and junior officers of the *Freikorps* were the 'youths of the trenches', many of their officers were former colonial soldiers, and a surprising number of the most important figures in the movement had taken part in the genocides against the Herero and Nama, or been involved in Germany's other colonial wars. The first *Freikorps* unit, which provided the model for the entire movement, was formed by General Ludwig von Maercker, who had served in German South-West Africa. In the aftermath of the Nama War, von Maercker had overseen the internment of the Nama survivors of the Shark Island concentration camp in the former stables at Okawayo, where they had remained until the arrival of the South Africans in 1915.

By 1918 von Maercker was a veteran not only of the wars for *Lebensraum* in South-West Africa, but also of Germany's attempt to create an empire in the East, leading the 214th Infantry Division. In late 1918 von Maercker found himself back in Berlin as the German Revolution began. A traditional Prussian conservative, he was deeply fearful of revolution and of socialism, so in December 1918 he took the fateful step of re-forming what was left of his division into the *Freiwillige Landesjägerkorps* (the Volunteer Riflemen's Corps). This was a force dedicated to confronting socialist revolutionaries, upholding law and order, and defending the borders of the Reich. Von Maercker also forged the ethos of the *Freikorps*, in which the intense camaraderie of the trenches was invoked to bond officers and men together, replacing the suffocating hierarchy of rank and class that had, it was claimed, been a factor in the army's defeat.

By Christmas 1918 von Maercker's *Freikorps* had received official recognition from the government in Berlin. In January 1919 the *Freiwillige Landesjägerkorps* and several other newly formed *Freikorps* units entered Berlin and crushed the uprising of the Marxist Sparticist League in open battle on the streets of the capital. They then marched on to the city of Weimar and the northern ports of Bremen and Hamburg before confronting communist and revolutionary forces in the industrial cities of the Ruhr. As was the case with many *Freikorps* units, several of the men who served under von Maercker went on to hold key positions during the Third Reich. By far the most important of von Maercker's former comrades was the young Reinhardt Heydrich, later the head of the Reich Main Security Office and architect of the Final Solution.

Another veteran of the Herero and Nama genocides who formed a *Freikorps* unit in 1919 was Paul Emil von Lettow-Vorbeck, who had conducted a brilliant four-year-long guerrilla war in German East Africa finally surrendering two weeks after the Armistice in Europe had been signed. In one of his last acts before abdicating, Kaiser Wilhelm had promoted von Lettow-Vorbeck to the rank of Major General, and when he returned to

Germany, von Lettow-Vorbeck and his East Africa *Schutztruppe* were the only unit in the entire German army to be permitted a victory parade through the Brandenburg Gate.

Within months of his return von Lettow-Vorbeck had formed a *Freikorps* unit, and in May 1919 they saw action in the violent suppression of renewed left-wing rioting in Hamburg and Berlin. Although now fighting on the streets of Germany, von Lettow-Vorbeck continued to wear his *Schutztruppe* uniform and broad hat. An ardent monarchist and a conservative, von Lettow-Vorbeck did not become a member of the Nazi party. However, many of the men who fought under him made an effortless transition from the ranks of the *Freikorps* to the rallies of the early Nazi party.

The largest of the Bavarian *Freikorps* that assembled for an assault on 'Red Munich' in April 1919 was commanded by a man who had fought alongside von Lettow-Vorbeck at the battle of the Waterberg and in the Omaheke Desert. Knighted, elevated to the rank of General, and a recipient of Germany's most prestigous military decoration, the Pour le Mérite, Franz Xavier Ritter von Epp was a war hero and now commander of a menacing new force – *Freikorps von Epp*. They were 600 strong, had retained their field grey army uniforms but on their *Stalhelm* (steel helmets) they had painted a white 'E' – for Epp. On their sleeves they wore their unit's badge, a black diamond out of which stared a lion's head – an appropriate symbol for a unit commanded by a colonial soldier. General von Epp's fanatical belief in Germany's great racial destiny was undiminished by four years of war, much of it spent in the East. Two years after the formation of his *Freikorps* unit, von Epp was formally reprimanded by his superiors in *Reichswehr* (the official post-war German army) for distributing racist pamphlets to soldiers under his command.[7]

In 1919, however, most of the men who had been recruited to the *Freikorps von Epp* were in no need of indoctrination. The membership of von Epp's unit reads like a *Who's Who* list of the later Nazi elite. Among the future Nazis who marched on

Munich with an 'E' on their steel helmets was Wilhelm Stukart, the Nazi lawyer who was involved in drafting the Nuremberg Laws and attended the Wannsee Conference, at which the Nazis devised their 'Final Solution' to the Jewish question. Another of von Epp's men, Karl Astel, went on to become leader of the Nazis' Racial Hygiene Office in Munich and co-publisher of the magazine *Volk und Rass*. Astel also sat as a judge on Nazi Genetic Health courts in Jena and authorised thousands of forced sterilisations of the mentally ill and socially undesirable. Gerhard Wagner went on to hold the Nazi title 'Führer's Commissioner for National Health'. As such, Wagner was one of the men behind the sterilisation programmes of the Jews and the pre-war Nazi adult euthanasia programme. Walther Schultze, another of von Epp's followers, was one of the earliest members of the Nazi party and rose to become their Reich Leader of University Teachers. He too was implicated in the euthanasia of the mentally ill. Gregor Strasser was the Nazis' Reich Propaganda Leader, former commanding officer of Heinrich Himmler and the man who recruited Joseph Goebbels into the party. The figure from the *Freikorps* who was to play the most critical role in the birth of Nazism was General von Epp's *aide-de-camp* Ernst Röhm, Hitler's right-hand man and the driving force within the Nazi Brown Shirts.

Alongside *Freikorps von Epp* on the march on Munich in April 1919 was another *Freikorps* unit commanded by a veteran of German South-West Africa. Hermann Ehrhardt had fought as a marine in the war in the south against the Nama between 1905 and 1906. Having risen to naval lieutenant-commander, Ehrhardt was a proud veteran of the battle of Jutland, and by the end of April 1919 he had formed a *Freikorps* unit that had fought with von Maercker's men across central Germany. *Freikorps Ehrhardt* were renowned for their fanaticism and excessive violence. Like the Thule Society, they had already adopted the swastika as their emblem, painting it on their steel helmets. *Freikorps Ehrhardt* even sang a marching tune that, with a few small changes, became the official song of Hitler's personal bodyguard.[8] From the ranks of Ehrhardt's unit came yet more future Nazis. In fact, most of the men who dominated the Nazi party, Martin Bormann, Reinhardt Heydrich, Hans Frank, Otto Strasser, Wilhelm Keitel and many others, had been members of one or other of the *Freikorps*. Hitler was a notable exception.

In late April 1919, *Freikorps* units, including those of von Epp and Ehrhardt, were marshalling their forces on the outskirts of Munich. In the city itself, the more determined members of Munich's 'Red Army' had taken around one hundred members of the city's bourgeoisie hostage in the Luitpold Gymnasium. On 30 April, the order was given to kill them; of the twenty or so who were shot, seven were members of the Thule Society. News of these atrocities was carried out of Munich by right-wing students and members of the Thule Society, who slipped through the frontlines to join the *Freikorps* on the edge of the city. Among them was Rudolf Hess, Hitler's future deputy, who now joined the ranks of *Freikorps von Epp*.

When reports of the massacre in Luitpold Gymnasium reached von Epp and Ehrhardt, they redrafted their plans and launched an early assault on the city. On 1 May, as Lenin stood before an enormous May Day crowd in Moscow's Red Square and declared that 'The liberated working class is celebrating its anniversary freely and openly not only in Soviet Russia, but in Soviet Hungary and Soviet Bavaria', the *Freikorps* were breaking into Munich.[9]

There was determined resistance in some working-class areas, but in much of the city opposition melted away as the Red Army volunteers deserted their posts. In the attack on Munich, the *Freikorps* and the other units of the 'White Guard' deployed machine-guns, artillery, aircraft and even an armoured train. Within three days the city was pacified, but it was after the resistance had ended that much of the worst violence took place. With the population cowed, the *Freikorps* began a wave of retribution and executions. Citizens who had welcomed von Epp, Ehrhardt and others as their liberators now recoiled in revulsion as over a thousand communists, communist sympathisers and many hapless innocents were murdered. Some of the killings were carried out in the Hofbrauhaus, later the scene of Hitler's failed coup. The *Freikorps* were aided in this grim work by members of Munich's far-right organisations, including the Thule Society, who now emerged from hiding.[10]

The coming of the *Freikorps* marked the end of Munich's brief civil war and the beginning of the period during which the city became a sanctuary for disparate elements of the far right, including many disaffected former *Freikorps* men. For much of 1919 Munich was run directly by the army, with General von Epp at one point installed as a virtual dictator. In August the Bamberg government-in-exile returned to the city. However, the army soon overthrew the civilian regime they had ostensibly fought to defend. In its place a right-wing, anti-republican government, with strong links to the army, was installed under the presidency of Gustav von Kahr. With the arrival of the *Freikorps* and the transformation of Munich into a haven for the ultranationalist, much of the cast who were to take leading roles in the Nazi epic tragedy were assembled in one city: the future Nazis of the Thule Society were joined by their future comrades from the *Freikorps*.

In one of his later essays Arthur Count de Gobineau, the nineteenth-century philosopher regarded by many as the spiritual father of modern racism, described the fate that would befall an authoritarian state such as Germany if the ruling elite were toppled and a weak government set in their place. A firm believer in aristocracy, Gobineau claimed:

> It is from above that inspiration and direction are fated to descend to the people; and when in these spheres of authority there no longer is any belief, no more confidence, no more will, no more striving for good and for the better, one may state with all the certainty of a mathematical proposition that power will fall to the first corporal who, in passing, will seize it.[11]

In the Munich of 1919, as the *Freikorps* of Ritter von Epp and Hermann Ehrhardt rampaged through the street with swastikas on their helmets, in a corner of the Türken-Strasse barracks of the 2nd Bavarian Infantry Regiment sat Gobineau's corporal.

Hitler's meteoric rise to political prominence has been well documented elsewhere. Less well explored is the importance of a series of patrons who eased Hitler's ascendancy. One of the most important and most often overlooked of these figures was von Epp.

Von Epp's initial involvement with the Nazis was somewhat detached. Under the terms of the Treaty of Versailles, *Freikorps von Epp* was incorporated into the 21st Bavarian Infantry Brigade – part of the *Reichswehr*, Germany's official post-war army. One of the units that came under von Epp's influence was a new intelligence and propaganda unit commanded by Captain Karl Mayr. In May 1919 Mayr had come across Adolf Hitler, and recruited him as an informer and political re-educator. In September Hitler had been assigned the task of monitoring the Deutsches Arbeiterpartie, one of the fifty or so parties that had emerged on the *Völkisch* fringes of Munich beer-hall politics. The Deutsches Arbeiterpartie (DAP) had been founded in January 1919 by Anton Drexler, an associate member of the Thule Society. It had just a handful of committed members, but within three months Hitler became its public face, later renaming it the Nationalsozialistische Deutsche Arbeiterpartei – the NAZIS for short.

There is no evidence that Adolf Hitler, the working-class corporal, had met von Epp, the upper-class general, at this point. However, Hitler certainly had extensive dealings with von Epp's former adjutant and *Freikorps* comrade, Ernst Röhm. Hitler was first introduced to Röhm by Captain Mayr in the autumn of 1919. Röhm is known to have attended the first German Workers' party meeting at which Hitler spoke on 16 October 1919, and he joined the party shortly afterwards. In early 1920 Mayr took Hitler to a meeting of Röhm's Iron Fist Club, a band of extremist nationalist officers, and it is around this time that

Röhm seems to have decided Hitler was 'the man for Germany' and worth supporting. In the Munich of 1920, the support of Ernst Röhm was no small matter.

In the chaos of the immediate post-war period, politics and organised political violence had become inextricable, particularly in Munich. Just months before Hitler became leader of the Nazi party, the Bavarian Minister President Gustav von Kahr, under pressure from the victorious Allies, was forced to disband the *Einwohnerwehr*, a right-wing citizens' militia formed in the aftermath of the *Freikorps*' 'liberation' of the city. The resulting power vacuum was filled by a plethora of new paramilitary formations. From von Epp's *Freikorps* emerged the *Bund Oberland*. Hermann Ehrhardt and his men formed the *Wiking Bund*. But the National Socialists had no paramilitary wing, only a small gang of thugs to keep order during its beer-hall meetings. In November 1920 these strongmen were formed into the party's 'Gym and Sports Section', which concentrated on providing physical training for young party members. A year later, Hitler redesignated them the *Sturmabteilung* 'Storm Section', or SA. They quickly became known as the Brown Shirts. The final transformation of the SA, from a training programme for young party members into a fully-fledged paramilitary force, was primarily the work of Ernst Röhm and Hermann Ehrhardt.

By the time he began his association with the Nazis, Ernst Röhm had become the key link between Munich's paramilitary organisations and the regular army.[12] His official role was to supply von Epp's *Reichswehr* brigade with weapons, but in this position he also channelled *Reichswehr* funds and weapons into those paramilitary groups that the army believed might be deployed as reserves in time of trouble. Secure under the protection of General von Epp and the Bavarian Minister President von Kahr, it was Röhm who decided which groups received financial support and access to the large cache of arms and ammunition he had been busily stockpiling, in flagrant contravention of the terms of the Versailles Treaty and the Allied Disarmament Commissions. As the 'Machine-Gun King' of Munich, Röhm supported the slow growth and development of the SA and helped strengthen the party's connections to the real brokers of power in the city, including General von Epp. As the fledgling party learned how to spread its new paramilitary wings, Hitler and the Nazis increasingly found themselves in legal difficulties and Röhm's influence with von Epp became ever more beneficial.

What Hermann Ehrhardt brought to the SA was not guns, but men and money. After playing a critical role in a disastrous attempted coup in Berlin in 1920, Ehrhardt and his men became virtual fugitives and naturally sought sanctuary in Munich. With Röhm most likely acting as an intermediary, Hitler and Ehrhardt agreed that former members of Ehrhardt's *Freikorps* would be channelled straight into the SA, and funds to train them into a paramilitary force would be provided.

General von Epp did not become directly and personally involved with the Nazi party until late in 1920. In the middle of that year, the Nazis had learned that the *Völkischer Beobachter*, the newspaper of the Thule Society, formerly the *Münchener Beobachter*, had fallen upon hard times and was on the verge of folding. Unable to secure the funds to buy the paper outright and aware of a number of rival bidders, Hitler and his supporters approached General von Epp, who agreed to illegally supply the party with a loan of 60,000 marks, taken from the funds of the *Reichswehr*. This allowed the party to seize control of the paper that remained its prime propaganda organ until 1945, and made von Epp one of its greatest benefactors.

The critical role of the colonial soldiers of the Second Reich in the birth of the Third has been almost completely forgotten. The best visual record that reveals the links between the colonial army and the Nazi movement is stored in the film canisters of the Bundesarchiv in Berlin. The first and most striking feature of the early Nazi films is their amateurism. More accustomed to the later films of Leni Riefenstahl, we have come to imagine the Nazis en masse as ordered, symmetrical, purposeful and always on the move. These early films are static and banal by comparison. They show the first Nazis and their supporters in Munich's squares, and on rain-soaked parade grounds waiting for speeches or assembling for marches. Most of the framings are wide shots, capturing as much of the action and as many of the players as possible. Only occasionally are there close-ups of groups or individuals; even Hitler rarely appears alone. The framing hints at the confusion of the times, as if the cameraman was uncertain as to the significance of the events he was recording and, to be safe, filmed as widely as his lens would allow, in case some figure in the margins was destined for greatness or power.

In Riefenstahl's films of the vast Nuremberg rallies of the 1930s, the Nazis appear in the uniforms and symbols of the Third Reich. In these early party gatherings the men filmed shuffling together for the photographers wear a bewildering array of uniforms, hats, insignia, tunics and medals – the symbols and honours of the Reich that had so recently collapsed. Through this muddle of uniforms, the spectrum of various military and paramilitary subcultures from which the Nazis drew their early support is clearly visible. Alongside the old Prussian generals with their spiked *Pickelhaube* helmets and ex-*Freikorps* commanders proudly wearing their modern *Stalhelm* is a uniform that is now almost completely unrecognisable: that of the *Schutztruppe* officers. The desert-brown tunic and wide-brimmed hat of the men who had avenged Germany after the Boxer Rebellion and exterminated the Herero and Nama appears time and again in these films. In the 1920s the uniform was a potent reminder of the painful loss of Germany's colonies and their living space. Today the *Stalhelm* is an instantly recognisable icon of Nazi aggression and the *Pickelhaube*, although rendered slightly comical by historical distance, is firmly associated with the sabre-rattling militarism of the old Prussian-dominated Germany of the Kaisers. The *Schutztruppe* uniform, in its obscurity, is untarnished by any association with Nazism.

One feature of the *Schutztruppe* uniform has a direct association with Nazism, though that connection has been obscured.

The brown shirts of the SA, the first symbol of Nazi brutality, were surplus *Schutztruppe* uniforms. They had been manufactured for von Lettow-Vorbeck's *Schutztruppe* units in German East Africa, but as von Lettow-Vorbeck and his men had been cut off from Germany for the entire duration of the war, the uniforms had become unwanted army surplus. They were procured for the SA probably by Gerhard Rossbach, another former *Freikorps* commander and reputedly the homosexual lover of Ernst Röhm.

Nazism as a political ideology emerged, half-formed and half-baked, from the primordial, *Völkisch* soup of the Munich beer halls. Just as the soldiers of the lost colonial empire in Africa were key players in the emergence of the party as a political and paramilitary force in Munich, the philosophers of colonial expansion, racial inequality and *Völkisch* nationalism were among its most important intellectual benefactors.

In this early stage – between 1919 and 1923 – what is most striking about Nazism as an ideology was its unoriginality. There was little within the party's manifesto – the 'twenty-five points' – that distinguished the Nazis from many of the other conservative parties that had sprung up in Munich and across Germany. Other than its opposition to the Treaty of Versailles, the party's programme was remarkably similar to the stated aims of innumerable pre-war *Völkisch* parties, such as the Pan-Germanic League and the Fatherland party.

Nazism's roots in *Völkisch* mysticism and nationalist politics of the Second Reich have encouraged some historians to look for a single inspirational figure from whom Hitler might have derived political inspiration. The fact is that Nazism was not so much invented as reassembled from the enormous array of traditional nationalist obsessions and the racial pseudo-sciences that had mushroomed in the last decades of the nineteenth century. The acute fear of encirclement by other European powers, a determined belief that Germany was chronically overcrowded and an unshakeable suspicion that the nation was being denied her rightful place in the world – these were all concerns that exercised the Kaiser and his clique as much as the future Führer and his party. The prejudices and neuroses of the Second Reich were passed down to Hitler and the Nazis like family silver.

Perhaps the most critical stage of the synthesis and appropriation of old ideas took place between 1923 and 1925. In November 1923 the Nazis attempted to seize power in Bavaria by force. The Munich Beer Hall Putsch was a spectacular mistake, an absurdly premature grasp for power. General von Epp considered it to be so badly organised that he refused to participate, but was persuaded to help clean up the political mess left in its wake. Yet this crass miscalculation provided Hitler with the time and space to complete his political education.

Imprisonment at Landsberg Castle, on the edge of Munich, should have been the end of Adolf Hitler and the beginning of the end of the Nazi party. He was, to all intents and purposes, a washed-up beer-hall agitator, yesterday's man. As his trial began, the newspapers confidently predicted the end of his political career. Yet when Hitler was released at the end of 1924, he was politically stronger, and had codified and ordered Nazism into a political ideology. At the heart of that process was his autobiography and political manifesto – *Mein Kampf*.

Away from the Munich beer halls and the task of organising the party and dominating its membership, Hitler peered back into the history of German mysticism, *Völkisch* nationalism and the history of German colonialism, in both Africa and the East. He communed with the philosophers and scientists who had travelled the same intellectual paths before him and took from his fellow travellers only what he needed to support his own simplistic ideas. With fellow prisoner Rudolf Hess taking dictation in their comfortable suite of prison rooms – and they were more rooms than cells – Hitler explored the scientific racism that had flourished during the age of empire. His reading took him back to Friedrich Ratzel's *Lebensraum* theory, Arthur Gobineau's theories on racial mixing and the principles behind Francis Galton's pseudo-science of eugenics – by then distorted by an army of eugenicists and race hygienists, including Eugen Fischer. Years later, when describing his time in Landsberg, Hitler claimed to have also read Nietzsche's philosophy, the memoirs of Bismarck and the works of Heinrich von Treitschke, the nationalist German historian and teacher of Heinrich Class, the leader of the Pan-Germanic League. Although many aspects of the political credo that appear in *Mein Kampf* had certainly begun to emerge before Hitler's imprisonment, it was within the walls of Landsberg Castle that his ideas crystallised. Many of the conclusions he reached remained unshakeable convictions for the rest of his life.

At the core of the ideology outlined in *Mein Kampf* was Hitler's dedication to the Social Darwinian notion of the struggle for existence. *Mein Kampf* is littered with analogies of the struggle for life taken from the natural world – as were the speeches that Hitler gave in the months leading up to the Beer Hall Putsch. What was true for animals and plants, he believed, was true for humans: life was a perpetual battle for existence in which the strong were predestined to overwhelm and destroy the weak. Hitler's belief in 'the struggle' provided him with a theoretical framework through which to see the world and a pseudo-scientific language with which to describe it. Social Darwinism also permitted Hitler, like the militarists and racists of the previous century, to explain away terrible acts and justify the destruction or enslavement of other peoples as being natural, inevitable and therefore somehow moral. Of course, many Germans who accepted the apparent logic of Social Darwinism did not support imperialism, anti-Semitism or militarism. Yet much of the medical profession, the criminal justice system, the army and the ruling elite had by the 1920s come to view conflicts between races, nations and classes in similar ways to Hitler. This great cultural shift had taken place long before the Nazis emerged as a major political force, and similar ideas had taken root in most European nations, as well as in America and Japan. However, the widespread acceptance of the general principles of Social Darwinism and equanimity with which millions in Germany had come to view the displacement or destruction of the 'weak' eased Hitler's rise to power. The same phenomenon later helped soothe the conscienses of those millions of Germans, soldiers and civilians who chose to follow Hitler's orders.

Of all the theories to come from the nineteenth-century world of Social Darwinism and scientific racism, the one Hitler accepted most unquestioningly was Friedrich Ratzel's *Lebensraum* theory. Hitler was probably well versed in the principles of *Lebensraum* theory long before his incarceration but, as with a range of other ideas that became central to Nazi ideology, he was able to explore it further at Landsberg Castle. Before he had become embroiled in the Nazi party, Hitler's deputy Rudolf Hess had been the protégé of the foremost living authority on *Lebensraum* theory and the work of Friedrich Ratzel: Professor Karl Haushoffer. Haushoffer lectured in geopolitics at the University of Munich, and at one point had appealed to Hess to abandon politics and return to his studies. The evidence suggests that, while in prison, Hitler read Haushoffer's theories and discussed them with Hess. After the war Haushoffer claimed that Hitler had read Ratzel's *Political Geography* while at Landsberg.[13]

Professor Haushoffer is known to have visited his former pupil Hess and Hitler in Landsberg. Speaking years later, Haushoffer recalled discussing *Lebensraum* theory, claiming that 'Hitler never understood these things and did not have the right outlook for understanding them.' Haushoffer also stated that during his visits he had always made special efforts to avoid being left alone with Hitler. 'I always had the feeling', he told an interviewer, 'that he felt the distrust of a semi-educated person towards a scientifically educated person.'[14]

Whether or not Hitler was inspired by Haushoffer and Hess, or took his ideas directly from Ratzel, it is clear that the notion of *Lebensraum*, as outlined in *Mein Kampf*, was little different from that of the Pan-Germans or Second Reich colonialists like Paul Rohrbach. Like them, he believed that nations were essentially organisms whose health was determined by their ability to expand. Borders, in Hitler's view, were mere lines on maps. The limit of a people's geographic spread was determined by their racial vitality.

In 1923 Hitler believed that Germany's future *Lebensraum* lay in the East, the lands from which her armies had so recently been expelled. He regarded his crusade for *Lebensraum* as the continuation of a tradition of German conquest and colonisation of the East that had begun in the thirteenth century and been briefly revived during World War I. There was, however, one critical grain of originality in the way Hitler viewed the East and its people. In World War I, the most prominent supporters of Eastern colonisation, including General von Ludendorff, the Pan-Germanic League and the various nationalist movements, had envisioned an Eastern empire in which the Slavic and Jewish peoples would be rendered economically dependent and culturally subservient to Germany. Germany's role in the East had been one of *Kulturträger* – the bringers of culture and civilisation. The introduction of German *Kultur* in the East would help raise the Poles, Ukrainians and Baltic peoples from their current state of backwardness and lethargy. Hitler's vision was profoundly different. He cast people of the East into racial categories devised in the nineteenth century, giving them the status of 'colonial peoples' – a term Hitler used to describe the Ukrainians.

Before the German *Volk* could take on the great task of creating 'living space' in Russia and apply Hitler's racial policy to the Slavs and Jews, they would need to undergo a process of racial purification. The degenerate, defective and alien elements that had, in Hitler's view, contaminated the Aryan bloodline had to be weeded out. The Reich was to be purged of the weak, and foreign races would have to be driven out or prevented from breeding with Germans. The National Socialist state, Hitler declared in *Mein Kampf*, 'must set race in the centre of all life'.[15]

Like much of Hitler's core ideology, his dream of a racial state was in large part unoriginal. The Pan-Germanic League and the Deutschbund, two of the most influential *Völkisch* societies of the Second Reich, had, in the late nineteenth century, declared their determination to keep 'fighting intermarriage with non-Aryans'.[16] Hitler believed that medical and racial science had advanced to such a point that it was now possible in a practical sense to forge a state in which the racially undesirable and the weakest in society could be excluded from the German bloodline. In his quest for evidence to substantiate this vision and for inspiration as to how it might be realised, Hitler turned to the pseudo-science of race hygiene – the Germanic strain of Francis Galton's science of eugenics. Hitler's search for scientific legitimacy again brought him into contact with the men of the lost colonial empire and the ideas that had been partly developed in Africa.

German race hygiene was born in 1895 when Alfred Ploetz had published *The Foundations of Racial Hygiene*. In 1904, the year Germany had begun her war to annihilate the Herero people, Ploetz had helped launch the eugenics journal *The Archives of Race Science and Social Biology*, a periodical which was published by Julius Lehman's family company. In 1923, as Hitler began to draft *Mein Kampf*, Julius Lehman re-enters our story. Following his arrest as a member of the Kampfbund Thule in 1919, Lehman had been briefly imprisoned, and was incarcerated when a fellow Thule Society member, Anton Drexler, founded the German Workers' party. On his release, Lehman quickly joined the party in 1920 and even published some of its early propaganda literature.[17] By 1923 he had become one of the wealthy patrons who helped bankroll the party. Lehman had also developed close personal links to Hitler himself. Unlike many of Hitler's other influential backers, Lehman was willing to get his hands dirty and had even played a marginal role in the Beer Hall Putsch, allowing his villa to be used to hold hostage a group of Bavarian government officials whom Hitler needed out of the way for the duration.[18]

The year Hitler was sent to Landsberg Castle, Lehman's publishing house was busy producing the second edition of what fast became the most influential German book on race hygiene and biological racism. *Human Heredity and Racial Hygiene* was co-written by Erwin Baur, Fritz Lens and Eugen Fischer. Fischer's chapters were based on his research into the Rehoboth Basters in South-West Africa. The book had been warmly received and well reviewed in Germany, translated into English for wider publication and had helped advance the careers and reputations of all three of its authors. For Eugen Fischer, *Human Heredity and Racial Hygiene* was the first step in his journey to becoming one of the most powerful figures in Nazi racial science.

Fischer's contribution to the book set his study of the Rehoboth Basters within the context of a wider survey of the various racial types of humanity, as he categorised them. Fischer argued that for the highest races to mix with the lowest was a degenerative act, a pollutant that threatened the health of the higher race. To address this acute danger, Fischer and his co-authors suggested that a programme of positive selective breeding was needed. This would help purify the Aryan race and accentuate its inherently noble qualities and innate talents, creating a true and undiluted Master Race.

While he was in Landsberg, Hitler was given a copy of *Human Heredity and Racial Hygiene* by Julius Lehman. Historians have long argued that *Human Heredity and Racial Hygiene* helped shape Hitler's views of race and racial purity, and one of the authors, Fritz Lens, was himself utterly convinced that the book had been one of the key influences on Hitler as he wrote *Mein Kampf*. In 1931 Lens claimed that 'many passages in it [*Human Heredity and Racial Hygiene*] are mirrored in Hitler's expressions'.[19] Although there is much in the book that Hitler might have disagreed with, if he read his copy he would have surely taken from it, as always, only those passages that supported his own opinions.

Hitler's personal copy of *Human Heredity and Racial Hygiene* survived the war. It is housed in the rare books division of the

US Library of Congress. The dedication to Hitler, written by Lehman on the frontispiece, reads: 'To Adolf Hitler, the primary fighter for the meaningful recognition of the race question as the most important cornerstone in our deepening knowledge.'[20]

17

A People without Space

When the Nazis came to power in January 1933, they set out to rule Germany according to the twin principles at the heart of their revolution: the expansion of German living space and the creation of a pure Aryan 'racial state'. Both of these projects would involve the revival of practices, concepts and theories that had been developed in Germany's former African empire. Soldiers and scientists whose careers began on the pastoral deserts of South-West Africa or in the killing fields of East Africa, Togo and Cameroon were to play leading roles in the Nazi tragedy.

The other legacy of the Kaiser's lost empire that was exploited by the Nazi regime was the powerful sense of nostalgia for the colonies that infused inter-war Germany. Much of this nostalgia was focused on the memory of German South-West Africa and the era of the 'settler paradise' between the Herero and Nama genocides and World War I. Alongside pro-colonialist tracts and pamphlets, a number of popular novels and memoirs were written between the wars by both former settlers and their ideological supporters. Many of these books glamorised the lives of the men and women who had made their homes amid the vast spaces of the south-west. This potent image became linked to a profound and widespread bitterness over the confiscation of Germany's empire at Versailles. These sentiments were skilfully manipulated by Nazi propagandists to connect the memory of the lost colonies to the party's incessant efforts to convince the German people of the *Lebensraum* theory and the need for German territorial expansion.

Although acquisition of *Lebensraum* was central to Hitler's grand vision, it could be seized only through war, for which

Germany was ill prepared until the late 1930s. By contrast, forging what Hitler described as a state that placed 'race in the centre of all life' was a task that could begin almost immediately.[1] The party turned to a generation of German race scientists, eugenicists and anthropologists, many of whom had been trained in the colonial institutes or were veterans of field expeditions to the former colonies. Most, though not all, of these scientists embraced the Nazi revolution with palpable enthusiasm, as did their colleagues in medicine, engineering, geography and a host of other disciplines. The research these men and women had carried out on the peoples of Africa and Asia was used to lay the scientific foundations of the 'racial state'. Those scientists whose work best supported the party's central racial theories were rewarded with power and money. Their institutes and research programmes received lavish funding and party apparatchiks attended their lectures. The most prominent became wealthy, celebrated figures and were encouraged to apply their theories on race and purity in ever more radical ways. Ultimately they were given the power of life and death over their fellow citizens, and later over the peoples of Eastern Europe.

In an 'Appeal to the German People' issued on 31 January 1933, the day after the Nazis came to power, Hitler claimed that the Nazi state would 'not recognise classes but only German people'. The new Führer demanded that his people enter into a pact of 'mutual reconciliation'.[2] Through such a process the old divisions of class and regional affiliation were, on the surface at least, to be expunged. The only social divisions that would remain in the new Germany were those of race and blood. These fissures were to be widened, made absolute and inviolable.

When designing the laws needed to create the 'racial state' and persecute those the regime defined as 'non-Aryan', the Nazis found a number of definitions and legal precedents, along with a whole lexicon of racial terminology, in legislation passed in

Germany's former colonies. Aspects of laws that had been designed to secure the racial privileges of white settlers in Africa were adapted by Nazi lawmakers and applied to the German nation itself.

The largest group whose bloodline the Nazis sought to extricate from that of the German *Volk* were the Jews. Since the late nineteenth century, various *Völkisch* movements had campaigned for a prohibition against mixed marriages between Jews and 'Germans', on the grounds that Jews were biologically separate and an 'alien' race. In May 1933, just three months into the Third Reich, Minister of Justice Franz Gürtner called for an initial investigation into how a law to ban mixed marriages might practicably work. It was not until September 1935, at the end of a summer during which Nazi street thugs had attacked Jews known to be married to Aryans, that the party finally acted.

The new laws were formally announced by Hitler at the 1935 party rally in Nuremberg. The Reich Citizenship Law and the Law for the Protection of German Blood and German Honour were known as the Nuremberg Laws. The former defined those of German blood as *Reichsbürger* (Reich citizens). The latter forbade Jews from marrying or having sexual relations with *Reichsbürger*. As the Nuremberg Laws also applied to the other racial groups caught in the dragnet of the racial state – 'Negroes' and Gypsies – the same terms, definitions and laws were also applied to them.

The earliest precedents the Nazi legal experts looked to when drafting the Law for the Protection of German Blood and German Honour were the laws banning intermarriage passed in German South-West Africa in 1906. Similar sanctions had later been introduced in German East Africa in 1906 and German Togo in 1908.[3]

In drafting the supplementary decrees to the Nuremberg Laws, the party's lawmakers also adopted a term first used in the colonies' race laws – *Mischlinge*, of mixed race. The *Mischlinge* concept provided the lawyers and civil servants with both a conceptual framework and quasi-legal terminology, allowing them to formulate a system by which Germany's ancient Jewish community, with its deep and complex roots, could be classified, isolated and ultimately extracted. Among the race scientists whose work was quoted by civil servants drafting the Nuremberg Laws were Eugen Fischer and his erstwhile co-author, Fritz Lens.[4]

Other terms that had first been applied in the drafting of colonial racial laws seeped into Nazi racial legislation and public discourse during the 1930s: the notion of *Rassenschande* (racial shame) and *Bastardisation* were both transmitted in this way. The censures imposed on German citizens who contravened the new race laws were very similar to those pioneered in Germany's African colonies. In the same way that settlers who maintained relations with African women in South-West Africa had been disenfranchised and denied financial assistance, Germans whose spouses were of 'lesser racial value' – a term which included those with hereditary diseases – were denied certain tax benefits, child benefits and income tax relief by the Nazi state.[5]

In February 1941 Dr Oskar Hintrager, the former Deputy Governor of German South-West Africa, published a three-page article in the *Illustrated Colonial and Foreign News* in which he suggested that Germany's colonies had allowed the Reich the opportunity to see the dangers of racial mixing at first hand. It had been 'a good experience for the Volk to possess colonies', Hintrager claimed. 'Among colonial Germans the experience of living with other races underscored the importance of race itself; the most important lesson was that mixed marriages between white men and coloured women have appalling results and must, for many reasons, be utterly condemned.'[6]

The Nuremberg Laws, although regarded as race laws, in fact defined 'Jewishness' according to the religious affiliation of the individual and their ancestors. A medical or biological test to determine Jewishness had yet to be developed. For the state to determine and record the racial status and genetic health of every individual, through medical, physiological examination, a considerable infrastructure of laws, training and institutions was required. Here again the Nazi regime drew on the expertise of the generation of race scientists, anthropologists and eugenicists, many of whom had learned their skills and acquired their knowledge in the lost colonial empire.

German race science had flourished in the years leading up to World War I. As military control over the various subject peoples of the empire had tightened, the colonies had been opened up to the scientists of Germany's booming universities, institutes and museums. This was a process that had been energetically championed by Friedrich von Lindequist in his role as Secretary of the Colonial Department. In the first decades of the twentieth century, aspects of German racial science and aspects of the research carried out in the colonies became fused with ideas and principles taken from eugenics. In the 1920s and 1930s, German 'race hygiene' became increasingly influenced by the ideas and research of eugenicists in the United States, where eugenics laws had been passed in several states, a development that was praised by Hitler.

When the Nazis seized power, the most important institute dedicated to the racial sciences and eugenics in Germany was the Kaiser Wilhelm Institute for Anthropology, Human Genetics and Eugenics, situated in Dahlem, a leafy suburb of Berlin. The directors of the Kaiser Wilhelm Institute were Eugen Fischer and Fritz Lens, who with Erwin Baur had co-authored *Human Heredity and Racial Hygiene*. The other director was Otmar von Verschuer, who specialised in the study of twins and with whom Fischer worked closely.

The Eugen Fischer of 1933 was a very different man from the ambitious field scientist in his mid-thirties who had travelled to Rehoboth in 1908. Now almost sixty, Professor Fischer was arguably the most respected racial anthropologist in Germany. His academic reputation, initially founded upon his supposedly groundbreaking study on the Basters of Rehoboth, was international, and his work had been published in both Britain and the United States. He enjoyed strong personal links with the key players in the powerful American eugenics movement and was able to attract funds from their wealthy supporters.

Even though Hitler had probably read *Human Heredity and Racial Hygiene* while writing *Mein Kampf*, Fischer had not been immediately embraced by the Nazis. Not only had he conspicuously failed to join the party, but his theories on race, and on the Jews in particular, were not fully in accordance with Nazi doctrine. Early in 1933 Fischer was called to a meeting at the SS Office of Population and Genetic Health, during which he seems to have been persuaded to support the party. Although he never fully jettisoned his ideas that clashed with Nazi ideology, Fischer became a fervent and vocal supporter of the new order and eventually a party member. His willingness to participate in the racial revolution was amply demonstrated in 1933 when Fischer wrote a paper stating that racial mixing between Jews and Germans was damaging the German race and suggesting that laws be devised to prevent it. On becoming Rector of the University of Berlin in July, he used his inaugural lecture to declare his support for the Nazis and oversaw the dismissal of all Jews from the university's staff. In 1934 he began teaching anthropology to SS doctors at the Kaiser Wilhelm Institute.

Fischer's role, like that of many prominent racial anthropologists and experts in race hygiene, was not merely to support the racial revolution in their papers and at the lectern. He also played a practical role in the building of the 'racial state'. Alongside Jews and Gypsies, another racial group whom the Nazis wanted removed from the German 'community of blood' were the 'Rhineland Bastards'.

At the end of World War I, the French army that had occupied the western Rhinelands of Germany included several thousand troops of various races from across France's colonies. When these units took up their duties within the army of occupation, an international campaign against them was launched. They were condemned as 'Senegalese savages'; the occupation itself was attacked (by a British journalist) as 'The Black Horror on the Rhine'. In Germany, the campaign spread lurid and unsubstantiated allegations that the black troops had embarked on a spree of rapes and attacks on German women. When the French withdrew in 1921, the focus of German outrage fell on around four hundred mixed-race children left behind. Although mere infants, they were seen as racial outsiders and living reminders of Germany's humiliation and defeat. Reflecting Eugen Fischer's now widely accepted terminology, they were named the 'Rhineland Bastards' and both they and their white mothers were subjected to years of abuse and discrimination.

Within just three months of coming to power the Nazis turned their attentions to the 'Rhineland Bastards problem'. In April 1933 Hermann Göring ordered that the local authorities collect information on their numbers and whereabouts. Churches and schools cooperated, handing over information to the authorities. Even at this very early stage, one of the key institutions assisting in the persecution of the Rhineland children was the Kaiser Wilhelm Institute under Eugen Fischer.

Dr Wolfgang Abel, one of the departmental heads at the Kaiser Wilhelm Institute, carried out a series of 'racial-biological' examinations on a small sample of Rhineland children. Abel, who had come to Eugene Fischer's attention thanks to his work examining Nama and San-Bushmen skeletons in a Viennese collection, concluded that the mixed racial heritage of the Rhineland children had rendered them physically and mentally deformed, and their genetic inferiority was so pronounced that action needed to be taken to 'prevent their reproduction'. That same year Walther Darre, the Nazi Minister of Agriculture and later one of the architects of German expansion into the USSR, wrote, 'It is essential to exterminate the leftover from the Black Shame on the Rhine . . . as a Rhinelander I demand sterilisation of all mulattoes with whom we were saddled.' Darre suggested that sterilisation take place within two years before the 'Rhineland Bastards' became sexually active. 'Otherwise', he warned, 'it is too late, with the result that hundreds of years later this racial deterioration will still be felt.'[7]

In March 1935, a 'committee of experts on population and race policy' was assembled by the Reich Ministry of the Interior, to find a solution to problem of the 'Rhineland Bastards'.[8] One suggestion was that with the help of the church they might be deported to Africa. Yet as Germany no longer possessed any African colonies in which to dump the Rhineland children, it was feared this might lead to some sort of diplomatic incident. Two years later, with the oldest Rhineland children reaching puberty, the Nazi regime consulted Eugen Fischer, whose study of the Rehoboth Basters had been used to legitimise the Nazis' stance against racial mixing.

In the case of the 'Rhineland Bastards', like that of the Gypsies, the Nazi Hereditary Health Courts were bypassed. Instead, Special Commission No. 3 was formed by the Gestapo, who placed both Eugen Fischer and Dr Wolfgang Abel on its board. The commission's task was to identify and then sterilise the Rhineland children, as efficiently and discreetly as possible. In the spring of 1937, the children were taken directly from their homes or classrooms by the police and subjected to an examination by a board of race scientists. After it had been medically confirmed that they were of mixed race, they were taken to a local hospital where the operation was performed. By 1937 almost four hundred, all in their teens, had been forcibly sterilised. In *Mein Kampf* Hitler had warned that under Nazi rule the Germans would 'not allow ourselves to be turned into niggers as the French tried to do after 1918'.

Eugen Fischer was the most prominent race scientist with a colonial background promoted to a position of power within the Nazi state, but he was not alone. Although there were some German scientists who had carried out racial and anthropological work in the colonies but later rejected Nazism, most wholeheartedly embraced the opportunities offered by the regime. One of the most prominent, at least in the early years of the regime, was Dr Philalethes Kuhn, a Nazi eugenicist and co-author of the eugenics tract *From German Ancestors to German Grandchildren*. Kuhn was a former *Schutztruppe* who had fought against the Nama under Theodor Leutwein. During the Herero genocide he had been the military surgeon at the Karibib concentration camp. After leaving German South-West Africa he continued his research at the Institute of Tropical Disease in Berlin, before joining the *Schutztruppe* in Cameroon. A founding member of Alfred Ploetz's Society for Racial Hygiene, Kuhn lectured in *Rassenhygiene* at the University of Giessen. He joined the Nazi party in 1923 but died in 1937, before the full scope of the Nazis' eugenics programmes was realised.

Another scientist who transferred his skills from the Kaiser's empire to the Nazi regime was Ernst Rodenwaldt. As a colonial doctor Rodenwaldt had served in Togo and, like Fischer, had made his name studying the effects of 'bastardisation'. Along with Alfred Ploetz, to whom he was linked by marriage, he co-edited the race hygiene journal *The Archives of Race Science and Social Biology*. When the Nazis came to power, Rodenwaldt began to apply his ideas on bastardisation to the subject of Jewish *Mischlinge*, pre-empting certain aspects of the Nuremberg Laws.

The Nazi race scientist Otto Reche first came to prominence as a lecturer at the Hamburg Institute for Colonial Sciences, perhaps the most prestigious of the establishments set up during the Second Reich to advance the study of the colonies and their people. Reche was a physical anthropologist and a close affiliate of both Eugen Fischer and Fritz Lens. He had taken part in the Hamburg South Seas Expedition, a project yielding hundreds of skulls and skeletons that were later used for anthropological research at the Hamburg Museum of Ethnology. Reche became a committed Nazi and devoted himself to studying the distribution of blood types across the human races in the hope of discovering a means by which Germanic racial ancestry could be proved and racial impurities detected in the blood. Reche also drafted recommendations for settlement and population policy of Eastern Europe for the Race and Settlement Main Office of the SS. He warned that, like all colonial projects, the settlement of Poland posed a potential danger of 'bastardisation of German immigrants'. These dangers could only be overcome, Reche prophesied, if the areas in which Germans were to be settled were ethnically cleansed.[9]

Finally, there was Theodor Mollison, who assisted Eugen Fischer in his work on the Rehoboth Basters and who had undertaken fieldwork in German East Africa. In 1937 Mollison wrote to a colleague, 'If you think that we scientists do not join in the call "Heil Hitler", you are very much mistaken. We, the German scientists, are very much aware of what we owe to Adolf Hitler.'[10]

The Nazi state transformed the place of race scientists and eugenicists in German society. They were entrusted with nothing less than the genetic health and racial purity of the German people, and with transmitting their ideas and prejudices to their students. As lecturers, research supervisors, mentors and teachers, they trained the eugenicists and anthropologists of the Third Reich. It was this generation, young and enthusiastic for the racial revolution, who left the laboratories, institutes and colonial schools and went out into the field and to the new territories of the East after 1941 and applied the lessons they had learned from men like Fischer, Reche and Mollison.

The connections between the colonial race scientists and the stars of Nazi race science are startling. Joseph Mengele was a student of Theodor Mollison at the University of Munich. After completing his Ph.D. on the racial anatomical differences in the structure of the human jaw, Mengele was drawn into the orbit of Otmar von Verschuer, professor at Frankfurt University's Third Reich Institute of Hereditary Biology and Race Hygiene. Von Verschuer was a close associate of Eugen Fischer, and, on Eugen Fischer's retirement, in 1942 became Director of the Kaiser Wilhelm Institute. When Mengele was wounded on the Eastern Front that same year, von Verschuer invited him to come and work at the Kaiser Wilhelm Institute, which had by then been renamed the Eugen Fischer Institute. A year later, Mengele left Berlin to take up a post as Senior Doctor at Auschwitz.

In 1943 von Verschuer helped his protégé attain funds for his work, writing in support of a grant application made to the German Research Council. The money awarded for Mengele's work paid for a new and well-equipped pathology lab at Auschwitz in which Mengele conducted a series of horrific experiments.

The extent of Mengele's involvement with von Verschuer and the Kaiser Wilhelm Institute will never be fully known, as much of the institute's documentation was burned by von Verschuer in 1945 as the Russians closed in on the city. However, what is known is that in the darkest traditions of racial experimentation Mengele sent body parts and skeletons of his victims at Auschwitz back to the Kaiser Wilhelm Institute. On one occasion a family of eight were killed by Mengele so their eyes, which displayed a rare discolouring, could be sent for examination by scientists at the Kaiser Wilhelm Institute.[11] For the second time in German history, the victims of a racial genocide were used to advance the racial theories that had justified their killing.

In the name of their racial and eugenic revolutions, the Nazi state turned upon its own citizens: Jews, Gypsies, black people and the disabled. The struggle to secure *Lebensraum* beyond the borders of the Reich would not be fought against such a weak opposition; it required the mobilisation of the entire nation. Alongside the process of rearmament, the Nazis embarked upon a concerted propaganda campaign that aimed to exploit the deep sense of nostalgia that millions of Germans felt for the lost colonies in Africa.

By the 1930s, the idea of the lost colonies was perhaps a more potent and mobilising force than colonialism itself had been during the Second Reich. The story of the former colonies had become a powerful narrative of fortitude, loss and injustice. The importance of this colonial longing for the political parties of the right and centre cannot be overstated. Germany had lost her empire under the terms of the hated Treaty of Versailles. It was therefore politically impossible for any party – other than those of the far left – openly to accept their loss. To do so risked being linked with the 'November Criminals', the civilian politicians who had supposedly stabbed the army in the back in 1918 and betrayed the nation at the negotiating table a year later.

The potency of Germany's claim to her former territories was in part a reaction against the arguments that had originally been used by the British and South Africans at Versailles. The Allies' case for summarily expelling Germany from the club of colonial powers rested on the atrocities Germans had committed in their empire, most shockingly in German South-West Africa. These crimes, the Allied powers maintained, had shown Germany to be 'unfit' to rule over 'backward races'. This claim was dismissed in inter-war Germany as the 'Colonial Guilt Lie', and huge efforts were made to discredit the Blue Book. Major O'Reilly's report was loudly denounced as a work of fiction. Others accepted its veracity but retorted by claiming that Germany's colonial record had been no worse than that of any other great power. Despite such protestations, the 'Colonial Guilt Lie' festered throughout the inter-war period and was resented as much as the confiscation of the colonies itself.

Before the Nazis came to power, the campaign for the return of the lost colonies had been coordinated by the German Colonial Society, a movement that outlasted the Second Reich and the Weimar Republic, as well as the colonies themselves. Most of the society's leading members were former colonial administrators or veterans of the *Schutztruppe*, men for whom the shame of defeat and the loss of empire were mixed with their own personal bitterness. The end of empire had abruptly foreshortened their careers and rendered their expertise utterly irrelevant. Tapping into a groundswell of resentment, the German Colonial Society had harnessed massive popular support.

For sections of the Nazi elite and for millions of party supporters, the demand for the return of the German colonies was a genuine and heartfelt call, a passionate rejection of the 'Colonial Guilt Lie'. For others, it was primarily a political stance, necessary to unify the party's supporters during their election struggles of the 1920s and early 1930s. Nazism was a movement built on its ability to bring together the forces of the right. The party had achieved this remarkable balancing act by appealing to as many prejudices and obsessions as possible: they embraced anti-Semitism, anti-Marxism, *Völkisch* Romanticism, Nordic mysticism, atheism, anti-capitalism, eugenics and colonial imperialism. The result was a wild and at times unstable mix of traditionalism, conservatism and radicalism. Colonial imperialism was one of the more important of these political strands, and while campaigning at the ballot box, the Nazis skilfully exploited the nostalgic longing for the lost colonies to great effect.

Even after coming to power in 1933 and dismantling the democratic apparatus of the Weimar state, it is remarkable how acutely sensitive to public opinion the party remained. Despite the totalitarian nature of Nazi rule, the party machine, oiled from a decade of electioneering, was primed to keep its disparate support blocks moving in the same direction, constantly assuring each of them that their particular concerns and preoccupations were at the core of the party's programme and in the forefront of the Führer's mind.

While the recapture of the lost colonial empire was in reality a policy of secondary importance to the Nazis, it was never abandoned. Although in *Mein Kampf* Hitler had dismissed colonialism in Africa as an outdated policy that risked diverting German energies away from her true destiny in the European East, the party actively campaigned for the return of the Kaiser's former colonies while pursuing power through the ballot box in the late 1920s and early 1930s. Hitler's vision was ultimately global, but he was adamant that Germany's priority was to forge a vast continental empire. When the East had been conquered and colonised, Germany would have the raw materials and access to food supplies needed to make her impervious to naval blockade.

As the masters of Europe, with the resources of the whole continent at her disposal, she would expand further and take back the German colonies in Africa.

The Nazis were so convinced that Germany was destined to return to Africa that when in power, the regime set about planning for the new overseas empire. Under Hitler, the *Mittelafrika* fantasy of a giant central African block, centred around the Congo and linking the four former colonies together, was reborn. The Colonial Institute in Hamburg was revived to train a new generation of German colonialists, and by 1935 there were thirty-one institutions in Germany offering courses in all aspects of colonial administration, as well as in ethnography, colonial history, tropical medicine and agriculture. In 1940, as Western Europe came under Nazi occupation and the British were driven from the continent, German confidence reached its apex. In that year, the work of the Colonial Policy Office went beyond simple planning and embarked on preparations for a new age of empire. Guidelines for a colonial code governing the conduct of the *Wehrmacht* in Africa were produced, new uniforms for men who would administrate the colonies were designed and ambitious bureaucrats clamoured for places in night classes in Swahili and the Yoruba language of southern Nigeria. A Colonial Act for the civilian administration of Germany's future African territories was drafted. The terms of this law that banned miscegenation and enforced strict racial segregation were based upon the Nuremberg Law for the Protection of German Blood and German Honour, which itself had adopted the legal terminology developed in the African colonies of the Second Reich. Going further than any laws passed in peacetime Germany or in the Kaiser's African colonies, the draft Colonial Act stipulated that 'members of the African and mixed-race communities . . . who have sexual intercourse with a white woman in the German colonies shall be punished by death'.

The extent to which German attentions wandered to Africa in 1940 is also shown by the Nazi plan for the resettlement of the Jews in Madagascar, a colony that they imagined could be acquired from the defeated French and transformed into a 'reservation', in the colonial sense. This 'territorial solution' to the Jewish problem was only abandoned at the end of 1940.

Much of the planning for the future German empire was directed by private companies. In 1940 IG Farben, the manufacturers of Zyklon B gas used at Auschwitz, established an 'African Committee' which helped the company win concessions to supply chemicals to the future Nazi empire in Africa. Both Dresden Bank and Deutsche Bank were also involved in planning the exploitation of Nazi Africa. It was not until January 1943, when the German army trapped in Stalingrad disintegrated, that preparations for German rule in Africa were halted and the seemingly irrepressible fantasy of *Mittelafrika* was finally laid to rest. Later that same year the German Colonial Society was closed down and its assets transferred to the party coffers, on the orders of Martin Bormann.

Before 1943 the planning for an expanded African empire had been accompanied by a vocal campaign for the return of the colonies lost at Versailles. To mastermind this, the party had turned to von Epp. In May 1936 von Epp was given control of the German Colonial Society, which was subsumed within the party, as the *Reichskolonialbund* – the Reich Colonial League. By 1938 it had six thousand branches nationwide. Its Senior Manager was Wilhelm Rümann, a former *Schutztruppe* who had fought under von Epp in the 4th Field Company during the Herero genocide.[12] Together, von Epp and Rümann battled to keep demands for the return of the colonies high on the party's programme. Von Epp travelled extensively, both inside and outside the Reich, seeking support, maintaining contact with the numerous *Schutztruppe* veteran associations and cultivating close ties with prominent German settlers who still resided in the former colonies.

While von Epp coordinated the colonial campaign, the party also set out to link itself and its leadership with the lost empire – and here the memory of German South-West Africa took on a particular significance. Part of this process involved the construction of a historical myth around Hermann Göring's father, Dr Heinrich Göring, the first Reich Commissioner to South-West Africa. Hermann Göring's official party biography, published in 1938, enormously inflated his father's role in the development of German rule in the colony. It also maintained that the elder Göring's supposed bravery in the face of the Herero had inspired his son and helped shape his character. The summit of this process of historical reinvention came in August 1940 when a museum in honour of Dr Heinrich Göring was opened in Hanover. Although the *Völkischer Beobachter* described the Dr H. E. Göring Colonial House as the 'centre of the [party's] colonial political work', the curators were faced with the not inconsiderable problem that Dr Göring's colonial career had in fact been ineffectual, embarrassing and short. They overcame this impediment by skimming over the actual details of Göring's time in South-West Africa and created what was in effect a mausoleum to the lost empire. The centrepiece was a large bronze bust of Dr Göring surrounded by wreaths. The various exhibition halls that housed the museum's inventory of curios and exhibits were themed. One explored the idea of *Lebensraum*, another showed examples of the raw materials the empire had once provided. To create a genuine African ambience a number of stuffed monkeys were distributed in hallways and corridors, and some springbok horns were mounted on the walls. The entrance of the Göring Colonial House was flanked by the Nazi blood banner on one side and the Imperial War Flag of the Second Reich on the other. In the main hallway there hung a huge portrait of the Führer flanked by suitably smaller portraits of the heroes of the empire, including Adolf Lüderitz and Paul von Lettow-Vorbeck.[13]

While many prominent colonial figures played roles in the emergence of the party or flocked to the colours once it was in power, not all Second Reich colonialists supported Hitler's Third Reich. Despite having been a prominent *Freikorps* commander

Paul von Lettow-Vorbeck was a conservative monarchist who never joined the party. Wilhelm Solf, the former governor of German Samoa and the official who drafted Germany's colonial demands during World War I, is better known as the husband of Hannah Solf, the organiser of the anti-Nazi intellectual group the Solf Circle. Even Paul Rohrbach, the man who fully accepted the cold logic of settler colonialism and wrote that black Africans only had a right to exist if they were of use to the 'higher' white race, rejected Nazism. However, these voices were drowned out in the late 1930s, by the general background chatter of the Nazi propaganda machine as it geared up for war.

One aspect of the increasingly vocal campaign for the return of the colonies was the use of feature film and documentary. In 1939 the documentary director Karl Mohri produced the feature-length documentary *Deutsches Land in Afrika* (German Land in Africa.) The film was commissioned by the Reich Film Chamber and sanctioned by Joseph Göbbels in his capacity as Propaganda Minister. It inter-cut the history of German colonialism with anthropological scenes of the people of East Africa and South-West Africa. Much of the film takes place in South-West Africa, then under the South African mandate. It set out to show that a successful and prosperous German settler community had forged a place for itself on the colonial frontier, and that these expatriate Germans had embraced Nazism from afar. The film was shown across Germany. An educational pamphlet was produced to accompany it, to help teachers use the film to educate their classes in the story of Germany's lost colonies. *Deutsches Land in Afrika* appealed to the young by showing the youth of East Africa (then Tanganyika) and South-West Africa as the vanguard of the Nazi revolution in Africa. The Lüderitz chapter of the *Pfadfinder*, the German Boy Scouts, were shown marching across the southern deserts with their fluttering banners, and staring out across the South Atlantic, their faces silhouetted against a dramatic sunset.

In this regard at least, *Deutsches Land in Afrika* was accurate. By the mid-1930s large sections of the German settler community of South-West Africa were solidly behind the Nazis, and the movement was indeed strongest among the young. The para-militarisation of childhood, a defining feature of Nazi rule in Germany, had been imported into South-West Africa. Just before the outbreak of the war in Europe, Benjamin Bennett, a travelling American journalist, stumbled upon a secret Hitler Youth ritual being performed in the deserts outside Swakopmund.

Crouching behind a tamarisk bush late at night I watched the 'Sonne und Wald Tag', the Nazi ceremony of 'Ordeal by Fire'. Flames crackled and spiralled across a course formed by long ranks of boys and girls. Voices chanted, softly at first, then shriller, 'Ein Reich, Ein Volk, Ein Führer'. The small boys, ten or twelve years of age, braced themselves, grasped the hands of their elders and vaulted the flames. Sparks and glowing embers showered over them. Their legs and clothes were singed. Gasps of pain gave way to cries of triumph – they had survived the 'Ordeal by Fire'.[14]

Fittingly, the Nazi stronghold in South-West Africa was the town of Lüderitz. Not only did the town have its own party office and branch of the Hitler Youth, it was also home to a chapter of the *Stahlhelm*, a fanatic grouping of former frontline soldiers and *Freikorps*, who in Germany were eventually incorporated into the Brown Shirts. Wilfried Lubowski, a former member of the Lüderitz Hitler Youth, recalled in an interview that after the Nazis had come to power in Germany, the Jewish population were jeered at in the street. Rotten eggs and even rocks were thrown at their shops and some emigrated to South Africa.

By the mid-1930s Hitler's birthday was openly celebrated in South-West Africa, a tradition that outlived the Third Reich and Hitler. In 1936, when the Windhoek Brewery failed to hoist the Nazi banner in honour of the Führer, a boycott by German settlers was only narrowly averted.

In the 1930s, the potent image of South-West Africa under the spell of the Nazi revolution proved to be a less powerful propaganda device than the nostalgic image of German South-West Africa before the Great War. A disproportionate number of the more successful pro-colonial novels and memoirs published between the wars were set in German South-West Africa, the colony that attracted the largest number of German settlers and had always been most firmly associated with romantic, frontier fantasies.

The memoirs of Margarethe von Eckenbrecher, *Was Afrika Mir Gab und Nahm* (What Africa Gave to Me and What It Took Away), although originally published in 1909, went through a series of reprints during the inter-war years and continued to woo readers well into the Nazi era with its highly romanticised recollections of the life of a settler woman in German South-West Africa.

Another important book set in German South West Africa was *Verschüttete Volksseele: Nach Berichten aus Südwestafrika* (The Buried Folk Soul: Reports from South-West Africa). It was the work of Dr Mathilde Ludendorff, the mystic philosopher and wife of General Erich Ludendorff – the man who had been one of the driving forces behind schemes for German settlement in Poland, the Baltic and the Ukrainian Crimea during World War I. *Verschüttete Volksseele* was based on a collection of letters from settlers in German South-West Africa that had been collated by Mathilde Ludendorff over several years. It painted the settler society, as it had existed in German South-West Africa just before World War I, as one in which the settlers had discovered their true German identity. Not only was *Verschüttete Volksseele* deeply nostalgic for the lost colony, it continued the tradition – begun by Friedrich von Lindequist – of rewriting the history of the wars that had led to the virtual extermination of the Herero and Nama peoples. Mathilde Ludendorff claimed that the wars against the Herero and Nama had been racially justified. She also wildly exaggerated the numbers of settlers who had died in the initial outburst of violence.

Similar historical distortions characterised another hugely popular book from the inter-war period. Gustav Frenssen's

Peter Moor's Fahrt nach Südwest (Peter Moor's Adventures in South-West Africa) was a simplistic dramatised account of the Herero-Nama genocides, based closely on interviews with veterans of the German *Schutztruppe*. The novel gripped its (mainly young) readers with tales of danger and heroism. Repeatedly, over the course of the story, Frenssen justified the destruction of the Herero and Nama by allowing his characters to regurgitate the traditional racist caricatures found in the German press during the genocides. Peter Moor, the central character, discovers the Herero to be untrustworthy and primitive. He dismisses them as barbaric peoples, doomed to a just and inevitable extinction. Frenssen's novel was the best-selling children's book in Germany until 1945.

The most important colonial novel of the inter-war era was *Volk Ohne Raum* (People Without Space). It was the work of Hans Grimm, Germany's greatest purveyor of colonial fairy tales. A former professor of law, Grimm had briefly lived in German South-West Africa and spent many years in South Africa. The novel is set partly in German South-West Africa during the Herero-Nama genocides. But *Volk Ohne Raum* is more than mere nostalgia: it is a political tract posing as a novel. It tells the barely believable story of Cornelius Freibott, a naive Candide-like figure whose journey across the globe and through his troubled life leads him to adopt the same political opinions as his creator. The book was so popular, and so important in keeping alive the memory of the colonies and popularising the *Lebensraum* theory in inter-war Germany, that its somewhat ridiculous plot is worth describing in detail.

Freibott's misadventures begin when he and his father are forced to abandon their lives as traditional peasant farmers, and seek employment in industry. Denied a pure *Völkisch* life on the land, Freibott escapes industry and, after joining the navy, finds himself in Africa, the continent that is to change his life. In the British Cape Colony, he learns of Britain's enormous colonial power and imbibes the classic Pan-Germanic hatred of Britain as a force holding Germany back for her own selfish interests. In

Africa, Freibott also recognises that colonial expansion has provided Britain with an enormous 'living space'. The empire, he concludes, has permitted millions of British emigrants to avoid the ravages of industrialism and modernity, the forces that had atomised his own family in Germany.

Freibott is then swept up into the Boer War and persecuted by the British for fighting with the Boers. Interned in a prisoner-of-war camp, he finally grasps the message that the Pan-Germans and colonial societies had been trying to explain all along: German emigrants can only be free in colonies of their own, and Germany herself can only be rid of her problems when she acquires enough colonial living space to accommodate her people without space. Inspired by his epiphany, Freibott journeys to the only place on earth where German settlers have found *Lebensraum* – German South-West Africa. The date is 1907.

As Hans Grimm had lived in South Africa between 1897 and 1911 and was briefly resident in German South-West Africa, he knew the crimes his countrymen had committed against the Herero and Nama. However, he was equally well versed in the alternative history used to cover up the genocides, and it is this myth that provides the backdrop for Freibott's adventures in the colony. There is no mention of the concentration camps or the Extermination Order in *Volk Ohne Raum*. By contrast, British misdeeds committed during the Boer War are covered in exhaustive detail.

After further adventures in Africa, Freibott returns to Germany in the early 1920s in order to preach the importance of *Lebensraum* to his fellow countrymen. On his return he learns another critical lesson: that the Jews, although masters of the German language, are not members of 'the tribes which constitute the Germans and the German Reich'. In a final twist, Freibott is murdered by a misguided socialist at the very moment he comes fully to understand Germany's mission in the world.

Grimm's *Volk Ohne Raum* is today dismissed as a work of breathtakingly poor quality. It weighs in at over 1,500 pages, is badly written (even compared to Grimm's other works) and populated entirely by two-dimensional characters who are little more than mouthpieces for the author's own racial and political views. Grimm's formula – crude and simplistic though it may have been – was nevertheless a sensational success. Between its publication in 1926 and 1935, 315,000 copies of *Volk Ohne Raum* were sold. By 1942 sales had reached over half a million.[15]

Volk Ohne Raum – the most successful of Grimm's books – was in effect Friedrich Ratzel's *Lebensraum* theory told through the experiences of a German everyman, and Grimm's book arguably did more to keep the concept of *Lebensraum* current, during the interregnum between the Second and Third Reichs, than any propaganda campaign. Critically for the Nazis, who praised the book and its author effusively, *Volk Ohne Raum* reminded the German people that *Lebensraum* – the ideological foundation upon which South-West Africa had been conquered and ethnically cleansed – was the same concept that underpinned the Nazis' calls for territorial expansion and national renewal. Germany needed *Lebensraum* now as much as it had before the Great War, Grimm told his readers. A Nazi propaganda poster of the 1930s made the same connections. It showed a map of Africa with the four lost colonies highlighted. The text read: 'Here also is our living space.' The 'also' is critical. It spoke of the belief that while the African empire might be won back, Germany had other and equally valid claims to living space elsewhere.

Through Ratzel's *Lebensraum* theory, Nazi ambition could be linked with the supposed injustices of the past. The word *Lebensraum* itself, along with the phrase *Volk Ohne Raum*, became constant refrains on the streets and in the meeting halls of Hitler's Germany. As well as appearing on posters and being incorporated into the plots of novels, arguments for the expansion of Germany's Raum were slipped into the subtexts of films and hammered home from the lectern and in innumerable political tracts. By the late 1930s it was taken as axiomatic that Germany was chronically overcrowded, and *Lebensraum* was transformed from a dubious nineteenth-century Social Darwinian theory to something akin to a national religion. Millions believed that as a strong and vigorous race the Germans had a right to expand beyond the borders ascribed to their nation at Versailles, and to do so at the expense of other nations and other races.

The two regions of the earth in which millions of Germans earnestly believed their nation had legitimate claims to seek *Lebensraum* were the former colonies in Africa and the European East. Both shared a common narrative. Both, it was felt, had been unjustly stolen. Bitterness about both losses was palpable in inter-war Germany, a land that abounded with veterans' organisations and fellowships of old comrades. While veterans of the Western Front comforted themselves with the myth of the 'stab in the back', veterans of the East, along with the former *Schutztruppe* of the colonial empire, harboured a different grievance. They railed against the loss of the *Lebensraum* they had conquered on two continents, and alongside their bitterness grew a sense of entitlement to the lands from which they had been expelled.

18

Germany's California

On the afternoon of 16 July 1941, a secret conference was held on Hitler's private train, the *Amerika*. In a siding outside the Polish town of Angerburg, this fifteen-carriage armoured behemoth was an awesome sight. Propelled by two locomotives, she had armour-plated flak cars at each end, both equipped with heavy anti-aircraft guns. Other carriages contained the offices and sleeping berths of Hitler's numerous adjutants, bodyguards and servants. There was a fully equipped dining car and carriages of additional accommodation for visitors. The Führer's private coach consisted of a large drawing room with table and chairs, as well as sleeping quarters. The nerve centre of the *Amerika* was in the 'command coach', with its map room, communications centre and conference room. She was a miniature Chancellery on wheels, and that July the whole train hummed with activity as communiqués were sent and received via teleprinters and radio-telephones.

Five hundred miles away on the great Russian Steppe, 3 million German soldiers were coming to the end of day twenty-five of Operation Barbarossa, the invasion of the USSR. For over three weeks, the mechanised brigades of the Blitzkrieg had destroyed everything in their path. Great fleets of Panzers had sailed across the vast golden wheat fields, silhouetted against a dark-blue summer sky that was regularly punctuated by columns of smoke rising from burning farms and homes. Hundreds of thousands of Russian prisoners of war marched past the invader. The majority of the Germans who looked down from the trucks and Panzers and the majority of bewildered Russians who squinted up to see the faces of their conquerors were to die in the coming months and years. Neither captives nor captors had any idea of the catastrophes awaiting them.

If the men on board the *Amerika* in mid-July 1941 had wanted to look for early indications of disaster, they had already begun to appear. On 3 July Hitler's Chief of the Army General Staff, Franz Halder, had confided in his diary that the Russians were almost defeated. Entries made days later reveal not only a dramatic change of opinion but Halder's shock at the breathtaking inaccuracy of the military assessment of the Red Army, on which Germany had planned the invasion. The confident predictions about the likely behaviour of Soviet soldiers and the technical abilities of their officers had been proved completely false by recent experience. Pre-invasion assessments on the morale and equipment of the Russians had also been proved catastrophically inaccurate, and whole Russian divisions – of whose existence German Intelligence had been completely unaware – had already been thrown into battle.

But on 16 July the Nazi leadership, and much of the army, dismissed the Intelligence failures and other ominous portents as defeatism. They remained electrified by the daily dispatches from the front. The unimaginable scale of the battle itself and the incredible speed of the German advances blinded even the generals to the impossibility of their task.

If success blinded the generals, it expanded Hitler's vision. His dream of destroying the USSR with one gargantuan blow was slowly becoming a reality. Exactly as he had predicted, the German armies had kicked down the door and the USSR, eaten from within by 'Jewish Bolshevism', had begun to collapse. With victory seemingly in sight, Hitler felt confident enough to draw up plans against his other enemies. On 14 July he had signed a decree that diverted armaments production away from the army, which was to be drastically reduced in size. The factories of the Reich were to concentrate their efforts on aircraft production and expanding the German navy for a renewed struggle against Britain and her supporters in America.

Hitler, now more than ever, was convinced of his own genius. He was fifty-two and had reached the apex of his life. In power for almost a decade, he had erased the shame of the Versailles

Treaty, reclaimed much of the nation's lost territory and overseen the rebuilding of Germany's economy – or at least taken credit for its revival. As a former soldier who had spent four years in the filth of the Western Front, he had had the unimaginable satisfaction of arriving in Paris at the head of a conquering German army and chasing the British off the continent. Yet these conquests, critical though they were, had been merely geopolitical. Victory against the USSR was of a different order. The fight against 'Jewish Bolshevism', the 're-invasion' of the East, was a crusade steeped in the *Völkisch* and colonial traditions from which Nazi ideology had emerged.

From the windows of the *Amerika*, a new world was slowly becoming visible – a world without Bolshevism, without Stalin and eventually without the Jews in Western Europe. The time had come to set out the shape and character of the 'New Order' that would fill the void left by the USSR, and Hitler's deepest-held ideological passions came to the fore; the racial obsessions and distorted Social Darwinism that underpinned his most fundamental beliefs were liberated by military victory. Freed from the pragmatic considerations that had limited his plans only weeks earlier, Hitler had a vision of appalling clarity and set about planning the ethnic cleansing, resettlement and ruthless exploitation of what he later called 'the future German empire'.

At three o'clock on 16 July, Hitler sat at the long conference table in the *Amerika*'s command coach. He had gathered around him the men who were going to administer and exploit the new empire in Russia. Göring was there, not as Air Reich Marshal, but as overseer of the Four-Year Economic Plan. Alfred Rosenberg, 'the philosopher of National Socialism', had come to the meeting in the fervent hope that his vision of a network of national states bound to Germany and turned against Moscow might win his leader's approval. But Hitler had no interest in these visions for the East. Another of the National Socialist luminaries at the conference table was Heinrich Lammers, Hitler's legal adviser, Chief of the Reich's Chancellery and honorary SS General. Lammers, along with Hitler's personal secretary Martin

Bormann, were men on their way up in the party. Representing the army was Wilhelm Keitel, the Chief of Staff who had threatened to resign in the hope of dissuading Hitler from invading Russia. It was his only act of resistance. Now utterly convinced of the Führer's genius, Keitel was not a man to stand in the way of the colonial fantasy unveiled a on board *Amerika*. His compliance ultimately led him to the Nuremberg gallows.

The minutes of the meeting on 16 July were taken by Martin Bormann. They reveal that Hitler was adamant that Germany's task in Russia was not occupation but colonisation. In the privacy of his inner sanctum and in the company of the party elite, Hitler spoke with clarity and without rhetoric. He began with a warning. 'It is essential', he said, 'that we should not proclaim our aims before the whole world. Rather Germany should emphasise that we were forced to occupy, administer and secure a certain area . . . we shall act as though we wanted to exercise a mandate only.' With this veil in place the real work of colonisation could begin. 'We can', Hitler reassured his audience, 'take all the necessary measures – shooting, resettling etc. – and take them we shall . . . It must be clear to us', he insisted, 'that we shall never withdraw from these areas.'[1]

Over the course of this five-hour meeting, many of the states of Eastern Europe were redesigned as colonial administrative districts. Their borders were to be redrafted for the convenience of future German administrators. The Balkans would be renamed Ostland, other states were to be bisected or amalgamated. The Crimea was to be evacuated of its entire population – whom Hitler referred to as 'foreigners' – and resettled with ethnically German farmers. The Ukraine would become a sort of plantation colony with the produce of its wheat fields redirected into German mouths.

Towards the end of the meeting, the viceroys who would rule these colonies were appointed. A list of Nazi functionaries were plucked from semi-obscurity and set on the road to infamy. The names of some still resonate in parts of Eastern Europe. Fritz Sauckel became the Gauliter of Thuringia, Heinrich Lohse the

Reich Commissioner of the Baltic States. Erich Koch, whose brutal methods in Poland had gained Hitler's approval, was given the task of transforming the Ukraine into a twentieth-century slave state. Others were appointed prematurely. Siegfried Kasche, whom Himmler once dismissed as 'a man of the desk', was never able to take up his post as Gauliter of Moscow, though he still nursed ridiculous hopes of doing so as late as 1944.[2]

At eight in the evening the meeting was declared over. It was still light as the delegates left their seats and prepared for dinner. On a train called *Amerika*, on the outskirts of a Polish town, a German dictator had declared the birth of an empire in Russia. It was perhaps no more preposterous than the birth of any other empire.

We are not accustomed to think of imperialism as a phenomenon that touched the continent of Europe itself. Yet Hitler's war for *Lebensraum* was the greatest colonial war in history. It brought into existence a realm of genocide, slavery and barbarism that consumed half of Europe for four years. It saw slave-hunting parties, reminiscent of those sent into the forests of King Leopold's Congo, scouring the woods of the USSR. Thousands of villages were wiped off the map in punitive raids, and 11 million civilians, 6 million of them Jews, were systematically murdered, many in industrial killing factories.

By contrast, Germany's struggle against the Western powers was mostly fought according to a code of military ethics whose immediate origins stretched back to the middle of the nineteenth century. Although there were a number of infamous atrocities committed against combatants and civilians in Western Europe, they pale in comparison to the routine barbarity of the East – fought by the same regime during the same years. But the war against the Jews, Poles and the peoples of the USSR was not barbarous simply because established European conventions of war were abandoned. Rather, it was shaped and directed by another set of conventions, those developed in Europe's colonies and on the frontiers of America during the nineteenth and early twentieth centuries. Although European history is not without its wars and massacres, the Nazi war for *Lebensraum* took much of its inspiration from the colonial world.

In the 1870s and 1880s, colonialism in Africa and Asia had been transformed by the emergence of Social Darwinian racism. Its advocates had learned to reject the appeals of the missionaries and the 'sentimentalists' who believed that the dark races could be educated and raised to higher cultural levels. By the end of the nineteenth century imperialists had instead come to imagine the colonial process as the physical expression of racial superiority. Some envisaged its climax as the extinction of all but the higher Northern European race.

Half a century later, Germany's eastern colonial impulse underwent a similar shift. As it made the transition from the Second to the Third Reich, it entered its own Social Darwinian phase and fused with a strain of German anti-Semitism of appalling virulence. By the summer of 1941 the Nazis, and millions of their followers, had come to regard the Jews, Gypsies and Slavic peoples of the East in ways that were little different from how the *Schutztruppe* and settlers of German South-West Africa had regarded the Herero and Nama four decades earlier.

In the Nazi world view, the East had changed little since General von Ludendorff's armies had been driven out in 1918 and 1919. Without German leadership, the Slavs had supposedly remained in stasis, incapable of stamping even their limited culture on their landscape. The Jews – whom the Nazis regarded as a dangerous and parasitic race – had spent the inter-war years infecting Slavic USSR with the peculiarly Jewish poison of Bolshevism. Germany, by contrast, was a nation transformed: a 'racial state' in which marriage, reproduction, citizenship were governed by race laws. When the Nazis applied the same biological-racial certainties that governed the lives of German citizens to the peoples of the East, the sheer folly of her former policies became clear. By 1941 the paternalist belief that through spreading her language, wealth and

Kultur, Germany could uplift the peoples of the East – both Slavs and Jews – was dismissed by the Nazis as a deluded fantasy, based on unscientific ideas. Nine months into the war against the USSR, Joseph Goebbels noted in his diary that the 'nationalist currents' encouraged by the Kaiser's armies could be seen in the former Baltic States, then under German occupation. In the same entry, he went on to mock those among these Slavic minorities who erroneously 'imagined that the German Wehrmacht would shed its blood to set up new governments in these midget states . . . One would have to take the imperial regime of Kaiser Wilhelm as a model if one were to inaugurate so short-sighted a policy. National Socialism is much more cold-blooded and much more realistic in all these questions. It does only what is useful for its own people.'[3]

What is perhaps most surprising is not that the Nazis were capable of using against fellow Europeans ideologies and methodologies previously restricted to the frontiers and the colonies, but that the connections between the Nazi empire and the colonial violence of the age of empire should have been so little explored and little discussed in the decades since.[4] This is especially surprising since there were those living and writing during the years of the Third Reich who recognised exactly that continuity.

In 1942 Karl Korsch, a German Marxist émigré, became one of the first intellectuals to acknowledge that 'the Nazis have simply extended to "civilised" European peoples the methods hitherto reserved for the "natives" or "savages" living outside so-called civilisation'.[5] The eminent German political economist Moritz Bonn recognised the true face of Nazism even before the war had begun. In a paper probably written in the thirties, though never published, Bonn argued that Nazi violence against the Jews drew directly upon the racial ideologies that Germany had used to justify the Kaiser's holocaust in German South-West Africa forty years earlier. The Nazis, Bonn argued,

> accept and amplify the racial theories by which General von Trotha had justified his policy of extirpating the rebellious Hereros by making them

> die of thirst in the Omaheke Desert: that according to the law of nature inferior races must die out when brought in contact with superior races. The Nazi creed is based on the same cheap conception of Darwinism, and like their colonial predecessors, they do not believe in the unaided working of this supposed law of nature.

He went on, 'They are now doing on a much larger scale to the Jews what had been intended as punishment for the Hereros.'[6]

Korsch and Bonn were not isolated voices. The Nazi elite themselves understood that they were part of a historical continuum. When speaking in private, Hitler, Himmler and Göring, along with many of the apparatchiks they appointed to administer the occupied territories, repeatedly compared their war in the East and the empire it was intended to create to earlier colonial ventures. The British Empire, as Göring and others pointed out, had been won by conquest. Its existence was routinely justified by claims of British racial supremacy over the subject peoples. Germany's conquest of the European East was merely an extension of the same principles to Europe. Göring continued to insist that German colonialism was little different from that of Britain, France or the United States right up to the days before his suicide in Cell 5 of Nuremberg prison.

It was Hitler who felt the greatest need to place his brutal policies within a wider historical framework. On numerous occasions he spoke lucidly of his genuine admiration for the British Empire and the pragmatic professionalism of the men who ruled over it. A month after launching Operation Barbarossa, he told guests at his headquarters that Germany needed to 'learn from the English, who, with two hundred and fifty thousand men . . . govern four hundred million Indians'. A week later he stated: 'What India is for England the territories of Russian will be for us. If only I can make the German people understand what this space means for our future.'[7]

While Hitler praised the way the British had 'learned the art of being masters', he often turned his attention to the historical myths of the North American frontier for precedents as to how the war in the East was to be fought, and when explaining what

Lebensraum in the East would mean for the German people.[8] In Hitler's mind, the rise of the United States as a world power demonstrated what might be achieved when 'race' and 'space' were combined. He believed that the North American continent had been a vast, blank canvas on which the Aryan race had been able to express its innate superiority. Through a series of historic and genocidal wars, the Aryan core of the American population had driven out or exterminated the racially inferior indigenous peoples. With the living space of a whole continent, they had created a nation of enormous industrial power with incalculable military might. In the summer of 1942, in discussions on the brutal war being fought behind the German frontlines against Stalin's army of Partisans, Hitler warned that such a conflict would inevitably degenerate into 'a real Indian war'. On another occasion he predicted that the German empire that would emerge from the war would become 'Germany's California'.[9]

To Hitler, the decades of genocide and extermination visited on the peoples of Africa, Asia and the Americas were proof of his deepest conviction: that the unstoppable process of Social Darwinism was in operation across the globe. Yet when discussing the Nazi empire in private conversations, recorded by Martin Bormann during the years 1941 and 1942, Hitler focused not on the fates of the weaker races – the Jews, Slavs and Gypsies – but on how the endless *Lebensraum* and vast resources of the region would expand the power and enhance the racial health of his own German people. In this endeavour, too, he looked to European colonial history – including that of Kaiser Wilhelm's Germany – for precedents, inspiration and cautionary tales.

In his most expansive fantasies, Hitler looked forward to a time after the war and beyond his own lifetime. He described a vast empire populated by 100 million German settlers. Even when imagining the near future, Hitler spoke of an empire built on an awe-inspiring scale and at a ferocious speed. 'In ten years' time', he said in May 1942, 'we must be in a position to announce twenty million Germans have been settled in the territories already incorporated in the Reich and those which our troops are at present occupying.'[10]

Detailed planning of the geography, economics and ethnic make-up of the future empire had begun long before the Panzers started to roll East. It culminated in late 1941 with *General Plan Ost* (General Plan East). The Plan described how the Nazi empire would stretch from the borders of an expanded German Reich to the Ural Mountains. The eastern border, known as the 'Eastern Wall', was to be a living barrier of German settlements and fortresses, manned by a colonial militia of veterans and their families. Against this bulwark, future waves of Slavic barbarians would crash and be repulsed. Like many aspects of Nazi colonialism, the 'Eastern Wall' was a concept that had first emerged during the years of the Second Reich.

On the western side of the wall, a new world was to be brought into existence. The first phase of Nazi colonisation envisaged the repopulation of European Russia with ethnic Germans. It was suggested that this aspect of the plan might be completed around the year 1970. Despite its astounding ambition, *General Plan Ost* was conservative and restrained when compared to some of the wild fantasies of the Führer. Whereas the planners estimated that initially only 10 million Germans could be resettled – and that even this would take thirty years to achieve – Hitler believed double that figure might be settled in a third of the time.

The farms and villages to which these millions were to be sent, like the fields in which they would toil, would all be redesigned. National Socialism, like much of the right-wing German *Völkisch* theorising from which it was born, remained convinced of the existence of a mystical link between the soil and the *Volk*. The Slavic peoples of Russia and her satellites had shaped the landscape only as much as their lowly racial status would allow. The 'East' – as it was usually vaguely described in Nazi documents – was a landscape completely unsuited to the character of the higher German race. A wholesale transformation would have to take place: fields expanded, marshes drained and rivers re-channelled. The farms created for the settlers were to be modern and spacious and, along the best roads outside Germany, 'a belt of handsome villages' would run.

Hitler believed that the task of transforming Russia into what he described as a 'Garden of Eden' would bring about an equally dramatic transformation of the German people themselves. Both Hitler and Himmler were convinced that through the task of taming the Russian wilderness, the Germans would realise their destiny and become 'a frontier people'. The building of the German empire would draw the bravest and the best from the Reich. The East would be 'a country where they will not find their bed nicely made for them', Hitler warned. Having been toughened by life on the frontier, Germany's new colonialists would become the future racial bedrock upon which the Thousand-Year Reich would stand.[11] From among their ranks, a new generation of leaders would emerge. 'In ten years' time', Hitler predicted in 1941, 'we'll have formed an elite whom we'll know that we can count on . . . whenever there are new difficulties to master. We'll produce from it all a new type of man, a race of rulers, a breed of viceroys.'[12]

The Nazis' 'breed of viceroys' would spring not just from the farmer settlers, but also from the SS – the masters of the master race. To the leaders of the SS, the Eastern empire was to become a sort of racial gymnasium in which the new German elite would be made fit for future struggles. It was Himmler who most clearly articulated how the empire would become the incubator of the new SS. In an infamous speech given at Posen in 1943 to the SS leadership – during which he openly discussed the extermination of the Jews – Himmler outlined his vision for the East after the war:

> If the peace is a final one, we shall be able to tackle our great work of the future. We shall colonise. We shall indoctrinate our boys with the

laws of the SS . . . In twenty to thirty years we must really be able to provide the whole of Europe with its ruling class. If the SS together with the farmers . . . then run the colony on a grand scale, without any restraint, without any questions of tradition, but with nerve and revolutionary impetus, we shall in twenty years push the national boundary 500 kilometres eastward . . . We shall impose our laws on the east.[13]

The collapse of Operation Barbarossa and the move to defensive warfare in the winter of 1941–2 meant that the extent of German colonisation during World War II was limited to a few small settlements in the Ukraine and Poland. The driving force behind these projects was Himmler and the SS. In his capacity as Reich Commissar for the Strengthening of Germandom, Himmler pushed through the creation of twenty-eight separate villages populated with German settlers and clustered around his field headquarters at Hegewald, in occupied Ukraine. The original Jewish inhabitants of the area were almost all exterminated and those of Slavic origin either retained as slave labour or 'evacuated' into the labour camps. Other German settlements were created at Zhytomyr, again in the Ukraine, and at Warthegau in Poland.

Although short-lived, there were deliberate attempts to draw links between these settlements and the memory of Germany's lost empire in Africa. In the colony of Zhytomyr, members of the Togo Ost Society applied models of colonial agriculture developed in the former African colony to the black soil of the Ukraine. The following year, German farmers from Eastern Africa were transplanted into the Warthegau settlement, in the hope that their colonial expertise would inspire other Germans to come forward and take up the challenge of colonising the East, a task for which few of Hitler's countrymen ever showed any great enthusiasm.[14]

—

The purification by ordeal of the Aryan 'master race' would be only one effect of the Nazi's *Lebensraum* policy. The other would be the displacement of the 'lower' races of the East. By the end of 1941 Germany had not only acquired a vast colonial territory, she had also brought a subject population of anything from 40 to 65 million under her control; 11 million were Jews, the rest mainly Slavs. In Nazi ideology and in modern historical memory, the Nazis' racial contempt for the Slavs is overshadowed by their more fanatical and obsessive hatred of the Jews. Nazi anti-Semitism had Darwinian elements but was deeper, more complex and multi-layered. The Slavs' place in the Nazis' racial world-view was more directly shaped by colonial thinking.

In preparing the army for the brutality of a 'war of annihilation', the Nazis found within the traditions, language and methodologies of European colonialism, pre-existing categories in which to reclassify the Slavs. By reducing the nationalities of the East to what Hitler was to call 'colonial peoples', the violence and excesses of both colonial war and colonial administration provided the regime with an inventory of military practices, terms and justifications. These practices, even within Germany's own relatively modest colonial experience, included slavery, ethnic cleansing, concentration camps and genocide.

Even before the launch of Barbarossa, both Joseph Goebbels's Propaganda Ministry and the SS had waged campaigns specifically designed to reinforce the low racial status of the Slavic peoples. Propaganda onslaughts were directed at both the German public and the army. In 1942 the SS issued a pamphlet titled *Der Untermenschen* (The Subhumans) that stressed the racial differences between Slavs and Aryans. *Der Untermenschen* was designed to harden racial attitudes against the Slavs within the ranks of the army by setting photographs of supposed Aryan perfection alongside images of Slavic subhumanity. Four million copies were printed, helping to bring the phrase *Untermenschen* into the lexicon of wartime terminology. In the months before the invasion, the army command also encouraged its troops to make racial distinctions between the various ethnic minorities who filled the ranks of the Red Army. A directive of May 1941 on the behaviour of troops in the upcoming Russian campaign warned that 'The Asiatic soldiers of the Red Army in particular are devious, cunning and without feeling.'[15]

Categorised as 'colonial peoples', the Slavs could not expect the protection of European law. The conventions of warfare that secured the rights of combatants and prisoners of war had never been fully applied to Africans, Asians or the Native Americans. The Nazis withdrew the same rights from the Slavs, in part, by denying their status as Europeans.

The re-categorising of the Slavic peoples was not only critical in encouraging the army to abandon the rules of 'civilised warfare', it was also a prerequisite for colonial rule. Unlike the Jews who were to be entirely removed from the German living space, between 14 and 15 million Slavs would remain under *General Plan Ost*. They were to form a class of virtual slaves and their labour used to construct the farms and villages of the German East and work their fields under the watchful settlers.

To confirm the Slavs' position, the Nazis, in both their own thinking and their propaganda, employed stereotypes inherited from the colonial tradition. Unable to point to external racial differences like skin colour, they fell back on some of the oldest racial characterisations. The Russians, like the Africans, were described as brutal monsters capable of terrible violence and as being 'natural born slaves who feel the need of a master'.

They were viewed as Erich Koch described the Ukrainians: as 'white niggers'.[16] This caricature of servility and brutality came straight out of European colonial racism, and was exactly how Rudyard Kipling had described the Africans and Indians of the British Empire in verse forty years earlier: 'Half Devil and half child'.

In taking up the white man's burden in the East, the Nazis completely rejected the principle of using German *Kultur* to lead and uplift the people of the East, an idea promoted by various nationalists during the years of the Second Reich. The 'civilising mission' was one of the very few aspects of the nineteenth- and early twentieth-century colonial tradition that Hitler rejected utterly. When railing against this outdated and discredited form of colonialism, Hitler claimed that the greatest mistakes had been made by the missionaries and colonialists of Germany's pre-war colonies, who he was convinced had been overly concerned with the health, education and spiritual well-being of the native peoples. In one of his after-dinner rants, he explained to his guests that such impulses had been central to the failure of Germany's pre-war colonies, 'No sooner do we land in a colony than we install children's crèches, hospitals for the natives. All that fills me with rage . . . Instead of making the natives love us, all that inappropriate care makes them hate us.'[17] In another of his conversations Hitler assured his audience that there would be no attempt to 'civilise' the Slavs in the new German empire:

> As for the ridiculous hundred million Slavs, we will mould the best of them to the shape that suits us, and we will isolate the rest of them in their own pigsties; and anyone who talks about cherishing the local inhabitant and civilising him, goes straight off into a concentration camp.[18]

Hitler was especially adamant that 'nobody must let loose the German schoolmaster on the eastern territories . . . The ideal solution would be to teach this people an elementary kind of mimicry. One asks less of them than one does of the deaf and dumb.'[19] On another occasion he suggested that

> A loudspeaker should be installed in each village, to provide them with odd items of news and, above all to afford distraction. What possible use to them would a knowledge of politics or economics be? There is also no point in broadcasting any stories of their past history – all the villagers require is music, music and plenty of it. Cheerful music is a great incentive to hard work, give them plenty of opportunities to dance and the villagers will be grateful to us.[20]

In the Nazi East, there were to be no missionaries and no schools. Those Russians, Poles, Ukrainians and others permitted to remain would be slaves with no hope of manumission or education. The only technological advances made available to them would be abortion and contraception, in an effort to keep their populations down to acceptable levels.

The Slavs were to be completely segregated. 'The life of the German colonist', Hitler warned, 'must be kept as far separate from that of the local inhabitants as possible . . . the easiest way of preventing any fusion between the German and the native population is to encourage the latter to adhere to their own ways and discourage them from aping ours.'[21]

Plans for racial separation in the East clearly resemble the schemes and draft laws that were developed in the same years by the Nazis' Colonial Policy Office for the administration of Germany's future colonies in Africa. They also built on Nazi rule in occupied Poland where the imagined racial inferiority of the Poles was emphasised in almost every aspect of daily life. As with all truly racialised systems, Nazi colonialism placed racial status above the abilities and achievements of the individual. In September 1941 Hitler explained that, 'The least of our stable-lads must be superior to any native.'[22]

The Slavic population of the Nazi East were to be kept submissive through the colonial policy of divide and rule. Every ethnic division and religious divide was to be magnified by their German overlords. Hitler's enthusiasm for the policy is palpable in his private conversations. At dinner in April 1942, he delivered a long monologue on how Germany was to divide and then dominate the Slavs:

> Even the village communities must be organised in a manner which precludes any possibility of fusion with neighbouring communities; for example, we must avoid having one solitary church to satisfy the religious needs of large districts, and each village must be made into an independent sect, worshipping God in its own fashion. If some villages as a result wish to practise black magic, after the fashion of Negroes or Indians, we should do nothing to hinder them. In short, our policy in the wide Russian spaces should be to encourage any and every form of dissension and schism.[23]

As in Apartheid South Africa and nineteenth-century colonial Africa, segregation was to be accompanied by a tightly controlled system of economic exploitation. In 1915, the colonial writer Paul Rohrbach had argued that only by labouring in the service of the white race did the black peoples of South-West Africa earn any right to existence. In April 1942 Hitler expressed an almost identical conviction, but with the Russians in mind. 'These people', he raved, 'have but one justification for existence – to be used by us economically.'[24] The people of the fertile Ukraine were to justify their continued existence by becoming a class of serfs ruled over by German settlers:

> At harvest time we will set up markets . . . There we will buy up all the cereals and fruit, and sell the more trashy products of our own manufacture. In this way we shall receive for these goods of ours a return considerably more than their intrinsic value . . . It will also be a splendid market for cheap cotton goods – the more brightly coloured the better . . . Why should we thwart the longing of these people for bright colours?[25]

In Hitler's plans for the East, only a proportion of the Slavs were to be enslaved. The rest, along with the entire Jewish population, were to be removed – one way or another – from Germany's *Lebensraum*. The details of this immense act of ethnic cleansing were at first left to the planners. In the months leading up to the invasion of the USSR, Nazi racial scientists, economists, geographers and agriculturalists began in earnest to grapple with the population problems of the East. Through its various drafts and revisions, the authors of *General Plan Ost* concluded that in order to make way for German settlers, around 30 million of the current inhabitants of European Russia would have to be pushed out. Other estimates suggested even higher figures: 45 million and more. In some proposed schemes, these tens of millions of people were to be 'evacuated' east over the Urals into Siberia. A directive issued in May 1941 showed that the planners had fully grasped what a colonial war in the East would mean for the populations of Poland and the USSR. It stated that 'The population . . . especially the urban will have to look forward to the severest of famines. It will be essential to drive the population into Siberia. Efforts to save the population from starving to death by bringing surplus food from the black soil region can be made only at the expense of feeding Europe.'[26]

Three months later Hitler told his entourage that the peoples of the East were to suffer the same fate as the 'Red Indians'. They were to be exterminated and then simply forgotten. 'We also eat Canadian wheat,' he reminded his audience, 'and don't think about the Indians.' Three months later Hermann Göring, the man tasked with the economic exploitation of the former Soviet territories, informed the Italian Minister of Foreign Affairs, Count Galezzo Ciano, that between 20 and 30 million Soviets would be confronted by famine in 1942. 'Perhaps it is as well that it should be so,' he added, 'for certain nations must be decimated.'[27]

It was Göring who ordered Reinhardt Heydrich to begin work devising a 'Final Solution' to the Jewish problem, in July 1941. Sometime in the autumn of that year, as 2 million Soviet prisoners of war were being starved to death in holding pens and the death squads of the *Einzatzgruppen* were massacring thousands of Jews each week, the notion of a 'territorial solution' – the expulsion of the Jews from the German *Lebensraum* – was overtaken by plans for their complete extermination as a race.

At the start of the war in June 1941, no such plans were in place. Operation Barbarossa was launched as a war for *Lebensraum*. Hitler did not invade with Auschwitz in mind. While it is certainly true that Nazi plans for the East demanded that it be made a 'Jew-free space', few had imagined this could be achieved through the wholesale liquidation of the 11 million Jews within the zone under German occupation. The Jewish Holocaust, the ultimate expression of Nazi violence, emerged from the context of the Nazis' racial colonial war.

While the decision to exterminate the Jews was taken sometime in late 1941, the methodology developed slowly, taking shape amid a maelstrom of accidental happenings and coincidences. At times it was driven by the personal sadism of a small number of relatively minor Nazi administrators. Although motivated above all by the fanatical anti-Semitism that lay at the very heart of Nazism, the final nature of the Final Solution was partially determined by a wider process of radicalisation that impacted on almost every aspect of the Nazi project, and which began the moment the war was launched – accelerating perceptibly in the aftermath of German military defeat at the gates of Moscow in late 1941. In the summer of 1940, the regime had seriously investigated the possibility of deporting the Jews of Europe to Madagascar. The failure of Operation Barbarossa ended all possibility of a 'territorial solution', even in the East, although it must be remembered that the 'territorial solutions' proposed in documents like *General Plan Ost* would have proved genocidal to both Jews and Slavs.

Labour camps and death camps were a policy of last resort for the Nazis, just as concentration camps had been for the British in South Africa and the Kaiser's army in South-West Africa. General von Trotha had sought to annihilate the Herero in the great encirclement at the Waterberg or – when this proved impractical – to push them into the Omaheke. He had not envisaged that they would be slowly worked and starved to death by the civilian authorities and private companies in concentration camps.

In 1942, the Nazis' war in the East ran into the same crisis and contradictions that had halted von Trotha's war in South-West Africa in 1905. The desire to exterminate or expel their racial enemies ran counter to a growing and desperate need for labour and concerns for the well-being of the fighting men. These contradictions were never fully solved, but as in South-West Africa, one solution was the creation of forced labour camps in which labour became a means of liquidation. The Nazis termed this 'extermination through labour'. The direct impact that the labour shortage had on treatment of the peoples of the Nazi East was demonstrated most dramatically by the Nazis' attitudes towards Soviet prisoners of war. During the terrible winter of 1941–2, around 2.2 million Soviet soldiers were starved, frozen and beaten to death in vast open-air pens. Six hundred thousand were simply shot and a small number gassed in the first mobile gassing vans. This was the first Nazi genocide.[28] Although a further 1.3 million Soviets died in German captivity between the end of February 1942 and the end of the war, the faltering war economy dictated that the prisoners of war be exploited as slave labour rather than simply liquidated, preventing a repetition of the mass extermination seen during the first winter of the war.

The Nazis had begun to exploit the labour of their racial and political enemies in concentration camps (*Konzentrationslager*) even before the war. Yet in 1941 the camps housed fewer than 1 million prisoners. By 1945 the system had evolved into a vast network of facilities of various types and had exterminated 11 million people, enslaving another 6 million. This was realised through an incessant and furious process of invention and radicalisation. Like the colonial authorities of German South-West Africa, who adapted the original concentration camp concept inherited from the British and the Spanish, the Nazis added their own modifications. Count von Stillfried's 'confined areas' and regime of forced labour were replicated in the Nazi East, as was the practice of selecting the work-able from the work-unable. The scale was vastly different but the principles broadly the same.

Yet even on Shark Island, the worst of the South-West African camps, there had been a half-hearted attempt to harness the labour of the prisoners. Shark Island can be considered a death camp in that extermination of the prisoners clearly took precedence over the work they were ostensibly deployed to carry out. The equanimity with which the civilian colonial authorities accepted the failure of the infrastructure projects on which the Nama worked demonstrated that such works were of secondary importance and the extermination of the prisoners the primary function of the camp. The critical Nazi refinement of the death camp concept was to create camps in which any pretence at forced labour was abandoned. Auschwitz, Sobibor, Treblinka, Majdenek, Belzek and Chelmno differed from Shark Island, and from the other Nazi camps, in that they were simply factories for killing. There the regime made no effort to exploit the labour of the vast majority of those who passed through their gates. Indeed, the Final Solution absorbed men and resources, and ran counter to military pragmatism. These were camps with no alibi, no cover story and no 'product', other than liquidation.

Epilogue
The Triumph of Amnesia

During World War II, both German scholars and members of the Nazi elite came to recognise that the war in the East, and the regime's murderous treatment of its racial enemies, were redolent of the bloodier episodes in colonial history. Yet during the Nuremberg Trials in 1946 and 1947, the International Military Tribunal and the governments it represented avoided making similar connections. The memory of the German genocides committed in South-West Africa, so important at Versailles in 1919, were overlooked at Nuremberg a generation later. This is partly explained by 'colonial amnesia' – Europe's propensity for ignoring or forgetting the colonial past. However, in 1945, with the greater part of Asia and almost all of Africa still under colonial rule, the victorious and liberated powers of Europe had more immediate reasons for wanting to close their eyes to the darker aspects of colonial history.

Throughout the war, the British had put millions of her colonial subjects into uniform and called on them to fight Fascism. Yet their status as colonial subjects, without a political voice and on the wrong side of the colour-bar, was not widely regarded as being at odds with the propaganda of a war against Nazism. The hypocrisy of the Western democracies, who condemned the racism of the Nazis while ruling over 600 million colonial subjects, was ridiculed by socialists of various shades. Some characterised the war between the Western democracies and Germany as a clash between a group of imperialist powers and a would-be imperialist power.

Although wartime Allied propagandists had rightly condemned the Nazi East as a 'slave empire', post-war governments maintained that the horrific depths to which Nazi imperialism had sunk had no bearing on the future of their own empires or on the general principle of colonialism. But the experiences of the war forced post-war advocates of empire to denounce the model of colonialism that had emerged from the Social Darwinian revolution in the late nineteenth century. When Germany had drawn the line between 'superior' and 'lower' races across the continent of Europe itself, and condemned the Jews as a parasitic race and the Slavs as a 'colonial people', a nexus of a biological anti-Semitism, *Rassenkrieg* and *Lebensraum* had been unleashed. Only then had the general populations of the colonial powers who confronted Hitler been able to see at close quarters what the colonial 'conquest of the world' could mean, and where the clinical logic of biological racism could lead. That the victims of Nazi imperialism were white Europeans helped overcome the barrier of racism and made the realisation easier.

Rather than reject the colonial project in the wake of Nazism, the Western colonial powers evoked the alternative vision of colonialism: the nineteenth-century notion of the 'civilising mission'. They used it to claim that their systems were distinct from Nazi imperialism and therefore fit to continue in the twentieth century, perhaps beyond. The British in particular spoke of their empire as 'communities' or 'families' of nations.[1] Pointing to the successes in their territories (where they could be found), colonialists across Europe sought both to placate indigenous independence movements, and to demonstrate to the world and the multi-ethnic United Nations that the violence and genocidal racism of the Nazi colonial experiment was not an innate feature of all imperial ventures.

The cold facts of 1945 were that the British were almost bankrupted by the war and needed the foreign exchange from their colonial produce to support a faltering currency. The French, Belgians and Dutch were seeking to re-establish themselves as powers on the international stage, unable to accept their status as geopolitical minnows in a world of Super Powers. At the very moment the European powers needed their empires financially and geopolitically, they claimed more vociferously than ever that colonialism was motivated not by self-interest but by Christian paternalism.

As in the lead-up to the Paris Peace Conference and the Versailles Treaty, the Americans had, at first, seen things differently. Attracted to the principle of international supervision of post-war dependent territories, they had gone so far as to predict that the war would see the age of empire brought to an end. However, by 1945 America's traditional antipathy towards European empire-building, and British expansionism in particular, was drowned out by deeper fears. The slow dawning of the Cold War convinced Truman's administration that the European empires were needed as a balance against the power of Stalin's USSR. When France, Belgium and the Netherlands – all of whom had been occupied by the *Wehrmacht* only months earlier – returned to their colonies in Asia and Africa and imposed their own occupation on the local populations, they encountered little resistance from across the Atlantic.

As the Nazi defendants at Nuremberg were being condemned as the masters of a 'slave empire', a new age of European colonialism in Africa and Asia was stuttering into life. Those who stood in its way were the colonial subjects themselves, who had dared to imagine that the defeat of Nazism might herald the new era of racial equality and self-determination that wartime propaganda had alluded to.

In the context of the post-war renewal of European colonialism, the history of exterminatory wars and slavery in Africa and Asia was an unwelcome intrusion that risked demonstrating how Western colonialism had, in the past, been capable of atrocities similar in character (if rarely in scale) to those so recently seen in Europe. But if colonial history was brushed under the carpet, the genocides committed by Germany in South-West Africa had, by 1945, been comprehensively buried.

In 1919, South Africa had dramatically revealed to the world the atrocities carried out in German South-West Africa. Yet in the years after Versailles, the same nation had quietly and efficiently entombed the history they had gone to such efforts to unearth. Despite all their condemnations of German colonialism, the South African administrators of the Mandate of South-West Africa had established a white settler society in the colony, which was in most respects indistinguishable from that which Germany had spent three decades struggling to build. In 1921 the Herero and Nama lands that had been confiscated by Kaiser Wilhelm II were incorporated into the 'Crown Lands of South-West Africa'. Eight thousand square miles of territory were set aside for white settlers who were encouraged to migrate north from South Africa. The same year, the policy of native reserves begun by the Germans in 1903 was revived. From a total of 57 million hectares, 2 million were set aside for the 'natives', who made up 90 percent of the colonial population.[2] With the best farmland earmarked for whites, the native reserves were situated on unproductive, marginal land. One reserve, at Aminuis in the Omaheke Desert, in which thousands of Herero were made to settle, was described as being 'deadly for cattle', by the South African's own Reserves Superintendent.[3]

After the last Nama uprising had been crushed and the will of the Herero to resist dampened by an intimidatory campaign of aerial bombardment, they, along with the other 'native' tribes, were bound to the white economy by a taxation system carefully designed to force them to seek work on white-owned farms for part of the year. In 1927, the South Africans completed the disempowerment of the black population by suppressing their history.

At the core of South African policy in South-West Africa was the ambition to erase the nationalism and jingoism of the war years, and instil in the white population a sense of unity that placed racial consciousness above nationalism and language. Of the twenty thousand whites resident in the Mandate of South-West Africa in 1921, almost eight thousand were Germans who had remained in the colony after 1918. Over the course of the early 1920s, the South African administration became increasingly aware that the history contained in the Blue Book of 1919 was a significant obstacle to the unity of the white population. The leaders of the German settler community were open in their desire to see the Blue Book obscured, or perhaps officially repudiated as a 'war pamphlet'.[4] Chief among their complaints was that Major O'Reilly's report had been based, in part, on the testimonies of 'uneducated blacks'.

In July 1926 August Stauch, a German settler respected as the overseer who had identified the first diamonds found outside Lüderitz, put forward a proposal to the newly elected Legislative Assembly, calling for the destruction of all copies of the Blue Book. In support of Stauch, the *Windhoek Advertiser* assured its readers that 'The Germans were ready and anxious to cooperate in the building up of South West Africa . . . [but] could not do so fully until the stigma imposed by the publication of the Bluebook in question had been removed from their name.' Further encouragement for the proposal came from D.W. Ballot, leader of the ruling Union party, who reminded his fellow settlers that 'Few civilized races could look back over their colonial history without regrets in regard to some of the incidents that have darkened their past.'[5]

In 1927, all copies of the Blue Book were recalled from public libraries and government offices and burned. Copies held in British colonies abroad were transferred to the Foreign Office and the testimonies that had shocked delegates at Versailles were purged from the Official History.[6] In a eulogy to the Blue Book, the editor of the *Windhoek Advertiser*, J. D. L. Burke, concluded that its destruction would allow the white nations in South-West Africa to 'go forward together unhampered by the suspicion and rancour of the past'.[7] The burning of the Blue Book was the moment the South African authorities, with the acquiescence of the British, took over the process of historical fabrication and distortion begun by the German authorities two decades earlier.

By the end of World War II, the white population of the Mandate of South-West Africa had reached almost thirty thousand. United and racially privileged, this tiny minority ruled over a black African population of well over a quarter of a million.

In January 1946, Britain placed the former German colonies of Togoland, the Cameroons and Tanganyika, which had been awarded to her as mandates by the League of Nations, under the trusteeship of United Nations. France, Belgium, Australia and New Zealand all pledged to do the same with their mandates. But Pretoria refused to loosen her grip on South-West Africa. Two years later, elections brought the National Party to power in South Africa and their government immediately set about expanding existing laws into the Apartheid system. After a farcical sham referendum, South Africa informed the United Nations in 1949 that she would continue to rule South-West Africa as a mandate. The territory was effectively incorporated into South Africa. As independence movements grew in strength across the continent, South Africa slipped into her age of isolation, dragging South-West Africa with her. The 'wind of change', like the early Portuguese explorers, were unable to penetrate the Namib or reach the people of the south-western interior.

Just as there were connections, both personal and historic, linking Germany's colonial empire in Africa and the Nazi regime, South African Apartheid had its own links to German South-West Africa. Several young Boer nationalists who studied in Germany in the 1930s were at one time or another the house-guest of Oskar Hintrager, the former Deputy Governor of German South-West Africa. A vocal supporter of Boer Nationalism, Hintrager, assisted by General von Epp, wrote a regular column in support of the Boers in the Nazi colonial press. In the 1950s, as the Apartheid system was being established, he wrote the book, *Geschichte von Südafrika*, in which he claimed that the Boers were not Dutch, but of Germanic racial descent. As members of the virile Germanic *Völk*, Hintrager suggested, the Boers had quite naturally risen to power over the other, lesser races of South Africa.

Hintrager had been one of the principal authors of the race laws passed in German South-West Africa. The similarities between the legislation he helped devise and the laws passed by the South Africans in the Mandate of South-West Africa meant that, for many German South-West Africans, the transition from German colonial rule to South African Apartheid was effortless. In 1948 two South-West African senators were selected to represent 'the reasonable wants and wishes of the coloured races' in the South African Assembly. One was Dr Heinrich Vedder, the former missionary who had witnessed the suffering of the Herero in the Swakopmund concentration camp. In a speech to the South African Senate, Vedder claimed that the separation of the races had been pioneered not in South Africa but in South-West Africa under German rule, where 'from the very beginning the German government carried out that which has unfortunately not yet been attained in South Africa – namely Apartheid'.[8]

During the 1950s the intricate architecture of Apartheid was put in place, piece by piece, on both sides of the Orange River. On Human Rights Day 1959, thirteen Africans were killed by police armed with sten-guns while demonstrating in the 'Native Location' on the outskirts of Windhoek. Five months later, sixty-nine black South Africans were shot – again by police armed with sten-guns – at a demonstration in the Sharpeville township near Johannesburg. Both South Africa and her colony became pariah states.

For South-West Africa, political ostracism compounded her geographic isolation and exacerbated the cultural gulf between the white population and a fast-changing Europe. Many German South-West Africans, like their British and Boer neighbours, became increasingly culturally disconnected from the continent of their birth or their ancestry. For some, this was deliberate. Post-war South-West Africa became a bizarrely backwards land in which small German communities, living in isolated settlements on the endless grasslands of the fertile plateau, lamented the defeat and collapse of both the Second and Third Reichs. Alongside the last of the ageing *Schutztruppe* veterans, another community was washed onto the South West African shore by the tides of German history. Well into the 1990s, South-West Africa was renowned among journalists and travellers for the 'Bush Nazis': Germans, some veterans of Hitler's armies, who defiantly celebrated Hitler's birthday in the local *Biergarten* or flew the swastika flag above their farmhouses.

In the small town of Omaruru, one baker celebrated the Führer's birthday by marking his bread rolls with the swastika. In 1987, on the death of Rudolph Hess, a group of German Namibians placed an advertisement in the Windhoek newspaper the *Allgemeine Zeitung* describing Hitler's deputy as 'the last representative of a better Germany'. As late as 2005, a Windhoek magazine published an article paid for by a group calling themselves International Action Against Forgetting, celebrating the death of the Nazi hunter Simon Wiesenthal. 'With joy and satisfaction', it read, 'we take notice of the death of the big monster. On September 20th, the earth and its inhabitants were delivered from Simon . . . His biggest crime was to live 96 years.'

Pro-Nazi statements such as these have been repudiated by many German Namibians in recent years, and the Nazi-sympathising and neo-Nazi elements within the community are no doubt small, and getting smaller with each passing year. But the refusal of that minority to condemn the Nazi past tends to go hand-in-hand with a rejection of Namibia's own history. A culture of denial has developed, that regards attempts by the Herero and the Nama to uncover and commemorate the extermination of their ancestors as an attack on Germany and German Namibians in particular.

Supporters of this position dismiss the genocides as a historical 'theory' and tend to be most defensive on the subject of concentration camps. In early 2009 the Windhoek-based *Allgemeine Zeitung* published a letter by a German Namibian condemning the use of the word 'concentration camp' (*Konzentrationslager*) on a memorial erected by the Herero, near the site of one of the Swakopmund camps. Yet *Konzentrationslager* was the term used by von Schlieffen in the order he sent to von Trotha to establish the camps and was used by the *Schutztruppe* themselves.[9] The issue of forced labour is similarly vexed, but is more usually ignored than denied. Another article published in 2009, in a supplement of *Die Republikein*, the main Afrikaans newspaper, contrasted the slow pace of work on Namibia's new southern railway line with the lightning speed by which a similar line had been constructed between 1905 and 1906. The article claimed that the original Aus–Lüderitz railway line had been completed in a matter of months by one hundred German soldiers. It made no mention of the thousands of prisoners, most of them Herero women and children, who actually built that railway, or of the almost two thousand of them who died of exhaustion in the southern deserts.[10]

The story of the Herero and Nama genocides is not of consequence only as an unheeded augury of the calamities that were to befall Europe in the twentieth century. Neither is it a historical cudgel with which to beat Germany and the German population of Namibia, or force them to accept guilt for the crimes of their forefathers. It is of consequence in and of itself. To the descendants of its victims, the genocides are not a distant memory but an open wound that shapes their day-to-day existence.

South-West Africa was the continent's last colony, only achieving independence in 1990, after the collapse of Apartheid South Africa. Pretoria's grip on the colony she had seized in 1919 was broken only after a bitter and protracted war, fought by the forces of SWAPO (The South West African People's Organization) and her Angolan and Cuban allies. That final and emphatic rejection of white colonial rule is regarded by many Namibians as a direct continuation of the wars fought against German rule at the beginning of the twentieth century by the Herero, Nama and others. Among the Namibian leaders who confronted the South Africans in the 1950s and 1960s was the Herero chief Hosea Kutako, a veteran of the battle of the Waterberg and a survivor of the Omaruru concentration camp. One of the Nama leaders who worked alongside him was Hendrik Samuel Witbooi, the great-nephew of Hendrik Witbooi.

Among the freedoms that were opened up to the black citizens of the new nation of Namibia in 1990 was the freedom to challenge the Official History that had been established by the white minority. Over the course of the twentieth century, South-West Africa had become a nation assured of its own creation myth: a distorted frontier fantasy that had hardened into a state mythology, underwritten by Pretoria and underpinned by the pact of racial unity between Boer, Briton and German that had been consecrated in 1927 on the pyre of the Blue Book.

Yet the black majority – Herero, Nama, Owambo, San, Damara and many others – had kept their own histories alive, handing both stories and artefacts down through the generations. The old had shown the young where their ancestors where buried, and told them of the 'holy ground' where blood had been spilt. Survivors of the camps and the forced-labour regime had given their children the brass identification tags they had been forced to wear, physical tokens of their family's part in their people's calamity. Even today the very last Herero and Nama people born into post-genocide German slavery can recount the stories passed on to them by relatives and elders. Ms Unjekererua wa Karumbi, an elderly Herero woman, lives on a former reserve on the edge of the Omaheke Desert. Now in her eighties, she can still recall the names of all eight members of her family who were 'taken to Lüderitz' during the war. Only one of the eight survived. Throughout the years of South African rule, she dreamed of travelling to Lüderitz in order 'see for myself how they died'. The South Africa Pass Laws and crippling poverty made this impossible. Elderly and bed-ridden, her memory is fading and she is beginning to stumble over the list of names told her by her uncle.[11]

For many Herero, the victims of the war and the camps live on as more than names. Despite the catastrophes that have befallen them and the sustained efforts of the missionaries, the Herero have managed to maintain their ancient religion, with its visceral connection to the spirit world of their ancestors. To a people for whom the land can become the embodiment of the dead, the whole country, pockmarked with graves, is a memorial to the genocides. When the Herero town of Otjimanangombe was established in the 1920s, the local community refused to build their homes on two low hills that lie just to the east. In late 1904 a German patrol had encountered a group of Herero on the hills and in the skirmish that followed several German solders and Herero fighters lost their lives. For the Herero, the hills of Otjimanangombe became a place in which the living have no business.

In the 1990s the taboo was broken when a tree from one of the hills was felled and used to build a fence. A week later the town's main well stopped flowing. When government engineers were unable to solve the problem, the Herero elders took matters into their own hands. After communicating with the ancestors of the Oseu family, two of whom had fallen in the skirmish of 1904, they slaughtered a cow and buried its bones on the hill. The next week, to the satisfaction of the elders, the water returned. A few years later when the engineers of Namibia's Mobile Telecommunications Company considered erecting a mobile phone mast on one of the hills they were prevented by the people of Otjimanangombe.[12]

Despite their recent calamities and persistent poverty, the Herero are a highly organised people. Each year, they come together to mark the anniversary of their holocaust. In the last weekend in August, thousands converge on Okahandja, still nominally the Herero capital. The women wear long Victorian-style dresses and hats shaped like the horns of a cow, the men a military uniform based on that of the South African army which brought German rule to an end in 1915. Together they march from the Apartheid-era township on the edge of Okahandja. Passing the site of the old German fort where their uprising began, the procession makes its way to a small cemetery in which stand the graves of Samuel Maharero and his son

Friedrich. Silently circling the graves, running their fingers along the perimeter walls, the mourners pay their respects.

Colonialism left the Herero their memories and the spirits of their ancestors but little else. The war that exterminated 80 percent of the 1904 population cost them almost all of their land. Although some land redistribution has taken place since Independence, the vast majority of commercially viable farmland in Namibia is owned by around four thousand white commercial farmers. Around one hundred thousand Herero still live on the former 'native' reserves, onto which their grandparents were driven in the 1920s by the South Africans. Trapped by grinding poverty, they subsist by farming on communal land so overgrazed and under-watered that much of it can barely sustain goats, never mind cattle. A further two hundred thousand black Namibians work as labourers on the white-owned commercial farms. Conditions on some are a throwback to another age. Many farm labourers live in debt to their employers, who run farm shops selling basic supplies. The debt problem is in some cases exacerbated by an affliction that ravages isolated communities of repressed former colonial peoples across the world: alcoholism. The US State Department's *Country Report on Human Rights Practices* for Namibia, published in 2008, stated that 'Farm workers and domestic servants working on rural and remote farms often did not know their rights, and unions experienced obstacles in attempting to organize these workers. As a result, farm workers reportedly suffered abuse by employers.'[13]

Modern Namibia is one of the most unequal societies on earth. The concentration of wealth, land and privilege in the hands of a tiny racial minority remains entrenched. Yet some black Namibians, especially in the north and among the younger, post-Independence generation, have managed to escape the poverty trap and form an emerging black middle class. Black social mobility is centred on Windhoek, which has become one of the most racially and ethnically integrated cities in southern Africa. But although there are reasons to be optimistic about the possibility of change and development in the capital and the north, southern Namibia – seemingly frozen in time – is a cause for concern.

Life for black Namibians in the south is marred by acute poverty and rampant unemployment. The descendants of the Nama clans who once dominated the region live, like the Herero, either by subsistence farming or labouring on white farms. Gibeon, the capital of the Witbooi Nama since the 1840s, has fared as badly as any other southern town. Beyond the main road, with its old German colonial houses, lies a maze of unpaved backstreets leading to hundreds of desperate hovels, with neither running water nor adequate sanitation. Those fortunate enough to hold family farms keep goats and, where possible, cattle. Much of the rest of the population are maintained by the remittances of family members working in the cities or by the elderly, who receive a monthly pension of around $45.

Yet there are still sporadic flashes of the past in Gibeon, reminding visitors that this was once Hendrik Witbooi's realm. The occasional horse rider emerges from the desert and passes through Gibeon, seeking water from the nearby Fish River. The old German prison on the outskirts of town, with its barred windows and crumbing yellow bricks, is a reminder that this was once a town that was capable of revolt rather than in need of resurrection. The descendants of the Witbooi family still live in Gibeon. The 81-year-old great-granddaughter of Hendrik Witbooi, Alvina Petersen, the descendant of a leader whose name was heard in the Kaiser's Potsdam palace and along the corridors of power in Berlin, lives in a shack made from old rusty oil drums, hammered flat and painted bright pink. From her concrete porch, overlooking the Fish River, Mrs Petersen and her husband Hans sit and reflect on the century that brought their people little but disaster.

The act of remembering is perhaps what binds the Nama communities together. Despite the poverty, the cemetery at Gibeon, where the survivors of Shark Island are buried, is better cared for than much of the rest of the town. While the Nama lament the calamity of the genocides, they also revel in the old stories of Kaptein Hendrik, and the years when the Witbooi fighters, with their rifles and white bandanas, refused to yield to the might of Germany. Every other year representatives of each Nama community turn their attentions to Lüderitz. Gathering on Shark Island, they commemorate the three thousand who died on that desolate rock.

Across the bay, the town of Lüderitz retains the feel of frontier settlement, despite the new hotels and modern housing developments. It is a town trapped in the past: the chimney of one of the old factories was until recently painted in the red, white and black of Wilhelmian Germany, a nation that ceased to exist ninety years ago. Lüderitz is still the gateway to the diamond zone, but today most diamonds are discovered out at sea, by giant prospecting ships that literally hoover up the seabed and sift the sand for the precious stones. Interlopers who sneak into the waters of southern Namibia, and prospect without a government licence, are occasionally caught, and their ships impounded in the harbour. The other method of prospecting uses huge metal sea walls and powerful pumps literally to push the Atlantic Ocean back from the shoreline. In early 2008 such an excavation on the Namib coast uncovered the wreck of an Iberian caravel, from the late fifteenth or early sixteenth century. Around the disintegrated remains of the ship – perhaps the oldest ever found off the coast of sub-Saharan Africa – were thousands of Spanish and Portuguese gold coins, copper ingots, a stash of ivory, some exquisite fifteenth-century navigational instruments and human remains. In Namibia, the past seems to emerge of its own volition.

Ten years earlier, the Namib began to yield up human remains from another chapter of Namibia's history. In 1999 the existence of several mass graves near Lüderitz was brought to the attention of the post-Independence Namibian government. The graves lie within a radius of 3–4 miles from Lüderitz in the *Sperrgebiet*, the diamond fields that were sealed off from the outside world in 1908. For a century, only the employees of the diamond companies have had access to this area. The closest grave, only about an hour's walk north of the town, is a truly shocking sight. Femurs, vertebrae and skulls bleached and flaking are scattered across the sand, intermingled and disregarded. Interspersed with the bones are pieces of clothing: the collars of Victorian shirts with their blue and white pin-striping, leather belts and the hessian sacking. Nearby are the giant electric excavating machines, imported from Germany by the diamond companies just before World War I. Enormous and rusted, they are half buried, their chains of metal buckets like the vertebrae of a fossilised dinosaur. In 2006 representatives of nine of the Nama authorities came together to issue a statement requesting the Namibian government commission a forensic survey on the human remains in the mass graves. Namibia's history is on the march.

In Germany, too, it has been the dead as much as the living who have dragged the story of the Herero and Nama genocides from the historical shadows. In recent years, the skulls and even preserved heads of prisoners from the concentration camps have been found in the medical collections of a number of German universities. Freiburg University is said to have twelve skulls from Namibia in its anthropological collection, while the Medical History Museum of Berlin's Charitie Hospital is believed to hold forty-seven Namibian skulls. It is suspected that among the human remains at the Charitie Hospital are seventeen decapitated heads of Nama prisoners, prepared and dispatched from Shark Island in 1906 by the camp physician Dr Bofinger. These 'specimens' were later studied by Christian Fetzer, a Berlin medical student who endeavoured to identify anatomical similarities between the Nama and the anthropoid ape. Fetzer's theories were influenced by the work of Eugen Fischer. In October 2008, the Namibian government formally requested the repatriation of all Namibian remains held in German universities.

The history of German South-West Africa has returned to modern Germany, in part due to the campaigning of the Herero and Nama and their many supporters in Germany. Mixed-race German Namibians, some of whom trace their ancestry back to the wave of rapes in the concentration camps, have also demanded their history be acknowledged. In 2001 the Herero filed a legal case for reparations against the German government and a number of German companies which they claimed had profited from the genocides or played a part in the exploitation of their ancestors. Three years later, on the centenary of the battle of the Waterberg, the German Minister for Economic Cooperation and Development, Heidemarie Wieczorek-Zeul, travelled to Namibia and addressed a Herero gathering on the battlefield. In a speech that condemned the actions of General von Trotha, Minister Wieczorek-Zeul surprised many, in both Namibia and Germany, by asking for forgiveness and using the term genocide to describe Germany's treatment of the Herero and Nama. Although a brave and admirable step – for which Wieczorek-Zeul was roundly condemned by parts of the German press – the German government's apology made no mention of the concentration camps, and seemed to place blame for the genocides on von Trotha and the *Schutztruppe*. When von Trotha departed the colony in November 1905, around forty thousand Herero were still alive. The Nama had not even surrendered. Of those Herero still living in November 1905, perhaps only around ten thousand would survive the camps or escape capture.

What happened in Namibia between 1904 and 1909 cannot be ascribed to the murderous racism of a single fanatic general. The victims of these genocides were killed in the battles of 1904, by armies led by Leutwein as well as by von Trotha. They died of thirst and exhaustion in the Omaheke, in ambushes and attacks by the Cleansing Patrols. They were shot while trying to surrender to the Peace Patrols in 1906 and an unknown number were hanged or shot by settlers in early 1904, during the first few weeks of the uprising.

While the camps were established by the army, under the jurisdiction of von Trotha, much of the abuse and systematic murder that took place within them was directed by civilian administrators, bureaucratic killers like von Lindequist and Hintrager. At Shark Island, it was the army who attempted to have the camp closed and the Nama prisoners evacuated, only to be thwarted by von Lindequist and Hintrager. The camps and the regime of forced labour, although not responsible for the majority of deaths, may have cost as many lives as the two dreadful months of the Extermination Order.

As Namibia's history has slowly emerged since Independence, those who found it unpalatable have been unable to contest effectively the question of 'intent' – the historical litmus test of genocide. If the Extermination Order stands as proof of von Trotha's genocidal 'intent', his removal from office at the end of 1905 speaks of the physical impossibility of exterminating a whole nation in a country of 82.4 million hectares, with inadequate maps, almost no roads, pre-World War I military technology and the Nama still undefeated.[14] Yet 'intent' is stamped onto the Namibian genocides in all its ugly stages. It was implied in von Trotha's warning to the Nama of April 1905; that they should surrender or suffer the same fate as the Herero. It can be read in Lindequist's statement of December 1906, expressing his hopes that the Nama on Shark Island would be 'reduced somewhat' in number, and seen in the fact that his administration allowed the quay development at Lüderitz to grind to a halt, due to the deaths of the workforce.

While denialists have been unable to sidestep the test of genocidal 'intent', they have been more successful in focusing attention on von Trotha and the Extermination Order. By accident or design, this has diverted attention away from the aspect of this history that is perhaps most uncomfortable: the development in South-West Africa of Germany's first concentration camps *(Konzentrationslager)*, an instrument of mass killing that many find it difficult to accept as part of German history, outside of the context of Hitler's Third Reich.

What does the re-emergence of the dead from the Namib Desert, and the unearthing of documents and human remains from the archives and universities, mean for modern, liberal Germany? What is the significance of the fact that thirty years before Hitler came to power, in a forgotten German colony, her soldiers and bureaucrats attempted to exterminate two indigenous peoples, ultimately in concentration camps, and in the name of a Kaiser rather than a Führer?

The images held in the Namibian National Archives of healthy jackbooted soldiers guarding concentration camps or posing amid emaciated, skeletal prisoners have a resonance that today is all too obvious and all too powerful. So much of what took place in German South-West Africa at the beginning of the twentieth century horribly prefigures the events of the 1940s: concentration camps, the bureaucratisation of killing, meticulous record-keeping of death tolls and death rates, the use of work as a means of extermination, civilians transported in cattle trucks then worked to death, their remains experimented upon by race scientists, and the identification of ethnic groups who had a future as slaves and those who had no future of any sort. All were features of the German South-West African genocides that were replicated in different forms and on a much vaster scale in Europe in the 1940s.

There is, however, no direct 'causal thread' linking the Herero and Nama genocides to the crimes of the Third Reich. No unstoppable historical force carried Germany from Waterberg to Nuremberg. But the Herero and Nama genocides, along with the Nazi vision of race war and settlement in Eastern Europe, can both be seen as aspects of a larger phenomenon: the emergence from Europe of a terrible strain of racial colonialism that viewed human history through the prism of a distorted form of Social Darwinism, and regarded the earth as a racial battlefield on which the 'weak' were destined to be vanquished.

Notes

Introduction: Cell 5

1. Leonard Mosley, *The Reich Marshal: A Biography of Hermann Goering* (London: Pan, 1977), pp. 427–8.
2. *The Trial of German Major War Criminals: Proceedings of the International Military Tribunal Sitting at Nuremberg, Germany, 20th November, 1945, to 1st October, 1946* (London: HM Stationery Office, 1946–51), Part 9 (12–22 March 1946), p. 63.
3. Ibid., p. 81.
4. G. M. Gilbert, *Nuremberg Diary*, p. 202.
5. *Trial of German Major War Criminals* 9, p. 63.
6. Erich Gritzbach, *Hermann Goering: The Man and His Work* (London: Hurst & Blackett, 1939), p. 222.
7. Joseph Conrad, *Heart of Darkness* with *The Congo Diary* (Harmondsworth: Penguin Books, 1995), p. 58.

1 The World behind the Fog

1. Eric Axelson, *Congo to Cape: Early Portuguese Explorers* (London: Faber and Faber, 1973), p. 84.
2. Ibid., p. 87.
3. Ibid., p. 85.
4. Phillip D. Curtin, *The Image of Africa* (Madison, WI, and London: University of Wisconsin Press, 1973), vol. 1, p. 94.
5. See P. I. Hoogenhout, 'An Abbe and an Administrator', in *SWA Annual* 21 (1965), pp. 24–5.
6. F. Williams, *Precolonial Communities of Southwestern Africa: A History of Owambo Kingdoms 1600–1920* (Windhoek: National Archives of Namibia, 1991), pp. 30–5; P. Hayes and D. Haipinge (eds), *'Healing the Land': Kaulinge's History of Kwanyama* (Cologne: Ruediger Koeppe Verlag, 1997).
7. The matrilineal Lele people of the Congo (Kinshasa) also worship the deity called Njambi.
8. B. Lau, *Namibia in Jonker Afrikaner's Time* (Windhoek: National Archives of Namibia, 1987).
9. Oral history interviews with various Nama elders (NAN, NiD/NaDS Accession), some of which are published in C. W. Erichsen, *What the Elders Used to Say* (Windhoek: Namibia Institute for Democracy, 2008).
10. *Namibia in Jonker Afrikaner's Time.*
11. Ibid.

12. B. Lau (ed.), *Charles John Andersson: Trade and Politics in Central Namibia 1860–1864* (Windhoek: National Archives of Namibia, 1989); idem (ed.), *Carl Hugo Hahn: Tagebuecher 1837–1860* (Windhoek: National Archives of Namibia, 1984).

2 The Iron Chancellor and the Guano King

1. *The Times*, 27 August 1884.
2. *Journals of the London Mission Society* (Schmelen, 1819), Cape Archives, Cape Town.
3. J. C. G. Röhl, *From Bismarck to Hitler: Problems and Perspectives in History* (London: Longmans, 1970), p. 61.
4. Helmuth Stoecker (ed.), Bernard Zöller (trans.), *German Imperialism in Africa: From the Beginnings until the Second World War* (London: Hurst, 1986), p. 18.
5. Ibid., p. 31.
6. Hans Ulrich Wehler, 'Bismarck's Imperialism', *Past and Present* 48 (1991), p. 129.
7. Ibid., p. 269.
8. *The Times*, 25 June 1888.
9. *The Times*, 16 September 1885.
10. *The London Globe*, 11 December 1884. Quoted in Hartmut Pogge von Strandmann, 'Domestic Origins of Germany's Colonial Expansion under Bismarck', *Past and Present* 42 (1969), p. 127.
11. Woodruff D. Smith, *The German Colonial Empire* (Chapel Hill, NC: University of North Carolina Press, 1978), p. 30.
12. Stoecker, *German Imperialism*, p. 31.
13. H. Drechsler, *Let Us Die Fighting* (Berlin: Akademie-Verlag, 1986), p. 23.
14. Prosser Gifford and William Roger Louis, *Britain and Germany in Africa: Imperial Rivalry and Colonial Rule* (New Haven, CT, and London: Yale University Press, 1967), p. 68.
15. Mary Evelyn Townsend, *The Rise and Fall of Germany's Colonial Empire 1884–1918* (New York: Macmillan, 1930), p. 129.

3 'This Is My Land'

1. H. Vedder, 'Was Dr Göring vor 55 Jahren in Okahandja erlebte', in *Afrikanischer Heimatskalender* (Windhoek, 1940), pp. 33–5; O. Hintrager, *Suedwestafrika in der deutschen Zeit* (Munich: Kommissionsverlag, 1955); Anonymous, 'Dr Göring, Heinrich Ernst', in W. J. DeKock (ed.), *Dictionary of South African Biography*, vol. 1 (Cape Town: Nasionale Boekhandel for the National Council for Social Research, 1968); H. E. Göring, 'Anfang in Deutsch-Suedwest', in W. von Langdorff, *Deutsche Flagge ueber Sand un Palmen* (Guetersloh: C. Bertelsmann, 1936), pp. 29–40.
2. National Archives of Namibia (NAN), *Heinrich Göring*, 'Allerhöchste Vollmacht fuer den Kommissar in dem suedwestafrikanischen Schitzgeniete Dr. Jur. Heinrich Ernst Göring'.
3. G. Pool, *Samuel Maharero* (Windhoek: Gamsberg Macmillan, 1991), pp. 38–43.
4. Göring, 'Anfang', pp. 32, 35, 37. In the last week of September, Göring and his colleagues had similarly dressed up to meet the chief of Otjimbingwe; Vedder, 'Was Dr Göring'.
5. A. Heywood and E. Maasdorp (eds), *The Hendrik Witbooi Papers* (Windhoek: National Archives of Namibia, 1995), pp. xiv, 6–13.
6. H. Vedder, 'Was Dr Göring'; Heywood and Maasdorp, *Witbooi Papers*, pp. 6–13.

7. Göring, 'Anfang', p. 38.
8. Heywood and Maasdorp, *Witbooi Papers*, p. 7.
9. T. Leutwein, *Elf Jahre Gouverneur in Deutsch-Suedwestafrika* (Berlin: Ernst Siegfried Mittler und Sohn, 1907), quoted in Heywood and Maasdorp, *Witbooi Papers*, p. 224.
10. Heywood and Maasdorp, *Witbooi Papers*, p. 12.
11. Ibid., p. 15.
12. Ibid., p. 33.
13. H. Drechsler, *Let Us Die Fighting* (Berlin: Akademie-Verlag, 1986), p. 34.
14. Ibid.
15. Ibid., p. 38.
16. Archives of the Evangelical Lutheran Church in Namibia (ELCN), RMS I, *Konferenzen und Synoden* 1.3 (1873–1905), 'Protokollbuch der Konferenzen in Hereroland/Bericht Uber die Verhandlungen zwischen der Herero Konferenz und Maharero gehalten zu Okahandja am 17–18 Dec 1888' (courtesy of Dr Jan-Bart Gewald).
17. Drechsler, *Let Us Die Fighting*, p. 41.
18. J. Gewald, *Towards Redemption* (Leiden: CNWS, 1996), pp. 40–6.

4 Soldier of Darkness

1. J. Gewald, *Towards Redemption* (Leiden: CNWS, 1996); idem, 'Learning to Wage and Win Wars in Africa' (Leiden: ASC Working Paper 06/2005); H. Drechsler, *Let Us Die Fighting* (Berlin: Akademie-Verlag, 1986); W. Tabel, 'Die literature der Kolonialzeit Suewestafrikas: Memoiren beruehmter Persoenlichkeiten: Curt von Francois', in *Afrikanischer Heimatskalender* (Windhoek, Informationsausschuss der Deutschen Evangelisch-Lutherischen Kirche in Suedwestafrika, 1984); G. Pool, *Samuel Maharero* (Windhoek: Gamsberg Macmillan, 1991).
2. Drechsler, *Let Us Die Fighting*, p. 43.
3. Ibid.
4. Tabel, 'Die literature', p. 78.
5. Klaus Dierks, *Chronology of Namibian History* (Windhoek: Namibia Scientific Society, 2002), p. 68 (18 August 1889).
6. Gewald, *Towards Redemption*, pp. 39–46.
7. Drechsler, *Let Us Die Fighting*, p. 43.
8. C. von François, *Deutsch-Suedwestafrika: Geschichte der Kolonisation bis zum Ausbruch des Krieges mit Witbooi, April 1893* (Berlin, 1899), pp. 75–6; H. von François, *Nama und Damara* (Magdeburg, 1895), p. 122.
9. A. Heywood and E. Maasdorp (eds), *The Hendrik Witbooi Papers* (Windhoek: National Archives of Namibia, 1995), p. 98. Witbooi might also have been referring to the Anglo-German Conference of 1890.
10. Ibid., p. 50.
11. Ibid., pp. 84–9.
12. Ibid., p. 102.
13. Ibid., p. 101.
14. Drechsler, *Let Us Die Fighting*, pp. 70–4; Union of South Africa, *Report on the Natives of South-West Africa and Their Treatment by Germany* (London: HMSO, 1918), section V; K. Schwabe, *Mit Schwert und Pflug in Deutsch-suedwestafrika* (Berlin, 1904); Heywood and Maasdorp, *Witbooi Papers*, pp. 126–41, 207–10; National Archives of South Africa, GG office 9/269/3, Witbooi to Cleverly

(2 May 1893).
15. Heywood and Maasdorp, *Witbooi Papers*, pp. 207–210.
16. Ibid.
17. For Petrus Jafta Statement, ibid., p. 210.
18. Schwabe, *Mit Schwert.*
19. Ibid.
20. Heywood and Maasdorp, *Witbooi Papers*, p. 210.
21. H. Drechsler, *Let Us Die Fighting*, p. 71.

5 'European Nations Do Not Make War in That Way'

1. Sven Linqvist, *Exterminate All the Brutes* (New York: New Press, 1996), p. 135.
2. William Winwood Reade, *Savage Africa* (London: Smith, Elder & Co., 1864), p. 452.
3. Ibid.
4. Richard Weikart, *From Darwin to Hitler* (New York and Basingstoke: Palgrave Macmillan, 2004), p. 10.
5. A. Heywood and E. Maasdorp (eds), *The Hendrik Witbooi Papers* (Windhoek: National Archives of Namibia, 1995), p. 130.
6. Ibid.
7. H. Drechsler, *Let Us Die Fighting* (Berlin: Akademie-Verlag, 1986), p. 71.
8. Ibid., p. 72.
9. Ibid., p. 73.
10. Heywood and Maasdorp, *Witbooi Papers*, p. 148.
11. Ibid.
12. Ibid., p. 175.
13. Ibid., p. 177.
14. L. Von Estorff, 'Kriegserlebnisse in Suedwestafrika', in *Militaerwochenblatt* (1911), Beiheft 3.
15. Heywood and Maasdorp, *Witbooi Papers*, p. 207–8.
16. Ibid., p. 209.
17. Ibid.
18. Drechsler, *Let Us Die Fighting*, p. 78.

6 'A Piece of Natural Savagery'

1. J. C. G. Röhl, *From Bismarck to Hitler: Problems and Perspectives in History* (London: Longmans, 1970), p. 61.
2. R. d'O. Butler, *The Roots of National Socialism, 1783–1933* (London: Faber and Faber, 1941), p. 193.
3. Alexandra Richie, *Faust's Metropolis, A History of Berlin* (London: HarperCollins, 1998), p. 228.
4. Graf von Schweinitz et al, *Deutschland und seine Kolonien im Jahre 1896: Amtlicher Bericht ueber die Erste deutsche Kolonial-Ausstellung* (Berlin: Verlag von Dietrich Reimer, 1897); G. Meinerke (ed.), *Deutsche Kolonialzeitung: Organ der Deutschen Kollonialgesellschaft*, Compendium, vol. 9 (Berlin: Verlag der Deutschen Kolonialgesellschaft, 1896); Felix von Luschan, *Beitraege zur Voelkerkunde der deutschen Schutzgebiete: Erweiterte Sonderausgabe aus dem 'Amtlichen Bericht ueber die erste deutsche Kolonial-Ausstellung' in Treptow 1896* (Berlin: Verlag von Dietrich Reimer, 1897); J. Zeller, 'Friedrich Maharero: Ein Herero in Berlin', in U. Van der Heyde and J. Zeller, *Kolonial metropole Berlin* (Berlin: Berlin Edition, 2002), pp. 206–11.

5. Schweinitz, *Deutschland und seine Kolonien*, p. 25.
6. Luschan, *Beitraege zur Voelkerkunde*, p. 221.
7. Ibid.
8. A. Zimmerman, *Anthropology and Antihumanism in Imperial Germany* (Chicago: University of Chicago Press, 2001), p. 27.
9. Schweinitz, *Deutschland und seine Kolonien*, p. 63.
10. J. Gewald, *Herero Heroes* (Oxford: James Currey, 1999), p. 112; H. Drechsler, *Let Us Die Fighting* (Berlin: Akademie-Verlag, 1986), pp. 88–119; N. Waterberg, *Mossolow* (Windhoek: John Meinert (Pty) Ltd, 1993).

7 King of Huns

1. J. C. G. Röhl, *Wilhelm II: The Kaiser's Personal Monarchy, 1888–1900* (Cambridge: Cambridge University Press, 2004), p. 1053.
2. M. Goertemaker, 'Deutschland im 19. Jahrhundert', *Schriftenreihe der Bundeszentrale fuer politische Bildung* 274 (1996), p. 357.
3. Dietlind Wünsch, *Feldpostbriefe aus China* (Berlin: Chr. Links Verlag, 2008), p. 197.
4. Richard Weikart, *From Darwin to Hitler* (New York and Basingstoke: Palgrave Macmillan, 2004), p. 205.
5. Theodore Roosevelt, *The Winning of the West* (Lincoln, NE: University of Nebraska Press, 1995), vol. 1, p. 63.
6. The US census of 1890 suggested that westward migration into unsettled regions had, to all intents and purposes, come to an end and the frontier had ceased to exist – other than in the American psyche.
7. See for example K. May, *Winnetou* (Bamberg: Karl-May-Verlag, 1953) or discussion thereof in S. Friedrichsmeyer, S. Lennox and S. Zantop, *The Imperialist Imagination: German Colonialism and Its Legacy* (Ann Arbor, MI: University of Michigan Press, 1998).
8. F. Ratzel, *Deutschland* (Berlin: Walter de Gruyter & Co., 1943); idem, *Anthropo-Geographie* (Stuttgart: Elibron Classics Series, 2005); A. Dorpalen, *The World of General Haushofer* (New York: Farrar & Rinehart, Inc., 1942); C. O. Sauer, 'The Formative Years of Ratzel in the United States', *Annals of the Association of American Geographers* 61.2 (June 1971); G. Buttmann, *Friedrich Ratzel: Leben und Werk eines deutschen Geographen 1844–1904* (Stuttgart: Wissenschaftliches Verlagsgesellschaft, 1977).
9. See, for example, Bayerische Staatsbibliothek, *Ratzeliana* I.2, Luschan to Ratzel (March 1897).
10. Sven Linqvist, *Exterminate All the Brutes* (New York: New Press, 1996), p. 144.
11. Weikart, *From Darwin to Hitler*, p. 194.
12. Jon M. Bridgeman, *The Revolt of the Hereros* (Berkeley, CA: University of California Press, 1981), p. 57.
13. Paul Rohrbach, *Der Deutsche Gedanke in der Welt* (Düsseldorf: Langewiesche, 1912), pp. 141–2.
14. Clarence Lusane, *Hitler's Black Victims* (New York and London: Routledge, 2002), p. 43.
15. Rohrbach, *Der Deutsche Gedanke*, pp. 141–2.
16. H. Drechsler, *Let Us Die Fighting* (Berlin: Akademie-Verlag, 1986), p. 106.
17. Helmut Bley, *Namibia under German Rule* (Hamburg: LIT, 1996), p. 130; Brenda Bravenboer and Walter Rusch, *The First 100 Years of State Railways in*

Namibia (Windhoek: TransNamib Museum, 1997), p. 16.

18. Bley, *Namibia under German Rule*, p. 133.
19. NAN, BKE 222, B.II.74.d, vol. 6, p. 48.
20. Quoted in Klaus Dierks, *Chronology of Namibian History* (Windhoek: Namibia Scientific Society, 2002), p. 92.
21. Bley, *Namibia under German Rule*, pp. 139–40.
22. Drechsler, *Let Us Die Fighting*, p. 136.
23. J. Silvester and J. Gewald, *Words Cannot Be Found: German Colonial Rule in Namibia* (Leiden: Brill, 2003), p. 96.
24. C. W. Erichsen, *What the Elders Used to Say* (Windhoek: Namibia Institute for Democracy, 2008), pp. 22–3.

8 'Rivers of Blood and Money'

1. G. Pool, *Samuel Maharero* (Windhoek: Gamsberg Macmillan, 1991); J. Gewald, *Herero Heroes* (Oxford: James Currey, 1999); H. Drechsler, *Let Us Die Fighting* (Berlin: Akademie-Verlag, 1986); I. Hull, *Absolute Destruction* (Ithaca, NY: Cornell University Press, 2005); J. Zimmerer and J. Zeller (eds), *Genocide in German South-West Africa: the Colonial War of 1904–1908 and Its Aftermath* (Monmouth: Merlin Press Ltd., 2008); C. W. Erichsen, *What the Elders Used to Say* (Windhoek: Namibia Institute for Democracy, 2008).
2. J. Gewald, *Towards Redemption* (Leiden: CNWS, 1996), pp. 188–9.
3. Ibid., p. 193.
4. Ibid., pp. 185–6.
5. National Archives of Namibia, Accession 71, 'Ludwig Conradt', Erinnerungen aus zwanzigjährigem Händler- und Farmerleben in Deutsch-Südwestafrika, p. 250.
6. A. Zimmerman, 'Adventures in the Skin Trade', in H. Glenn Penny and Matti Bunzl (eds), *Worldly Provincialism: German Anthropology in the Age of Empire* (Ann Arbor, MI: University of Michigan Press, 2003), p. 175.
7. This official tally is inscribed at the foot of a German colonial monument still standing in the Namibian capital Windhoek.
8. Pool, *Samuel Maharero*, p. 211.
9. C. Rust, *Krieg und Frieden im Hereroland* (Berlin, 1905), pp. 190–5.
10. *Cape Times*, 23 April 1904.
11. One of very few voices of reason came from Missionary Irle, who wrote to the influential newspaper *Der Reichsbote*: 'Certain newspapers report that the Herero have perpetrated terrible atrocities, alleging that they have massacred settler wives as well as castrating many men. With reference to the latter allegation, they have done this with the whites who have raped their women in a most brutal manner. With reference to the [white] women who are supposed to have been butchered and disembowelled, this is pure fabrication. Mrs Pilet and her sister Frauenstein, Mrs Külbel and her children in Oriambo, Mrs Lange and her sister in Klein Barmen, Mrs Bremen and her five children in Otjonjati . . . all are alive and well, they are not dead.' Quoted in Drechsler, *Let Us Die Fighting*, p. 146.
12. See Gesine Kruger, 'Beasts & Victims', in Zimmerer and Zeller (eds), *Genocide in German South-West Africa*.
13. Drechsler, *Let Us Die Fighting*, p. 142.
14. Quoted ibid., p. 147.
15. J. Krumbach, *Franz Ritter von Epp: Ein Leben Fuer Deutschland* (Munich: NSDAP, 1940), p. 185.

16. M. Bayer, *Der Krieg in Südwestafrika und seine Bedeutung für die Entwicklung der Kolonie* (Leipzig: Verlag von Friedrich Engelmann, 1906), p. 9.
17. A. Eckl, *S'ist ein uebles Land hier* (Cologne: Ruediger Koeppe Verlag, 2005), p. 220.
18. Bundesarchiv Berlin (Lichterfelde-West), Colonial Department, File 2133, pp. 89–90.
19. Pool, *Samuel Maharero*, pp. 232–9; I. Hull, *Absolute Destruction*, pp. 13–22; NAN, Accession 510, 'Tagebuch von Emil Malzahn 1901–1904 (Unteroffizier)', pp. 20–4.
20. Drechsler, *Let Us Die Fighting*, p. 149.
21. Hull, *Absolute Destruction*, pp. 26–7.
22. Drechsler, *Let Us Die Fighting*, p. 154.
23. G. Pape, *Lorang* (Göttingen: Klaus Hesse Verlag, 2003), p. 186.
24. H. Kuehne, 'Die Ausrottungsfeldzuege der "Kaiserlichen Schutztruppen in Afrika" und die sozialdemokratischen Reichstagsfraktion', *Militaergeschichte* 18 (1979), p. 211.
25. Quoted in Hull, *Absolute Destruction*, p. 33, from Otto Dannhauer.
26. NAN, Accession 453, 'Helene Gathman's Diary', Sunday 17 July 1904, p. 69.
27. Pool, *Samuel Maharero*, p. 251.
28. Helmut Bley, *Namibia under German Rule* (Hamburg: LIT, 1996), p. 156.
29. J. Gewald, *Towards Redemption*, p. 205.
30. Eckl, *S'ist ein uebles Land hier*; NAN, Acession 510, Tagebuch Malzahn; Pape, *Lorang; Kriegsgeschichtlichen Abteilung I des Grossen Generalstabes, Die Kaempfe der deutschen Truppen in Suedwestafrika* (Berlin, Ernst Siegfried Mittler und Sohn, 1907).
31. B. von Bülow, *Denkwürdigkeiten: Band 2* (Berlin: Ullstein, 1930) p. 21; Drechsler, *Let Us Die Fighting*, p. 155.
32. M. Bayer, *Mit Haputquartier in Suedwestafrika* (Berlin: Wilhelm Weicher Marine und Kolonialverlag, 1909), p. 161.
33. Adolf Fischer, *Menschen und Tiere in Suedwestafrika* (Berlin: Safari Verlag, 1914).
34. NAN, Accession 109, 'Major Stuhlman Diary'.
35. NAN, Accession 569, 'Memoirs of Pastor Elger', pp. 38–40.
36. *Kriegsgeschichtlichen Abteilung I des Grossen Generalstabes, Die Kaempfe der deutschen Truppen in Suedwestafrika* (Berlin: Ernst Siegfried Mittler und Sohn, 1907), pp. 193 and 218.

9 'Death through Exhaustion'

1. J. Gewald, 'The Great General of the Kaiser', *Botswana Notes and Records* 26 (1994), pp. 67–76; A. Eckl, *S'ist ein uebles Land hier* (Cologne: Ruediger Koeppe Verlag, 2005); H. Drechsler, *Let Us Die Fighting* (Berlin: Akademie-Verlag, 1986).
2. Most historians mistakenly refer to this event as taking place on 2 October, as this is the date that appears on von Trotha's so-called Extermination Order.
3. Gewald, 'The Great General', p. 68.
4. Eckl, *S'ist ein uebles Land hier*, p. 284.
5. Drechsler, *Let Us Die Fighting*, pp. 160–1; Helmut Bley, *Namibia under German Rule* (Hamburg: LIT, 1996), p. 164.
6. Ibid.
7. Drechsler, *Let Us Die* Fighting, p. 157.
8. Ibid., p. 159.
9. ELCN: RMS: V 12 Karibib, 1904.

10. Union of South Africa, *Report on the Natives of South-West Africa and Their Treatment by Germany* (London: HMSO, 1918), pp. 117–18.
11. J. Silvester and J. Gewald, *Words Cannot Be Found: German Colonial Rule in Namibia* (Leiden: Brill, 2003), pp. 106–7; BAB, Colonial Department, File 2117, pp. 112–16.
12. Silvester and Gewald, *Words Cannot Be Found*, pp. 106–7.
13. Bundesarchiv Berlin (BAB), Colonial Department, File 2117, pp. 112–16.
14. Anonymous, *Tagebuchblaetter aus Suedwest-Afrika* (Berlin: Boll und Pickardt, 1906), pp. 35–6.
15. Drechsler, *Let Us Die Fighting*, p. 161.
16. Ibid., p. 163.
17. BAB, Colonial Department, File 2089, pp. 7–11.
18. I. Hull, *Absolute Destruction* (Ithaca, NY: Cornell University Press, 2005), p. 30.
19. Ibid., p. 65.
20. BAB, Colonial Department, File 2117, p. 59b (insert: pp. 1–57).
21. Ibid.
22. Ibid.
23. 'Concentration Camps during the Boer War', Stanford University Library Collection: http://www-sul.stanford.edu/depts/ssrg/africa/boers.html.
24. C.W. Erichsen, *'The Angel of Death Has Descended Violently among Them': Concentration Camps and Prisoners-of-War in Namibia, 1904–08* (Leiden: African Studies Centre, 2005), p. 22.
25. Ibid., pp. 24–8.
26. NAN, Accession 569, Memoirs of Pastor Elger.
27. Hull, *Absolute Destruction*, p. 71.
28. Erichsen '*The Angel of Death*'; J. Zimmerer and J. Zeller (eds), *Genocide in German South-West Africa: the Colonial War of 1904–1908 and Its Aftermath* (Monmouth: Merlin Press Ltd., 2008); J. Gewald, *Herero Heroes* (Oxford: James Currey, 1999); Drechsler, *Let Us Die Fighting*; Hull, *Absolute Destruction*; J. Gaydish, 'Fair Treatment is Guaranteed to You: the Swakopmund Prisoner-of-War Camp 1905–1908', Unpublished conference paper (Windhoek: UNAM, 2000).
29. NAN, Zentralbureau (ZBU) 454, D. IV.l.3, vol. 1, pp. 58–9.
30. The Herero elders in the Swakopmund concentration camp wrote a letter to the Mission Head asking for access to translated books of the Old Testament, especially the Book of Moses. According to the author of the letter, the enslavement of the Israelites had some resonance with the prisoners. Evangelical Lutheran Church Namibia (ELCN), RMS, Missions-berichte 1906, p. 120.
31. ELCN, RMS, Chroniken 31, Swakopmund.
32. J. Zeller, 'Ombepera I koza – The Cold is Killing Me', in Zimmerer and Zeller, *Genocide in German South-West Africa*, pp. 65–83.
33. Erichsen, '*The Angel of Death*', pp. 48–53.
34. *Kommando der Schutztruppen im Reichskolonialamt, Sanitaets-Bericht Ueber die Kaiserliche Schutztruppe fuer suedwestafrika waehrend des Herero und Hottenttotenaufstandes fuer die Zeit vom 1. Januar 1904 bis 31. Maerz 1907. Erster Band, 1. Administrativer Teil.* (Berlin: Ernst Siegfried Mittler und Sohn, 1909), pp. 45–50.
35. NAN, ZBU 454, D.IV.l.3, vol. 2, pp. 336–40; NAN, ZBU 454, D.IV.l.3, vol. 1, p. 163; NAN, BKE 224, vol. 2, 74.d. spec. I, pp. 29–31.
36. Erichsen, '*The Angel of Death*', pp. 22–3.
37. NAN, ZBU 2372, IX. H. vol. 1, pp. 58–61.

38. Cape Archives, GH 23/97, 'Statement under oath by: Jack Seti, John Culayo and James Tolibadi', Ministers to Governor, 22 August 1906.
39. See, for example, B. Lau, 'Uncertain Certainties', in *History and Historiography* (Windhoek: Namibian National Archives, 1995).
40. ZBU 454, D. IV.l.3, vol. 1, pp. 58–9.
41. Deaths in the military concentration camp, which was begun early February 1905, until 29 May were 399 prisoners out of 1,100 – 111 of these died in the last two weeks of May. ZBU 454, D. IV.l.3, vol. 1, pp. 58–9.
42. Ibid.
43. Ibid.
44. BAB, Colonial Department, File 2118, p. 157.
45. Ibid., pp. 152–6.
46. ELCN, RMS Correspondence VII 31.1, Swakopmund 1–7, Eich to Vedder, 19 June 1905.
47. NAN, BSW 107, VA/10/6.

10 'Peace Will Spell Death for Me and My Nation'

1. C.W. Erichsen, '*The Angel of Death Has Descended Violently among Them': Concentration Camps and Prisoners-of-War in Namibia, 1904–08* (Leiden: African Studies Centre, 2005); H. Drechsler, *Let Us Die Fighting* (Berlin: Akademie-Verlag, 1986); Jon M. Bridgeman, *The Revolt of the Hereros* (Berkeley, CA: University of California Press, 1981); T. Leutwein, *Elf Jahre Gouverneur in Deutsch-Suedwestafrika* (Berlin: Ernst Siegfried Mittler und Sohn, 1907); W. Nuhn, *Feind Ueberall* (Bonn: Bernard & Graefe Verlag, 2000); W. Hillebrecht, 'The Nama and the War in the South', in J. Zimmerer and J. Zeller (eds), *Genocide in German South-West Africa: the Colonial War of 1904–1908 and Its Aftermath* (Monmouth: Merlin Press Ltd., 2008), pp. 143–59.
2. Leutwein, *Elf Jahre*.
3. Drechsler, *Let Us Die Fighting*, pp. 182–3; Union of South Africa, *Report on the Natives of South-West Africa and Their Treatment by Germany* (London: HMSO, 1918).
4. NAN, Accession 507, Missionary Berger Memoirs: 'Drie Jare by Hendrik Witbooi', pp. 14–15.
5. BAB, Colonial Department, File 2133, pp. 32–4.
6. I. Goldblatt, *The History of South West Africa: From the Beginning of the Nineteenth Century* (Cape Town: Juta and Co. Ltd, 1971), pp. 147–8.
7. *South African News*, 31 May 1904.
8. Drechsler, *Let Us Die Fighting*, p. 143.
9. Ibid., p. 184.
10. ELCN, RMS, Missions-berichte January 1905, pp. 25–31, 39–45.
11. Ibid., pp. 39–45.
12. C. W. Erichsen, *What the Elders Used to Say* (Windhoek: Namibia Institute for Democracy, 2008), pp. 20–31.
13. *Kriegsgeschichtlichen Abteilung I des Grossen Generalstabes, Die Kaempfe der deutschen Truppen in Suedwestafrika: Band 2* (Berlin: Ernst Siegfried Mittler und Sohn, 1907), pp. 17–19.
14. A German solider present at Auob remembers how the Nama taunted them mid-battle. 'Scorning remarks were shouted at us, like "Are Deutschmanns thirsty? Here is plenty of water." They displayed filled canteens of water in

front of us. Again, one of our officers was severely wounded, shot from behind. Another Lieutenant charged the enemy alone. Four bullets struck him down, dead.' C. Jitschin, *Als Reiter in Suedwest* (Breslau: Flemmings Verlag, 1937), pp. 89–90.

15. O. Trautmann, *Im Herero und Hottentottenland* (Oldenburg: Gerhard Stalling, 1913), p. 121.
16. Jitschin, *Als Reiter*, p. 130.
17. Paul Emil von Lettow-Vorbeck, *Mein Leben* (Biberach an der Riss: Koehlers, 1957), pp. 87–8.
18. Drechsler, *Let Us Die Fighting*, p. 187.
19. *Cape Times*, 29 May 1906.
20. In an official communication to the parents of E. L. Presgrave upon his death at German hands in 1907, he was described in the following manner: 'Mr. E. L. Presgrave is reported to have acted as "Secretary" and adviser to Marengo, one of the Rebel leaders, and His Majesty's Government are informed by the German authorities that it has been ascertained that he took part in the fight at Narugas on 11 March and in a patrol fight at Bissiport [aka Pisseport] in April 1905.' Cape Archives, Correspondence file no. 868, p. 1.
21. Drechsler, *Let Us Die Fighting*, p. 220 n. 16.
22. Ibid., p. 193.
23. Ibid., p. 187; M. Bayer, *Mit Haputquartier in Suedwestafrika* (Berlin: Wilhelm Weicher Marine und Kolonialverlag, 1909), p. 225.
24. NAN, BKE 220, B.II. & 4.a. spec. 1, pp. 7–8.
25. Some sources note that Lieutenant Thilo von Trotha was the general's son. However, Maximilian Bayer, who travelled through most of the operational areas with the general, claims the younger Trotha was a nephew. Bayer, *Mit Haputquartier*, p. 261; *Kriegsgeschichtlichen Abteilung I*, pp. 119–20.
26. Nuhn, *Feind Ueberall*, p. 175.
27. ZBU 465, D.IV. m.3. vol. 1, p 30; BKE 305, G.A. 10/2 'Secret Files: Uprising 1904–05', pp. 77–86; *Kriegsgeschichtlichen Abteilung I*, pp. 180–83.
28. BKE 305, G.A. 10/2 'Secret Files: Uprising 1904–05', p. 79.
29. NAN, Accession 507, Missionary Berger, p. 37.
30. BKE 305, G.A. 10/2 'Secret Files: Uprising 1904–05', pp. 77–86; *Kriegsgeschichtlichen Abteilung I*, pp. 180–83.
31. See, for example, von Estorff's dire assessment of the situation facing the German army. L. von Estorff, 'Kriegserlebnisse in Suedwestafrika', *Militaer-wochenblatt* 3 (1911), p. 95.
32. Nuhn, *Feind Ueberall*, p. 176.
33. *Kriegsgeschichtlichen Abteilung I*, p. 185.

11 'You Yourselves Carry the Blame for Your Misery'

1. NAN, Photo Library: Arrival of Lindequist; Bundesarchiv Koblenz, Kl. Erwerbungen, Nachlass Lindequist, File 275; NAN, *Biographies: Lindequist*; H. Vedder, *Kurze Geschichten aus einem langen Leben* (Wuppertal-Barmen: Verlag der Rheinischen Missions-Gesellschaft, 1953), pp. 145–7; ELCN, RMS, Missions-berichte 1906. G. I. Schrank, 'German South-West Africa: Social and Economic Aspects of Its History, 1884–1915', unpublished Ph.D. thesis (New York: New York University, 1974), p. 206.
2. S. Shaw, *William of Germany* (Dublin: Trinity College, 1913).

3. G. I. Schrank, 'German South-West Africa', p. 206.
4. NAN, Vedder Quellen, 29A, p. 99.
5. NAN, ZBU 454, D.VI.l.3, vol. 1, pp. 187–8.
6. Vedder, *Kurze Geschichten*, pp. 145–7; ELCN, RMS, Missions-berichte 1906, pp. 34–6.
7. Ibid.
8. ELCN, RMS, Missions-berichte 1906, pp. 36–7; NAN, Vedder Quellen, 29A, pp. 99–100.
9. ELCN, RMS, Missions-berichte 1906, pp. 36–7; H. Drechsler, *Let Us Die Fighting* (Berlin: Akademie-Verlag, 1986), pp. 207–10, 227 n. 161.
10. C.W. Erichsen, *'The Angel of Death Has Decended Violently among Them': Concentration Camps and Prisoners-of-War in Namibia, 1904–08* (Leiden: African Studies Centre, 2005), pp. 28–44.
11. ELCN, RMS, Missions-berichte 1906, p. 167.
12. NAN, ZBU 2369 Secret Files: Witbooi-Hottentotten, VIII.g. vol. 1, p. 8; ELCN, RMS, Missions-berichte 1906, pp. 67–8.
13. ELCN, RMS, Missions-berichte 1906, pp. 67–8.
14. W. Nuhn, *Feind Ueberall* (Bonn: Bernard & Graefe Verlag, 2000), p. 179.
15. *Kriegsgeschichtlichen Abteilung I des Grossen Generalstabes, Die Kaempfe der deutschen Truppen in Suedwestafrika: Band 2* (Berlin: Ernst Siegfried Mittler und Sohn, 1907), pp. 180–3; NAN, ZBU 2369 Secret Files: Witbooi-Hottentotten, VIII.g. vol. 1, p 44 (old pagination).
16. NAN, ZBU 2369 Secret Files: Witbooi-Hottentotten, VIII.g. vol. 1, pp. 52–5.
17. F. Dincklage-Campe, *Deutsche Reiter in Suedwest* (Berlin: Deutsches Verlagshaus Bong, 1908), p. 14.
18. Erichsen, *'The Angel of Death'*, pp. 42–51.
19. *Windhuker Nachrichten*, 22 March 1906.
20. Ibid.
21. G. Pool, *Die Herero-Opstand 1904–07* (Cape Town: Hollandsch Afrikaansche Uitgevers Maatschappij, 1979), p. 270.
22. J. Silvester and J. Gewald, *Words Cannot Be Found: German Colonial Rule in Namibia* (Leiden: Brill, 2003), p. 178.
23. NAN, ZBU 456, D IV.l.3, vol. 5, p. 170.
24. Ibid.
25. L. Schultze, 'Südwestafrika', in H. Meyer (ed.), *Das Deutsche Kolonialreich*, vol. 2 (Leipzig: Verlag des Bibliographischen Instituts, 1914), p. 295.
26. *Der Deutsche*, 1 August 1906, as cited in Nuhn, *Feind Ueberall*, p. 266.

12 'The Island of Death'

1. H. F. B. Walker, *A Doctor's Diary in Damaraland* (London: Edward Arnold, 1917), Chapter X, 18 July.
2. C.W. Erichsen, *'The Angel of Death Has Descended Violently among Them': Concentration Camps and Prisoners-of-War in Namibia, 1904–08* (Leiden: African Studies Centre, 2005), pp. 65–9.
3. ELCN, RMS, Correspondence VII. 31, Swakopmund 1–7, Eich to Vedder 24 May 1905.
4. Ibid., Eich to Vedder 16 December 1905.
5. H. Vedder, *Kurze Geschichten aus einem langen Leben* (Wuppertal-Barmen:

Verlag der Rheinischen Missions-Gesellschaft, 1953), p. 139.

6. NAN, ZBU 456, D IV.l.3, vol. 5, p. 98.
7. Ibid., p. 106b.
8. Kuhlmann as quoted in I. Hull, *Absolute Destruction* (Ithaca, NY: Cornell University Press, 2005), p. 78.
9. *Cape Argus*, 28 September 1905.
10. Ibid.
11. Erichsen, '*The Angel of Death*', pp. 88–94.
12. L. Sinclair (ed.), *Collins German Dictionary Plus Grammar* (Glasgow: HarperCollins Publishers, 2001).
13. See J. Grobler, *Mail* and *Guardian* (Johannesburg), 13–19 March 1998.
14. B. Auer, *In Suedwestafrika gegen die Hereros* (Berlin: Ernst Hofmann & Co., 1911), pp. 189, 208.
15. F. Cornell, *The Glamour of Prospecting* (New York: F. A. Stokes, 1920).
16. NAN, ZBU 2369, Witbooi Geheimakten, pp. 103–4.
17. There were two missionaries in Lüderitz due to the many prisoners sent there, because these were seen by the mission as souls still in need of saving. Missionary Laaf was the first to arrive, in December 1905, and was later followed by Nyhof.
18. NAN, ZBU 2369, Witbooi Geheimakten, pp. 103–4.
19. Union of South Africa, *Report on the Natives of South-West Africa and Their Treatment by Germany* (London: HMSO, 1918), Chapter XX, testimony by Samuel Kariko.
20. Cornell, *Glamour of Prospecting*.
21. NAN, ZBU 2369, Witbooi Geheimakten, pp. 93–6.
22. NAN, HBS 52, 28 November 1906.
23. Ibid., 24 December 1906.
24. NAN, ZBU 2369, Witbooi Geheimakten, p. 116.
25. Ibid., pp. 102–3.
26. Archiv der Vereinten Evangelischen Mission Wuppertal-Barmen, RMG 2.509a, C/h 23a, Bl. 348, letter the Rhenish Mission Society in Barmen, Inspector Spiecker by hand.
27. NAN, ZBU 2396, Witbooi Geheimakten, pp. 96a–96b.
28. Ibid.
29. Ibid., pp. 97–8.
30. Ibid.
31. H. Drechsler, *Let Us Die Fighting* (Berlin: Akademie-Verlag, 1986), p. 211.
32. NAN, ZBU 2369, Witbooi Geheimakten, 'Todesinsel', Bezirksamtman Zülow to Gov. 6/01/07, pp. 120–30.
33. Cape Archives, PMO 227–35/07, British Military Attaché, Col. F. Trench to British Embassy, Berlin, 21 November 1906.
34. Erichsen, '*The Angel of Death*', p. 155.
35. Ibid.
36. Notably this debate was watched by a contingent from German South-West Africa including Governor Lindequist and Major Bayer, who had come to support the cause. *Stenographische Berichte uber die Verhandlungen des deutschen Reichstages*, 11. Legislature, II. Session. 1905/1907. Reichstag. – 140. Sitzung. 13 December 1906, p. 4367.
37. Union of South Africa, *Report on the Natives of South-West Africa*, Chapter XX.
38. J. Zimmerer and J. Zeller (eds), *Genocide in German South-West Africa: the*

Colonial War of 1904–1908 and Its Aftermath (Monmouth: Merlin Press Ltd., 2008), pp. 76–7.

39. Zürn to Luschan, 25 June 1905. MfV,1B 39, vol. 1 775/05. Quoted in A. Zimmerman, *Anthropology and Antihumanism in Imperial Germany* (Chicago: University of Chicago Press, 2001), p. 245.
40. C. Fetzer, 'Rassenanatomische Untersuchungen an 17 Hottenttotenkoepfen', *Zeitschrift fuer Morphologie und Antropologie* 16 (1912).
41. Dr Stabsarzt Bofinger, 'Einige Mitteilungen uber Skorbut', *Deutsche militaer-arztliche Zeitschrift* 39.15 (1910).
42. ELCN, RMS, V.16, Chronik der Gemeinde Lüderitzbucht, pp. 28–9.
43. BAB, Colonial Department, File 2140, 'Note for the Reichstag about the Native Prisoners of War on Shark Island', p. 88.
44. Ibid.
45. NAN, ZBU 2369, Secret Files, p. 113.
46. Ibid., p. 115.
47. BAB, Colonial Department, File 2140, 'Note for the Reichstag About the Native Prisoners of War on Shark Island', p. 157.
48. Ludwig von Estorff, *Wanderungen und Kaempfe in Suedwestafrika, Ostafrika und Suedafrika 1894–1910* (Windhoek: John Meinert (Pty) Ltd, 1996), p. 134.
49. NAN, ZBU 456, D IV.l.3, vol. 5, p. 135.
50. NAN, ZBU 2369, Witbooi Geheimakten, pp. 152–3.
51. 'Population statistics in Lüderitz (German) as of end-1906: 836 men, 94 women and 49 children under 15 years.' NAN, ZBU 154, A.VI.a.3, p. 207. For a further discussion on these figures see Erichsen, '*The Angel of Death*', pp. 134–45.
52. They had, in a grotesque mirror image of the literal sense of the word, been decimated.
53. NAN, ZBU 2369, Witbooi Geheimakten, p. 153.

13 **'Our New Germany on African Soil'**

1. NAN, Photo collection, ref no. 2857; J. Zeller, 'Symbolic Politics', in J. Zimmerer and J. Zeller (eds), *Genocide in German South-West Africa: the Colonial War of 1904–1908 and Its Aftermath* (Monmouth: Merlin Press Ltd., 2008), pp. 231–49; *Kolonial-Post*, 1937, p. 6 (courtesy of Joachim Zeller); D. J. Walther, *Creating Germans Abroad* (Athens, OH: Ohio University Press, 2002); J. Gewald, *We Thought We Would Be Free* (Cologne: Ruediger Koeppe Verlag, 2000).
2. U. van der Heyden and J. Zeller, *Kolonial Metropole Berlin* (Berlin: Berlin Edition, 2002), p. 164.
3. *Kolonial-Post*, 1937, p. 6.
4. K. Epstein, 'Erzberger and the German Colonial Scandals: 1905–1910', *The English Historical Review* 74, No. 293 (Oct. 1959) pp. 637–63.
5. NAN, ZBU 456, D IV.l.3, vol. 6, p. 88.
6. NAN, ZBU 465, D IV. M.3, vol. 2, p. 147.
7. Ibid., p. 119.
8. Ibid., p. 239.
9. G. I. Schrank, 'German South-West Africa: Social and Economic Aspects of Its History, 1884–1915', unpublished Ph.D. thesis (New York: New York University, 1974), p. 212.
10. Walther, *Creating Germans*, pp. 58–9.
11. BAK, Kl. Erw. NL 1037, Nr 8, p. 6.
12. Walther, *Creating Germans*, p. 20.

13. Ibid., p. 30.
14. Ibid., pp. 90–1.
15. Ibid., p. 93.
16. Ibid., p 103.
17. L. Wildenthal, 'She Is the Victor', in G. Eley (ed.), *Society, Culture, and the State in Germany, 1870–1930* (University of Michigan Press, 1998), p. 374.
18. J. W. Spidle, 'Colonial Studies in Imperial Germany', *History of Education Quarterly* 3.3 (Autumn 1973), pp. 231–47.
19. M. Baericke, *Luederitzbucht: 1908–1914* (Windhoek: Namibia Wissenschaftliche Gesellschaft, 2001), p. 33.
20. Klaus Dierks, *Chronology of Namibian History* (Windhoek: Namibia Scientific Society, 2002), p. 138.
21. Walther, *Creating Germans*, p. 46.
22. There are still black Namibians today who carry the name von François, and trace their ancestry back to the von François family.
23. Decree of the Governor of German South-West Africa on the Half-Caste Population, 23 May 1912. *Deutsches Kolonialblatt* (1912), p. 752. Quoted in Helmuth Stoecker (ed.), Bernard Zöller (trans.), *German Imperialism in Africa: From the Beginnings until the Second World War* (London: Hurst, 1986), p. 211.
24. R. Gordon and S. S. Douglas, *The Bushman Myth: The Making of a Namibian Underclass* (Oxford: Westview Press, 2000); R. Gordon, 'The Rise of the Bushman Penis: Germans, Genitalia and Genocide', *African Studies* 57.1 (1998), pp. 27–54; E. Fischer, *Die Rehobother Bastards und das Bastardierungsproblem beim Menschen* (Jena: Gustav Fischer, 1913); idem, *Begegnung Mit Toten* (Freiburg: Hans Ferdinand Schulz Verlag, 1959); M. Bayer, 'Die Nation der Bastards', *Zeitschrift fuer Kolonialpolitik, Kolonialrecht und Kolonialwirtschaft* 8.9 (1906), pp. 625–48.
25. E. Fischer, 'Das Rehobother Bastardvolk', *Die Umshau* 13 (1910), p. 1049.
26. Fischer, *Die Rehobother Bastards*, p. 57.
27. Ibid., p. 302.
28. Richard Weikart, *From Darwin to Hitler* (New York and Basingstoke: Palgrave Macmillan, 2004), p. 118.
29. Henry Friedlander, *The Origins of Nazi Genocide: From Euthanasia to the Final Solution* (Chapel Hill, NC, and London: University of North Carolina Press, 1995), p. 12.

14 Things Fall Apart

1. H. Brodersen-Manns, *Wie Alles Anders Kam in Afrika* (Windhoek: Kuiseb Verlag, 1991); General Staff, *The Union of South Africa and the Great War 1914–1918: Official History* (Pretoria: The Government Printing and Stationery Office, 1924); C. C. Adams, 'The African Colonies and the German War', *Geographical Review* 1.6 (June 1916), pp. 452–4; D. E. Kaiser, 'Germany and the Origins of World War I', *Journal of Modern History* 55.3 (Sept. 1983), pp. 442–74.
2. E. M. Ritchie, *With Botha in the Field* (London: Longmans, Green and Co., 1915), section 1.
3. H. F. B. Walker, *A Doctor's Diary in Damaraland* (London: Edward Arnold, 1917).
4. Ibid.
5. Helmuth Stoecker (ed.), Bernard Zöller (trans.), *German Imperialism in Africa: From the Beginnings until the Second World War* (London: Hurst, 1986), p. 272.
6. *The Times*, 10 July 1915.
7. Prosser Gifford and William Roger Louis, *Britain and Germany in Africa: Imperial

Rivalry and Colonial Rule (New Haven, CT, and London: Yale University Press, 1967), p. 280.
8. J. Silvester and J. Gewald, *Words Cannot Be Found: German Colonial Rule in Namibia* (Leiden: Brill, 2003), pp. xv–xvi.
9. Ibid., p. xvii.

15 'To Fight the World for Ever'

1. Quoted in Fritz Fischer, *Germany's Aims in the First World War* (London: Chatto & Windus, 1967), p. 618.
2. Ibid., p. 588.
3. Vejas Gabriel Liulevicius, *War Land on the Eastern Front: Culture, National Identity and German Occupation in World War I* (Cambridge: Cambridge University Press, 2000), p. 59.
4. Woodruff Smith, *The Ideological Origins of Nazi Imperialism* (Oxford: Oxford University Press, 1986), p. 195.
5. *The Times*, 12 September 1918.
6. John Horne and Alan Kramer, *German Atrocities, 1914: A History of Denial* (New Haven, CT, and London: Yale University Press, 2001), p. 135.
7. Quoted in Alan Kramer, *Dynamic of Destruction Culture and Mass Killing in the First World War* (Oxford: Oxford University Press, 2007).
8. *The Times*, 12 September 1918, p. 7: The 'Militarist' and Colonist.
9. William Roger Louis, 'The South West African Origins of the "Sacred Trust", 1914–1919', *African Affairs* 66.262. (Jan. 1967), pp. 20–39.
10. Prosser Gifford and William Roger Louis, *Britain and Germany in Africa: Imperial Rivalry and Colonial Rule* (New Haven, CT, and London: Yale University Press, 1967), p. 346.

16 A Passing Corporal

1. Gregor Dallas, *1918: War and Peace* (London: John Murray, 2000), p. 274.
2. Ian Kershaw, *Hitler 1889–1936: Hubris* (London: Allen Lane, 1998), p. 99.
3. David Clay Large, *Where Ghosts Walked: Munich's Road to the Third Reich* (New York and London: W. W. Norton, 1997), p. 25.
4. Richard Weikart, *From Darwin to Hitler* (New York and Basingstoke: Palgrave Macmillan, 2004), p. 122.
5. Large, *Where Ghosts Walked*, p. 91.
6. Count von Arco-Valley survived the left-wing governments that followed the regime of Kurt Eisner. He also outlived both the Nazis and the war, only to be run over and killed by an American army jeep in 1945.
7. Harold J. Gordon, Jr, *The Reichswehr and the German Republic 1919–1926* (Princeton, NJ: Princeton University Press, 1957), p. 281.
8. Nigel Jones, *The Birth of the Nazis: How the Freikorps Blazed a Trail for Hitler* (London: Robinson, 2004), p. 176.
9. John Toland, *Adolf Hitler* (Garden City, NY: Doubleday, 1976), p. 81.
10. Nicholas Goodrick-Clarke, *Occult Roots of Nazism* (London: I. B. Tauris, 2004), p. 148.
11. John Lukacs, *Tocqueville: The European Revolution and Correspondence with Gobineau* (New York: Doubleday, 1959), p. 187.
12. Kershaw, *Hitler*, p. 174.
13. Weikart, *From Darwin to Hitler*, p. 225.

14. Toland, *Adolf Hitler*, p. 199.
15. *Mein Kampf*, trans. Ralph Manheim (London: Hutchinson, 1969), p. 367.
16. Annegret Ehmann, 'From Colonial Racism to Nazi Population Policy: The Role of the So-Called Mischlinge', in Michael Berenbaum and Abraham J. Peck (eds), *The Holocaust and History: The Known, The Unknown, The Disputed and The Reexamined*, p. 115.
17. Weikart, *From Darwin to Hitler*, p. 222.
18. Edwin Black, *War Against the Weak: Eugenics and America's Campaign to Create a Master Race* (New York: Four Walls Eight Windows; London: Turnaround, 2004), p. 274.
19. Quoted in Weikart, *From Darwin to Hitler*, p. 223.
20. G. E. Schafft, *Racism to Genocide* (Urbana, IL: University of Illinois Press, 2004), p. 62.

17 A People without Space

1. M. Burleigh and W. Wippermann, *The Racial State: Germany 1933–1945* (Cambridge: Cambridge University Press, 1991).
2. J. Noakes and G. Pridham (eds), *Nazism: A History in Documents and Eyewitness Accounts, 1919–1945* (University of Exeter Press, 1983), vol. 1, p. 133.
3. Annegret Ehmann, 'From Colonial Racism to Nazi Population Policy: The Role of the So-Called Mischlinge', in Michael Berenbaum and Abraham J. Peck (eds), *The Holocaust and History: The Known, The Unknown, The Disputed and The Reexamined* 1998, p. 123.
4. Henry Friedlander, *The Origins of Nazi Genocide: From Euthanasia to the Final Solution* (Chapel Hill, NC, and London: University of North Carolina Press, 1995), p. 25.
5. Burleigh and Wippermann, *Racial State*, p. 48.
6. O. Hintrager, 'Das Mischehen-Verbot von 1905, in Deutsch-Suedwestafrika', *Africa-Nachrichten* 22.2 (Feb. 1941), pp. 18–19.
7. Clarence Lusane, *Hitler's Black Victims* (New York and London: Routledge, 2002), p. 138.
8. Ehmann, 'Colonial Racism to Nazi Population Policy', p. 121.
9. Ingo Haar and Michael Fahlbusch, *German Scholars and Ethnic Cleansing, 1920–1945* (New York and Oxford: Berghahn Books, 2005), p. 15.
10. Ehmann, 'Colonial Racism to Nazi Population Policy', p. 121.
11. Benno Müller-Hill, *Murderous Science* (Oxford: Oxford University Press, 1987), p. 71.
12. L. H. Gann and Peter Duigan, *The Rulers of German Africa, 1884–1914* (Stanford, CA: Stanford University Press, 1977), p. 254.
13. NAN, WH/SMA 'erster Jahresbericht der Kolonialen Lehrschau und Schulungsstaette Dr H. E. Göring-Kolonialhaus Hannover 1939/40'.
14. B. Bennett, *Hitler over Africa* (London: T. Werner Laurie, 1939), p. 1.
15. S. Friedrichsmeyer, S. Lennox and S. Zantop (eds), *The Imperialist Imagination: German Colonialism and Its Legacy* (Ann Arbor, MI: University of Michigan Press 1998).

18 Germany's California

1. J. Noakes and G. Pridham (eds), *Nazism: A History in Documents and Eyewitness Accounts, 1919–1945* (University of Exeter Press, 1983), vol. 1, p. 622.

2. Alexander Dallin, *German Rule in Russia: 1941–1945* (London: Macmillan, 1957), p. 296.
3. *The Goebbels Diaries 1942–1943*, ed. and trans. Louis P. Lochner (London: Hamish Hamilton, 1948), p. 126.
4. Hannah Arendt was among the first historians to suggest such a link, while recent publications by Adam Toze and Mark Mazower have done much to set Nazism within the wider context of colonialism and colonial violence.
5. Enzo Traverso, *The Origins of Nazi Violence*, trans. Janet Lloyd (New York: New Press, 2003), p. 50.
6. Thanks to Robert Gordon for both of these quotations.
7. *Hitler's Table Talk 1941–44: His Private Conversations*, trans. Norman Cameron and R. H. Stevens (London: Weidenfeld & Nicolson, 1953), p. 24.
8. Ibid., p. 574.
9. *Monologue im Führerhauptquartier, 1941–4: die Aufzeichnungen Heinrich Heims, herausgegeben von Werner Jochmann*, p. 377: 30 August 1942.
10. *Hitler's Table Talk*, p. 469.
11. Ibid.
12. Ibid., p. 19.
13. Noakes and Pridham, *Nazism*, pp. 918–20.
14. Wendy Lower, 'Hitler's Garden of Eden in Ukraine: Nazi Colonialism, Volkdeutsche and the Holocaust, 1941–1944', in Jonathan Petropoulos and John K. Roth (eds), *In Gray Zones: Ambiguity and Compromise in the Holocaust and Its Aftermath* (New York and Oxford: Berghahn, 2005), p. 187.
15. Noakes and Pridham, *Nazism*, p. 1090.
16. Robert Cecil, *Hitler's Decision to Invade Russia, 1941* (London: Davis-Poynter, 1975), p. 206.
17. *Hitler's Table Talk*, p. 319.
18. Ibid., p. 617.
19. Ibid., p. 354.
20. Ibid., p. 425.
21. Ibid., p. 575.
22. Ibid., p. 34.
23. Ibid., p. 424.
24. Ibid.
25. Ibid., p. 617.
26. Alan Bullock, *Hitler and Stalin: Parallel Lives* (HarperCollins, 1991), p. 773.
27. William L. Shirer, *The Rise and Fall of the Third Reich: A History of Nazi Germany* (London: Secker and Warburg, 1960), p. 854.
28. Noakes and Pridham, *Nazism*, p. 915.

Epilogue: The Triumph of Amnesia

1. Mark Mazower, *Hitler's Empire: Nazi Rule in Occupied Europe* (London: Allen Lane, 2008), p. 593.
2. P. Katjavivi, *A History of Resistance in Namibia* (London: Currey, 1988), p. 14.
3. J. Gewald, *We Thought We Would Be Free* (Cologne: Ruediger Koeppe Verlag, 2000).
4. J. Silvester and J. Gewald, *Words Cannot Be Found: German Colonial Rule in Namibia* (Leiden: Brill, 2003).
5. As quoted in J. Silvester, *The Politics of Reconciliation: Destroying the Blue Book*

(Windhoek: forthcoming), p. 13.

6. Silvester and Gewald, *Words Cannot Be* Found, p. xxxii.
7. 'The Native Bluebook', *Windhoek Advertiser*, 31 July (1926).
8. Klaus Dierks, *Chronology of Namibian History* (Windhoek: Namibia Scientific Society, 2002), p. 211.
9. 'Nuwe spoorlyn ontspoor by Tsaukaib', *Die Republikein*, 17 March 2009, Suiderland.
10. Ibid.; a widely available book on the history of Namibia's railways, Brenda Bravenboer and Walter K. E. Rusch, *The First One Hundred Years of State Railways in Namibia* (Windhoek: TransNamib Museum, 1997), is similarly mute on the matter of forced labour used to construct the Lüderitz–Aus Railway.
11. Ibid.
12. Ibid.
13. Namibia Country Reports on Human Rights Practices 2007. Released by the Bureau of Democracy, Human Rights, and Labor 11 March 2008. http://www.state.gov/g/drl/rls/hrrpt/2007/100496.htm
14. Labour Resource and Research Institute (LARRI), 'Farm Workers in Namibia: Living and Working Conditions', research paper (Windhoek: LARRI, 2006).

Acknowledgements

David Olusoga:

I would like to thank Casper W. Erichsen whose ferocious passion for the history and people of Namibia made this book possible. Susie Painter for her support, informed criticism and assistance. Marion Olusoga for her help with early drafts and translation. Neil Belton and Kate Murray-Browne at Faber & Faber for their enthusiasm and endless patience.

Further thanks for support and inspiration goes to:

Sally-Ann Wilson at the Commonwealth Broadcasting Association whose financial support and belief in the story of Namibia and its tragic past first allowed the authors the opportunity to work together. Michael Poole and Roly Keating at the BBC who executive-produced and commissioned (respectively) a television documentary that allowed me to further explore the history of Namibia. Our agent Charles Walker at United Agents. Jeremy Silvester who introduced the authors, leading not only to this book but to a valued friendship. Thanks goes, also, to the great writers and scholars with whom I've had the opportunity to discuss this history: Adam Hochschild, Mike Davis, David Dabydeen and Henry Reynolds.

Casper W. Erichsen:

I would like to thank Inatu Indongo Erichsen for her loving support through it all, my son Helao David Wulff Erichsen and my mother Elisabeth Erichsen.

Further thanks for support and inspiration goes to:

David Olusoga, one of the most intelligent people I have ever had the pleasure of meeting and a true friend, Susie Painter for surviving four mad years with us, Neil Belton and Kate Murray-Browne at Faber & Faber, Teis Wulff Owens, Janet Owens, Natascha Wulff, Angelo, Hannah and Mika Carlsen, the Indongo family, Bes, Gitte and Claus, Grandma Leona and Grandpa Joe.

Jeremy Silvester, Werner Hillebrecht and Ellen Namhila, Jan-Bart and Gertie Gewald, Aulden and Rachael Harlech-Jones, Helao and Jane Shityuwete, Kanjoo and David Lush, Robert and Rinda Gordon, Uno Katjipuka Sibolile, David Benade, Rudiger, Jessica, Finn and Narla Gretschel, Tim Huebschle, Steffen List, Robert Ross, Carsten Norgaard, the Muurholm clan, Alex Kaputu, Isak Fredericks, Gabs, Moonira and Momo Urgoiti, Patricia Hayes and Ciraj Rasool, Simon Wilkie, Gerhard Gurirab, Memory Biwa, Ivan Gaseb and Mette Gases, Hage Iyambo, Irleyn Kuhanga, Anette and Tommy Bayer, Bastian Schwarz and Hannelie Coetzee, Flemming G. Nielsen, the Vigne family, Mburumba Kerina, Utandua Austin, Mimi Mupetami, Naomi Boys, Nelson Garay Perez, Neville, Mandela, Martha, Abena and the rest of the History Society crew, Peter Pauli, the Feltons, Jens Friis, Steve, Judy and Nyasha Murray, Morten Levy, Sean Neary, Chris Lappin, Jata Kazondu, Shasheeda Mberira, Ndapewa Ithana, Adam Ross, my colleagues at Positive Vibes, Anders Thomsen and Kim Isenbecker.

Index